AF552456

INTERNATIONAL MARKETING MANAGEMENT

International Marketing Management

B.S. Sharma

ANMOL PUBLICATIONS PVT. LTD.
NEW DELHI - 110 002 (INDIA)

ANMOL PUBLICATIONS PVT. LTD.
H.O.: 4374/4B, Ansari Road, Darya Ganj,
New Delhi-110 002 (India)
Ph.: 23278000, 23261597

B.O.: No. 1015, Ist Main Road, BSK IIIrd Stage
IIIrd Phase, IIIrd Block,
Bangalore - 560 085 (India)
Visit us at: www.anmolpublications.com

International Marketing Management

First Published, 2006

ISBN 81-261-2941-7

PRINTED IN INDIA

Printed at Mehra Offset Press, Delhi.

Contents

Preface

"International Marketing Management" as a paper is being taught at B.B.M., B.Com., M.Com., M.B.A. and Other Management Courses at various universities and institutions. This book is designed as an introductory text to the above paper, encompassing vital information on all pertinent aspects. Thus the material presented here would be of interest as well as of great use to the students, teachers and professionals of Business Management. This book will provide complete knowledge of international marketing, economic environment, constraints of marketing, India and World Trade, institutional infrastructure for export promotion, legal dimensions of international marketing, documents for export, marketing mix, pricing and distribution strategy for export, joint ventures and turnkey projects, export promotion, export finance etc. to the students.

The major topics dealt in this book are—International Marketing—An Introduction; Economic Environment of International Marketing; Constraints of International Marketing; India and World Trade; Institutional Infrastructure for Export Promotion; Legal Dimensions of International Marketing; Procedure and Documents for Export; International Marketing Mix; Pricing and Distribution Strategy for Export; Joint Ventures and Turnkey Projects; Export Promotion; Export Finance etc.

It is hoped that all those will benefit from the contents of this book for whom it is meant. The author will feel amply rewarded, if motive is achieved.

Editor

Internat
It refers
activiti
the same
the informa
simple
the co
systen
polluc
countr
and so
and cou
countr
growth
perform
servic
may b
wants
mean
satisfy
for th
Interna
marke

1

International Marketing—An Introduction

International marketing is the marketing across the national frontiers. If refers to the strategy, process, and implementation of the marketing activities in the international arena.

International marketing may be defined as an activity related to the sale of goods and services of one country in the other, subject to the rules and regulations framed by the countries concerned. In simple words, it refers to marketing activities and operations among the countries of the world following different political and economic systems. International marketing is marketing abroad *i.e.*, beyond the political boundaries of the country. International marketing brings countries closer due to economic needs and facilitates understanding and co-operation among them. It is essentially a constructive economic and commercial activity which is useful and beneficial to all participating countries. International marketing act as an instrument of global growth and development.

According to Hess and Cateora international marketing is 'the performance of business activities that direct the flow of goods and services to consumers or users in more than one nation.' Marketing may be understood as human activity directed at satisfying needs and wants through exchange process. It means working with markets. It means attempting to actualise potential exchange for the purpose of satisfying human needs and wants. It includes analysing the markets for their potentials in order to assess the needs of the customers. International marketing is a part of total marketing process. It is marketing activities carried on by a marketer in more than one nation.

It may be defined as 'marketing carried on across national boundaries.' Marketing activities, *i.e.*, buying, selling, transportation, storage and warehousing, financing risk bearing, pricings, standardising, advertising and sales promotion etc. may be called international marketing when performed in foreign markets across the national border.

SCOPE OF INTERNATIONAL MARKETING

The scope of international marketing essentially includes exporting of goods and services in foreign markets. The exporter performs various activities, other than exporting the goods and services. These activities are:

(1) Establishing a branch in foreign market for processing, packaging or assembling the goods according to the needs of the markets. Sometimes complete manufacturing is carried out by the branch through direct investments.

(2) Joint Ventures and Collaborations. International marketing includes establishing joint ventures and collaboration in foreign countries with some foreign firms for manufacturing and/or marketing the product. Under these arrangements, the company works in collaboration with the foreign firm in order to exploit the foreign markets.

(3) Licensing Arrangements. The company, under the system, establishes licensing arrangements with the foreign term whereby foreign enterprises are granted the right to use the exporting company's know-how, *viz.*, patents, processes or trade marks according to the terms of agreement with or without financial investment.

(4) Consultancy Services. Offering consultancy services are also covered in international marketing scope. The exporting company offers consultancy services by undertaking turnkey projects in foreign countries. For this purpose, the exporting company sends its consultants and experts in foreign countries who guide and direct the manufacturing activities on the spot.

(5) Technical and Managerial Know-how. The scope of international marketing also includes the technical and managerial know-how provided by the exporting company to the importing company. The technicians and managerial personnel of the exporting company guide and train the technicians and managers of the importing company.

Characteristics of International Marketing

(1) Large Scale Operations. International marketing transaction is always conducted in large or bulk quantity. It is not conducted on a retail basis, but on the wholesale basis. This is necessary for securing the advantages of large scale operations as regards transportation, handling and warehousing.

(2) Dominance of Multinationals. Multinational corporations dominate the international marketing scene. Such enterprises have world wide contacts. They conduct business operations more efficiently and economically. They are in a better position to adopt global approach which is necessary in international marketing. Multinational corporations usually market thei· products in large number of countries and thereby dominate developing countries. Along with multinationals, industrially developed countries like the USA and Japan dominate international marketing due to their massive production capacity. Such countries :upply goods to all countries and earn huge profits.

(3) International Restrictions and Trading Blocs. International marketing is not free like internal marketing. There are various restrictions or barriers (tariff and non-tariff) because of the protective policies followed by different countries. Tariff barriers are adopted practically by all countries. Foreign exchange regulations also impose various restrictions on imports and exports. The scope of international marketing is also restricted due to various trading blocs like CMEA, ASEAN and LAFTA. These blocs impose artificial barriers on free movement of goods and services among the countries. Regional trading blocs or regional groupings like EEC also impose restrictions on international marketing. Such restrictions may be in the form of quotas and other direct restrictions on free imports. Efforts of GAIT and UNCTAD are not very effective in removing such trade barriers. The growth of international marketing is adversely affected due to such trade restrictions.

(4) Need of Marketing Research. International marketing requires marketing research in the form of marketing surveys, product surveys and product testing as it is highly competitive.

(5) Sensitive Character. International marketing is also highly sensitive and flexible in character. A product may suddenly become unfavourable or the market may come down quickly due to political and economic reasons. Even the use of advanced technology by the competitors or the introduction of new products by a competitor may affect the sale.

(6) Importance or Advanced Technology. International marketing is extremely dynamic and competitive. In such a type of marketing, an enterprise must be able to sell the best quality articles at competitive prices. Countries like the USA, Japan and Germany have a dominating position in international marketing because of the use of advanced technology in production and marketing of goods. They are able to promote exports and capture world markets due to their ability to sell superior quality goods at competitive prices. At present, world markets are flooded with Japanese goods. This is the result of intensive use of automation and advanced computer technology in Japan. Expansion of international marketing is basically due to the growth of modern technology. Technological developments facilitate large scale production. This brings the need to find out new markets. Secondly, technological developments are required to maintain these markets.

(7) Keen and Acute Competition. International marketing is highly competitive. Moreover, this competition is between developed and developing countries which are unequal partners. Such competition is made severe due to special facilities and incentives provided by the government to the exporters for export promotion. World markets are dynamic and this makes it necessary to use competitive techniques for export promotion.

(8) Need for Specialised Institutions. International marketing is risky and complicated. It requires lengthy procedures and formalities. Professional experts are necessary for dealing with various aspects of international marketing. Similarly, financial support is also necessary. Specialised institutions like indent houses, exchange banks and export houses are established world over for effective participation in international marketing.

(9) Need for Long Term Planning. International marketing requires long term marketing planning. The marketing situation in different countries changes because of social, economic and political factors. This stresses the need for long term planning in international marketing. A comprehensive and dynamic marketing programme can be prepared through such planning.

(10) Develops Cultural Relations and Maintains World Peace. International marketing brings different countries closer and also develops cultural relations among them. Closer cultural relations improve the quality of life of people in different countries. Finally, international marketing brings interdependence among the countries of the world. The participating countries have to maintain friendly relations among themselves. This situation ensures cordial relations among the nations of the world and also ensures world peace.

International Marketing, even though it has certain distinct characteristics, is essentially similar to domestic marketing in terms of certain technical attributes. Marketing can be conceived as an integral part of two processes, *viz.*, technical and social. So far as the technical process is concerned, domestic and international marketing are identical. The technical process includes non-human factors such as product, price, cost, brand, etc. The basic principles regarding these variables are of universal applicability. But the social aspect of marketing is unique in any given stratum, because it involves human elements, namely, the behaviour pattern of consumers and the given characteristics of a society, such as customs, attitudes, values, etc.

It is obvious that marketing as a social process will be different in varying environments and international marketing, to the extent it is visualised as a social process, will be different from domestic marketing.

Needs of International Marketing

International Marketing grows and prospers because of certain economic and political factors. The existence of global marketing over many centuries justify its existence. Some of the industrially advanced nations enjoy huge production capacity and surplus of goods. National market becomes inadequate to them. They must export so that their economies develop and expand. The need for international marketing is universally accepted because it is beneficial to all the countries. More than ever before international marketing has become important, now, because fastest means of transport and communication has well-linked all the countries. The following factors necessitate international marketing:

(1) Rapid Industrialisation. Countries are economically dependent on one another. Every country has to import certain goods and also to export so as to pay for imports. The third world countries are deperdent on the western countries for superior technology to achieve faster economic growth. International marketing has become. prominent because of international interdependence and growing industrialisation.

(2) Cost Benefits. Due to certain favourable factors, some countries can produce certain commodities with low cost of production. International marketing is favoured by all in order to enjoy the comparative cost benefits. International marketing becomes the only option to exchange goods and export such goods where the countries enjoy cost benefit. A country will import such goods which either it cannot produce or will produce at a higher cost.

(3) Raised Standard of Living. There is consciousness all over the world and people desire to raise their standard of living through the consumption of best quality goods procured from nook or corner of the world. International marketing also mobilises foreign investments, superior technology and international understanding. The standard of living of the people can be raised only by enabling them to consume quality products at reasonable prices, no matter from where they are procured. Even perishable goods are marketed within minimum possible time due to well-organised network of transport and communication.

(4) Cultural Exchanges. Peaceful co-existence to a very great extent depends on economic, social and cultural exchanges. International relations can improve when people move to different countries on goodwill visits. Cultural differences separate the countries from one another. This gap can be well connected through international trade and exchange of culture.

(5) Fulfils Economic Needs. The increase in the rate of population growth has brought pressure on the Government to fulfil economic needs of growing number of its people. In order to provide basic amenities and luxuries to the increasing population imports and exports become obligatory. The growth of international trade is certainly because of increasing world population.

(6) Maintaining International Prices. It is not possible that varying prices will prevail in international marketing for long. Various countries market their goods at competitive rates. The comparative cost benefits enjoyed by one country in a particular item can be shared by other countries.

(7) Helps Both Developed and Developing Countries. International marketing is also required to narrow the gulf between advanced countries and less developed or developing countries. Even advanced nations must export their surplus so that under-developed countries can obtain their requirements. In turn, advanced countries must provide concessional terms so that developing countries have no option but to import superior technical know-how from developed countries. It is through international marketing that industrially advanced nations provide assistance to developing countries in their struggle towards economic growth. International marketing improves economic relations and reduces the chances of international conflicts.

Advantages of International Marketing

International Marketing has number of advantages. Some of these briefly summarised below:

(i) Availability of goods which cannot be produced in the home country due to geographical factors and other natural limitations.

(ii) Provision of better standard of living to citizens by providing them with wide variety of goods and services.

(iii) Industrial development of the country, provision of massive employment opportunities to the people and full utilisation of natural resources available.

(iv) Rational allocation of resources and the best use of the resources available at the international level.

(v) Benefits of comparative cost difference as suggested in the theory of comparative costs. The benefits of division of labour and specialisation at the international level are also available through international marketing.

(vi) Social and cultural exchanges between different countries of the world.

(vii) International economic, political and cultural co-operation and world peace.

(viii) Effective utilisation of surplus domestic production, introduction of new varieties of goods, improvement in the quality of production and promotion of mutual co-operation among countries.

(ix) Special benefits during the period of emergency like famines and floods.

(x) Removal of deficit in the balance of trade and payments of participating countries through export promotion and import substitution.

(xi) Easy availability of foreign exchange for import of capital goods, modern technology and other essential requirements.

(xii) Rapid expansion of teritiary sector which includes transport, insurance and shipping.

It may be noted that the above mentioned advantages or benefits are available only when international marketing is reasonably free from various restrictions and regulations. Unfortunately, almost all countries have imposed various restrictions on the free movement of goods. Such commercial restrictions are undesirable as they restrict the scope of free and fair international marketing.

Importance of International Marketing

Foreign trade or exports make a significant and necessary contribution to the economy and the country's development and particularly in underdeveloped countries. It provides a sound base for the country's economy. The rapid progress of underdeveloped countries in the industrial field is mainly due to their exports.

J.S. Mill has pointed out that "Efficient employment of the productive forces of the world is a direct economical advantage or foreign trade. But there are, besides indirect effects, which must be counted as benefits of a high order. One such is the tendency of every extension of the market to improve the process of production. A country which produces for a larger market than its own can introduce a more extended division of labour, can make greater use of machines, and is more likely to make inventions and improvements in the process of production."

Thus exports extend the market and the scope of the division of labour, permits a greater use of machinery, stimulates innovations, overcomes technical invisibilities, raises the productivity of labour and generally enables the trading country to enjoy increasing returns and economic development. In practical, these effects are very real and visible. The exports of our engineering goods has developed the engineering industry in India and now our engineering goods can compete with the best in the world. The experience gained by the exporter in foreign markets enables the exporter to improve the designs and incorporate the necessary changes in the product at the earliest. These improvements can be carried over to domestic production, thus giving improved product and performance. Prof. Gerald Muir puts the idea more succinctly. "The export trade helps considerably in the importation of technical. know how and skills which is an indispensable source of technological progress. It provides an opportunity to learn from the achievement and the failures of the advanced countries. By selective, judicious borrowing and adaptation, it can act as exellent stimulus for speedy economic development."

India is rather in a unique position among the developing countries. There is already available with us the prior development: and sufficiently broad-based infrastructure, which can provide a positive and self reinforcing response to the stimulus, it receives from foreign trade.

One of the used indicators referred to in this connection is the rate of economic growth compared to the export trade. The rate is continuously increasing but still it is very low as compared to other western countries. The same case is with the share of India's export in the world exports. In this light, India should increase its share in the world exports. Thus export marketing is very important for a nation's economy and for the individual business firm as well.

(A) Importance of Export Marketing in the National Economy

From the point of view of national economy, the importance of export marketing can be understood under the following heads:

(1) To Meet Imports of Industrial Needs. No country today can survive in isolation. The developing countries need imports of capital equipments, raw materials of critical nature, technical knowhow for building the industrial base in the country with a view to rapid industrialisation and developing the necessary infrastructure. The share of oil imports in the total import of the underdeveloped countries is much higher and its imports cannot be avoided all it is required as a means of energy to run the industries.

There is only option to avoid the situation is to establish the export-oriented industries and to increase the existing installed capacity of units producing goods for export markets. Industries should also be given stimulus to utilise their unutilised capacity and export the surplus production. Thus export is a must for meeting the import requirements of a country because by exporting the surplus or additional production, a country can also earn valuable foreign exchange that is necessary to meet the import bill.

Moreover, if a country fails in meeting the import bill by exporting the goods and services from the other country, the difference is trade deficit which cannot be said to be a pleasant situation. Thus, positive measures, and encouragement for the steady and substantial increase in the export trade is necessary to balance the imports.

In this way, export should be increased steadily and substantially especially by an underdeveloped country where trade deficit has become a regular feature.

(2) Debt Servicing. Almost all underdeveloped countries, including India, have been receiving external aid over the years for their industrial development. The natural consequence of aid has been the need for debt servicing *i.e.* arrangement of foreign exchange every year equal to the instalment and interest assumed thereon as per terms of the aid or loan. Hence, it is necessary to aim at sufficient export earnings to cover both imports and debt servicing. This will lead to the availability of higher amount of foreign aid for development and consequently higher amount for debt servicing.

(3) Rapid Economic Growth. An expanding export trade can be a dynamic factor in a country's development process. However, one has to plan imaginatively in increasing the production of exportable surpluses. The country should have to utilise domestic resources and to provide technological improvement and improved production at lower costs. For this purpose industrial development is inevtable which is not possible wilhout making exports. Export and economic development of a country are interrelated without exports economic development of high order cannot be imagined. In a study on The relation of exports and economic growth" conducted for a group of 50 countries by R.F. Emery, it was found that a higher rate of economic growth tends to be associated with a higher rate of export growth. The study also revealed that a significant correlation exists between exports and GNP and that real GNP per capita recorded an increase of 1 % for every 21 % rise in exports.

It is now amply clear that countries that desire to grow economically should take serious view for creating exportable surpluses (surpluses after meeting domestic demands). In the best interest of the economy and exports, emphasis should be on increasing the overall production and expanding the export of non-traditional products. This will lead to:

(i) Earning of more valuable foreign exchange which can be judiciously allocated for the import of necessary plants, machinery and equipment for the development of industries in the country in order of preference as spelt out in the development plans of the country. The foreign exchange can be used for the import of agricultural implements and fertilisers to raise the production of agricultural produce and that can provide a base for many agriculture based industries. New agricultural produce can be grown to established new industries that may provide import substitution and may save necessary foreign exchange.

(ii) 'Spin off' benefits for the domestic consumer by exposing the industry to international markets and making it more competitive as well as conscious of costs and quality.

(iii) Mitigate unemployment in labour-intensive industries.

(iv) Established new and new industrial unit for contributing towards export after making their domestic demand, sometimes, 100% export-oriented units are established.

(v) Full utilisation of idle resources.

(4) Profitable use of Natural Resources. Natural resources are valuable assets of a country which should be exploited ideally keeping the interest of the country in mind. This can be well done by export marketing. Earning from exports can be utilised in establishing industrial unit based on different natural resources available in the country by making the necessary imports of plant and machinery for the purpose. Moreover, necessary equipments can be imported for the exploitation of natural resources such as digging machines to be used in oil exploration etc. In this way, an increase in the conservation of natural resources and their profitable use in the industry will reduce imports of a country.

(5) Facing Competition Successfully. In a thrust to export more, the Government of the country, announces several concessions and incentive plans. Domestic producer in order to avail these concessions, concentrates his mind towards the improvement of quality of goods produced and reducing the cost of production so as to face the acute competitive situation in the foreign markets by making intensive use of latest technology. As because he is already marketing the goods in the domestic market, the advantage of other-quality at reduced price is also made available to the domestic customers and face competition successfully in the local market. Moreover, better quality and lower prices improve the image of the producer as well as of the country in minds of foreign customers.

(6) Increase in Employment Opportunities. In an effort to increase the export, many export. oriented industrial units are established, on the one hand, and the existing units produce more to get exportable surplus, on the other hand. This generates new Opportunities for employment and increases the existing level of employment. In underdeveloped countries, particularly in India, the problem of the employment and under-employment is very serious that can be solved to some extent by increasing the level of export. Moreover, new markets are surveyed exporting the goods and so many other persons are also engaged directly or indirectly in the export trade. Employment opportunities can also be explored by entering new areas for exports.

(7) Role of Exports in National Income. Export play an important role in the national inceme of the country and it can be increased to a sizable extent through organised export marketing. Shares of export income in the national income of some countries are Hungary 43%. Netherland 42%, Japan 11%. Canada 21%, Belgium 42%, West Germany 19%, England 17%. This shows the contribution of exports in the national income of the country.

(8) Increase in the Standard of Living. Export marketing improve the standard of living of the countrymen in the following ways:

(i) The imports of necessary items for consumption can be made which may help improve the standard of living of the people. Such imports can be managed out of foreign exchange fund earned from exports.

(ii) Exports increase the employment opportunities which, in turn, increase the purchasing power of the peoples by which they can purchase more for this consumption.

(iii) Exports are responsible for the rapid industrialisation of the country. New items are produced for consumption in the domestic market. It increases the level of standard of living.

(iv) In order to face the competition in the international market, the producers improve the quality of the product by applying the latest technology. Moreover, cost of production is also reduced because of large-scale production and use of improved technology. In this way, people gets better quality products at cheaper rates. It helps improve the standard of living of the people.

(B) Importance of Export Marketing from the Point of View of Individual Firm

Business and industrial firms are also benefited from the export trade. Due to these benefits, they are motivated to export. The following are some benefits from exports to the individual firm:

(1) Insufficiency of Domestic Demand. If the domestic demand for the product is not sufficient to consume the production the firm may take a decision to enter the foreign market. In this way he can equalise the production and the demand.

(2) To Utilise Installed Capacity. If the installed capacity of the firm is much more than the level of demand of the product in the domestic market, it can enter the international market and utilise its unutilised installed capacity. In this way, it can export the surplus production.

(3) Relative Profitability. The export trade in more attractive for its higher rate of profitability. The rate of profitability is also increased by export assistance measures offered by the Government of the country. The higher profitability rate also gives extra strength to the firm for its competitive position in the domestic market.

(4) Legal Restrictions. Sometimes the Government of a country impose certain restrictions on the growth and expansion of certain firms or on the production an distribution of certain commodities in the domestic market in order to achieve certain social objectives. Such firms or producers of such commodities then sell their production in export market. As a part of its import policy, Government of the country may impose certain export obligations on the industries and, therefore, they will have to export their production to meet the obligation.

(5) Less Business Risk. A diversified export business helps the exporting firm in mitigating the risk of sharp fluctuations in the business activity of the firm. Downward trend in one market may be partly or fully counterbalanced in other markets.

(6) Social Responsibility. In order to meet the social responsibility, some business firms take the decision to contribute to the national exchequer by exporting their products. They are committed to exports.

(7) Increased Productivity. Due to certain social and has technological developments, the industrial production has increased to a great extent. The production, therefore, will be higher at a cheaper rate. The surplus production can, therefore, be exported. The company can, now, spend more money on research and developmental activities.

(8) Technological Improvements. Technological improvements also attract the business firm to enter foreign markets. It introduces new products with latest technological improvements and faces the competition successfully in the overseas markets.

(9) Product Obsolescence. If a product becomes obsolete in domestic market it may be in demand in foreign markets. The firm has to make a survey for introducing the product in those markets.

(C) Importance from Other Viewpoints

The importance of export marketing can also be viewed from some other angles:

(1) International Collaboration. Export marketing results in international collaboration. Developed countries fix their import quotas for different countries and for different commodities. A country can export various commodities to these developed countries to the extent of its quota. In order to settle certain common issues some countries from a group or a common platform to discuss various issues concerning their international trade and take decision jointly. OPEC and EEC are such groups. In, this way, international trade leads to international collaboration.

(2) Closer Cultural Relations. International trade brings various countries closer. Better trade relations are established among the countries. Government and non-Government trade commissions or trade representations visit other countries from time to time. The local representatives and other related persons came into contract with foreign representatives and come to know their habits and customs. Apart from this, exporting firms open their selling deposits, agencies or manufacturing units abroad. Their employees also come into contract with the persons of the countries of their posting. In this way closer cultural relations among various countries develop.

(3) Help in Political Peace. The economic relations between two countries help improve their political relations. Various countries having different political ideologies import or export their products. The USSR imports foodgrains from America, though they have a different rather opposite, political ideologies. Thus, to some extent, international trade help maintaining political peace in the world.

TRANSITION FROM DOMESTIC TO INFERNATIONAL BUSINESS

Export business in different in many ways from domestic business; especially the risks and complexities associated with exports tend to be higher. Therefore, the decision to enter foreign markets must be based on strong economic factors. Temperamental decision to export is transient in character and is totally unsuitable for export marketing. Success in exporting requires total involvement and determination which can come only out of basic economic necessity as perceived by the corporate unit.

Pre-Export Behaviour

Every firm at some point of time starts as a non-exporter. The point to be studied is what made some of these firms get involved in export business. This might give a clue to the question as to whether a present non-exporter will become an exporter and, if so, why and when.

The factors which influence a non-exporting firm's decision to go in for export business can be classified under the following categories:

(i) Firm Characteristics. These characteristics include:

(a) Product characteristics,

(b) Size and growth of the domestic market,

(c) Optimal scale of production, and

(d) Potential export markets.

If the firm is manufacturing a product which is internationally marketable and the present and future market prospects in the domestic market are not encouraging, the motivation of the firm to get involved in export business will be considerable.

(ii) Perceived External Export Stimuli. Under this falls the management's recognition of the external market conditions. This will include:

(a) Fortuitous order,

(b) Market opportunity; and

(c) Government's stimulation/assistance.

(iii) Perceived Internal Export Stimuli. These refer to the management's expectations about the effects of exports on the firm's business. This covers:

(a) The level of capacity utilisation,

(b) Higher level of profits; and

(c) The growth objectives of the firm.

(iv) Level of Organisational Commitment. The decision-makers must agree on the level of export commitment. This is crucial because it will determine whether adequate resources will be made available for embarking on international marketing. Resources will be required for hiring new staff specialised in international marketing, hiring of consultants for carrying out overseas market potential studies, etc.

The interaction of these variables can be shown diagrammatically.

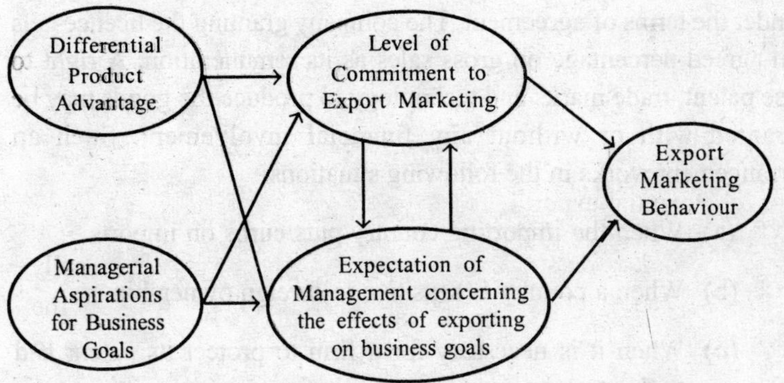

METHODS OF ENTERING FOREIGN MARKETS

If a firm has decided to go international it has six alternative methods to choose, amongst, for getting the entry into the foreign market. The choice very much depends on the resources of the firm and the market potentials for its product in the importing country. The level of export commitment call also be considered for the choice of methods of entering foreign markets. But, the firm should assess its strength and weakness. Following are the methods of entering foreign markets:

(i) Exporting. By exporting its surplus production through any of the following forms, a firm may choose to enter the international market for the first time. These forms are the most common and the simplest for entering the overseas markets for the first time because the risk attached to such venture is minimum.

(a) By approaching the consumers directly in overseas markets.

(b) By selling the production to an import house or buying agent in India.

(c) By selling the product to an exporting house in India for export purpose.

(ii) Licensing. Another easy method of entering international market is to grant a licence to a foreign firm to manufacture the product by using the firm's name, patent trade mark and technology under the terms of agreement. The company granting the licence gets an agreed percentage on gross sales as its remuneration. A right to use patent, trade marks and technology to produce the goods may be granted with or without any financial involvement. Such an arrangement works in the following situations:

(a) When the importing country puts curbs on imports.

(b) When a country is sensitive to foreign ownership.

(c) When it is necessary for a firm to protect its patent and trade mark against cancellation for non-use.

(d) Where there is a danger of its patent and trade mark being imitated.

This strategy gained prominence in the seventies, because a large number of countries were sensitive to foreign ownership. This form is generally suitable for small and medium sized firms. It does not require a huge capital investment.

(iii) Joint Ventures. Joint ventures mean joining the management and sharing the profit of the firm in the importing country. This venture may be for manufacturing or marketing the product. This strategy got prominence in seventies because most of the developing countries viewed direct foreign investment with suspicion. The other reasons for gaining prominence may be summarised as following:

(a) Lack of adequate capital or human resources inhibiting a company's plan of internationalising its operations;

(b) Prospects of a company in the foreign market if it utilises the skills of a partner in the importing country;

(c) A company's desire to take advantage of the local firm's distribution system.

In joint ventures, the firm enters into collaboration with a local company in the importing country to share the management and profits of such venture. It reduces the political and economic risks substantially, associated with the internationalisation. However, it might lead to loss of absolute control and perhaps also loss of freedom of action in production marketing operations.

(iv) Manufacturing in a Foreign Country. A firm finds that it is not possible or profitable to export the goods to a foreign country due to the following reasons:

(a) The high cost of exporting;

(b) The lower cost of materials and labour in a foreign country and hence lower cost of production;

(c) Tariff and non-tariff barriers on its goods in the importing country.

(d) A firm may decide to manufacture and market the goods loyally in the importing country. Thus, it may keep itself away from the importing country's barriers on the import of goods and other restrictions on imports.

The decision to manufacture and market the goods locally is very risky because the success depends very much in the fair assessment of the market potential in the foreign country concerned. This strategy works well when the market for a specific type of goods in a particular country is substantial and is likely to expand further. The competitive position of the firm in the importing country's market is also a deciding factor in this regard. The firms should also take into consideration the political and economic conditions prevalent in the importing country and their likely effects on the firm manufacturing.

(v) Management Contracts. This method of serving a foreign country it is the result of the external political pressures from the host country Government. It is rarely adopted by the firm itself. It generally comes into being when the firms' investments in a foreign country are expropriated by the host country's Governments and when no suitable and adequate managerial capability exists in the host country. The firm gets specific fees to manage its former investments for a specific item period. Although no firm likes this type of arrangement, it has no choice but to enter into such type of contract as the only viable solution possible.

(vi) Offering Consultancy Services and Undertaking Turnkey Projects. In this arrangement, the countries which are lagging behind in technical field offer facilities to firms from other countries to serve the host country and invite them to participate in their developmental programmes through their expertise services in different specialised fields. Firms having such expertise may enter into contracts with the host country's Government or firms for the export of such project exports which may include the following:

(a) ***Turnkey Projects.*** There are projects which involve the rendering of services like designing, civil construction, erection and commissioning of plant-or-supervision thereof, along with the supply of equipment.

(b) ***Engineering Services Contracts.*** These involve the supply of engineering services along.

(c) ***Consultancy Services Contracts.*** These involve consultation on various matters for the commissioning of plant and include feasibility report, preparation of designs and advice to the project authority on the specifications for plant and equipment etc.

(d) ***Civil Construction Contracts.*** These may be with or without preparation of designs or drawings.

LEVELS OF INVOLVEMENT

Once a decision to enter into foreign market or 'go international' is taken, the next question arises as to the degree of commitment (the level of involvement) towards the international marketing. The level of involvement is not the same for all the firms. It varies from firm to firm depending upon its internal factors like its monetary and non-monetary resources, and external factors like Government policies and market potential. A firm may get itself involved in foreign marketing in any of the following four distinct but overlapping categories:

(1) No Marketing Involvement. In this alternative, the firm does not involve itself in export marketing. It continues to operate predominantly in the domestic market. No serious efforts are made by the firm to enter the foreign market, however its products enter the international markets indirectly. The strategies adopted in this stage by a firm are:

(a) The firm sells the product or products to foreign buyers, coming of their own accord and purchasing their own requirements. Here the responsibility of taking the goods across the border, is that of foreign buyers; and

(b) The firm sells its product to export houses, or to some domestic manufacturers or to other agencies for being ultimately exported by them.

(2) Temporary or Casual Involvement. In this type of involvement, the firm gets involved in foreign business just to dispose of its temporary surplus or to utilise temporary excess capacity. Temporary surpl.ıses may be caused by fluctuations in production levels or demand may result in a firm infrequently marketing its goods abroad. Export of aluminium in the last decade was only of temporary nature because its export was allowed only when its domestic demand was much lower than its production. But with the power situation getting worse and the domestic demand continuing to grow, aluminium manufacturers had no motivation to export.

(3) Regular Marketing Involvement. Here the firm is serious to foreign market commitment. It earmarks a fixed percentage of production capacity which is specifically devoted to the production of goods meant for export. The firm makes serious efforts to develop the foreign markets. It appoints foreign or domestic middlemen or sets up its own distribution channels and sales force in foreign markets to explore the marketing potentials. Visits to foreign countries are more frequent. Here also the primary motivation of the firm remains producing for home markets and producing for overseas markets is only an extension of markets for the products, being already produced at home with some modifications, if any, for foreign markets.

(4) Intensive or Global Involvement. In this case, a firm becomes truly international firm as it starts treating the entire world as its market and seeks to maximise its profits globally. The firm involves itself in international operations intensively and establishes branches for producing and marketing the goods in a number of countries of the world. The products that such a firm sells in markets are not its surpluses but they are purposely produced for markets. Such firms are generally termed as 'multinationals,' or 'transnationals'.

As the firm gets itself more and more involved in international business and relies more on foreign markets to absorb its surplus production, the basic marketing orientation changes. Generally, when firm goes through the above four categories of involvement, one at a time, it is possible if for it to skip one or the other stage. With each subsequent stage, international marketing becomes more sophisticated and complex. In the first two stages of involvement, the firm relies more on other for marketing its products in foreign markets while in the later stages, it may engage its own personnel in selling the product, to specific foreign buyers. The marketing task in the earlier stages is simple, *i.e.*, only selling while in later stages, serious research is necessary and serious attempts are made to locate and satisfy the needs of the customers.

However, before entering into the export market the firm should undertake a thorough analysis of the markets and its resources to get a success.

PROBLEMS AND PRACTICES OF INTERNATIONAL MARKETING

We have earlier discussed the importance of export marketing in various fields in detail but there are certain hindrances as well in undertaking international business. The international marketing is quite different and more complicated than the domestic business because there are certain basic points of difference which make the export marketing more complex. Different Governments different political entities, different currencies, restrictions and barriers, social differences etc. create complications and make the free flow of goods and services among different countries difficult. However, in domestic marketing, the rules and regulations, restrictions and barriers, currency and other factors are the same from market to market within the country. Hence the task of international marketer is more difficult than that of domestic marketer because of the complexities in export trade. These complexities create the following problems:

(1) Different Trade Patterns. International marketing has primarily to deal with the trade patterns among the various countries of the world. It has also to take into account those trade policies of various countries which govern their imports and exports. Naturally, those policies and practices impose certain constraints and restrictions on international trade. Hence the task of international marketer is to solve the problems by experience and expertise and evolve a marketing strategy which will get the best possible results for one's own country.

(2) Regulatory Measures. Every country in the world aims at exporting more than its imports in order to achieve a favourable trade balance. Further, the trade pattern of a country is dictated by its desire to achieve its national objectives which are, by and large, to export its surplus natural resources, agricultural produce and manufactured goods to the extent, it can, and import only those goods and products which are not produced, extracted or manufactured within the country. This automatically brings about certain limitations in its trade with other countries, resulting in regulatory measures such as tariff barriers (custom duties) non-tariff barriers (quota restrictions, foreign exchange restrictions, technological and administrative regulations, consular formalities, state trading and preferential arrangements etc.), trade agreements and joint commissions etc. come in the way of a free and unfettered flow of foreign trade.

(3) Lopsided Development or Developing Countries. The developing countries are equipped with sophisticated technologies capable of transforming raw materials into finished products on a large scale. The developing countries, on the other hand, lack technical knowledge and latest equipment and therefore they have to subsist on old and outdated technologies. It leads to the lopsided development in the international marketing and trade has been the concern of most of the developing countries in the world because the present trade pattern, unfortunately, has been such that the raw material wealth of developing countries flows into developed countries and is converted there, into sophisticated manufactured goods with the help of latest technologies available with them and there is channelised back into the developing countries at a price disproportionate to their intrinsic valae.

(4) Economic Unions. Another negative aspect of international marketing is the increasing tendency among nations to form small groups of economic unions. As a result, apart from ensuring a free flow of trade among themselves, the member countries as a group and in a better position to negotiate terms for their trade with other countries. ASEAN, COMECON, EEC, LAFTA are a few examples of economic unions which, to a certain extent, inhibit growth and world trade on a free and fair basis.

(5) National Policy or Development. Aspirations of individual countries of the world to achieve self-sufficiency in industrial production by developing necessary infrastructure of their own with a view to converting their raw materials into finished products have tempted many countries for the imposition of restrictions and erection of barriers on international trade. The strategy of other countries in international marketing should, take into account such barriers created by many countries. The country, desirous of achieving self sufficiency, follows a strategy of importing capital goods equipped with latest and sophisticated technology and restricting imports of less important consumer goods with a view to lowering down its import bill.

(6) Procedural Difficulties. Different countries have evolved different procedures, practices and documents in order to regulate the export trade. Some of these—such as foreign exchange control regulations and others—have been formulated after keeping in view the national objectives, and have posed certain procedural problems to exporters and importers.

(7) Other Problems. Apart from the problems generally faced by an exporter in international marketing, there are many other internal difficulties which restrict the export trade and consequently affect the foreign exchange earnings. We are explaining certain internal problems as our exporters are facing in India which come in the way of our export trade.

(i) Business and industry have not recognised the importance or export marketing. They have not decided to make exports a 'must'. They, therefore, do not dare to step in the foreign markets. In some cases, our businessmen are ignorant of the export facilities and assistance available in the country.

(ii) Inflation, high prices and black marketing are staring us in the face. If this situation persists, it may put our price level beyond the means of our customers abroad, no matter, how badly they need our export.

(iii) Our internal economy is being managed very badly in recent years. If it continues, we may find ourselves impoverished to the point where we cannot supply our own essential need, what to say about supplying to other nations.

(iv) Poor business ethics is also responsible for our poor foreign trade.

In order to solve our export marketing problems the following efforts should be made by heart:

(a) Our business and industry should have an international outlook.

(b) Export targets must be realistically assessed and the export market segments be focussed or should be selected.

(c) Relevant environmental factors in the export market must be fully analysed.

(d) An export marketing strategy must be designed with regard to the following factors:

(i) size and extent of export market,

(ii) buyers behaviour in the world market,

(iii) foreign competition,

(iv) legal, political and business factors, and

(v) final price and terms of sales with reference to costs.

In export marketing, service also counts. The product-exported must be of acceptable quality and for this purpose a constant study of consumers abroad should be made.

Keeping in mind the problem which are really faced in the international marketing by an exporter and some internal difficulties, it can be safely argued that the task of international marketer is more difficult than that of domestic marketer.

INTERNATIONAL MARKETING V/S. DOMESTIC MARKETING

Marketing can be conceived as an integral part of two processes, *i.e.*, technical and social. So far as technical aspect is concerned, international and domestic marketing are identical. Technical aspect includes non-human factors in marketing such as product, price, brand, packaging, warehousing, costs etc. and the basic principles regarding these variables have universal applicability. The social aspect, on the other hand, is unique in any given stratum as it involves human elements, namely, the behavioural pattern of the consumers and characteristics of the society such as customs, attitudes, values etc. Thus, international marketing is identical to the domestic marketing as far as technical aspect is concerned but international marketing, to the extent, it is visualised as a social process, differs from domestic marketing.

Similiarities

The following points of similarities may be observed between international and domestic marketing:

(i) In both the markets—domestic as well as international, satisfying the basic needs of the consumers is of prime importance. The success of exporting company depends very much on this factor. It involves finding out what the customers want and how to meet their needs accordingly.

(ii) Creation of goodwill is necessary in both the markets. If a firm is able to win the faith of the consumers in the market, the task of marketing will be much simpler and easier in comparison to those who are not able to do so. For this purpose, the marketer should after liberal guarantees and after sale services to the customers on fairly extensive scale.

(iii) Research and development with a view to product improvement and adaptation is necessary both for international and national marketing. By research, several new facts are found out and in the light of those facts, products are improved.

(iv) The technique of marketing, *i.e.*, non-human factors such as product, price, costs etc. are similar to both the market.

Differences

(i) Sovereign Political Entities. Each country is a sovereign political entity. Therefore, several restrictions are imposed by them for importing and exporting the goods and services in order to safeguard their national interest. The traders in international marketing have to observe such restrictions. These restrictions fall in any of the following categories.

(a) Imposition of Tariffs and Customs Duties. This is done both on import and export of goods and services in order to make them costly in the importing country and not to ban their entry into the country completely: By the efforts of General Agreement on Tariffs and Trade (GATT) in the post-war period their has been a significant reduction in tariff globally and on regional basis due to the emergence of regional economic groupings.

(b) ***Quantitative Restrictions.*** These are imposed in order to :restrict trade in some specific commodities. The major objective behind this is the protection of home industries from the competition of the foreign commodities.

(c) ***Exchange Control.*** The Government, in some countries, not ban the entry of goods in the country but the importer is not allowed the necessary foreign exchange to make the payment for the goods imported. In some cases, exchange control and quantitative controls are put together along with the grant of import licence.

(d) ***Imposition of more Local Taxes on Imported Goods.*** This is done in order to make the imported goods costly.

(ii) **Legal Systems.** Different countries operate different legal systems which differ from each other. Most of the countries follow English Common Law as modified from time to time. However, Japan and Latin American countries are important exceptions to this rule. The existence of different legal systems makes the task of businessmen more difficult. They are not sure as to which particular system will apply to their transactions. As laws are the same for the whole country this difficulty does not arise in the domestic trade.

(iii) **Mobility of Factors of Production.** Mobility of different factors of production is less between nations than in the country itself. However, the mobility of labour has increased manifold with the advent of air transport. The development of international banking has also increased the mobility of capital and labour. In spite of these developments, the mobility of labour and capital in international market is not as much as it is within the country itself.

(iv) Monetary Systems. Each country has its own monetary system. Thus the exchange rates for each country's currency are fixed under the rules framed by the International Monetary Fund. Therefore, these are more or less fixed. However, in recent years the exchange rates have been fluctuating and being determined by demand and supply forces. Some countries operate multiple rates, in which different rates are applicable to different transactions.

(v) Market Characteristics. Market characteristics such as demand pattern, channels of distribution, methods of promotion etc. are different from market to market. Taking each country as separate market, one can assume different market characteristics there. These differences are accentuated due to the existence of Government controls and regulations. However, within one single country, like India and USA, these differences in market patterns may be found from state to state.

(vi) Procedures and Documentation. The laws of the country and the customs of trade in each country demand different procedures and documentary requirements for the import and export of the goods and services. The traders residing within the country have to comply with these regulations and customs if they want import or export of goods and services.

Thus international and domestic trade are quite different as there are differences in legal and monetary systems, in Government regulations and controls, in market characteristics, in mobility of factors of production and in procedures, practices and documentation. Each country has to protect its own interest-political, financial and social. It has to put certain restrictions on foreign trade which is quite different as compared to domestic marketing. Restrictions are also made in domestic marketing but the procedures, systems and the rules and regulations are applicable equally in all the parts of the country and these are well-known to the traders concerned.

INTERNATIONAL MARKETING V/S EXPORT MARKETING

1. Scope

(i) International Marketing. The scope of international marketing includes the following activities:

(a) To set up a branch abroad for processing, packaging, assembly or even undertaking direct manufacturing through direct investment.

(b) To enter into licensing arrangement.

(c) To set up joint ventures and collaborations in the foreign markets.

(d) To offer turnkey projects and consultancy.

(e) To conduct research into the needs of the foreign markets and evolve a suitable marketing strategies to meet them.

(ii) Export Marketing. On the contrary, the scope of export marketing is very limited. It includes only the activity of exporting goods and services to the foreign country and related matters thereto. A manufacturer tries to sell his surplus production in foreign markets as and when the demand for it arises either directly or through some agency. He does not make any attempt to have an insight into the potential of foreign market by conducting research. Nor does he make any attempt to differentiate his marketing mix to match such needs.

2. Approach

(i) International Marketing. A firm's approach in entering the international market is not to avail the Government incentives or to counter the domestic market conditions *i.e.*, intensive competition or the small size. As the approach in entering the international markets is to explore the marketing opportunities in the host country or countries, therefore, the exporting firm's actions are governed mainly by the host country's environment. It aims at countering Government and competitive pressures in the host country. Also at this stage the firm undertakes international market research to identify consumer preferences in the host country and develop an appropriate marketing mix. Here too, the centre of reference remains the parent firm and its headquarters.

(ii) Export Marketing. It approach towards the firm's orientation in the case of export marketing, a firm is ethnocentric or home oriented and produces and sells goods to foreign buyers visiting home country or to an importer in the host country or to an export house for being sold in the foreign market. In exporting the goods by the firm the philosophy here is either:

(a) To counter domestic competition and export the surplus product, or;

(b) To avail of the incentives provided by the home government.

Most of the present day multinationals started their international operations because of compulsion of their domestic market conditions, *i.e.*, intensive competition and their small size. On the other hand most of the Indian firms attracted towards international operations started exporting mainly to avail Government incentives. However, the firm majors into international marketing as the foreign marketing deepens and involves any or all of the above listed alternatives.

To conclude, while international marketing approach presupposes serious marketing involvement of a firm in its foreign markets, export marketing approach is opportunistic. In this case the involvement of a firm in its overseas operations is at best casual.

❒

2

Economic Environment of International Marketing

There is difference between various international markets as it differs from the domestic markets. The diversity in the environments of these factors are to be considered before planning any strategy of international marketing.

Following are the factors that act a determinants of the international marketing policies:

(1) Cultural Factors. Social values become the distinguishing factor between domestic and international marketing. Before stepping in the international market in any way, it is essential to understand the cultural dynamics of these foreign markets. The marketer must consider the cultural factors of the country in which it wants to enter in the international marketing. Culture has a board meaning. According to M.J. Herks Kovits, "culture may be viewed as the sum total of man's knowledge, beliefs, arts, morals, loves, customs and any other capabilities and habits acquired by man as a member of society". To be more precise, culture is the, "distinct, way of life of a group of people, their complete design for living". Man has tried to solve the problems by borrowing from other cultures the various alternatives and by adopting it according to his environment and what is more appropriate for his society.

The borrowing by one society from another society is a process which is systematic and unending. It rather goes on inter-stingly. The adoption of a borrowed system or techniques is restricted to the environment of the society which is borrowing. This is why one product which is radially acceptable by one society is not liked by another society. In the like manner, a technique of selling workable in one society may not be successful in another society. These differences occur because of differences in the way of living, customs, habits, beliefs, morals etc.

The existence of subculture *i.e.*, a culture within a nation's culture, is again a matter that attracts serious thought. Sub-culture arises due to differences existing within a culture. For instance in India, there is a distinction between the northern and the southern part of the country. Sub-cultures, may exist in the geo-political boundaries and sometimes they spread across all the political boundaries. For example, Bangladesh is very much like the West Bengal in India, as far as the cultural similarities are concerned. From the point of view of international marketing these differences between cultures and sub-customs, are very important because of their influence on the marketing plan as well as on the decisions about the selection of these markets. The demand for a product, influenced by cultural factors, must be ascertained to achieve success in the field of international marketing.

A marketer willing to enter an international market, must study following aspects of cultural background of a foreign market:

(a) ***Material Culture.*** This includes, technology and Economic aspects of that country.

(b) ***Social Institutions.*** This includes, the consideration of social organisation, education system, and political system of the foreign country.

The belief and family system its kinds is also be considered.

In addition to these, the Aesthetic part of culture including graphic and plastic art, folk love, folkways and mores, music, drama, dance, etc. are also the aspects to be given consideration. And the last but not the least, is the language of the foreign market.

Regarding culture, the changes that often take place in every society from time to time must also be considered as these caste effective impact on various aspects of peoples life. A firm desirous of entering international market must consider these factors and it should also evaluate the degree of influence and involvement of these factors, on the decision of international marketing policies.

There exists a feature of resistance of the Cultural change. This reflects a certain degree of surprise on and apprehension about new products, ideas, and techniques. The degree and extent of this resistance differ from economy to economy. It has also been noticed that changes affecting the very basic structure of the culture face maximum resistence.

There is also a tendency, commonly present in all economies, to regard foreign goods as the things of social status. One more reason for the indication towards foreign products is the inferior nature of the domestic products, this feature is more common to the developing economies.

Thus for a successful international marketing, proper understanding of the culture is essential.

(2) Political Considerations. Political environment is another factor affecting the foreign market. It is necessary for an international marketer to assess the political environment since these affect has success as well as existence in such markets.

The study and assessment of the political environment include the following:

(a) ***Political Systems.*** The type of government *i.e.*, whether it is Socialistic, Capitalistic, Democratic etc. must be analysed, since the philosophy of the government is reflected in its policies.

(b) ***Philosophy of the Govemment.*** It is essential to study government's philosophy in particular about, policy towards private sector and foreign business. Generally, the governments of the target foreign countries, specify their priority areas in which foreign business is encouraged.

Many rules exist in the different countries. For example in India Foreign Exchange Regulation Act 1973, specifies guidelines for foreign private investment.

Infact, the government's philosophy towards foreign capital goes under change with the change of the party in power at a given period of time. From all this view points, it is essential for an international marketer, to assess the philosophy of the government in power, as well as the long run political prospectives.

(c) Permanency and Stability of the Policy of the Government. It is necessary to examine the extent of permanency and stability of government policy of the target foreign market. The marketer must always be careful about such changes in policy that lead to its destabilisation. It also involves the assessment of the long-run predicability of the governments policy.

The policy of a government in the field of trade may be rendered unstable, because of anyone of the following factors :

(i) Change in Governments.

(ii) Growing aspirations of nationalism.

(iii) Shifting of political parties reaching the government at different levels.

Due to certain causes, the products become politically vulnerable. The attempt of the international marketer should be to minimise it.

(3) Economic Factors. An international marketer should assess the level of economic development of the concerned country. Since the level of development of the countries is not the same, so marketer must act according to making his best contribution to the economic development. It is also essential to assess the economic aspirations of the concerned countries. The factor of 'market potential' should always be kept in mind while studying the levels of economic development of a country.

A marketer should study following indications, in regard:

(a) Gross National Product.

(b) Per Capita Income.

(c) Purchasing power of the consumers.

(d) Rate of Economic Growth.

(e) Level and degree of industrialisation.

(f) The form of marketing channels and related infrastructure.

These factors play tremendous role in chalking out the marketing strategy of the firm deciding to enter the international marketing arena.

In addition to these factors, an international marketer should also study the policies, programmes and objectives of the international economic institutions like GATT, UNCTAD, UNIDO, IMF, World Bank, Asian Development Bank etc.

PRESENT INTERNATIONAL MARKETING SCENARIO

When we look at the current international marketing scenario, the following points attract our attention:

(i) Free trade at the global level is the ideal situation and is beneficial to all countries. However, at present, various types of restrictions (tariff and non-tariff) are imposed on international trade by all countries developed and developing.

(ii) The GATT (now WTO) and other international organisations have failed to introduce new international economic order under which international trade will be free and fair to all participants.

(iii) Regional trade blocs (regional groupings) exist in the field of international marketing. Such blocs (*e.g.*, EEC, EFTA, ASEAN, etc.) may be useful to members of the blocs but they create obstacles in the free movement of goods at the global level. Such blocs are harmful to less developed countries. There is growing trend for such regional groupings among less developed countries of the world.

(iv) In spite of trade restrictions, trade blocs and other obstacles, world trade is growing. World merchandise trade volume rose by eight per cent in 1995 and value of trade in goods and services over $6,000 billion for the first time as per the report of WTO.

(v) Rich and developed countries dominate present international marketing scene. They put pressure on less developed countries to accept certain decisions which are not a favourable but actually harmful to less developed countries.

(vi) The US is the world's leading single goods exporter and also the top importer followed by members of the European Union.

(vii) International marketing is rapidly becoming global marketing. The countries of the world are coming closer under global village. This tendency will lead to integration of economies of different countries. As a result, rapid expansion will take place in the field of export marketing.

(viii) Efforts are urgently required (under the leadership of WTO) for the creation of new international economic order in which free trade in the world will be a reality and just and fair treatment will be given to all countries of the world irrespective of political and economic factors.

(ix) The domination of MNCs on export marketing is fast increasing. These corporations are making huge profits by planning their marketing activities to the global level. MNCs and TNCs are also creating many problems for developing countries as regards their export marketing plans and programmes.

(x) The setting up of the World Trade Organisation (WTO) would see a major shift in the style of the world trade ushering in a new era in which countries would be bound by common rules.

Bilateral Trade Agreement

When two countries make agreement for mutual trade and commercial benefits their agreement is called bilateral trade agreement. The agreement contains all aspects governing import-export transaction and the measures to solve dispute arising thereform if any. The developing countries do make such agreements. Their agreement may be with another developing country or even with the advance country which may be of capitalist or socialist ideology. These agreements depend upon mutual trust and political relationship.

India, has entered into bilateral trade agreements with many countries in the world. India being the developing country still, she needs these agreements to meet the increasing demands of her industrialisation and economic development. India and Russia, India and Germany, India and South Africa are some of the best examples of bilateral trade agreements.

Multilateral Trade Agreement

When more than two countries enter into trading agreement for the common benefit, the agreement is called multilateral trade agreement. After Second World War, multilateral trade agreements have been entered into to resolve the problems arising out of their trading relationships. Maximisation of world welfare, uniform trading pattern and reduction in the duty so as to benefit more to the developing countries and related matters are the objectives of multilateral trade agreements. Multilateral trading agreements are also entered into to ease but the customs and non-tariff barriers which made free trade difficult.

The post war period is fast becoming a global village. Advancement in technology and transport *vis-a-vis* international communication have facilitated international trade. Restrictions once imposed by governments (communist governments) upon imports and exports have been relaxed, as a result of multilateral trade agreements.

Two important multilateral trading agreements are: General Agreement on Tariffs and Trade (GATT), and United National Conference on Trade and Development (UNCTAD).

MOTIVATION TO EXPORT

There are some basic economic reasons which might influence a company decision regarding export business. These are:

(1) Relative Profitability. The rate of profit to be earned from export business may be higher than the corresponding rate on the domestic sales. Export assistance measures as may be instituted by the Government from time to time may substantially affect the relative profitability. Further, experience shows that there has been a progressive improvement in the unit value realisation of certain export products.

(2) Insufficiency of Domestic Demand. The level of domestic demand, either at a point of time or over time, may be insufficient for utilising the installed capacity in full. Export business offers a suitable mechanism for utilising the unused capacity. This will reduce costs and improve the overall profitability of the firm. Recession in the domestic market often serves as a stimulus to export ventures. In fact, export of engineering goods from India picked up momentum at the time of recession in the Indian economy during 1967-69, when Indian manufacturing units faced with large inventories and weak order book position, turned to export markets. Developing diversified export markets thus provides firm with a degree of protection against cyclical domestic economic showdown. But it must be emphasised that there is an inherent danger in looking at exports to merely supplement the domestic business at the time of crisis. Penetrating foreign markets is a difficult job but sustaining them is even more onerous. Therefore, once a decision is taken to enter international markets, every effort will have to be made to retain them. An this can be done only when export marketing operations are recognised as an integral part of the total corporate activity. In fact, what is needed is full involvement in and commitment to exports.

(3) Reducing Business Risks. A diversified export business may help in mitigating sharp fluctuations in the overall activity of a company. When a firm is selling in a number of markets, the downward fluctuation in sales in one market, which may be the domestic country, may be fully or partially counter-balanced by a rise in the sales in other markets. Secondly geographic diversification also provides the momentum to growth inasmuch as a single or a few markets will have only limited absorptive capacity.

(4) Social Responsibility. In many cases, businessmen themselves feel a sense of responsibility and contribute towards the national exchequer by increasing their exports. Incidentally, by exporting at a time when it is difficult to export they build up their image in the domestic market. They also look at exporting to attain status and prestige.

(5) Legal Restrictions. Governments may impose certain restrictions on further growth and capacity expansion of some firms within the domestic market in order to achieve certain social objectives. But there may not be any such restrictions on making investments overseas or the restrictions may be relaxed even in the domestic market, provided the additional capacity envisaged by the company is utilised for exports. In such situations, a firm may contemplate export operations, because it offers a way to achieve corporate growth, which may otherwise not be possible.

Nations have to export to pay for imports of materials, technology or processes not available within their national boundaries. Governments, therefore, may be compelled to impose export obligations on the firms specially those in need of imported inputs.

(6) Increased Productivity. Increased productivity is necessary for ultimate survival of a firm. This itself may lead a company to increase production and then seek export markets. Moreover, in these days of technological developments, bigger companies have to spend a lot on research and development. To meet the increase costs of research and development, larger markets become a necessity and exports become unavoidable.

(7) Technological Improvement. Entry into export markets may enable a firm to:

(a) Pick up new product ideas and to add to product line,

(b) Improve its producer,

(c) Reduce costs, and

(d) Discover new applications for its product.

As was pointed out by Telco Chairman at its 1980 annual General Meeting, 'Export exposes us to the fiercely competitive international market and compels us to update our products. This upgradation of our vehicles unmistakably benefits the Indian customer also.'

ECONOMIC REASONS FOR EXPORT

Why should a firm take a decision to export its goods and services? The simple answer to the question is that the exporting firm exports something more than it gains in the domestic market. The following are some basic reasons whkh might influence a company decision regarding export business:

(1) Insufficiency of Domestic Demand. If the installed capacity of the firm is much more than the level of demand in the domestic market at a point of time or over time, the firm may take a decision to enter into foreign market to utilise its installed capacity in full. Export business offers simple opportunity to utilise the unused capacity. This will reduce the total and per unit cost of production to improve the overall profitability of the firm. Recession in the domestic market often serves as a stimulus to export trade. If we peep into the past, the export of engineering goods in India got momentum during recession in 1967-69 when there was large inventories and weak order book position. Thus developing diversified export markets provide protection to the exporters against cyclical domestic showdown.

One thing must be emphasised here that there is an inherent danger in looking at the export only at the time of crises. The exporter, before entering the foreign market, must think seriously and should take a decision to export only if he is in a position to sustain foreign markets even after the crises is over. Every effort should be made to retain foreign markets: This can be done only when the export operation is recognised as an integral part of the corporate activity.

(2) Legal Restrictions. Governments if almost every country impose certain restrictions on further growth and expansion of some firms or on production and distribution of certain types of commodities for the domestic markets in order to achieve certain social objectives and in the better interest of the country. But, such restrictions may not be for export or for marketing investments in overseas markets or such restrictions may be relaxed if the additional capacity envisaged by the company is utilised for exports. In such situations, a firm may undertake overseas operations to avail the relaxations in order to achieve corporate growth which may otherwise be not possible.

Nations have to export to pay for imports of inputs, materials, technology or processes which are not available within the country. Governments, therefore, may be compelled to impose certain export obligations on firms specially those in need of imported inputs. Governments may impose a condition on the import of the inputs that the importing firm will have to export the whole or a part of its output to meet the imports. Thus; the firm may take an advantage of this obligatory export for the development and growth of the firm.

(3) Relative Profitability. The profitability rate of export business is relatively higher than the rate of profitability in the domestic business. The relative profitability of export trade is also effected by export assistance measures as may be instituted from time to time by the national Governments because, they reduce the cost of production or distribution. Further, it increases the competitive strength of the firm. Experience shows that thrre has been a progresseve improvement in the unit value of certain export products.

(4) Reducing Business Risk. A diversified export business helps the exporting firm in mitigating the risk of sharp fluctuations in the business activity of the firm. When a firm is selling its product in a number of markets, a downward trend in one market may be partially or fully counterbalanced by a rise in sales in other markets in the domestic country or in overseas countries. Secondly, geographic diversification also provides momentum to growth in as much as a simple or a few markets will have only limited absorptive capacity. Thus exporting may reduce the business risks.

(5) Social Responsibility. Some businessmen feel a source of responsibility towards society and prefer to contribute awards the national exchequer by exporting or by increasing the exports of their products. They are committed to exports. Incidentally, by exporting at a time when it is difficult to export, they build up their image in domestic as well as in overseas markets. They take up export activity to attain their status and prestige in tbe society. In this way, exporting of goods is a method of satisfying their ego.

(5) Increased Productivity. Increased productivity is a must in modern day business for the survival of the firm. Due to certain social and technological developments, the industrial productivity has increased a lot. Moreover, bigger companies have to spend a lot on research and development. Due to increased productivity, the production of the company shall also be increased. Moreover, it has also become necessary to increase the production of goods in the industry in order to meet the increased costs of research and developments. This may lead company to enlarge its markets in order to absorb the increased production. As the domestic markets have limited capacity, the exports become unavoidable.

(7) Technological Improvement. Export exposes a company to the fiercely competitive international market and compels a company to update its products. It leads a company to introduce new products with latest technological improvements that it may face the competition in the domestic and foreign markets. Thus entry into export market may enable a firm to-*(i)* pick up new product ideas and to extend the length, width and depth of the product line. *(ii)* improve the product, *(iii)* Cut its production costs, *(iv)* discover new applications for the product; and *(v)* utilise its production capacity to the maximum extent.

(8) Competition in Domestic Markets. Almost in every country, the existing firms are increasing their level of production to meet the domestic demand. But, on the other hand, it is also true that new and new firms are entering the domestic marketing. It leads to cut throat competitive in the domestic marketing. Firms, facing severe competition in the local markets, may take a decision to enter overseas markets, in order to reduce the severity of the problem. It may be argned here that the competition also exists in the foreign markets. But there is a difference in the form and level of competition there. In foreign markets competition quality and standards of products exists. Price competition poses not a big problem in foreign markets. It is, therefore, a challenge to local busnessmen to improve the quantity and standards of their products and increase the export to avoid the domestic competition. Many foreign firms entered domestic markets only due to severe competition in their home countries and are running their business successful here because the quantity of their products is much better than that of many Indian products in the line. One more example may be cited to clear the point. The Indian engineering goods entered the foreign markets due to intense competition in domestic market but they have fared well in international market even though cut-throat competition from many advanced countries is there and it becomes possible only because their quality is much better as compared to products of other countries.

(9) Product Obsolescence. Every product has its own life cycle and is to die as soon as the cycle (innovation, growth maturity and obsolescence) is over. Some products (which are generally used by well-to-do people) may become obsolescent in domestic markets but there may be markets for such products overseas. There are so many products which have reached a stage of obsolescence in developing countries yet they can be sold easily in under developed or undeveloped countries. For example lantern(oil lamps) in most of the developing countries has become out of date but there is a good demand of lanterns in Indian and other underdeveloping countries. Thus, the firm producting a product that has become obsolescent in domestic market may take a decision for its export in market where it can be sold easily.

EFFECTS OF NON-TANGIBLE FORCES

Apart from certain financial factors which are considered by the management mainly at the time of making decision for the entry into foreign markets, there are certain non-financial or non-tangible forces that affect the decision-making process of a firm. Such forces are necessarily originating from the environmental dynamics. Three major forces have been identified. These are:

(1) Commitment Effect. The Government role in business and industry has been increasing day by day. Its role can be viewed as a two-edge force, with one edge, making demands on management and on the other bringing benefits to it. As a result the management must be ready to meet the Government expectations. It should make the business policies and objectives consistent with the state policies and objectives. Though this cannot be attained by force, yet an agreement between Government and public sector policies must be present keeping in view the national interest. The Government expects full employment, price stability and growth from the business and the business is supposed to commit to these social objectives and this commitment will serve the interest of the business and industry. Private sector should recognise its responsibility to the society. In the changed context of social values, validation of the concept of private property needs to be in terms of the business, commitment to the objectives the society has set before itself.

This philosophy of social commitment is now being accepted by the progressive business leaders in India. It is being realised that the rapid change in the political, economic and social values of the emergent India is bound to have its reflection on the business concepts as well.

It is needless to say that Government has stressed the price importance on export and offered various concessions including legal sanctions proyision of financial incentives, appeals and exhortation as fa strategy for export promotion. As a consequence, many progressive firms did take into account this national objective of export promotion seriously, despite adverse financial considerations, including assistance and concessions from the Government. It cannot be suggested in the interest of the business that it will go on incurring losses to adhere to the national goal but that a policy objective stressed repeatedly by the Government gives a motivational stimulus to see whether the objective can be attained.

The national awards of outstanding export performance have also helped in creating a psychological climate which is conducive to export consciousness. Also industrialists are increasingly realising the indirect benefits which stem from export activity.

(2) Image Effect. Every firm try to project an image in the minds of those social groups with which the firm deals, *viz.*, customers, competitors, dealers, Government, shareholders and so on. At the same time these social groups hold an image of the firm which may or may not be identical of the image which the firm aspires. The octroi of the firm must be oriented to the task of bringing all the images in line with the image the firm wants to project for itself. Firms in India want to project an image which may reflect two basic qualities. First, their product is quality product and secondly, they are socially progressive. They try to develop and project such image through their export involvement.

We in India tell recently considered the mark 'Made in England or Germany' as the hallmark of quality. After independence, the supply of foreign goods became scarce but the domestic products completely failed to meet the public thirst of quality goods. Since it is generally recognised that exportable products are of standard quality, attempts were make to produce exportable items to be of standard quality as compared to those produced for being sold only in the domestic market. A firm which is successful in marketing its products in the foreign market may claim that its products are of superior quality and it will help in projecting the image of the firm as producer of quality goods. It satisfies the first ingredient of the desired image.

As far as the second ingredient of the desired image, *i.e.*, an image of socially progressive firm, is concerned, it can be sought to be achieved through export involvement. If a firm is successful either:

(a) In promoting exports to earn foreign exchange, or

(b) In conserving foreign exchange by promoting import substitution, it can be justifiably claim to have contributed to the national objective and thereby projects its image as socially responsible and progressive firm. Public relations of the firm can emphasise this image in advertisements.

(3) Organic Effect. Organic effect refers to the changes in the management decision-making process effected by changes evolving within the management. The one significant change in the social structure of management in India is the emergence of professional management class. In developed countries, the professional management class is in full control of the management, *i.e.*, proprietorship and management have been separated. Naturally, ambitions and aspirations, values and attitudes to work affect the decision-making process of the organisation, where they are employed.

Maslow has classified all human needs in five distinct levels in hierarchical order, *i.e.*,:

(a) Physiological needs,

(b) Safety or security needs,

(c) Social needs,

(d) Ego needs, and

(e) Self-fulfilment needs.

First three needs are most probably satisfied in case of the managerial cadre, only last two remain to be satisfied. The managers work in full devotion in the company only to satisfy their ego and self esteemed needs.

An export manager knows it pretty well that his standing in the company depends on the success, he may achieve in getting increasing volume of export business. Even if his job is secure, the urge to get acclaims from his superiors will motivate him to work to his best.

Similarly self-esteemed needs which are related to self-development and growth also push him to the same end. Extending the earlier example, an export manager who is fully satisfied from his work knows that he may be assigned a more challenging task by the board of directors if the board feels satisfied. It does not only increase his remuneration that goes with the assignment but also it gives boost to his self-confidence and a thrill to play a more important role in the decision-making process for the policy formulation and so on.

Organic effect can also be traced to another change that taken place in the hierarchy of business organisation due to the process of cooperation. If the management seeks cooperation from the juniors in the policy determining structure of an organisation, it will naturally absorb new elements into the leadership as a means of averting threats to its existence or stability. These new elements will induct new values and judgements to the policies and thus will change the original system of values. Appointment of Government representatives or nominees of the financed institutions to the Board thus helps in making the policy of the firm in consistent with the social objectives.

INTERNATIONAL INSTITUTIONS

Following are some international institutions and their objectives.

World Bank

The International Bank for Reconstruction and Development (IBRD), also known as the World Bank, was set up in 1945 to provided international capital for reconstruction and development of Western Europe which was devastated during the Second World War. The objective has since been achieved. The main function of the World Bank is now to provide loans to the developing countries for development projects and programmes. Since the credit rating of many developing countries is poor, they find it difficult to raise resources in international capital markets. The World Bank is, therefore, a vital source of finance to the developing countries. The Bank's subscribed capital as on June 30, 1985 was $58.9 billion and its membership was 148.

The basic rules governing the World Bank operations are:

(i) It must lend only for productive purposes and must stimulate economic growth in the developing countries where it lends.

(ii) It must give due regard to the prospects of repayment.

(iii) Each loan is made to a Government or must be guaranteed by the government concerned.

(iv) The Bank's decisions to lend must be based on economic considerations.

(v) Loans must be used to meet the foreign exchange component of the projects.

(vi) The rate of interest is somewhat lower but related to market rates.

(vii) The use of loans cannot be restricted to purchases in any particular member country. In other words, loans are not 'tied'.

Functions of the World Bank

The World Bank is an inter-governmental institution, corporate in form, the capital stock of which is owned by its member-governments. The principal functions of the bank as enumerated in Article 1 of the Articles of Agreement are :

(i) To assist in the reconstruction and development of the territories of its member Governments by facilitating investment of capital for productive purpose;

(ii) Where private capital is not available on reasonable terms, to make loans for productive purposes out of its own resources or out of the funds borrowed by it; and

(iii) To promote foreign private investment by guarantees of or through participation in loans and other investments made by private investors;

(iv) To promote the long-range growth of international trade and the maintenance of equilibrium in the balance of payments by encouraging international cooperation.

"World Bank's loan are mainly directed to help the member countries to Bank Except in special circumstances, for the purpose of specific projects of proceeds of any loan are used only for the purposes for which the loan was granted."

Objectives of World Bank

(1) To Assist in the Reconstruction and Development of its Member Countries. This is by facilitating the investment of capital for productive purposes, thereby promoting white long range growth of international trade and improvements in standard of living ;

(2) To Promote Private Foreign Investment. This is done by guarantees of, and participation in, loans and other investments made by private investors; and

(3) To Make Loans for Productive Purposes. When private capital is not available on reasonable terms this is done out of its own resources or the funds borrowed by it.

Financing

(1) Direct Lending. IBRD may lend funds directly, either its capital funds or from the funds it borrows in private investment markets.

(2) Guarantee. IBRD may guarantee loans advanced by others or it may participate in such loans.

(3) Loans to Member Countries. Loans may be advanced to member countries directly or to any of their political sub-divisions or to private business or agricultural enterprises in the territories of members.

As credit rating of many developing countries is poor, they feel difficulties in raising funds an international capital markets. In its efforts to advance loans for developmental purposes, the World Bank has provided loans to the developing countries for developmental projects and programmes. It is a vital source of finance to the developing countries. When the member Government, in whose territory the project is located, is not the borrower the World Bank asks the member Government for a guarantee.

Subsidiaries of the World Bank

(1) International Development Association (IDA). In order to structure the economy of less developed countries, the World Bank set up the International Development Association (IDA) in 1960. It is an aiding centre for several developing countries who look up to it for financial assistance. It is an association of donor countries who have come under the aegis of the World Bank to help the developing or less developed countries whose paying capacity is limited due to their socio-economic problems.

Credits

(a) Criteria. The main criterion for the allocation of IDA credit is the per capital income of the recipient country. Countries which have an annual per capital Gross National product (GNP) of less than $681 (in 1979 dollars) are eligible for IDA credits. Other parameters taken into consideration are a country's credit worthiness, its accessibility to commercial borrowing, its economic performance, the density of its population and the existence of viable projects in the borrowing nations.

(b) Terms. IDA interest-free credits available to Government only may be obtained on payment of nominal service charges at 0.75% per annum. The period of repayment is 40 years, excluding 10 years for initial grade period. This is in contrast to World Bank loan which carries an interest at 12% per annum and the repayment period is 20 years. Thus less developed countries have benefited immensely from IDA. The number of beneficiary till June 1982 was 78.

(c) Purposes. The purposes for which the IDA has advanced the credits are agriculture, rural development, education, energy, industrial development and finance, industry, population and nutrition, transportation and tourism, telecommunication etc.

(d) Credits to India: As the largest beneficiary from IDA, India's share is 40% of IDA funds. During Third Plan India got aid from IDA $578 m (Current). During the fourth plan his was tripled to about $1,556 m (Current). During fifth Plan it touched a new height of nearly $5,581 m (Current). This increasing trend halted during the Sixth Plan as the amount of aid authorised during the plan was about $4,568 m. However, both because of infrastructural difficulties at home and the adverse conditions imposed by donor countries governing such aid. India has not been able to utilise this aid fully. IDA credits have helped various sectors of Indian economy such as agriculture, rural development, construction, irrigation, power, telecommunication, ports, industrial imports, fertilizer production, shipping etc. Some of the important projects financed by IDA credit project, are : Gorakhpur fertilizer expansion projects, Bombay development project, Railway project etc. IDA has also been providing funds to the Industrial Development Bank of India (IDBI) and the Agricultural Refinance and Development Corporation (ARDC) for their developmental activities pertaining to industry, agriculture and rural development.

(2) International Finance Corporation (IFC) Establishment. An affiliate of the World Bank it was set up in 1956. It extends credits to private business enterprises. It provides equity and loan capital for private enterprises in association with private investors and managements, and encourages the development of local capital. Particularly, it supports joint ventures which provide opportunities to combine domestic knowledge of market and other conditions with the technical and managerial experience available in the industrial nations. Organisation IFC had 124 members as on 30th June 1983. On the date its paidup capital was 544 million dollar and its retained earning were 204 m. dollars. It has authority to borrow up to 732 m dollars. It had made commitments totalling 5520m dollars to 711 private enterprises. In the fiscal year 1982, it approved investments totalling 612m dollars for 65 projects. In 1983, the approved investment amounted to 612 m dollars for 58 projects.

Conditions of Assistance

The project, for which IFC advances assistance, must satisfy the following conditions:

(a) It should have the prospects of earning profits.

(b) It should boost the economy of the country.

(c) Local investors should be able to participate in the project in the beginning of the project or later.

(d) The required funds for the project are not available from private investors at reasonable terms.

(e) The management should be capable and experienced.

(f) The sponsor of the project has a substantial holding in the enterprise.

India and the World Bank Group

Until June 1983, cumulative landing by the World Bank to India amounted to 5553 m dollars in 76 loans out of a total of 89.6 billion dollars and by the IDA, the cumulative lending was 11,529 m dollars in 149 loans out of a total of 30.1 billion dollars. Till then India received 17083 m dollars for 225 projects out of cumulative combined assistance of 119.7 billion dollars from World Bank and IDA taken together so far. The IFC has advanced 220 m dollars for 22 companies till June 1983.

Because of constraints on resources the prospects of getting larger funds frc'n V'orld Bank seem to be bleak, because of the failure of the USA to provide funds for its replenishment, the situation is not much better as regards IDA loans. Due to the entry of China as a member of IDA, India's share of aid has been adversely affected. However, the prospects of getting assistance from IEC have improved substantially due to a positive turn in Government of India policy in this respect.

International Monetary Fund (IMF)

Even before the Second World War came to an end, monetary experts in USA and UK started thinking over the monetary problems likely to be faced after the war. Two different plans were chalked out, one by Mr. Keynes an American author and the other by Mr. White-a British author, and were named after them as Keynes Plan and White, Plan. The two sets of proposals were subjected to intensive discussion and served as the basis for the Brettonwoods conference. The conference decided to set up two organisations:

(i) International Monetary Fund (IMF), and

(ii) International Bank for Reconstruction and Development popularly known as IBRD.

The International Monetary Fund was established on 27th December 1945 but it actually started operations from 1st March 1947 and the first transactions were made in May 1947. The funds of the IMF are subscribed to by the member countries. Each member country subscribes to the Fund as per its quota fixed by the IMF at the time of its joining the Fund 25% of the quota or 10 per cent of the members holdings of gold and U.S. dollar, whichever is less, is subscribed to in gold and the remainder in national currency. Now, the system of depositing gold as a part of its subscription, has been discontinued and the accounts of IMF are kept in SDR (Special Drawing Rights).

The Fund has 146 member countries, accounting for about 80 per cent of the total world production and 90 per cent of the total world trade. Russia is a member of the Fund.

Aims of the Establishment of the IMF

The IMF was established with following aims:

(i) Establishment of Monetary co-operation between the countries on the durable lines.

(ii) To maintain and promote the international exchange rates.

(iii) To faciliate the increasing rate of employment and increase in the real national incomes of the countries.

(iv) To remove international foreign exchange problems which distort the economic development.

(v) To provide funds to the members and to help them in their monetary problems of international level.

(vi) To reduce the possibility of exchange depreciation complementarity among the nations.

(vii) To faciliate the system of international payments; but removing the problem before the countries.

(viii) To help in the eradication of maladjustments.

(ix) To remove the situations of disequilibrium lying among the countries.

(x) To strengthen the economic integrity of the member nations.

All these functions are enlisted in Article I of the Charter by which this Fund has been created.

Functions of the IMF

(i) Regulatory functions. The IMF administers a code of good behaviour in international payments. It regulates exchange rate practices and international payments.

(ii) Financial Functions. As a financial institution, the IMF offers medium-term loans to the national monetary authorities to enable them to make up their balance of payment deficits. Its resources come from the member countries based on an established quota as fixed in terms of SDR and member countries under certain conditions as set forth in the 'General Arrangements to Borrow'.

(iii) Consultative Functions. As a consultant, the IMF provides a forum for international cooperation. It is a source of counsel and technical assistance to its members.

In November 1983, the aggregate fund quotas were 6106 billion SDR approximately. As a result of Eighth General Review of Quotas these are expected to increase to SDR 90,035 billion. Quotas are used to determine:

(a) The voting power of members;

(b) Their contribution to fund resources,

(c) Their access to these resources, and

(d) Their share in the allocation of SDRs.

India's quota in the Fund is SDR 1,717.5 million. It is expected to increase to SDR 2207.7 million.

Board Functions of IMF

(i) Fixation of Exchange Rates. The procedure relating to the fixation of exchange rates was enumerated in Section I of the Article IV of the charter. According to the par value of the currency was to expressed in terms of gold or in U.S.A. dollar.

(a) Country must report about the par value in 30 days.

(b) Member countries cannot buy gold beyond the prices described by the upper and lower limits of the par value.

(c) 14% margin was as to be provided in the case (b) above.

(ii) Alterations in Exchange Rates. The exchange rate is not a rigid rate. It is subject to alteration with the alterations in the national and international monetary conditions. No member country is allowed to bring any feeling of complimentarity by adopting competitive Exchange Depreciation.

Article IV of the declaration has made certain obligatory rules for the states while changing the par value for instance; a change in the par value should be with the permission and consultation of the IMF. The change should be only to remove the disequalibrium. If a change in the part value by a country does not affect the international monetary system, then the consultation and approval of the IMF is not required.

In short a member-country can undertake an adjustment of 10 per cent only. If the Nation wants further adjustment then 10% is again allowed with the permission of the IMF. The adjustments are allowed only in the condition that it is to cure some acute disequilibrium.

(iii) Sale and Purchase of the Currency. As per powers vested by Article V of the Agreement, IMF can sell and purchase the currency of nations on the basis of gold. It is to facilitate the members in their international transaction in complexities. A country is empowered to buy only 25% of the quota in a year. A member state can only use the IMF's resources with its due permission.

Following table will explain the policy of the IMF selling currency to a member nation. It has been framed for to disinduce the member for buying more and more currency for long period).

I.M.F. Fund's Holding in excess of to quota	*Charge Payable*					*(In percent)*
	First 3 Months	*Next 9 Months*	*Second year*	*Third year*	*Fourth year*	*Fifth year*
Upto 25%	Nil	½	1	1½	2	2½
26-50% ½	1	1½	2	2½	3	
51-75% 1	1½	2	2½	3	3½	
76-100%	1½	2	2½	3	3½	4

(iv) Demand of Scarce Currency. A scarce currency is the currency whose amount has fallen down the level of quota which is kept with the IMF. In short the currency is available only in a very small amount. In short the currency is available only in a very small member nation (whose currency has fallen short) to re-evaluate its currency to raise prices and cost of production in the economy to induce imports. With the rise in imports more currency will start, coming in the international market. The member nation is obliged to follow the directions of the IMF.

(v) Technical Assistance. International Monetary Fund also provides technical assistance to the member nations. IMF sends its expert technical officers to the member countries to provide consultation on specific subjects. These officers also survey the member countries, economic prospects and provide guidance in the desired fields.

The Fund also takes the help of the experts from outside by assigning them the task of helping some member-nation. This is often done in case a member nation wants permanent expert on the subject.

To provide more efficient technical assistance IMF has created two departments.

(i) The Central Banking Service Department.

(ii) Fiscal Affairs Department.

These departments are entrusted with specialisation work in the respective fields.

Thus IMF has played a great role and it has to pay more complicated and vast role, as the development of the economies moves further.

TRADING BLOCS

The emergence of trading blocs has been a post-war phenomenon. Countries which possessed something in common began to get together as an Economic Union for mutual benefit. Such economic blocs could get extra advantageous terms, especially for the import of raw material from developing countries. Barriers to trade among the member countries were reduced and sometimes even eliminated. A free movement of factors of production, such as labour, capital, etc., was permitted within the Bloc so that each country could specialise in particular areas of production activity while enjoying at the same time the combined strength of the union *vis-a-vis* other countries.

Some of the powerful forces at work in the formation of these blocs are the geographical contiguity of the countries within the union, social, cultural and ethnic similarities among them, or a common ideology.

Some of these trade blocs are:

(1) European Economic Community (EEC). Also known as the European Common Market, it is a powerful economic bloc comprising the developed countries to Western Europe. It was established by a Treaty of Rome in 1957. It came into operation in 1959. The founder members of the community were France, W. Germany, Italy, Belgium, the Netherlands, and Luxemburg. Greece and Turkey are associate members. In 1973, UK joined the Community.

EEC is a customs and economic union. The EEC's aim is to coordinate the efforts of all member countries for the benefit of the entire community. Countries of the community have abandoned separate tariff schedules for import from member countries. Internally, member countries enjoy free movement of all goods and services and sometimes of even factors of production, such as labour and capital. Member countries help each other to speedily sort out problems of balance of payment experienced by any of the group.

As originally conceived, the EEC was a political union but to a large extent it has worked as an economic union.

(2) European Free Trade Zone (EFTA). It was created by the Convention of Stockholm in 1960 with members countries Austria, Denmark, Norway, Iceland, Portugal, Sweden and Switzerland. Finland is an Associate member. Its aim is to promote trade among member countries in a free and fair atmosphere, to achieve full employment, together with the optimum use of resources towards realising better standards of living. It aims to obtain an equitable distribution of raw material resources. To enable the free flow of trade among the protective import duties and other trade barriers among member countries would be removed wherever necessary.

(3) The Council for Mutual Economic Assistance (COMECON). It was started as a rival organisation of EEC, under the active control of the USSR at about the same time. It comprises all the socialist countries of East Europe and the Soviet Union. Its members are: Russia, Rumania, East Germany, Poland, Hungary,

Yugoslavia, Bulgaria and Czechoslovakia. Its objective is to achieve economic integration among member countries. It has made an attempt to coordinate their five-year plan, so that, ultimately, joint planning may become a reality. By achieving economic cooperation, they would be in a position to pool their resources with regard to technical skill and raw material supplies. This would enable them to present a joint front in international trade forums and trading activities. To some extent integration has been achieved in the field of raw material processing and mining industries. Recently, attempts were made to achieve at least semblance of economic integration in the field of energy. Unfortunately, in other areas of co-operation, member countries tend to keep the national interest alive, thereby hampering, to a certain extent, the concept of integration. COMECON discourages exports to capitalist countries of western Europe and North America. Despite these facts, a determined effort has been made by member countries to export their goods to developed countries. Some of the COMECON countries are even keen on signing long-term trade agreements with developed countries, particularly with the neighbouring countries of Western Europe.

(4) Association of South-East Asian Nations (ASEAN). It is a loose economic union of the five South-East Asian nations, namely, Malaysia, Thailand, Singapore, Indonesia and the Philippines. Its aim is to promote economic interdependence among member countries. Its members meet periodically to formulate their strategies. They present a united front with a view to obtaining concessions and favourable terms for the products exported by them to other countries, particularly to the developed countries. Like other economic unions, ASEAN aims at political understanding among member countries in order to strengthen their economic interdependence.

(5) Latin American Free Trade association. (LAFTA). It was set up in 1960, with its headquarters at Montevideo and ten member countries including Uruguay, Argentine, Brazil, Mexico, Chile and Venezuela. Its ultimate aim is to form an association that would create a South American common market. With this end in view, many discussions were held among them and steps were considered to eliminate tariff and trade restrictions. Unfortunately, owing to political instability and consequent economic imbalances among member countries, nothing significant has been achieved by LAFTA in the last decade and a half. In April 1977, at the Fifteenth Congress of the Inter-American Council for Trade and Production, it was strongly recommended that the much elusive Latin American Common Market be formed within the existing political framework of LAFTA. The chief aim of the Congress was to eliminate control over monetary policies and formulate equal legal norms for foreign and local investments.

(6) Andean Group. In 1968, a smaller group of countries joined together to form the "Andean Group" with Bolivia, Chile, Columbia, Equator, Peru and Venezuela as members. Chile subsequently dropped out. Unlike the earlier associations, the "Andean Group" has been successful in eliminating restrictions on trade, thus achieving a more or less free movement of trade among member countries.

GENERAL AGREEMENT ON TARIFFS AND TRADE (GATT)

GATT is the short form for General Agreement on Tariffs and Trade. As a multilateral treaty among the member countries it lays down certain agreed rules for conducting international trade. It came into being on 1st January 1948. At this time it was considered an interim arrangement pending the formation of U.N. agency to supersede it. When such agency failed to emerge, GATT was amplified and further enlarged at several succeeding negotiations. The member countries contribute together to four-fifth of the total world trade. Underdeveloped countries form a sizable majority in GATT.

'Ever since its creation in October, 1947 the GATT has been a major force in the reduction of tariffs and restrictions on imports. The GATT is also the meeting place of world's trading nations where the present day issues closely bearing on the world trade are discussed and decisions taken. The GATT has played, and will continue to play, in increasingly important role in the expansion of international trade.'

Origin of GATT

The GATT owes its existence to the efforts made by the Allied Powers during World War II to create new international institutions that would help promote more liberal system of international trade and payment and discourage the adoption of restrictionist practices. The depressed trade conditions that followed the great depression of 1929-33 and prompted the Governments of many countries to erect various kinds of protective trade barriers, high tariff protection, quota restrictions on imports, exchange controls and the like.

The GATT, which had been originally intended as a purely temporary arrangement, has now developed into a permanent international arrangement whose rules have been accepted by the greater proportion of the lending trading countries. The GATT is a treaty that is collectively administered by the contracting parties. Representatives of the contracting parties meet from time to time to discuss matters of common interest and give to effect to the provisions of the Agreement requiring joint action.

Administration and Membership

The increasing responsibilities of the GATT made it necessary to strengthen the organisation entrusted with task of administration, consequently at their sixteenth session in May and June 1960, following a review by a special group into the working methods and organisational structure of the GATT, the contracting parties decided to set up a Council of Representatives. The function of the Council is to consider urgent matters between the sessions of GATT's contracting parties, as well as to conduct regular business consisting of the supervision of the work of committees and preparation for sessions.

Basic Principles of the GATT

(1) Trade without Discrimination. Trade must be conducted on the basis of non-discrimination. All contracting parties are bound to grant to each other treatment as favourable as they would to any country (most favoured nation) in the application and administration of import and export duties and charges. Exceptions to this basic rule are allowed only in the case of regional trading arrangements and the developing countries.

(2) Protection only Through Tariffs. Protection should be given to domestic industries only through customs tariffs and not through other commercial measures. The aim of this rule is to make the extent of protection clear and to make competition possible. Exception is, however, made in the case of developing countries where the demand for imports generated by development may require them to maintain quantitative restrictions in order to prevent an excessive drain on their foreign exchange resources.

(3) A Stable Basis of Trade. A stable and predictable basis for trade is provided by the binding of the tariff levels negotiated among the contracting countries. Binding of tariffs means that these cannot be increased unilaterally. Although provision is made for the renegotiation of bound tariffs, a return to higher tariffs is discouraged by the requirement that any increase be compensated for.

(4) Consultation. A basic principle of GATT is that member countries should consult one another on trade matters and problems. They can call on GATT for a fair settlement of cases in which they feel that their rights under the GATT are being withheld or compromised by other members. The GATT Council has established panels of independent experts to examine trade disputes among member States and they are making increasing use of these panels. Panel members are chosen from countries which have no direct interest in the dispute being investigated. The panel procedure has often led to mutually satisfactory settlement.

Functions of GATT

Since its inception the GATT has adopted the following measures to cut the tariffs:

1. Trade Negotiations Under GATT. The GATT has organised seven trade negotiations so far. They are-1947 (Geneva), 1949 (Annecy, France), 1951 (Torquay, England), 1956 (Geneva), 1960-61 (Geneva, Dillon Round), 1964-67 (Geneva, Kennedy Round), and

1973-79 (Geneva, Tokyo Round). As a result of these negotiations, the tariffs rates on thousand of items entered into world trade were reduced or bound against increase.

(i) Kennedy Round Negotiations (1964-67). In 1964-67 Kennedy Round negotiations reduced the average level of the world industrial tariffs by about 1/3rd. Efforts were made to move toward linrear or across the board tariff reduction for industrial products, some countries achieved a 50 per cent reduction in many industrial products. Countries making tariff concessions in the 1964-67 negotiations were responsible for about 75 per cent of world trade.

(ii) The Tokyo Round (1973-79) or Multilateral Trade Negotiations. This was a landmark in the history of GATT. The negotiations were concluded in 1979. Ninty-nine countries participated. The agreements concluded in this round of negotiations include an improved level framework for the conduct of world trade. It includes recognition of tariff and non tariff treatment in favour of and among developing countries as a permanent legal feature of the world trading system. It includes various non-tariff measures covering subsidies and countervailing measures, technical barriers to trade, custom valuation, import licensing procedures and revision of the 1967. GATT antidamping code on bovine meat; dairy products; tropical products and an agreement on free trade in civil aircraft. The agreements contain most favourable treatment to developing countries.

(a) Tariff Measures. The participating countries agreed to cut tariffs of thousands of industrial agricultural products. The cuts were to be implemented gradually over a period of seven years commencing from January 1, 1980. The total value of trade affected by Tokyo Round MFN (most favoured nations) reductions, by bindings of prevailing tariff rates, amounted to more than US 155 billion, measured on MFN imports in 1977. It was estimated that the weighted average tariff on manufactured products in the world's nine major industrial markets will decline from 7.0 per cent to 4.7 per cent.

(b) Non-tariff Measures. The distorting effects of non-tariff barriers on world trade became more pervasive as the general level of tariff declined in Post-World War II period. The Tokyo Round tackled the problem of non-tariff barriers in a new perspective and aimed at reducing and bringing these non-tarrif measures (binding agreements or codes) under more effective international discipline. All the agreements provide for special and more favourable treatment for developing countries. The negotiations led to the following non-tariff measures:

(i) Restriction on Use of Subsidies. The signatories are committed not to use subsidies against the interest of any other signatory. Each has ensured that countervailing measures do not unjustifiably impede the international trade. These measures may be applied only if the domestic industry requests the Government that the subsidised imports are, in fact, responsible for causing material injury or threatening such injury.

(ii) Technical Barriers. The agreements provide certain technical barriers to trade (also known as tan-yards code). These barriers commit the signatories to ensure that if any Government or body adopt technical regulations or standards, and testing and certification schemes related to them, they should not create unnecessary obstacles to international trade.

(iii) The Import Licensing Procedures. These should be used in a neutral and fair way. The agreement aims at ensuring the procedures do not in themselves act as restrictions on imports. The signatory Governments are committed to adopt simple import licensing procedures and to administer them fairly.

(iv) Government Procurement. The provision of agreement will apply to individual Government contracts worth more than SDR 150,000 (about US dollar 1,70,000). It aims at securing greater international competition in the bidding for Government procurement contracts. It contains detailed rules as an invitation and award procedures and practices

regarding Government procurement more transparent, and to ensure that they do not protect domestic products or suppliers or discriminate among foreign suppliers or products.

(v) *Custom Valuation.* It sets a fair, uniform and rental system for the valuation of goods for customs purposes. It prohibits the signatory Governments to use arbitrary or fictitious custom values. It provides a precise revised set of valuation rules.

(vi) *Permision of Anti dumping Code.* The agreement revised GATT anti dumping code. The new code interprets the provisions of GATT's Article VI which lays down the conditions under which anti-dumpting of duties may be imposed as a defence against dumped imports. The code brings some of its provisions in line with the relevant provisions of the code on subsidies and countervailing measures.

2. Safeguards. The agreement provides proper safeguards for the domestic industry . Trade Article XIX of the General Agreement permits a member country to impose restrictions on imports or suspend tariff concessions on products if they are imported in excessive quantities and are causing or threatening to cause serious injury to competing domestic producers. The Tokyo declaration called for an examination of the adequacy of the multilateral safeguard system particularly the way in which Article XIX is applied. This issue was not resolved in Tokyo Round. A committee was formed within GATT to continue the safeguards negotiations.

3. Trade Negotiations Among Developing Countries. In order to increase the trade among developing nations eighteen GATT members joined in an agreement in 1973, known as the 'Protocol' relating to trade negotiations among developing countries, providing for an exchange of mutually advantageous tariff and trade concessions. These eighteen countries accounted for about half of the total exports of manufactured goods of developing nations. These are Bangladesh,

Brazil, Chile, Egypt, India, Israel, S. Korea, Mexico, Pakistan, Urguary, Peru, Philippines, Romania, Spain, Tunisia, Turkey, Uruguay and Yugoslavia. All developing countries whether or not they are members of GATT are allowed to join it. The participants negotiated for concessions on about 500 tariff headings or sub headings including agricultural, processed and manufactured goods and raw materials.

GATT has been successful in the accomplishment of its objectives. It contains an enabling clause that recognises the principle of granting special and differential treatment to the developing countries. It is helping to solve trade disputes among member countries impartially, amicably and quickly. The agreement identifies the measures to solve the problems of balance of payment without distorting or upsetting international trade. For balance of payment purposes developed countries have been restrained from imposing trade curbs as far as possible.

In November 1982 the GATT Ministerial meeting held in Geneva assessed the functioning of the multilateral trading system. The points noted were the protectionist pressures on Governments have multiplied; disregard of GATT disciplined has increased, and certain shortcomings of the GATT system have been accentuated. To overcome these threats the contracting parties of the GATT agreed to make concentrated efforts to ensure that trade policies and measures are consistent with GATT principles and rules and to resist protectionist pressures in the formulation of national trade policy and in proposing legislation. They undertook to restrain the Governments of signatory countries from adopting measures which are not consistent with GATT principles and which distort international trade.

UNITED NATIONS CONFERENCE (UNCTAD)

The United Nations Conference on Trade and Development (UNCTAD) was established in 1964 in order to provide a forum where the developing countries could discuss the problems relating to their economic development. This was set up essentially because it was felt that the existing institutions like GATT and IMF were not properly organised to handle the peculiar problems of the developing countries. With 167 members UNCTAD presently is the only body where developed as well as centrally planned countries are members.

It is a forum to discuss the problems of developing countries concerning their economic development. Although most of the developing nations joined the GATT, they were critical of it, insisting that more was required then the application of the most favoured national principle and the more reduction in tariff. They complained that in spite of the best endeavour to reduce or even eliminate trade barriers, the attempts have benefited the developed nations of the world. The prices of manufactured goods they had to import from developed nation were high whereas the prices of the primary commodities that they produced for export were low, thus frustrating their efforts to achieve a rapid growth. International Monetary Fund (IMF) had also failed to handle the peculiar problems of the developing countries. These frustrations and dissatisfactions led to the formation of UNCTAD. Presently it is the only body with member from developing, developed as well as centrally planned countries.

Objectives of UNCTAD

(i) Reduction of Barriers and Restrictions. UNCTAD has porevailed upon the developed countries into progressively reducing and eliminating trade barrriers and other restrictions which seriously limit trade with developing nations. It has worked on getting preferential terms of trade for the products of developing countries while they are exported to developed nations.

(ii) Formation of Principles and Policies. UNCTAD must meet at least once in four years. The Trade and Development Board is its permenent organ with four subsidiary organs:

(a) The committee on commodities;

(b) The committee on manufactures,

(c) The committee on shipping; and

(d) The committee on invisibles and financing.

The divisions have been made on the basis of administrative convenience for the smooth functionsing of the Board. The priorities for any action programme are decided in each of the plenary session and translated into action programme by the Trade and Development Board.

One of the principal achievements of UNCTAD has been to conceive and implement the Generalised System of Preferences (GSP). It was argued in UNCTAD forums that in order to promote exports of manufactures from the developing countries, it would be necessary to offer special tariff concessions to such exports. Accepting this argument, the developed countries formulated the GSP Scheme under which exports of manufactures and semi-manufactures and some agricultural items from the developing countries enter duty-free or at reduced rates in the developed countries.

Under the GSP, export of hand tools from India to the United States will not be subjected to that customs duty, whereas exports from Japan will be subjected to the 15 per cent customs duty. Thus Indian exports can be 15 per cent cheaper *via-a-vis* Japanese exports. The GSP Scheme had been introduced initially for a period of 10 years but has since been extended beyond 1985.

Another major achievement of UNCTAD has been to formulate the integrated Programme on Commodities. As is well known, prices of primary products undergo high level of fluctuations in the international market. This causes hardship to many developing countries as their total foreign exchange realisation from the export of primary products becomes uncertain. To stabilise the prices of primary products, UNCTAD has suggested the creation of a common fund which will stabilise the prices of primary products through buffer-stock. This fund, when it starts operations, will be of considerable benefit to the exporters and importers in the developing countries. Exporters of primary products will then be able to realise higher prices for primary products like rubber, cocoa, tin, copper, etc. Similarly, imports of such primary products also will not be subjected to the uncertainties of price fluctuations which sometimes are the result of speculative activity. India which is a major importer of nonferrous metals is likely to benefit from the operation of the common fund.

Two important characteristics of the Common Fund are:

(i) This is the first institution which has been formed by all members of the United Nations, including the East European countries and China.

(ii) This is the only organisation where the developing countries have a major say in the decision-making system. The developing countries as a group account for 47 per cent of the total votes whereas the percentages for the developed countries and the East European countries are 42 and 8 respectively.

UNCTAD is also endeavouring to reduce the debt burden of the developing countries. These countries have taken large amounts of loans from bilateral and multilateral sources. As a result, the servicing of the accumulated debts, *i.e.*, the interest payments and repayments, now account for a very substantial proportion of their foreign exchange realisation from exports. In fact, for some of the developing countries, the out go of foreign exchange on account of debt servicing is more than the current inflow of loans and credits. UNCTAD is trying to persuade the developed creditor countries to write off a part of the accumulated debts. Some of the developed countries, mostly Scandinavian group, have accepted the proposal. Further progress in this regard is expected in the coming years.

One major achievement has been the contribution by several countries to the creation of a commodity development facility, which aims at the development of product adaptation, processing and marketing skills and infrastructure in the developing countries. Popularly known as the Second Window, this facility is a part of the Integrated Programme on Commodities.

The central theme of UNCTAD VI held at Belgrade in 1983 was development and recovery. The meeting took place against the continued stagflation in the West which adversely affected the performance in the developing countries. The interdependent character of the world economy was never more evident. The UNCTAD Secretarial proposed to the world body that a two-pronged approach be initiated: a set of short-term measures for reactivating the world economy and long-term measures for structural adjustments in trade, money, finance and commodity trading.

The major problem with the UNCTAD has been that it has been trying to tackle too many problems at the same time. Partly it is due to the widely divergent interests of the developing country-members of the UNCTAD. As a result, due to the lack of any specific focus, it has not been able to achieve any tangible results. Experience shows that whenever UNCTAD discussed specific issues, it has been able to achieve significant success. GSP is one such example. It now appears that "UNCTAD has lost the initiative on trade to GATT, on debt to the IMF, on development to the world Bank."

FREE TRADE ZONES

Establishment of Free Trade Zones is an important aspect of Government Policy for encouraging exports. These are two such zones:

(i) Kandla Free Trade Zone, and

(ii) Santacruz Free Trade Zone.

The Santacruz Free Trade Zones at Mumbai is mainly for firms in electronics area. In these zones various facilities are provided by the Government for export production in the form of developed land, water, electricity and transport, taxes etc. supplies can be obtained in these zones for further production without payment of excise duty or import duty. Importation is possible without prior licensing. However, it is obligatory on the firms to export their 100 per cent production.

The following facilities are available, in addition to the above to the firms in these areas:

(i) All units in Free Trade Zones are eligible for a tax holiday for a period of five years from the year in which production is started under Income Tax Act.

(ii) Foreign investment in these areas is welcomed and conditions for investment are more liberal than in the domestic tariff area.

(iii) Export documentation and procedures for claiming exemption of customs duty on imported raw materials and components are simplified.

(iv) In so far as Kandla Free Trade Zone is concerned, the following facilities are available to units located in the zone:

(a) Transport subsidy is paid to the zone units to compensate for the extra expenditure incurred by them on import/export through Mumbai port.

(b) Gujarat Government pays cash subsidy @ 15% on fixed investment in plant, machinery and building subject to a maximum of Rs. 25 lakhs.

(c) Purchases within the State of Gujarat are exempted from Gujarat sales tax.

(d) The zone administration disburses the Central sales tax paid on purchases made from other states.

(e) Strap and rejects can be sold in the domestic market on payment of duty and to the extent prescribed. At present the limit is 25 per cent of total production.

(f) Zone units are assured of regular power supply. Power cuts are not applicable in the zones.

(g) Term loans and packing credits are also available at concessional rates.

The task force appointed to go into the working of the two Free Trade Zones and the scheme of 100 per cent export-oriented units has, *inter alia*, recommended that six or seven more such zones well located and well-serviced should be established to provide filling in the country's export promotion efforts. As a result, the Government is considering establishment of 4 more Free Trade Zones at NOIDA, Falta, Chennai and Cochin.

The rationale of Government decision to set up Free Trade Zones is to take advantage of producing and marketing those labour intensive products which were being run by the developed countries and were left out because of labour getting costly there. Consequently, such firms in developed countries prefer to export raw materials and components to developing countries having trained and skilled, manpower, and then market their products at competitive rates. India took advantage of that to earn additional foreign exchange, getting more employment and modem technology.

❑

3

Constraints of International Marketing

Every country has to regulate its own international trade mainly due to the specific reasons: *(i)* improving its balance of trade and balance of payments position. Most of the developing countries face balance of payments, problem and, therefore, they struggle hard to maintain the balance in their imports and exports, *(ii)* Protecting its own industries against the competition in the international market or in domestic markets from foreign products, and *(iii)* exploiting its manpower and natural resources to the maximum extent possible so that country's economic development may be done at a faster speed. In order to attain these objectives, almost every country imposes certain restricthns on its international trade, *i.e.*, imports and exports. These restrictions may be called trade barriers. Trade barriers may be: *(i)* Tariff barriers and *(ii)* Non-tariff or protictive barriers.

TARIFF

Tariffs refer to the taxes/duties imposed on internationally traded commodities when they cross the national boundaries. Tariff is a taxi import duty on the goods which are being imported from abroad. Tariffs are in the form of customs duties (imposed by the importing country) and operate through price mechanism. They raise the prices of imported goods and thereby restrict their sales as well as imports. Tariffs are imposed by the Government on imports and not on exports as all countries are interested in export promotion and if tax burden is imposed on exports, the exports will reduce. Tariffs make imported goods costly and discourage their imports. High tariffs provide additional revenue to the government and also give protection to home industries by providing domestic markets to them. The aim of tariffs is to raise the prices of imported goods in domestic market, reduce their demand and thereby discourage their imports. High tariffs are rarely imposed on export for such policy will make the goods costly in foreign markets and discourage their exports. High tariffs on imports and concessions and subsidies on exports are normally common in large majority of countries.

DIFFERENCE IN THE OPERATION OF TARIFFS AND QUOTAS

(1) Under the quota system, the quantity of imports is rigidly fixed in the upper direction. In the case of import duty, imports may increase for all kinds of reasons.

(2) Under a quota, the protected producers may feel more secure than under a tariff.

(3) A quota may induce the formation of a monoplastic organisation of producers with a view to keep output low and prices high.

(4) Quotas are often more flexible than tariff because the grant of import licences is usually a matter of official discretion in regard to their timing and quantity.

(5) Effective quotas may give rise to price differences between the importing and exporting countries which are not covered by the duty and transportation costs.

(6) Import quotas tend to make the business of importing restricted commodities a very lucrative one. Those traders who are able to import earn huge profits.

(7) Tariffs contribute to the revenue of the exchequer. Quotas do not yield any revenue unless licence fees are charged or licences are auctioned. However, under both these cases the revenue effect of quota will not be as much as that of tariffs even on imports under a quota.

(8) From administrative convenience point of view, tariffs are more simple to operate than quotas. Once tariff rates are fixed through legislation, no individual allocation or licensing is needed. Administration of quotas may laos result in some sort of political interference or corruption.

(9) Quotas are usually found to be more inflationary in their effect than tariffs because they restrict the quantity that could be imported.

Under tarrif, new importing firms in the country and new producers abroad are not discriminated against as they are when quotas are granted proportion to imports or output in some past representative period. Tariffs in particular deterinefficient as well as efficient units alike. Quotas tend to benefit those firms which are established and discrimate against newcomers.

KINDS OF TARIFFS

Tariffs may be classified according to:

(i) The purpose of taxes, and

(ii) How they are levied.

(i) According to the Purpose of Taxes. Tariffs may be classified into two categories: (a) Revenue tariff, and (b) Protective tariff.

(a) ***Revenue Tariffs.*** These intended to raise the Government revenue without protecting any industry of the country. It is levied at a fairly low rate. It does not obstruct the free flow of imports.

(b) ***Protective Tariffs.*** These aims at protecting the domestic industries.

These are generally levied at a very high rate, therefore, these obstruct the free flow of imports. Their main purpose is not to increase revenue but to provide a safeguard to the domestic industries against foreign competitions in the local market.

Tariffs are sometimes levied to discriminate between countries. For example, Tariffs are imposed on certain goods having certain specifications which are imported from a particularly country.

(ii) On the basis of method. Tariff may be put into two categories: (a) Specific tariffs, and (b) Ad valorem tariffs.

(a) ***Specific Duties or Tariffs.*** These are imposed on the basis of per unit of any identifiable characteristics of merchandise such as per unit of weight, volume, length, number or any other unit of quality of goods. These duty schedules must specify the rate of duty as well as the determining factor such as weight, number etc. and the basis of arriving at determining factor such as gross weight, net weight or fare weight etc.

(b) ***Ad valorem Tariffs.*** These are based on value of imports and are charged in the form of a specific percentage of the value of goods. The schedule should specify how the value of the imported goods would be arrived at. Most of the countries follow the practice of charging tariffs on the basis of cost of a product or cost mentioned in the invoice (FOB) As tariffs, under this method are levied on CIF or FOB price sometimes unethical practices of under-invoicing are adopted whereby the custom revenue is affected. In order to eliminate such malpractices, some countries adopt a fair value given in the schedule or the current domestic value of the goods as the basis for the computation of customs duty.

(iii) Other Tariffs. In order to protect these domestic industries, against competition, some other tariffs are also imposed. Among them are (a) Anti dumping duty, and (b) Counteracting duties:

(a) ***Anti-dumping Duties.*** Generally exporters from developed countries are eager to sell their products in the foreign markets with a view to capture a large market, at a very low price not proportionate to their cost of production. This method to introduce their products in a large quantity

into foreign market at a very low price, even lower than cost, is called 'dumping.' This adversely affects the domestic industries. Therefore the Government of the importing country, imposes customs duty on such goods at a very high rate to counteract this unfair competition. This duty is known as 'antidumping duties' which are charged in addition to the normal customs duty on the product. This additional charge would cover at least the differences between the export price and the normal price or market price in the exporting country.

(b) ***Counteracting Duties.*** Similar to the anti dumping duties, these are charged on goods imported from countries where the manufacturer exporter is paid, directly or indirectly a subsidy as an incentive for export. The amount of counteracting duty normally does not exceed the estimated amount of subsidy.

Preferential Tariff. This type of duty is of discriminatory nature. The importing country may charge lower duty to the imports of friendly countries and higher duty to the imports of non-friendly countries.

Alternative Duty. In case of some imports ad valorem as well as a specific duty are made applicable whichever is appropriate. Always the higher duty is imposed when protection is required to home industry from the low priced imports. In some imports lower rate of duty is imposed. Such duty is called the alternative duty.

Compound or Mixed Duty. In respect of some imports both the duties are imposed, the specific duty as well as ad valorem duty. Firstly, the duty of specific rate is imposed and then on the same imports the ad valorem duty is imposed. Suppose the import of cloth is charged at the rate of 25 paise per metre and also 2% on the total value of import of cloth. That is why it is also called the mixed duty.

Seasonal Duty. In some seasonal period higher duty is charged upon the imports. During off-season the normal rate of duty is charged. During particular season the higher rate of duty is charged to protect domestic seasonal product. During agricultural crop season the higher duty may be imposed on agricultural imports.

Single-Column and Multi-Column Duty. In case of single column duty the same rate of duty (standard rate) is imposed upon the imports of all countries. No discrimination against goods of any country is made.

However certain countries charge different rate upon the imports of different countries. Lower rate may be charged upon the imports of friendly countries and higher rate upon the imports of unfriendly countries.

Other Charges. In addition to the duties stated above the importing countries are free to levy other charges also, such as variable import levy which is similar to local tax imposed on imports to raise price of imports equal to domestically manufactured product. Compensatory agricultural duty is imposed by EEC countries upon price sensitive imports. Some countries impose temporary import surcharge to provide double protection to domestic goods Cascade (cumulative) tax is imposed upon imports every time when they change hands or on every process of products.

In addition, the licensing fees, stamp duty, sanitary inspection fees, deposits of certain types etc., are also charged upon the important commodities by certain countries.

Advantages or Benefits of Tariff Barriers

The usual benefits available from different types of tariffs are as noted below:

(i) Imports, from abroad are discouraged or even eliminated to a consideration extent.

(ii) Protection is given to home industries and manufacturing activities. This facilities increase in the domestic production.

(iii) Consumption of foreign goods reduces to a considerable extent and the attraction for imported goods is brought down considerably.

(iv) Tariffs give substantial revenue to the government. In addition, they also create employment opportunities within the country as there is encouragement to domestic industries and production activities.

(v) Tariffs remove or at least reduce the deficit in the balance of trade and balance of payments.

(vi) Tariffs encourage research and development activities within the country. They create favourable atmosphere for industrial development and generation of employment opportunities.

(vii) Tariffs may be used to influence the political and economic policies of other countries. A country, for example, may raise its tariffs to protect against tariffs raised by other countries.

(viii) Tariffs avoid competition from foreign manufacturers and this may Balance of Payments and Trade lead to monopolistic tendencies among domestic industries.

Non-Tariff Barriers

Recently, GATT has been endeavouring to achieve a reduced and rationalised tariff structure for trade among its member countries. As per terms of GATT, every member country will accord MFN treatment to all other member countries while importing goods from them. As importing countries are also concerned with the development of their own industries and trade they will have to protect them against unfair competition to give the domestic industry a fair chance for survival. Hence more and more countries are adopting non-tariff measures, to regulate their imports. Such measures are called 'non-tariff barriers'. Some of these non-tarff barriers are as follows:

(i) Quantity Restrictions, Quotas and Licensing Procedures. Under quantity restrictions, the maximum quantity of different commodities which would be allowed to be imported over a period of time from various countries is fixed in advance. The quantity allowed to be imported or quota fixed normally depends upon the relations of the two countries and the need of the importing country. There is, therefore, no effect of price level changes in foreign or domestic markets and the Government is in a position to restrict the imports to a desired level. Quotas are very often combined with licensing system to regulate the flow of imports over the quota period as also to allocate them between various importers and supplying countries. Under this system, a licence or a permit is to be obtained from the Government to import the goods specifying the quantity and the country from which to import, before concluding the contract with the supplier.

(ii) Technical and Administrative Regulations. The another measure to regulate the imports is the imposition of certain standards of technical production, technical specifications etc. to which an importing commodity must conform. Such types of technical restrictions are imposed in case of pharmaceutical products, etc. The importing country normally specifies certain standards which an importing commodities must satisfy before their import is permitted. Besides technical restrictions, administrative restrictions such as adherence to certain documentary procedure are adopted to regulate imports. These technical and administrative measures impede the free flow of trade to a large extent.

(iii) Foreign Exchange Restrictions. Exchange control measures have been widely used by a number of developing countries in the post-war period to regulate their imports and keep the balance of payments in controllable limits. Under this system, the importer must be sure that adequate foreign exchange would be made available to him for the imports of goods by obtaining a clearance from the exchange control authorities of the country before concluding the contract with the supplier.

(iv) Consular Formalities. A number of countries demand that shipping documents must accompany the consular documents such as certificate of origin, certified invoices, import certificates etc. Sometimes, it is also insisted that such documents should be drawn in the language of importing countries. In case the documentation is faulty or not drawn in the language of importing country, heavy penalties are imposed. Fees charged for such documentation are quite heavy.

(v) Preferential Arrangement. With the evolvement of multilateral trading system, a few member countries agree to a small advantageous group for their mutual benefit. The member countries of the group negotiate and arrive at a settlement of preferential tariff rate to carry on trade amongst themselves. These rates are much lower than ordinary tariff rates and applicable only to the member nations of the small group. Such type of preferential arrangements are outside the purview of the GATT. Some of the small groups are EEC, ASEAN, LAFTA etc.

(vi) State Trading. In most of the socialistic countries, foreign trade, *i.e.*, import and export transactions, is exclusively handled or canalised by certain state agencies. Separate state agencies are set up for each class of products. These agencies carry on the international trade strictly according to the Government policies. A few other countries of the world follow state trading in a restricted sense to achieve certain desired results especially where bulk imports are needed and Government wants to maintain price stability. India is a good example where state trading is followed in a restricted sense. Some articles, as decided by the Government, are imported only through the State Trading Corporation (STC). Likewise, exports of raw materials such as iron ore, mica etc. are canalised only through Minerals and Metals Trading Corporation (MMTC).

TARIFF V/S NON-TARIFF BARRIERS

(i) Revenue. With tariffs the Government receives the revenue. On the other hand no revenue is received by the Government by applying non-tariff measures. However, it is favoured as an appropriate measure to meet the demand of the country and to protect the industry.

(ii) Protection. Non-tariff measures protect the producers and make them feel more secure. Producers are inclined to produce more for domestic as well as for international market. Such incentives are not available under available tariffs.

(iii) Monopoly. Non-tariffs to trade induce the domestic producers to form monopolistic organisations in order to keep output low and prices high. This is not possible under tariffs. If the prices of products continue to rise due to the operation of monopolistic tendencies, imports become attractive even after the import duty is paid. Thus if monopolistic tendencies prevail in the country non-tariff barriers remain ineffective.

(iv) Custom's Classification and Valuation Procedures. These pose a problem before the customs authorities in tariff measures, no such problems arises under non tariff measures.

(v) Legislative. As imposition of tariffs and amendments therein are subject to legislative enactments these are more or less inflexible. In many cases, due to the commitment under GATT, the scope for adjustments especially an upward revision of tariffs is very limited. On the other hand, non-tariffs features are often more flexible than tariffs as the grant of import licence or release of foreign exchange is a matter of official discussion in regard to their timing and quantity.

(vi) Price Differences. Under tariffs, price differences between the importing and exporting countries are equal only to the costs of tariffs and transportation. Differences more than these are eliminated by competition. But if non-tariff measures are adopted the price differences are greater in two countries as there is no free flow of imports.

(vii) Profits. The importers earn huge profits because of the differences in prices of the product in two countries more than the costs of tariffs and transportation under non tariffs. This makes the business of importing more lucrative. However, there are no such complications under the tariff system because flow of goods is not restricted and the price differences cannot be more than the costs of tariffs and transportation for long. There are therefore, no huge profits in imports under tariff system.

(viii) Administration. From the point of view of administration, tariffs are more simple to operate. Once tariff rates are fixed through legislation, they require no individual allocation of licensing, quotas or exchange. On the other hand, there are a number of authorities for the administration of non-tariff measures. This may result in some sort of political interference or corruption.

(ix) Efficient Firms. Tariffs favour particularly efficient firms in the country because only they can bear the competition whereas non-tariff measures benefit the established firms because they get quotas or import licences on the basis of their past representation. Thus, non-tariffs discriminate against new comers whereas tariff increases do not do so.

(x) Discrimination. As both the measures-tariffs and non-tariffs are not free from defects therefore, both should be operated simultaneously to eliminate the ill-effects of each other and to get the best for the economy.

❑

4

India and World Trade

India is a very old participant in world trade. Its participation have been promoted by the opening of Suez Cannal and speedy development of the ship building industry supplemented by the spread of industrial revolution in Europe and fast expansion of the Indian Railways.

India's Foreign Trade During the re-Independence Era

Before independence, India exported raw-materials to Britain and imported finished consumer goods in return. India has not developed any industrial base and the Britishers exploited this situation to the maximum. There was no change in India's foreign trade before the Second World War.

The exports always exceeded imports and this was to facilitate the British Rulers, in meeting unilateral transfer of payments to Britain on account of salaries and pension of British civil and military officers as well as to meet the interest on sterling debts and dividends for the capital of Britishers invested in India.

There were changes in the foreign trade structure during and after the Second World War. During the war, India exported a variety of goods to Britain but could not get anything in the shape of imports because of British involvement in the war. There was a steep decline in imports due to following reasons:

(i) Shortages of shipping.

(ii) Non-availability of goods in foreign countries due to war.

(iii) Discontinuation of trade with enemy and the territories occupied by the enemies.

These factors were also responsible for decline in exports, too.

India's Foreign Trade Between 1947-51

The partition of the country in 1947, left serious challenges before the nation. It worsened the situation the foreign trade by creating strain on balance of payments.

During this period there was increase in imports. This increase was due to following factors:

(i) The demand for consumer goods was pushed up as a consequence of the pent up demand of the war and post war period.

(ii) To feed the hungry countrymen, there were large quantity of foodgrain imports from time to time.

(iii) Imports of basic raw materials like Jute and cotton, due to shortages caused by the partition of the country.

(iv) To meet the needs of the plans started immediately after the war, many equipment and machinery was imported.

India's exports did not present a fine picture during this period. The total exports in 1947-48 was Rs. 403 crores as compared to 179 crores during 1938-39. But the quantum index of exports came down to 51 in 1947-48. (Calculated as 1938-39 as the base year). The value of exports in 1950-51 was Rs. 647 crores and 650 crores respectively leaving an un favourable trade balance (trade deficit) of Rs. 3 crores. There were no exports of pulses and foodgrains due to rising demand in the domestic market.

Pattern of Trade During Plan Period

India's pattern of trade before Independence was traditionally that of a colonial and agricultural country. The bulk of her foreign trade was confined to Britain and other commonwealth countries. While exports were based on a few primary commodities, imports were restricted and consisted mainly of manufactured articles.

Though, on the surface, there was a favourable balance of trade it counsealed a low level of industrial production and economic development.

With the impressive industrial development since 1947, India's foreign trade has undergone a complete change and is no longer confined to few countries trading in a few commodities. She, now has trading links with practically all the countries of the world. The number of commodities being traded in India's foreign trade, either for purpose of exports or imports are now nearly 6.66. The exports cover a wide range of items of agricultural and industrial sectors and various handicrafts, handloom, cottage and craft articles. Project exports which include consultancy, civil construction and turn key contracts have made a significant progress in recent years.

1. Foreign Trade Up to Third Plan, (1951-52 to 1965-66)

(i) The First Five Year Plan (1951-56). In 1950-51 the imports and exports were 650 crores and Rs. 647 respectively thus leaving an insignificant unfavourable balance of trade of Rs. 3 crores only. During this period imports rose much faster than exports. Imports and exports were highest in 1951-52 being Rs. 963 crores and Rs. 730 crores respectively. They were at the lowest figure in 1953-54 : Imports Rs. 592 crores and exports Rs. 540 crores. The annual average value of imports, exports and trade deficit were Rs. 723 crores Rs. 609 crores and Rs. 114 crores respectively. This trade deficit was largely due to programmes of industrialisation which gathered momentum and pushed up imports of capital goods.

(ii) The Second Five Year Plan (1956-60). It initiated a massive programme of industrialisation as a strategy of long term development. It placed much reliance on import substitution as a means to restore equilibrium on the foreign exchange front, due to establishment of many heavy industries such as steel plants, heavy expansion and renovation of Railways and modernisation of many industries. Maintenance also increased imports during the period. However exports did not show any significant increase nor was there any attempt to increase them. Towards the end of the First Plan due to rising prices and a liberal import policy there was a substantial increase in imports so that by the middle of the Second Plan Indians foreign exchange reserves were reduced to a very low figure of Rs. 186 crores only. Imports would have been higher still but for a very tight import policy adopted thereafter. As the Plan proceeded and due to the serious foreign exchange crisis, attention was shifted to a need for promotion of exports. Some efforts were made in the form of establishment of export promotion councils, removal of export quotas and duties, concession in railway freights and taxes etc. However, the total effect of these measures one exports was negligible. The annual average figure of exports and imports during the period were Rs. 624 crores and Rs. 985 crores respectively thus leaving an annual average trade deficit of Rs. 361 crores.

(iii) The Third Five Year Plan (1961-65). It commenced with a recognition of urgent need of export promotion to balance trade deficit. A very tight import policy was followed. In order to finance the imports and correct the balance of payment position, the Government took several active steps to increase exports. These included Rupee Payments Agreements, export incentive measures, including import entitlements, and the establishment of a number of export promotion organisations. There was a significant increase in the annual average of exports, *i.e.*, from Rs. 624 crores in the Second Plan to Rs. 752 crores in Third Plan. However the annual import figure could not be restrained below an annual average of Rs. 1241 crores leaving an import surplus of Rs. 480 crores. During the three plans imports were financed with the help of foreign aid amounting to Rs. 382 crores in the First Plan, Rs. 2531 crores in the Second Plan and Rs. 2937 crores in the Third Plan. At the end of Third Plan the Rupee was devalued.

Reasons for Increase in Imports

From the commencement of the First Five Year Plan (1951-52) to the to the Third Five year Plan (1965-66) the imports have risen steeply. Following factors contributed to this phenomenon:

(i) Shortage of Food Grains. During this period, the imports of foodgrains were resorted to overcome shortage of food grains. PL 480 imports of foodgrains started and continued during this period.

(ii) Industrial Progress. In order to maintain the industrial progress created in the plan periods, larger imports for maintenance of plants and machinery were required.

(iii) The Increased Momentum of Industrial Development. It pushed the value of imports on account of capital equipment, raw materials and technical know-how.

(iv) Imports for Dependence. During these three Plans, India fought two areas with her neighbours once in 1962 with China and another in 1965 with Pakistan. Following these wars, India's defence needs were increased and consequently larger imports were allowed for defence purposes.

(v) The Prices of Imports. These had also shown and upward trend.

Reasons for Slower Growth of Exports

(i) Stagnant agricultural production and extensive failure of crops in 1965-66.

(ii) Development of synthetic substitutes for some of the major products like jute which India had been traditionally exporting.

(iii) Fierce competifion in world hade in control textile.

(iv) The policy of protection was followed by both developed and developing countries.

(v) Increased competition from China, Pakistan and Japan in the world market.

(vi) Reduction in export prices.

(vii) Reduction in exportable surplus due to:

(a) Increased utilisation of exportable agricultural produces as raw materials in the domestic manufacturing industries.

(b) More consumption of manufactured goods in home market due to increased income of the people.

(c) More demand of agricultural and manufactures goods due to increase in population.

(viii) Static demand of some of the staple export items.

2. Period after Third Five Year Plan (1966-67 to date). Due to adverse balance of payments, acute shortage of foreign exchange, extensive borrowing from other countries and international agencies like IMF etc., the Government of India was forced to devalue its rupee by 36.5% in June 1966 to overcome the above problems through *(a)* reducing the volume of imports, *(b)* boosting exports, and *(c)* creating a favourable balance of trade and balance of payments.

(i) Annual Plans (1966-69). As the Government of India could not start its Fourth Plan after 1965-66 it was decided to launch annual plans for three years and to start Fourth Plan from 1st April 1969. Devaluation was announced in June 1966 which was a year of drought. The following year also proved to be a bad weather year and the Government announced liberalisation of imports in case of 59 industries. Devaluation led to further aggravation of trade deficit due to inelasticity of imports. The imports soared to a figure of Rs. 1992 crores in 1966-67 and Rs. 2043 crores in 1967-68. Though exports also increased since devaluation of rupee in 1966-67 and Rs. 1255 cr. in 1967-68 the balance of trade situation worsened in these two years and the trade deficit was the highest since devaluation. However, the position improved in 1968-69 as the imports for foodgrains declined due to better crops and devaluation showed its healthy effects in stimulating exports. Consequently the balance of trade unfavourable to the tune of Rs. 788 crores during 1967-68 got reduced to Rs. 373 crores. This healthy development accounted for the export of non-traditional goods such as engineering goods, iron and steel, iron ore, and chemicals and allied products. Slack demand in domestic markets and various export measures also contributed to the situation. The effort of devaluation was nullified within the next three years due to high rate of inflation.

(ii) Fourth Plan Period (1969-70 to 1973-74). During the Fourth Plan period imports were at a figure of Rs. 1972 crores whereas it was at Rs. 1925 at the beginning of the Fourth Plan. The exports during this period jumped to Rs. 1810 crores from Rs. 1236 crores at the beginning mainly due to:

(a) General sluggishness of economy,

(b) India's capacity to manufacture much more than what she needed, and

(c) Vigorous export promotion measures.

In the year 1972-73 the country was able to have a favourable balance of trade for the first time since independence. This healthy development soon disappeared in 1973-74 because of several international factors which pushed up the prices of petroleum products. Although the spurt in the prices of exports helped to boost them up to a level of Rs: 2523 in 1973-74, the kick given to imports was much sharper and they reached a high level of Rs. 1973-74 to the tune of Rs. 432 crores.

(iii) Fifth Plan Period (1974-75 to 1978-79). During This period the average annual import jumped up steeply, from Rs. 1972 crores to Rs. 5540 crores. The primary cause of this sharp increase was the hike in international oil prices which led to a substantial increase in the import bill for petroleum products and fertilisers. Other factors were relaxation in restriction on imports of capital goods and equipment and liberal imports of edible oils to hold up the price line etc. Exports rose every year during the fifth Plan period. The average rate for exports increased from Rs. 1810 cr. to Rs. 4730 crores. The year 1976-77 was the best when there was a favourable trade balance to the tune of Rs. 72 crores second time favourable balance of trade since independence. This was due to substantial increase in exports of non-traditional items.

(iv) Sixth Plan (1979-80 to 1983-84). During this period imports and exports both showed a sharp increase. The reason of increase in import bill was a further hike in oil prices by OPE countries. The import and export figures for the period have been shown in the following table.

Table: Trade Balance During Sixth Plan

(In crores of Rupees)

Year	*Imports* *Rs.*	*Exports* *Rs.*	*Balance of Trade* *Rs.*
1979-80	9,143	6,418	–2,725
1980-81	12,549	6,711	–5,838
1981-82	13,608	7,806	–5,802
1982-83	14,356	8,908	–5,448
1983-84	15,763	9,872	–5,891

The above table shows that there was an increase every year in imports and exports but the rate of increase in imports was highest in 1980-81 and it was due to hike in oil prices. The increase in the value of exports fell much short of imports and the result was unprecedented trade deficit. This yawning trade deficit forced the Government to approach the Aid India consortium members including the World bank and the IDA which provided loans to India to the tune of Rs. 2472 crores in 1982-83, and Rs. 1356 crores in 1983-84.

(v) Seventh Plan (1984-90). 1984-85 was the first year of the Seventh Plan. The imports and exports for the year, were Rs. 16,485 crores and Rs. 11,297 crores respectively leaving an un favourable balance of trade for Rs. 5188 crores. The exports showed a mark up of 14.4 per cent over the previous year whereas imports showed a mark-up of only 14.4 per cent over the partially revised figure of Rs. 15763 crores. His phenomenal growth in exports was the fifth year succession when India's trade deficit continued to be more than Rs. 5,000 crores. However due to much smaller growth in imports it was substantially lower in 1984-85 than that in the previous year. During 1992-93 exports suffered due to collapse of ersrtwhile USSR, recession in the major industrial countries and sluggish growth in world trade.

During 1992-93, Asia and Oceania constituted a major market for Indian Products accounting for about 37 per cent of the total exports followed by West Europe, America, East Europe and Africa. In terms of individual countries, the biggest market for India's exports are USA, Japan, Germany, UK and Hong Kong.

As regards imports, during 1992-93, India's biggest suppliers were Asia and Oceania, followed by West Europe, America, Africa and East Europe. In terms of individual countries India's biggest suppliers were Belgium, Germany and UK (in the West Europe region) and Japan, Australia, Singapore (in Asia and Oceania) and USA.

Exports during seventh plan have not grown appreciably, but have also witnessed an increasing diversification over the years. The increase has been well spread over a number of commodities such as engineering goods, chemicals and related products, gems and jewellery, textiles, handicrafts, leather and leather manufactures, marine products, sports goods, carpets and processed food, etc. Emphasis has also been laid on exports of traditional items such as agriculture and allied products and ores and minerals.

Imports during seventh plan was effected to meet the essential requirements of domestic consumption, investment and production. Government has made efforts to make available all essential imports while at the same time cutting down non-essential imports. A major proportion of total imports of India consist of bulk imports accounting for roughly 32 per cent of total imports. These include fertilizers, newsprint, petrol and petroleum products. The other principal imports consist of pearls, precious and semi-precicus stones, machinery, project goods, medicinal and pharmaceutical products, organic and inorganic chemicals, coal, coke and briquettes, artificial resins etc.

(i) Growing Value of Trade. The total value of India's imports and exports both the quantum of trade and the price of goods constituting imports and exports have gone up. This rising trend in the total international trade is a healthy sign for the developing economy of India. The value and quantum of trade is bound to .increase further. However in spite of tremandeous growth, India's share in the world trade has gone down, *i.e.* from 2.1 per cent in 1950-51 to 0.41 per cent in 1981-82 which is much less than that of a small country.

(ii) Larger Imports. Between 1951 and 1982 the imports have risen 18 times. The value of India's imports has been going up due to following reasons:

- ***(a) The Frequent Hike in the Prices of Crude and Petroleum Products.*** India's payments for petroleum, oil and lubricants increased from Rs. 193 crores in 1971-72 to Rs. 5254 crores in 1980-81.
- ***(b) Need of Essential Goods.*** In order to ensure availability of essential goods and to control the domestic inflationary pressures, the Government imported mass consumption items like fertilizers, edible oils, cement and other consumption items.
- ***(c) Liberalisation of Imports After 1976-77.*** This was done to strengthen the domestic production base and to meet all legitimate requirements of industry for raw materials and components as also of capital equipment. Imports were further liberalised on the pretext of exports promotion, resulting not in only essential imports but even non-essential imports like colour TV etc.
- ***(d) Increase in Prices.*** Continuous increase in the prices of major items of imports other than crude, namely, food, fertilisers, machinery and equipment, edible oils, non-ferrous metals, cement, steel etc. had been the prime phenomenon after 1970.

(iii) Slow expansion of Exports. During the first three plans India's exports were almost stagnant due to predominance of traditional goods and the rising prices and high cost of production. After devaluation of Indian rupee India's exports got a price advantage. Some other export promotion measures also gave a momentum to exports. These factors recorded a rapid growth in 1970's but the increase in exports was never adequate and in the with imports except in two years over a period of 34 years. There were many reasons why export efforts did not match import requirements.

(a) ***Export of Agriculture Items.*** The major export items of India were till recently a agriculture based, the prices of which remained low in the international commodity market because the demand of these goods in developed countries is inelastic and partly because of no association of primary goods producing countries.

(b) ***Domestic Consumption.*** Ever-increasing domestic consumption and inadequate exportable surplus of certain commodities, *e.g.*, sugar, meat, vegetables etc. also contributed to the slow growth of exports.

(c) ***Inadequate Incentives.*** Export promotion incentives are in adequate particularly in the context of larger incentives provided even by advanced countries preventing the full flow of exports from developing countries.

(d) ***Protectionism.*** The policy of protectionism adopted by advanced countries prevented the full flow of exports from developing countries.

(iv) Widening trade deficit. In India the differences in the growth rate of imports and exports and the failure of the export to match the have been responsible for persistent trade deficit since 1951 except for two years-once in 1972-73 and again in 1976-77, when she had marginal trade surplus. The annual trade deficit which was only Rs. 3 crores in 1950-51 widened to Rs. 747 crores at the end of Third Plan and to Rs. 5891 crores at the end of Sixth Plan. It was only Fourth Plan period; where trade deficit came down to Rs. 162 crores. In 1984-85, the trade deficit was for Rs. 5188 crores. The deficit continued to be more than Rs. 15000 crores for the fifth consecutive year.

(v) Increasing Government Control over Foreign Trade. In India the Government control over foreign trade has been increasing day by day. The Government established State Trading Corporation in 1956 for importing and exporting the necessary goods. Thereafter several other organisations have been established for the purpose of exports in different commodities such as Cashew Corporation of India, Handicrafts and Handlooms Export Corporation, Indian Motion Pictures Export Corporation etc. Thus, the Government control over foreign trade has been increasing.

COMPOSITION OR STRUCTURE OF IMPORT TRADE

India's imports can broadly be classified into three parts:

(i) Capital goods,

(ii) Raw materials and intermediate goods,

(iii) Consumer goods.

The capital goods category includes machinery of all kinds, metals—iron and steel and other non-ferrous metals and transport equipment. The raw materials and intermediate category includes raw cotton, raw jute, dyestuffs, chemicals, mineral oils and fertilisers etc. Consumer goods category consists of electrical goods, drugs and medicines, textiles, paper and paper boards etc.

(i) Capital Goods Imports. The share of capital goods in total imports which was about 29 per cent during the First Plan period rose to 48.5 per cent during the Third Plan and thereafter it started declining. The spurt in import during first three plans was mainly due to the growing industrialisation of our economy. The strategy of growth adopted in our Five Year Plans banned heavily on the growth of capital goods industries and this objective was realised in the initial stage, only with the help of heavy imports. It showed a fall thereafter because in course of time, the country was in a position to dispense with the imports of those commodities.

(ii) Raw Materials and Intermediate Goods. In the context of economic development, the share of industrial and other raw materials and intermediate goods in the total imports was quite significant. In the First Plan period, the share of this category was only 29 per cent in the total imports but this share came down to 17 per cent in the next two plans and since then their share has shown a steady increase as to make them the dominant type of imports of the country, *viz.*, 26 per cent in the annual plans, 32 per cent in the Fourth Plan, 52 per cent in the Fifth Plan and 75 per cent in Sixth Plan. The main reason of low imports of raw materials and intermediate goods in Second and Third Plans was that India was industrialising itself through setting up new industries and, therefore, the imports of machinery and other capital goods was much more. The place of capital goods imports has been taken by raw materials. The main reasons for the imports of items under this category were:

(a) As the growth process moved, shortages and scarcity of different types of raw materials and intermediate goods began to be felt. As these raw materials were not available in India so the requirements were made up by imports otherwise the effective utilisation of capital goods would be affected adversely.

(b) The system of industrial planning in India was such that a number of industries were set up which required only imported raw materials.

(c) India's industrial development was typically modelled on western technology using oil based energy. Even new agricultural technology was based on extensive use of oil based fertilizers.

Consequently, India's imports of crude and petroleum products, fertilizers and chemical products, iron and steel and non-ferrous metals and fibres etc. shot up to such an extent that they constitute nearly 75 per cent of total imports. Of these, the import of crude has been causing much concern. The prices of crude and petroleum products and fertilisers alone have risen on seventies and eightees to an extent that they constitute nearly 50 to 60 per cent of total imports. The international prices of crude which are largely administered by the OPEC (Organisation of Petroleum Exporting Countries) countries shout up very fast during last decade which resulted in a sharp escalation in the oil import bill of the country, which went up to as high as Rs. 5160 crores in 1981-82. But subsequently, the prices of crude have been estimated to have came down to Rs. 3034 crores in 1983-84. This is mainly due to more domestic production of crude and use of other sources of energy. Efforts are therefore, required to consider the use of oil as fuel.

(iii) Consumer Goods and Foodgrains. The imports of consumer goods and foodgrains accounted for about 40 per cent of total imports during the First Plan. But the imports of these items gradually declined over the years, *i.e.*, 30 per cent during Second and Third Plans, 27 per cent during Fourth Plan, 24 per cent during Fifth Plan and only one per cent in 1980-81. The imports of consumer goods have been allowed only when they are required to meet the domestic shortage. Imports of foodgrains are generally allowed in the year succeeding the bad crops. From 1957 onward the imports of foodgrains continuously increased till the beginning of the Fourth Plan under PL-480 aid from USA. Since then their imports are negligible or virtually eliminated.

Major Imports

(i) Foodgrains. The imports of foodgrains were necessitated by the partition of the country in 1947 and the growing demand of foodgrains for the rising population. It showed an increasing trend during the first three Plans, *viz.*, Rs. 120 crores during first Plan, Rs. 161 crores during the Second Plan and Rs. 241 crores during the Third Plan period. The drought of 1965-66 further worsened the situation. Consequently, the imports went up to Rs. 400 crores annually during the three years *i.e.*, 1966-67 to 1968-69. The figure declined thereafter. It came down to Rs. 184 crore in the 1969-70. In 1970-71 it went down further to Rs. 28 crores. However, the trend was again reversed in 1973-74 when it jumped to Rs. 746 crores. During Fifth Plan, the imports of foodgrains were on an average of Rs. 686 crores. During the four year period (1979-80 to 1982-83) foodgrain imports averaged about Rs. 215 crores per annum.

(ii) Machinery and Transport Equipment. Imports of machinery include electrical and non-electrical equipment and locomotives. The imports of machinery rose averaged from Rs. 116 crores during the First Plan to Rs. 265 crores during the Second Plan, Rs. 472 crores during the third Plan, Rs. 484 crores during the Fourth Plan, Rs. 1010 crores during the Fifth Plan and Rs. 1854 crores during the Sixth Plan. This trend to mainly due to growing industrialisation which is also an indication of failure to develop India's own technology.

(iii) Mineral Oils. As India is short of mineral oils its imports of mineral oils, including petroleum and petroleum products, had been increasing. The imports of petroleum oil and lubricants which were only for Rs. 54.27 crores averaged Rs. 226 crores during the Fourth Plan period. On account of the sharp increase in the prices of crude announced by the OPEC countries, petroleum imports rose during the year 1973-78, import bill for petroleum rose to Rs. 1,556 crores. During 1979-80 to 1982-83, the imports of petroleum, oil and lubricants rose to a record level or Rs. 4846 crores annually.

(iv) Metals. Large-scale imports of metals, including iron and steel are necessitated for the rapid industrialisation programmes. The annual average imports of ferrous and non-ferrous metals were about 54 crores during the Fifth Plan. During 1979-80 to 1982-83, their imports have shot up steadily to Rs. 1394 crores annually. Now, India has made a tremendous progress in this sector. She has established a number of giant and mini iron and steel plants. It is expected that imports of iron and steel shall be reduced in the near future.

(v) Fertilizers. Following the adoption of the new strategy in Indian Agriculture, the imports of fertilizers were stepped up the annual average of the imports of fertilizers which stood at Rs. 28 crores during the Third Plan and rose to Rs. 121 crores during 1966-67 to 1968-69. However, the increase in domestic production, the imports of these items were slashed to Rs. 96 crores only. With the increase in the international price of fertilizers, its imports during the Fifth Plan increased to Rs. 423 crores and further during the Sixth

Plan period to Rs. 576 crores. Recently, in order to boos up the domestic production of fertilisers to meet the domestic demand the Government has decided to reduce the imports of fertilizers drastically. Many new fertilizer plants have been established to meet the countries demand.

(vi) Medicines and Chemicals. The annual average of these items during the First Plan was only about Rs. 55 crores during the Third Plan, Rs. 113 crores during the Fourth Plan, and during first four years of the Sixth Plan to Rs. 469 crores annually. Thus the imports of these items are increasing.

COMPOSITION OR STRUCTURE OF EXPORT TRADE

On the basis of nature of goods, the export items can be classified into three categories:

(a) Food beverages and tobacco;

(b) Raw materials; and

(c) Manufactured goods.

Food beverages and tobacco group includes tea, coffee, black papper, tobacco, cashew kernel, oil cakes etc. Raw materials group includes raw hides and skins, wool and other animal hair, raw cotton and cotton waste, mica, iron ore, maganese ore, lac, minerals and some fuel etc. Manufactured goods include jute manufactures, cloth, leather, woolen carpets and rugs, cement, chemicals, animals and vegetable oils and fats, art silk manufactures etc., machinery and transport equipment, iron and steel and engineering goods.

Major Items of India's Exports

Principally India exports the following items:

(1) Tea. Tea is one of the most important items of Indian exports. India exports nearly 75% of its tea production. Britain is the biggest customer of Indian tea. India exported tea worth Rs. 80 crores in 1950-51 which rose to Rs. 569 crores in 1977-78. It declined to Rs. 355 crores in 1979-80 and in 1982-83, there was no substantial increase in its exports. A 'Tea Trading Corporation' was set up in 1971 to promote exports of packet tea. The export of packet tea is expected to be about 34 m. kgs. During 1985 where as, it had never been above 16 m. kgs. Sri Lanka is our main competitor in this field.

(2) Jute and Jute Manufactures. Jute and jute manufactures have been our principal items of our export but during the past few years, export of Indian jute goods have been losing ground in the world markets primarily due to keen competition from synthetic substitutes and supplies from Bangladesh. The export of jute items had been Rs. 149 crore annually during the First Plan. It increased to Rs. 213 crores by 1960-61 and declined to Rs. 190 crores in 1970-71. During 1982-83 its exports were only to the tune of Rs. 264 crores. Jute Corporation of India was set up in 1971 to increase the exports of jute and jute manufactures and to stabilise prices of jute at remunerative levels. In 1973 'Jute International' was formed in association with Nepal, Bangladesh and Thailand to minimise the competition in foreign markets to search new markets and to engage in research in jute production.

(3) Cotton Textiles. During the First Plan period, the average annual exports of cotton yarn and cotton manufactures touched Rs. 81 crores but they declined to Rs. 76 crores during the Second Plan and to Rs. 55 crores during the Third Plan. The main reason of this downfall was high cost of production. It was only in post-devaluation period that the exports of Indian cotton textiles increased and touched a figure of Rs. 75 crores and in 1982-83 a figure of Rs. 366 crores. Exports of cotton textiles are subject to quantitative restrictions imposed by a number of countries.

In recent years, there had been a significant phenomenon that the export of ready-made garments have shot up from about Rs. 5 crores in 1965-66 to Rs. 196 crores in 1974-75, and Rs. 596 crores in 1981-82. The Indian ready-made garments are gaining popularity in foreign Countries.

(iv) Leather and Leather Manufacturers. One of traditional items of Indian exports is raw hides and skins. But in recent years, the export of leather and leather manufactures are on the increase. The export of these items were Rs. 39 crores in 1960-61 which rose to Rs. 371.8 crores in 1982-83. This is really a healthy development.

(5) Iron Ore. Exports of iron ore have increased substantially. In 1960-61, iron ore worth Rs. 26.8 crores was exported whereas its exports in 1982-83 was Rs. 373.8 crores. The main importer countries of Indian iron ore are USA and Japan. Actually this is an unhealthy development. India should utilise the iron ore in its own steel plants and try to increase exports of iron and steel.

(6) Engineering Goods. During Five Year Plan, the exports of engineering items have increased manifold. In 1960-61, the exports of these items were of the order of Rs. 13 crores only. In 1970-71, the exports of these items increased to Rs. 130 crores and in 1982-83 to Rs. 786.2 crores. In engineering goods are included railway wagons, chemical plants, telephone and telecommunication parts etc. The range of engineering goods exported not only showed a fair measure of diversification and specialisation but some of products also found their way to developed countries.

(7) Handicrafts. The exports of Indian handicrafts are assuming great importance since 1970. From a lower level of Rs. 70 crores in 1970-71, they increased to Rs. 120 crores in 1972-73 and to Rs. 1172 crores in 1982-83. The most important items among the handicrafts are gem, pearls, precious and semi-precious stones (worked and unworked). The increase of their exports was accounted for favourable market conditions abroad, particularly in USA. An appreciable increase was also recorded in the exports of hand-made carpets and rugs.

(8) Handlooms. The value of handloom exports has gone up manifold in the last decade and about 60 countries of the world are regular uses of Indian handloom products. Handloom products include fabrics made ups and garments. Currently one-tenth of the total production of the handloom sector is exported. The value of handloom exports was Rs. 186.98 crores in 1983 rising up to Rs. 242.12 crores in 1984. The important buyers of Indian handloom products are the USA, Australia, Canada, Singapore, Japan and USSR.

(9) Chemical Products. Chemical Products include drugs and pharmaceuticals, organic and inorganic chemicals and cosmetics. The exports of chemical products have shot up to a level of Rs. 451.73 crores during 1984-85 as compared to only Rs. 14.25 crores in 1963-64, the year in which the export of chemical products waS started. It means there is thirty times increase in their export value in 22 years. East Europe, including the USSR, remained the biggest customer of Indian chemical products followed by the USA, Canada and other American countries.

(10) Other Items. The other items of India's exports are sugar, unmanufactured tobacco, fruits and vegetables, iron and steel, mica, coffee, fish, oil cakes, spices etc.

The structure of Indian exports is typical of a developing economy. India has traditionally been an exporter of agricultural raw materials and manufactures. The exports of items under this class have declined in spite of the best export promotion efforts by the Government of India, one reason behind this is the increase of consumption of raw materials in domestic industries and increasing population. Consequently exportable surplus in many traditional commodities like tea, sugar, etc. has been decreasing or not increasing. Per capita consumption of these items have also increased.

The Indian exports have taken a new turn. Exports of manufactured goods consisting of machinery and capital goods have increased both in absolute and relative terms. For instance, exports of manufactured goods have increased from 45 per cent to 56 percent of the total exports. It shows a good progress in the industrial field of the country during plan period. Government exports have rose tremendously in recent years from almost nil in 1960-61 to Rs. 596 crores.

Traditional Exports

These are primarily products which India has been exporting over a long period. These include Jute, Tea, Cotton, Fabrics, Cashew, Spices, Coffee etc. The total exports of these products which used to comprise 72%-of exports in 1965-66, has gone down to 16% of the total exports in 1986-87. It should be remembered that the scope of exports in these products is limited, Some of these products are produced by other developing countries which provide us stiff competition.

Non-Traditional Exports

These are new avenues for exports for India related to the growth in the economy and the industries of the country, better exploitation of our natural resources, and where India has the potential to expand its export trade substantially. The products in the Group consist of Engineering goods, Marine products, Leather Products, Chemicals, Textile Garments, Gem and Jewellery etc.

The well planned export promotion measures taken by the Government from the late sixties, had an excellent impact on the export of manufactures. This led to the steady growth of the non-traditional Products in the export basket.

Pattern of India' s Exports

(i) Diversification. The Indian economy is being diversified. Both traditional and non-traditional items of exports are gaining importance. New marketing strategies have been developed in exports of traditional items.

(ii) Engineering Goods Exports. The engineering goods have emerged as the major item and the principal export earner. Due to the expansion of demand in industrial countries which have undertaken infrastructural projects like roads, ports and rail construction.

(iii) Crude Mineral Oil. Crude from Mumbai High can be considered as the major innovation of 1982. The crude being pumped out from Mumbai High is of superior quality. It is being exported in absence of proper refining capacity in the country. During the first year itself, India exported the crude worth Rs. 1000 crores. Now several refineries have been established in India.

(iv) Expansion. India is now in a position to take advantage of both favourable demand situation and attractive price situation in international markets. This explains the expansion in the exports of many traditional and non-traditional items.

(v) Mixed trends. While some commodities (like engineering, readymade garments and handicrafts) have fared well, some other like sugar, iron and steel have fluctuated hopelessly.

FUTURE OF EXPORT IMPORT IN INDIA

In today's context, the fast-growing sectors which India should concentrate on are: Engineering exports, leather and Leather Products Exports, Marine Exports, Gem and Jewellery Exports, Chemical Exports, Garment exports and Tourism.

The exports in this field can be broadly classified into:

(i) Plantation Sector. In the plantation sector of exports India has reasonable share of the exports in various plantation products.

(ii) Processed Food. In the areas of processed food, fruits and vestals, India's export is less than 1% of the world exports, and there is excellent scope for growth in this area. Following steps are called to increase exports in this area :

(a) India should concentrate on quality supplied and establish country's image as a quality conscious marketer in the international markets.

(b) Emphasis should be laid on high value products, such as mangoes, oranges, pineapples, grapes, and other horticultural products, and selected processed foods.

(c) Provision of adequate facilities and know-how should be made for post-harvest handling, storage and preservation.

(iii) Basmati Rice. The area where India has established a niche, and which can be exploited is in the export of "basmati" or high quality long grain rice. The exports of rice from India has been Rs. 164 crores in 1986-87 and

Rs. 324 crores in 1987-88. More organised marketing efforts increase of quality supplies, and attractive packaging will help us to increase these exports steadily.

(iv) Horticulture. In horticultural exports, the total world market is estimated to be $25 billion (Rs. 37000 crores). India's exports of fruits, vegetables and processed fruits is of the order of Rs. 203 crores (1986-87). India's share is less than one per cent since the early eighties, and we have the potential to increase the exports in this area tremendously. At present, India is producing approximately 50 million tons of vegetables and 25 million tons of fruits on just 4 per cent of the total area under cultivation. The most important horticultural crops in demand is the world market are all produced in India due to intensive cultivation in this area to increase the output and considerable amount of agricultural researching in the country. An organised and well planned effort is called for to improve the yields of most of the exportable vegetables like potatoes, garlic, tomatoes, onion, peas, cabbage, etc. as also fruits such as grapes, mangoes, pineapple, bananas, oranges, etc.

Government has formed a separate ministry for processed foods. It is hoped that this ministry will draw up an integrated action plan in the horticultural and processed food areas to give the necessary thrust in exports for this promising sector.

(v) Marine Products. Marine products exports is a very important and growing sector. International trade in marine products has witnessed a tremendous expansion and India has certainly taken advantage of this trend. Marine exports have increased to 158,900 tons valued at Rs. 960 crores in 1990-91 from hardly 70,000 tons in 1981-82.

(a) Fishing. India has a vast potential of fishing resources mainly because of a coastline of about 6,000 km. 29,000 km. of river, 1.7 million hectares of reservoirs, 0.9 million hectares of brackish water areas and 0.75 million hectares of tanks and ponds. In spite of this, fish production is just about 21.8 million tonnes, placing the country seventh among the fish producers countries of the world.

The tapping of this potential for exports began in the early sixties. In volume terms exports have increased from 15,732 tonnes in 1961-62 to 159,000 tonnes in 1990-91 a ten fold increase. Actually export stagnated between 1984 and 1987 at around 85,000 tonnes. There was a quantum jump in 1987-88 to 97,179 tonnes and today stands at 170,000 tonnes per year.

There has been a higher than proportionate increase in the value of exports because the average unit value realisation have been steadily increasing. It was just Rs. 40.80 per kg. in 1981-82, but increased to Rs. 54.66 in 1987-88, and 60.42 per kg. in 1991-92.

(b) Shrimps. A variety of marine products are exported for India, but the bulk consists of frozen shrimps which account for about 80% of the total marine exports. The other major products exported are frozen fish (Rs. 30.2 crores), frozen lobster tails (Rs. 24.7 crores) and frozen cattle fish (Rs. 22.3 crores). Hitherto frozen shrimps were exported in bulk to the major world market where in turn they were reprocessed and sold in the retail markets. However, the export of value added shrimps in individually quick frozen (lQF) form has been on the increase in recent years. In 1987-88, 2,000 tonnes of IQF) shrimps worth over Rs. 21 crores was exported to the US, West Europe, and Japan. According to the Marine Products Export Development Authority (MPEDA), 16 plants for the manufacture of IQF products are already in operation and more plants are in the offing.

Japan is by far the largest importer of Indian marine products. It accounts for 61.4% of the total and is followed by the US (14.1%), the UK (6.4%) and France (3%). However, it has been reported that India is losing out in the Japanese market to countries like Taiwan, China, Indonesia, the Philippines and Thailand. India accounts for about 30% of the Japanese market, but the MPEDA expects this to fall below 10% by 1990.

Given the foreign exchange crunch the country is facing the need to increase marine exports is imperative. In order to step up shrimp production, two large prawn hatcheries with technical know-how from Aquatic francs Ltd., USA, and France Agriculture, France, are being set up in Andhra Pradesh and Orrisa. MPEDA is setting up a fresh water prawn hatchery in West Bengal with DANIDA technical and financial assistance. Apart from setting up hatcheries, the policy for acquiring deep-sea fishing vessels through chartering and joint ventures has been liberalised. These and other measures taken by the Government should bring about an improvement in adding value to marine exports.

The Government is considering the formation of a National Fisheries Development Board to develop the fishing industry in a comprehensive manner. It has also been suggested that a technology mission on fish farming be set up. This should contribute considerably to the development of marine resources.

India's fishable resource base includes the long coastline of about 7,000 km. continental help extending to 4,15,000 sq. km. and the exclusive economic one of 2 million sq. km. Besides these, there are a large number of river beds, reservoirs, lakes, etc. which offer a good scope if properly nurtured.

The total marine fishable annual potential of India is estimated between 10 and 14 million tonnes. The present exploitation of this potential amounts to 1.7 million tonnes of marine landings per annum and it just a fraction of the total availability.

Hence a comprehensive, planned effort should comprise:

(i) Exploitation of deep sea fishing resources,

(ii) Development of brackish water and other resources of prawn cultivation,

(iii) Upgradation of processing technology, and

(iv) Market diversification.

Engineering Exports

Engineering Exports is a sector in which India has potential of increasing its exports. The export in this category which was of the order of Rs. 5 crores in 1956-57 has increased to Rs. 1335 crores in 1978-88 and to 3876 crores in 1990-91.

The Indian Engineering exports are made both directly and indirectly to over a hundred countries. Asia, and Middle East constitute our main markets; but there has been a gradual increase of our exports to the Western world. As against 95% of our export being made to Asia and Africa in 1957, the share of engineering goods to these destinations reduced to 48% by 1986-87. The exports of engineering goods to USA, Europe and Japan which was practically non-existent in the fifties, has risen today to 40% of our exports. This directional change clearly indicates the growing acceptance of Indian engineering goods in the developed world. The countries which figure prominently in the engineering goods exports are USA, West Germany, UK, Japan, Singapore, Nigeria, Ghana, Uganda, Kuwait, Saudi Arabia, UAE, Sri Lanka, Bangladesh and Malaysia. It was realised only in the late eighties that an integrated Policy was called for, which would encompass all aspects of the needs of the industry-such as availability of raw materials and components at International prices, complete freedom to buy, adopt and induct new technologies and upgradation, facilitating import of capital goods without heavy import duties, a continuous and steady policy frame-work for exports promotion for a decade, and planned removal of infrastructure bottle-necks. The Government of India seems to have accepted this approach, and efforts are being made to formulate separate "Policy Packages" for each industry. Products have been identified on this basis and its is expected that the policy framework for all the thrust areas will be completed soon.

In the total world trade of $800 billion in engineering goods, India's share in hardly 0.12% and this gives an idea of the strides the industry can make in exports in the years ahead. Even a share of 1% will increase India's engineering exports eight times.

It is essential that the Government and industry work together on a long-term plan to achieve substantial growth in exports in this dynamic sector. The main ingredients of this plan should be:

(i) To evolve suitable policy packages as indicated earlier, for each industry, if necessary, even for individual units, to enable them to plan for substantial increases. This has paid dividends in the past and certainly will do so on a long term basis.

(ii) The inflation at home should be contained to ensure that the price increases are minimal. This is vital especially when we start exporting to developed countries; the price increase in those countries every year is a minimal 2% in many cases.

(iii) In the year 1991-92, Government has announced a new Industrial Policy. It has also taken away the licensing of industries altogether, allowed foreign majority investment and partial convertibility of rupee. But Government has to go all the way, and removel all other restraints so that export of engineering goods increases considerably.

Leather Exports

Leather Export is an important growth area in India's exports, and has increased more than fourfold in the last decade. It was Rs. 28 crores in 1977-78, Rs. 440 crores in 1983-84, and Rs. 1245 crores in 1987-88 and has shot up to Rs. 2566 crores 1990-91.

The pragmatic Government policies, liberalising imports of capital goods, and large investment in modernisation, has turned the industry into a major foreign exchange earner for the country.

The change in the commodity composition of exports is very significant. The export of leather manufacturers has gone up from a share of around 20% in 1977-78 to 55% in 1987-88. Of these leather manufactures, footwear components constitute 47%, footwear 19%, garment 15%, and all other items like handbags etc. 19%.

Among the products exported from India, shoe uppers dominate followed by leather goods, footwear and leather garments in that order. It is imperative that we more towards providing modem facilities for the export of finished products. Even though shoe uppers we supply will continue to be in good demand for quite a while, we should simultaneously increase our capacity to make world class shoes which will take over in the future.

India has set a modest export target of Rs. 6000 crores to be achieved by 2000 AD., and even to achieve this target we may have to import not less than Rs. 2000 crores worth of raw materials.

Planning for Export

The broad trend in exports in the late eighties suggest that India is moving toward more manufactures in our total exports of 1987-88; and at the same time, the agricultural and allied products which was around 30% in 1980-81, have reduced to 21% in 1987-88, and ores and minerals from 6.2% to 5.4% during the same period. Hence the trend is clear that the growth in the nineties will be in the manufactures.

When India embarks on planning in the exports field, she will have to look at the short term as well as long term planning.

In the short-term, India had earlier identified half a dozen sectors which have good growth potential and these have to be concentrated upon to produce quick results. In doing so, many constraints have to be removed and certain steps are called for. These are:

(i) Solution of Problems. Having chosen the thrust sectors and products, Government should go all out to ensure that problems faced by the exporters are solved expeditiously. In this connection, it is essential to have an Inter-Ministerial agency, consisting of Commerce, Finance, and the concerned ministry for the product/ services, which should expenditiously dispose of all problems faced by the exporters, and which are not solvable by the commerce ministry alone.

(ii) Selection for Interaction. The time has come to select the industries and also specific organisations in the industry and interact with them on a continuous basis to provide all the help necessary to achieve a quantum jump in exports.

(iii) Check on Inflation. The domestic inflation and price rises have to be kept under check because we are becoming a high-cost economy in many areas and this is detrimental to exports. A close monitoring has to be done by the Government to ensure that cost escalations of a high order do not take place.

(iv) Transport, Power and Shopping. The infrastructural developments in the field of transport, power, shopping facilities etc., are to be attended to on a priority basis, with a view to ensuring that they do not become bottlenecks in our exports.

However, when looking for a long term plan, India has to project to a time frame of 2000 A.D., and beyond, since export is very vital for the growth and development of the country to evolve a National Export Plan with following ingredients:

(i) Resources. In the developing country like ours, the resources constraints will always be prevalent. But we should plan to set aside adequate resources for the development of exports, at the industry level as well as the national level. Hence, foreign investment will be reduced.

(ii) International Market Study. The international market place is continuously changing and will always be so there are six product groups where India has specific skills and advantages and can try for a substantial increase in exports. These product groups might change all of a sudden, and hence the National Export Plan should always provide for the development of new product group/ services on a continuous basis.

(iii) Manufactures. World trade is moving towards the exports of manufactures. Even Indian exports are moving in his direction and manufactures constitute 70% of our exports. In our plans, we should concentrate on high value added products, and gradually withdraw from areas where low value-added products are not worth our while.

(iv) Service Sector. In the international market, the services sector is assuming greater significance and we should plan for a substantial thrust in this sector. This will include areas like Banking, Insurance, Shipping and Tourism. We can also add computer software exports to this list.

The main raw material for the services sector is "trained manpower". India's should go in for more Functional Training establishments. We should endeavour to attract meritorious students for this specialised training, so that when they get into the main stream of exports they can stand up to the best in the world, and get a sizable share in the global market of services.

(v) Long Term National Plan. We have a penchant to lay down Government policies for a year at a time. Only every recently, have we move to a three year export import policy. We have to more away from these and evolve long term National Plans. This alone will enable organisations to plan their exports, new projects for exports, etc. on a long term basis, and also go in for substantial investments where necessary.

DIRECTION OF INDIA'S FOREIGN TRADE

In order to study the regional direction of trade, the world can be classified into four broad groupings, viz., America, Europe, Asia and Oceania, and Africa.

(1) American Region. So far as American region is concerned. North America comprising USA and Canada had strong trade relations with India. Really speaking USA is the dominant country in North America. The countries of Latin America and other American countries could not develop significant relations in our foreign trade. In 1951-52, our total exports to America region was 28 per cent, out of which 21 per cent was to USA and 6 per cent of Latin America. The share of Latin America declined over the years and it accounted for only less than 1 per cent in 1979-80, North America's share was also reduced to 19 per cent in 1979-80. After the Bangladesh war in 1971, the relations between India and USA were strained and consequently our exports to USA declined, but recently, they have improved slightly and in 1981-82, our exports of USA were 11.8 per cent of total exports.

On the import side, America contributed 36 per cent to out imports in 1951-52. It declined to 32 per cent in 1960-61 but due to large import of foodgrains under PL 480, it rose to 40 per cent in 1965-66 and to 35 per cent in 1969-70. As a consequence of hostile attitude of USA, after Bangladesh war, India decided to reduce her dependence on USA and thus in 1981-82, our imports from USA had declined to 10.4 per cent. It is now above 10 to 12 per cent.

(2) Europe Region. It consists of whole continent of Europe. Historically, India, being a colony of the British till August 1947, had close trade relations with UK. It had also trade relations with other countries of Europe. For purpose of trade, the continent of Europe may be grouped under three broad regions :

(a) Western Europe,

(b) Eastern Europe and other European countries.

(a) Western Europe. Western Europe can be broadly divided in two broad categories—the European Common Market (ECM) and European Free Trade Area (EFTA). In 1950-51, out of the total imports from Europe which accounted for 31.5 per cent Western Europe contributed 30.5 per cent. The share of Western Europe increased to 49 per cent in 1955-56. Two main factors were responsible for this increase—*(i)* UK had to pay her sterling debts to India and *(ii)* the share of West Germany increased sharply in our imports. Since 1973, when UK decided to in ECM, the importance of EFTA dwindled to barely 1.6 per cent in our total imports. But if me take ECM and EFTA countries together the share of western Europe has been on decline since 1955-56. It came down to 21 per cent in 1966-67. However, it improved slightly to 23 per cent in 1981-82. On the export side, UK and West Germany had been our principal customer. The share of Western Europe in 1951-52 was 33.4 per cent which declined to 20.1 per cent in 1969-70. In 1981-82 the share of ECM and EFTA countries jointly was only 18.1 per cent. Thus, the share of exports to Western Europe is also on decline.

(b) Eastern European Countries. Countries in this region are—USSR, Poland, Romania, Bulgaria, Hungary, East Germany, Czechoslovakia and Yugoslavia. This region contributes nearly one third of our international trade. The main items of exports to the countries of this region are tea, cashew kernels, tobacco, oil seeds, leather, metallic ores, jute manufactures etc.—the traditional items of Indian exports. In return, India imports iron and steel non-ferrous metals, chemical, capital equipment, railway stores, paper, medicines and pharmaceuticals and petroleum products. These items are crucial to our core projects and industries of strategic importance. Our balance of trade with this region is always favourable. In 1960-61, our imports from this region were only 4 percent of our total imports and our exports to this region were only 8 per cent of our total exports. But soon after the Indo-China conflict in 1962, and Indo-Pak war in 1965, our trade relations with this group improved remarkable. USSR is the chief contributor of our foreign trade in this region. This group of countries contributed about 18 per cent to our total imports and 22 per cent to our total exports. But in seventies, the trade with the countries of this region declined. In 1981-82, .our imports from these countries declined to 11 per cent and exports to these countries which declined tc 14 per cent in 1979-80 rose to 25 per cent in 1981-82.

(3) Asia and Oceania Region. Our trade with Asian and Oceanic countries has been of great importance. Our exports to these countries which were about 28 per cent in 1951-52 rose to 32 per cent in 1969-70. As against this, our imports declined from about 23 per cent to 19 per cent in this period. ECAFE region which is now called ESCAP (Economic and Social Commission for Asia and Pacific) region and includes Afganistan, Australia, Burma, Khymer, Sri Lanka, China (Mainland), Formosa, Hong Kong, India, Laos, Malaysia, Nepal, New Zealand, Bangladesh, Pakistan, Philippines, Singapore, Thailand and Vietnam was of great significance.

The other group in this region in OPEC (Organisation of Petroleum Exporting Countries), consisting of Algeria, Equador, Gabon, Indonesia, Iran, Iraq, Kuwait, Libya, Nigeria, Qatar, Saudi Arabia, UAE and Venezuela. Due to increasing importance of crude in our economy, OPEC countries have assumed a great significance in our imports. In 1970-71, the share of these countries in our imports was barely 8 percent which jumped up to 28 per cent in 1981-82. In 1983-84, their share has declined to 20%. The main reason of this share increase in imports from these countries is due to sharp hike in oil prices. The quantity index has not shown the corresponding increase. The reason of decline during 1983-84 is the increase of oil production in Mumbai High. On the export front, our exports to the countries of this region have also shown a remarkable increase, *i.e.*, from 6.4 per cent in 1971-72 to 12. per cent in 1981-82. In other words, it doubled during the decade.

The share of Japan and Australia in our exports has come down from 15 per cent in 1970-71 to 10 per cent in 1981-82. As regards imports from these two countries, their share in our total imports has slightly gone up from 7.2 per cent to 8.5 per cent during the same period.

India has great potential for increasing her foreign trade with Asian countries because there is a great scope for our commodities in these countries and they are readily acceptable. Similarly, India can import raw materials from relatively more developed countries in this region for our growing industries. This can be evidenced from the fact that our total imports from this region accounted for 36 per cent of our total imports in 1981-82 whereas they were only about 15 per cent in 1970-71. On the export side our exports have shown gradual and steady improvement to this region. They have increased from 21 per cent to only 23 per cent during 1970-71 to 1981-82. Keeping the available potential in this region in mind, there is a great need for exploiting them to the best of our exports.

(4) African Region. With African countries, our imports have sharply declined from 9 per cent in 1951-52 to 2 per cent in 1981-82 but our exports have witnessed a steady trend and have remained more or less to a level of about 6.7 per cent during the same period.

Taking an overall view, it can be stated that India has now more spatially dispersed pattern of foreign trade. Its excessive dependence an Western Europe and North America witnessed up to 1969-70 has now shown a declining trend and a shift is now in favour of East European socialistic countries and Asian countries especially OPEC countries. This is welcome development both from economic and political point of view.

STEPS TO HELP INDIAN EXPORTER

The Indian exporters like in under-developed countries are not aware of the prevailing environment of markets abroad : There are a few exceptions. The exporters in India an majority have no means to undertake surveys and marketing research. To facilitate the exporters of the country the Government of India has provided a variety of assistance in the field of international marketing. Notable among these are given below:

1. Marketing Pevelopment Assistance (MDA). The Government has a provision under which it gives grants to the exporters for certain activities, relating to export. These are as:

(a) Market and commodity research.

(b) Quality control programmes.

(c) Participation in trade fairs and exhibitions abroad.

(d) Publicity and dissemination of information regarding market for the export products.

(e) Sponsoring/inviting trade delegations from foreign countries in the country.

(f) Setting up of warehouses/showrooms, offices and branches abroad to assist the exporters in various fields.

According to the Government policies the Export promotion councils and other export organisations are entitled for grants in aid under the Marketing Development Assistance. The following are types of assistance available or exporters:

(a) "Cash compensatory support for exports of certain selected products, and

(b) Subsidy to the banks for providing export credit to the exporters at reasonable rate of interest."

The assistance available under the MDA scheme is restricted to the extent of 60% of the recognised expenditure of an exporter. The operation of Marketing Development Agency scheme is based on a appraisal of the proposals by the committee of MDA.

2. Quality Control and Preshipment Inspection. To ensure the quality of goods for export provision exists for inspection and quality control of these goods and it is performed by the Government officers to ensure that the goods being exported are of standard quality and to the satisfaction of foreign buyers. This scheme covers 877 items.

3. Meeting the Information Gap. A grievous malady before the exporters is the widening gap in information about export marketing. The Government of India has tried to improve the flow of information and for this, some of the steps taken are given below:

(a) Market orientation Visits and Tours. The Government together with the ITC, the SIDA and the IIFT sponsors many orientation tours relating to selected non-traditional products.

(b) Export management Development Programme. To provide information the Indian institute of Foreign Trade organises a 10 week programme every year in collaboration with ITC under SIDA assistance. The programme is directed towards exposing the selected young executives to various aspects of export marketing environment and development of analytical aptitude for proper appreciation and response to the immediate as well as long term marketing research conducted about selected products.

(c) Research Studies. Research studies are conducted every year by organisations like IIFT, IDA, EPC besides the Commodity Boards. A number of facts about the environment in different markets abroad are revealed by these studies, about the market potentialities for India's products in those markets. The report also suggest the manner in which these market opportunities can be exploited in the best interest of the nation's economic development.

(d) TDA's Buyer Seller Meets. The TDA also organises the buyer seller meets to enable the Indian exporters to expose their products to foreign buyers such meets also give opportunity to have conversation with them and to know their requirements. These help in making suitable changes needed in their products. These meets are organised to achieve following objectives:

(i) To help the Indian exporters in acquiring knowledge of the need for their products in abroad.

(ii) To facilitate the importer-manufacturers to familiarise with the quality and range of Indian products to enable them to understand the possible source of their supply.

(iii) To help the Indian exporters in identifying areas of capacity creation, product development, adaptation, quality control improvements as well as sales techniques. These are done to help them in changing their products as per the requirements of markets abroad.

(iv) To enable the exporters in exchanging market intelligence, information on prices, quality, packaging, designs, standards.

(v) To create market intelligence as well as information on prices, quality, packaging, designs, etc.

The TDA also invites delegations of foreign buyers to visit India and to see the latest Indian products. It also suggests ways how these products can be improved to meet the requirements of market abroad.

(e) Information Division of TDA. The Trade Information Division set up in TDA, has enhanced its information base through the development of contact with a number of organisations at all levels; national and international. The TDA procures catalogues from overseas manufacturers and other sources to enable the Indian exporters to know the price, quality and specifications of foreign competitors' products. It also sends catalogues of Indian exporters to its foreign offices to facilitate the overseas importers in getting to know about the products of Indian manufacturers for export.

(f) Participation in Trade Fairs and Exhibitions. The Indian manufacturers/exporter are encouraged to participate in foreign trade fairs and exhibitions. These fairs and exhibitions put forward an opportunity to know about the requirements of foreign buyers besides about their main competitors, as well as the specialities of the competing products and their prices. Through the exhibitions Indian exporter/manufacturers get the idea how their products can be adapted to the markets abroad.

(g) Publications. The various authorities and organisations publish journals/periodicals to inform the exporters manufacturers about world economy, India's economy, business possibilities of Indian products abroad and foreign products in India and other relevant information. The important regular journals are the following:

(i) ***Publications of TDA.*** Udyog Vyapar Patrika (Hindi monthly), Indian Export Bulletin (English weekly), and Economics Commercial News (English weekly), these journals are published by the Trade Fair Authority of India. These periodicals provide authentic information on India's economy, business possibilities offered by foreign markets, Government trade policies, facilities available for imports and exports etc. They also provide materials to Indian Missions for publicity.

(ii) Publication of Dept. of Commercial Intelligence and Statistics. The monthly journals—The Indian Trade Journal and the Monthly Bulletin of Imports Exports are published in English by the Department of Commercial Intelligence and Statistics.

(iii) Publications of the Export Promotion Councils. These also bring out their Home Bulletins to provide information of interest to their members. Some of the councils publish details of various procedural and other formalities to be followed by exporters and also various facilities available to them.

4. Foreign Exchange and Visa Facilities. These are made available to export houses for the following purposes:

(a) To obtain tender forms,

(b) To conduct market surveys,

(c) To participate in fairs and exhibitions abroad,

(d) To meet expenses of representatives deputed abroad,

(e) To advertise abroad,

(f) To purchase samples,

(g) To obtain other technical information.

5. National Award for Export Performance. Trophies and certificates of merit are awarded annually to exporteis for their outstanding export performance in the following areas :

(i) Development of a foreign market for a product which has not been exported previously;

(ii) Outstanding turnover of export of sales, especially of non-traditional commodities and of finished products;

(iii) Product development or successful introduction of a new products;

(iv) Successful breakthrough in foreign market where conditions are specially difficult etc.

The above steps taken by the Government to promote marketing skill, bridging yawning gap of communication and awards and grants have helped marketing the Indian products abroad successfully.

❐

5

Institutional Infrastructure for Export Promotion

EXPORT HOUSES

The origin of export houses in India dates back to 1958, when the Government gave a thoughtful consideration to the development of some specialised agencies for promoting exports mainly of non-traditional items. In 1960, Indian Government evolved criteria for the recognition of export houses with emphasis on the ability to diversify the export trade and to a large number of countries. The main objective of export houses is to effectively assist the small-scale units in exporting their goods and building up an export market. As the export houses are registered exporters holding a valid export house certificate issued by the chief controller of imports and exports, their recognition is based upon their export performance in the past three years and their capability of embarking upon export marketing.

Facilities Available to Recognised Export Houses

(i) Release of blanket foreign exchange for:

(a) Business travels abroad;

(b) Market studies conducted by specialists deputed from India or through market research organisations abroad;

(c) Publicity abroad;

(d) Participation in overseas exhibitions, trade fairs and Indian trade centres abroad; and

(e) Securing samples and technical information relating to export products and commodities.

(ii) Grants-in-aid under the Code of Grants for:

(a) Any project for developing new products for export;

(b) Exploration of new markets;

(c) Overseas market surveys;

(d) Publication of brochures, catalogues, price lists, etc., for use abroad;

(e) Advertisements for brand publicity;

(f) Display of exhibits in overseas showrooms; and

(g) Setting up foreign offices, warehouses and aftersales service.

(iii) Procurement to commercial intelligence from Indian Governments, trade representatives abroad as also from various departments and agencies of the Government.

(iv) Grant of Preferential treatment to their personnel for:

(a) Training programmes abroad as well as in institutions in Indian; and

(b) Inclusion as members of delegations sponsored by the Government of India or an export promotion organisation for visits to foreign markets.

(v) Import Facilities available to Export Houses. The following facilities have been extended to export houses:

(a) Import replenishment licences to which they are eligible as registered exporters;

(b) Import replenishment licences transferred to them by others.

(c) Import of items placed on OGL, including capital goods for the purpose of stock and sale to eligible actual users.

(d) Imprest licence to the extent of 100 per cent of the value of REP licences earned against their own exports made during the previous year.

(e) Import of non-OGL capital goods (other than those in the restricted list) up to Rs. 20 lakhs CIF against REP/ Additional licences, subject to indigenous clearance.

(f) Additional licences. Export Houses will also be granted Additional licences against exports of select products. Under the new policy, Additional licences will be granted at (a) 6 per cent of the net foreign exchange earned on total exports of select products plus (b) 5 per cent of the FOB value of exports of select products manufactured in SSI/cottage industrial units and effected during preceding year. The net foreign exchange earnings would be arrived at by deducting the value of Advance/Special Imprest/Imprest/REP licences/Import-Export Pass Book from the gross FOB value of exports of select products.

For purpose of calculating the value of Additional licences, export of select products having the REP rate of more than 50 per cent, shall not be taken into account. Export against Advance/ Imprest licences/Special Imprest Licences/Import-Export Pass Book with more than 50 per cent import content will also not be taken into account.

Additional licences can be used for import of items. Addition licences are also allowed to be used for import of capital goods (Appendix I, Part B).

Against Additional licences, Export Houses can also import spares. The spares so imported by the Export House can be sold to any person. However, under this facility the CIF value of the total imports of spares shall not exceed Rs. 2 lakhs. For export Houses with export turnover of Rs. 5 crores (FOB) or more for select products in the preceding financial year or Export Houses recording a growth rate of at least 50 per cent in preceding year subject to their exports of select products in the year, before the preceding year is at least Rs. 4 crores, the ceiling limit for import of spares will be Rs. 5 lakhs.

All additional licences shall be non-transferable. Raw materials and components imported against these licences will be disposed of only to eligible actual users. Spares can, however, be sold to any person.

Export houses with annual export performance of not less than Rs. 7 crores will be allowed IRMAC facilities for supply of raw material and components to actual users off the shelf against valid import licences held by them. This facility will also be allowed to Export Houses showing in 1984-85 a minimum growth of 50 per cent in their export of select products subject to their exports of select products being at least Rs. 4 crores in 1983-84.

An export house may be allowed to utilise foreign exchange up to 2.5 per cent of the FOB value of its total exports in 1984-85 for the following purposes:

(a) Foreign exchange expenditure on promotional activities permitted under the Code of Grants-in-aid for export effort;

(b) Import of testing instruments and equipment for packing and tagging and their spares duly cleared from indigenous angle and required for Setting up Common Service Centres.

The above limit of 2.5 per cent will be subject to a maximum of Rs. 10 lakhs and any amount in excess thereof shall be adjusted against the REP entitlement of the Export House on its own exports. The upper limit of Rs. 10 lakhs will be Rs. 20 lakhs for export houses with minimum exports of select products of Rs. 5 crores in 1984-85.

TRADING HOUSES

The concept of trading houses was for the first time introduced in the import policy of 1981-82 aiming at the development of new products in the foreign markets and also new markets particularly for the small and cottage industry sector. These trading houses were nothing but export houses fulfilling the following conditions for recognition purposes.

ANNEXURE

Details of the Appendices of Import Policy

Appendix I	**Part A** :	List of Restricted Items of Capital Goods.
	Part B :	List of Capital Goods allowed under OGL.
Appendix II	**Part A** :	List of Banned Items
	Part B :	List of Restricted Items
Appendix III	List of Limited Permissible Items	
	Part A :	Raw materials, components, consumable, tools and spares (other than iron and steel and ferro alloys).
	Part B :	Raw materials (iron and steel and ferro alloys).
Appendix V	Canalised Items	
	Part A :	List of Items import of which is canalised through public sector agencies.
	Part B :	Petroleum products, fertilizers, drugs, feature films/video films, oilseeds, cement, cereals, newsprint, fatty acids, etc.
Appendix VIII	Scientific and Measuring Instruments.	
Appendix X	List of equipment/machinery allowed as spares on a restricted basis.	
Appendix XVI	List of Selected Products.	
Appendix XVII	Import Policy for Registered Exporters.	
Appendix XIX	Duty Exemption Scheme.	
Appendix XXI	Duty Free Imports under REP Licences.	

(i) Export houses must have at least three years export experience and must be having an annual average export of select products of Rs. 10 crores during these three years, spread over atleast three product groups.

(ii) The exports should include export of products manufactured by small scale units to the extent of at least 10 per cent by way of direct exports or 20 per cent by way of indirect exports of the products manufactured by ancillary units.

(iii) For continuance as trading house after the first three years, they should also undertake to show an annual average growth of exports of at least 15 per cent.

(iv) Finally they should have financial and technical resources, including testing and quality control facilities.

Facilities Provided to Trading Houses

Trading houses will be eligible to the following facilities which are comparatively higher than those available to export houses in general:

(i) Import replenishment licences eligible to them as registered exporter or transferred to them by others.

(ii) Import of items place on OGL.

(iii) Imprest licence to the extent of 100 per cent of the value of REP licences earned against their own exporters made during the previous year.

(iv) Import of capital goods against REP licences/Additional licences to enable them to set up common service centres for the benefit of their supporting manufacturers and other exporting units.

(v) Import of non-OGL capital goods (not banned) up to Rs. 20 lakhs CIF against Replenishment/Additional licences subject to indigenous clearance.

(vi) Additional licences at 20 per cent of the value of exports of select products manufactured by small-scale and cottage industries and 7.5 per cent of the value of other exports of select products. The additional licences will be valid for import of restricted items with a value limit of Rs. 20 lakhs per item. These licences will also be valid for import of limited permissible and canalised items up to a maximum of 5 per cent of the value of the licence subject to a signal item not exceeding Rs. 5 lakhs in value.

(vii) A trading house may be allowed to utilise foreign exchange for exports promotion activities at 2.5 per cent of their total exports in the previous year subject to a maximum of Rs. 50 lakhs. Within their foreign exchange allocation, the trading houses are allowed to open warehouses and offices abroad without obtaining prior approval of the Reserve Bank of India.

(viii) The trading houses are allowed to provide IRMAC facility for supply of non-canalised items against actual user licence and REP licences/Additional licences.

AN EXPORT HOUSE

As 'Export House' means a Registered Exporter holding a valid Export House certificate issued by the chief controller of imports and exports. The origin of export houses in India dates back to 1958 when the Government of India gave serious consideration to the development of specialised agencies for promoting the export of non-traditional items. It was realised seriously that unless positive steps were taken to build up a number of merchant houses, concentrating mainly on exports and capable of undertaking trade on a sustained basis, it would not be possible to compete successfully against the highly experienced and resourceful trading houses of other countries. They were also expected to become focal points for organising exports of small scale sector for whom it may not he possible to embark upon directly on export trade. In 1960, Government evolved criteria for the recognition of export houses. The Government also decided to extend certain concessions to such recognised export houses. As a result of various facilities extended to export houses, their number has increased from 3 in 1962 to 80 in 1968 and about 1400 in 1982. Many public sector undertaking including the State Trading Corporation (STC) and the Mineral and Metals Trading Corporation (MMTC).

Functions of Export Houses

The export houses have performed valuable service to the exporting public. Their main functions are:

(i) The export houses pay a significant role in exporting the goods produced by small industrial units and helps small units in the following ways:

(a) They provide expertise and necessary information on market opportunities abroad.

(b) They provide financial assistance to small units in the form of trade credits, investments, direct loans, and loan guarantees.

(c) They provide sales opportunities in otherwise out-of-the way markets and get them recognised in the unknown markets.

(d) They handle the wide range of products and have ability to absorb many of the risks inherent in the trade.

Export houses, themselves, are keen to help small scale units in their export effort for two reasons:

(a) They are obliged to export products of small industrial units for getting their recognition renewed as an export house, and

(i) They get additional licences for imports against the exports of products manufactured by small scale and cottage industries.

(ii) The company prospects foreign markets through research, gets information on designs and product specifications.

(iii) An export house works with small scale manufacturers to make sure that their products meet rigid international quality standards.

(iv) The conduct market researches and surveys, collect orders from the foreign dealers (importers) and supply their requirements.

(v) They have world wide business connections and in some markets, they have market organisations to sell the products. They therefore, help new entrants to get their products introduced in such markets.

(vi) Export houses purchase the goods as per the orders of the importers, classify and brand them, conducting various marketing operations like packing, transporting, warehousing etc. and take other necessary steps to export them. They bear risks also.

(vii) The Export house promotes goods in export markets in its own name.

Thus, export house is an agency in indirect exporting system. its main aim is to help small industrial units which are not keen to export their products and introduce their products to world markets. As big industrial units organise their own export operations, they are, therefore, not supposed to be benefited by these export houses. Thus small industrial units are the prime beneficiaries.

Reasons for the Growth of Export Houses

The number of export houses has increased tremendously in the recent years. The main reason for the mushroom growth of export house are the various facilities provided to them by the Government of India. They generally collect orders in foreign markets, purchase the goods in Indian market, process them in accordance with the standards, and supply them to the importers. Thus, they deal in various lines and on large scale. Therefore, they also enjoy various advantages of large scale economies. Such as:

(i) They can avail themselves of the various economies of scale in transportation, bulk purchasing warehousing, and other areas related to physical distribution.

(ii) They can take advantage of export finance available at concessional rates from the various commercial banks and Export Import Bank.

(iii) They are in a position to employ qualified, experienced and specialised staff to look after the complicated tasks of customs, legal problems and documentation.

(iv) They can achieve economies in promotion efforts by using the most effective advertising and publicity media and by participating in many trade fairs and exhibitions.

(v) As they export different items on large scale, they can bargain with large trading companies in foreign markets on equal footings. This increased bargaining power enables them to earn higher profits.

(vi) They undertake to bear many of the risks inherent in international trade mainly because of the fact that they export a wide range of products to different world markets. The lose incurred by the export of one product may be absorbed by the profits earned by other products.

Thus, export houses enjoy large scale economies in exporting the goods.

Advantages for Merchant Exporter

(i) **Economies of Large Scale Shipments.** He can combine several shipments, thus gaining economies of large scale shipments.

(ii) **Specialisation in Marketing.** He can concentrate only on marketing aspects, unlike manufacturer exporter who looks after production as well as marketing.

(iii) **Export Incentives.** He can enjoy a number of export incenteves including 100% exemption of income tax on export income.

(iv) **Less Risks.** The merchant exporter is subject to less risks, *i.e.*, only marketing risks and not production risks.

(v) **Less Investment.** The merchant exporter requires less investment as he need not spend on assets and equipment for production purpose. He has to invest only in marketing infrastructure.

(vi) **Wide Range.** He can export a wide range of products. This is because he can sell a number of brands or products manufactured by several manufacturer suppliers.

Disadvantages for Merchant Exporter

(i) **Higher Prices.** Prices quoted by merchant exporter are less competitive because not only his profit margin is included but also that of his manufacturer-supplier.

(ii) **Difficulty to Execute Urgent Orders.** He may not be in a position to execute urgent orders as he has to depend on the manufacturers.

(iii) **Difficulty to Incorporate Last Minute Changes.** He may not be in a position to incorporate last minute changes in product design as he has to depend on his suppliers.

(iv) **Less Incentives.** The merchant exporter cannot claim all possible incentives that are offered to exporters in India. For instance, the IPRS benefit is provided only to manufactures.

(v) **Lacks Local Goodwill.** A pure merchant exporter who specialises only in export business, does not enjoy goodwill in the local or domestic markets.

(vi) Less Preferred by Importers. Regular or large sale importers may prefer to import directly from the manufacturers rather than depending on the merchant exporters.

Difference Between Manufacturer-Exporter and Merchant-Exporter

Manufacturer-Exporter	*Merchant-Exporter*
1. Manufacturer-exporter is basically a manufacturer but also takes interest in exporting his products abroad.	1. Merchant exporter is essentially a middlemen in export marketing and looks exclusively after exporting goods.
2. He gets profits out of his own export transactions. He exports products manufactured by him only.	2. He gets commission out of his export transactions. He exports products manufactured by many domestic manufacturers.
3. He requires huge capital for the business as he has to look after production and marketing (domestic and export) activities at one and the same time.	3. He requires limited capital for the business as he is not concerned with manufacturing but looks after the marketing of goods abroad.
4. For manufacturer-exporter, exporting is only one aspect of his total business activities.	4. For merchant-exporter, marketing abroad is the main aspects of the business.
5. He conducts marketing activities in domestic as well as in foreign markets.	5. He specialises in export marketing or marketing abroad.
6. Manufacturer-exporter acts as a seller in foreign markets.	6. Merchant-exporter acts as a connecting link-between Indian exporter (seller) and foreign Importer (buyer).

Difference Between Export House and Trading House

Export House	*Trading House*
1. **Meaning.** Export house is a registered exporter holding a valid export house certificate issued by the Chief Controller of Imports and Exports (CCI & E).	1. Trading House is a registered exporter holding a valid trad ding house certificate issued by the Chief Controller of Imports and Exports (CCI&E).
2. **Recognition.** The scheme for the recognition of export houses was formally adopted long back *i.e.*, in 1960.	2. The scheme for the recognition of treading houses was introduced recently *i.e.*, in 1981-82.
3. **Objective.** The objective of export house scheme is to diversify the range of export products.	3. The objective of trading house scheme is to develop new markets for exports, particularly for small/cottage industries sectors.
4. **Facilities.** Import licneces and foreign exchange facilities are provided to export houses.	4. Such facilities are provided but with larger incentives.
5. **Use of Foreign Exchange.** An export house is permitted by the RBI to utilise foreign exchange up to 2.5 per cent of the FOB value of its exports during the previous year subject to the maximum of Rs. 20 lakhs for promotional activities.	5. A trading house is permitted by the RBI to utilise foreign exchange upto 2.5 percent of the FOB value of its exports during the previous year subject to the maximum of Rs. 60 lakhs for promotional activities.
6. **Eligibility.** The eligibility for export house certificate is the	6. An export house having valid export house certificate is

Export House	*Trading House*
exports actually made during the previous three years.	eligible to apply for recognition as trading house.
7. **Qualifying Threshold.** Qualifying threshold for export house status is raised from Rs. 2 crore to Rs. 5 crore under the Exim Policy for 1990-93.	7. Qualifying threshold for trading house status is raised from Rs. 10 crore to 20 crore under the Exim Policy for 1990-93.

COUNTER-TRADING

In recent years, many countries have a tendency to resort to trading practices that constitute a retreat from multilateralism. These practices are collectively known as 'counter trade'.

There may be a variety of forms of counter trade. Basically it is a barter or a quasi-barter arrangement, where cash mayor may not involve but there is always a link between the imports and exports transactions. In other words, imports are paid out of exports in counter trade. For example, if India exports iron and steel against the imports of heavy machinery under contract is a counter trade transaction.

Counter-trade may involve one commodity on each side or may involve a number of products. Many counter-trade transactions are highly complex, involving several products, moving at different points in time, engaging several countries and may include financial payments as well.

Counter-trade involves trading arrangements between private firm and/or Government or Government agencies such as foreign trade organisation like Export Promotion Councils, State Trading Corporation etc. by which the seller is obliged to accept certain specific goods or services against the supplies of goods and services such as technology or industrial licences etc. from the buyer.

Principal Forms of Counter-Trading

On the basis of types of goods traded, the financial arrangements involved and the length of time it takes to complete the transactions, the following types of counter-trade may be distinguished.

(1) Barter. The simplest form of counter-trade is by means of barter. It is exchange of goods or services of equivalent value between the yeller in one country and the buyer in another. Suitable payment guarantees are obtained so as to complete these transactions over an agreed period. This is the oldest form of international trade and the source of origin of present day counter trade. In India private organisations are not allowed to enter into barter trade with other countries without the permission of the authorities.

(2) Buy Back. The exporter from a developed country who exports manufactured products agrees to buy back to the extent of his export or more the same product to be produced with his help from another developing country. He agrees to establish a factory in the country of the importer on a turnkey basis, for a specified amount. He is responsible for providing the technology, the machinery and to ensure that the production comes up to the agreed quality and output norms. He agrees to buy back the products produced out of this arrangement a portion or the entire output. It is resorted to ensure a reliable source for some of the exporting country's needs also in cases where it is phasing out certain types of production due to high cost of labour or pollution constraints.

(3) Switch Trade. When a third party is brought into the counter trade arrangement to accept the goods that the original foreign company is unable to use or market itself, it is switch trade, also known as a three-way counter purchase deal.

(4) Counter Purchase. As the very name implies, these transactions amount to selling and purchasing by two countries on specific precisely agreed time frames, depending upon products, consumption pattern and seasonal fluctuations. These amount to one separate contract for exporting and another separate contract for importing. The two contracts are linked by a separate agreement spelling out all conditions and terms agreed upon.

In counter-trade export from one country is compensated by goods, services or cash in agreed proportion; where necessary and mutual needs demand, more than two countries can be involved in the counter-trade.

(5) Compensation Counter-trade. Under compensation arrangement, the exporter agrees to accept a part of export consideration in cash and the balance in kinds. The exporter, then, enters into an arrangement with the third party who may be an end-user of the product or an export house to take over goods received by them in part payment of the goods exported. Thus, it involves cash and the third party who may agree to buy the purchasing commitment of the exporter. This type of arrangements are also not very common because it takes time to find a suitable third party to whom the exporter can transfer the purchasing commitment.

The above five types of counter-trade are usually in vague but there are certain other forms of counter trade.

(6) Swap. In a swap contract, to countries agrees to trade, products from different locations with a view to same transportation cost. This is ideally suited for commodities such as sugar, chemicals or and oil. An example is the swap of soviet oil bound for Cuba and Mexican oil to Europe and Asia Minor. In the 1978 agreement, the Soviets supplied oil to Mexico customers in Greece, Eastern Europe and Turkey and Mexico supplied oil to Cuba. Thus both countries saved considerable transportation cost. In swap transaction difference in quality of the goods being substituted are worked out in the swap contract.

(7) Evidence Accounts. Such accounts are monitored by the country's, bank that deals in foreign currency and where the company maintains its account. Under Evidence Account, the company sells its products or service to a local foreign trade organisation and purchase goods and services of its requirements from another local foreign trade organisation of the equal amount. The transactions are set to occur over a specified periods commonly one year.

(8) Blocked Currencies. When a company or individual cannot repatriate its accumulation of funds from a country because of currency restrictions. The individual or the company can use up the accumulated local currency in a number of ways. One such method is to purchase the local problems from the funds and then export them to the country of his choice according to the rules and regulations of the country concerned. The second method is to use up the local currency reserves in paying for the production of a movie then make money from the royalties when the film is shown in other foreign countries. A project began as effort to spend blocked currencies was the production of the movie, 'The Ninth Configurations' in Hungary. Thus, there are a number of forms of counter-trade transactions and any of them may be used taking the national interests into account.

Financial Structure for Counter-Trade

(1) Cost Factor. Counter-trade involves many inherent cost, which will have to be borne by the country which seeks counter-trade. If an Indian exporter wants to increase his exports by counter-trade and offers product X, he has to seek the help of an international counter-trade house or a national trading house. For rendering the service, the charges of such trading houses are the following:

(a) A share of the management time and overheads that the trading house spends on setting the deal.

(b) The specific service charge to be paid to the national or international trading house for handling the transaction.

(c) The implicit discount on the product price to be given so as to dispose of the product quickly or in a new market. All these costs as a rule have to be borne by the exporter offering product for counter-trade. These costs have to be paid by taking special permission of the authorities, if it is a foreign trading house. These costs tend to depress the ultimate realisation of the proceeds by the exporter.

(2) Mechanism. The mechanism or the financial structure is important in the case of counter-trade, as the transactions are not in line with the established norms of international finance such as, Letter of Credit, guaranteed deferred payment, official lines of credit etc. The flow of goods from one country to the other will not be simultaneous. It needs flexibility in the financial structure to ensure that the parties in the counter-trade do not face any shortfall in realisation. Some of these mechanisms are the following:

(a) ***Escrow Account.*** It is a bank account used specifically for the counter-trade transaction. It is opened in an International Bank jointly by the exporter and the importer. The purchaser pays the amount of this joint account as and when transactions take place, such amount paid by either of the parties will be kept in the escrow account, until the transactions are completed by both the parties in the agreed period. The debiting and crediting in the account is confirmed to the satisfaction of the parties, the account neutralised, and the interest which might have accumulated in the meanwhile, is shared by the parties as agreed to originally.

(b) ***Bank Guarantee.*** The goods are delivered under bank guarantees of both the parties: The bank guarantee is encased if either of the parties fails to fulfil the delivery commitment.

(c) ***Forfaiting.*** "Forfait" became popular in the early sixties. The transaction amounts to buying away the liability or a means of non-recourse financing for the exporter. The party, who agrees to export a certain product as countertrade has the facility of forfeiting or transferring its liability on to a financial institution for a certain consideration. The financial institution takes the responsibility of realising the amount and does not have any recourse on the exporter.

The practice is widely prevalent in transactions with Eastern Europe. It is resorted to, when insurance is not available for the national debt transaction from the official export credit agencies.

Some Typical Examples of Counter-trade

(1) Counter-trade between Brazil and Russia conducted in 1986. This was for a total value of US $35 million in which USSR imported microcomputers and products, food processing plants, services in the field of construction/engineering for hydro-electric plants, and also a joint venture in deep-sea fishing.

(2) Counter-trade in high-tech Products and Systems.

(a) ***Comter-trade in Malaysia with the Republic of Korea.*** This was for the import of naval patrol boats, against which they exported timber, rubber products, crude petroleum etc. This transaction was worth Malaysian $20 million. The period of delivery was sufficiently long to enable Malaysia to fulfil its commitment.

(b) ***Counter-trade between Malaysia and Germany.*** Malaysia purchased a complete Microwave Transmission System from West Germany, against which they exported rubber products, cocoa, refined pine oil etc. for a total value of M$56 million. In this case the counter purchase was to the extent of 80%.

(3) Examples of Indian Counter Trades.

(a) ***Counter-trade with Jordan.*** Earth moving equipment, and other engineering items of a value of $4 million were exported from India, against the purchase of rock phosphates and fertilisers by India from Jordan. A road construction project was also obtained by an Indian construction company.

(b) ***Counter-trade with Zimbabwe.*** India bought asbestos from Zimbabwe against which specific engineering goods were sold to her. Asbestos was imported, and the payment by India was kept in an escrow account which Zimbabwe used to buy tractors, sewing machines, covers and three-wheelers from India.

(c) ***Counter-trade with Madagascar.*** India imported cloves from Madagascar against which commercial vehicles and spares were bought by Madasgacar. The transactions were made by means of two independent letters of credit, each of which was conditional on the complete fulfilment of the contractual obligations on the parties concerned.

The volume of trade under counter trade arrangement is very difficult to estimate because no separate data are published on it. Moreover, counter-trade in the form of buy-back arrangement are often extended over several years, making it difficult to estimate the annual figure of volume of trade under such arrangements.

The magnitude of counter-trade technique can be estimated from the US Commerce Department estimates made 'in 1976 that 28 per cent of all East-West trade was in fact some form of counter-trade. In 1981, the figure was as high as 38 per cent. Mr. James Walsh, a senior economist in the US Department of Commerce, has predicted that counter-trade would be for no less than one-half -of the world trade by the year 2000. Counter-trade is increasingly becoming popular in the Chinese, East European, the USSR and third world markets. Many US corporations have set up their departments to deal with counter-trade. Banks have also established their new departments to provide services for counter-trade transactions.

Various Reasons Responsible for Counter-trade Growth

Considering the magnitude of counter-trade, it can be expected and predicted that there are good prospects of counter-trade. The various reasons for the growth of counter-trade may be enumerated as follows:

(1) In centrally planned East European countries, where local production can be planned but the foreign demand cannot be estimated and predicted. Counter-trade is, therefore, considered the best way of overcoming uncertainty of domestic production plans and, at the same time, maintaining the bilateral balance of trade-an important foreign trade policy in these countries.

(2) It is very easy to enter new markets through counter-trade. Goods purchased under counter-trade arrangement will be sold in foreign markets and will naturally have an edge over competitors.

(3) Shortage of convertible foreign currencies and the desire to stimulate foreign technology inflows have also motivated East European countries to enter into counter-trade arrangements.

(4) In many developing countries certain national and foreign trade activities are nationalised and some of the institutional characteristics which apply to counter-trade in East European countries are persent in those countries also.

(5) Developing countries, particularly those maintaining overvalued exchange rates have resorted to counter-trade for the following reasons:

(a) Adverse balance of payment situation arising from the sluggish export growth and increasing debt servicing burden, have prompted some of these countries to adopt some new ways of economising on scarce foreign exchange resources;

(b) More emphasis on industrialisation, originally aimed at import substitution has created over capacity and has produced pressures to find markets for their surpluses;

(c) It is a way of penetrating existing markets or establishing new ones, in an effort to gaining access to markets of the industrial countries for certain primary and manufactured products. Counter-trade arrangements that commit industrial country exporters to purchase a given quantity of products over a specified period can be used as a means of it;

(d) Counter-trade in the form of buy-back arrangements is seen by both industrially developed and more developed developing countries-as a means of securing reliable sources of essential raw materials while exporting equipment and technology that have become outdated at home;

(e) Counter-trade has become the only way to some exporters to overcome the restrictive trade practices and policies of some countries.

(6) As detailed trade data are not published, the Governments of many developing countries and also a number of communist countries, manage to conceal some facts of strategic importance from the public. Such circumstances are:

(a) Where Governments engage in counter-trade arrangements and strategic goods are involved and the facts are not desired likely to be made public. It is possible because commodity-wise trade data do not specify the separate figures for trade under normal trading arrangements and counter-trade.

(b) The desire of the Governments to conceal from the domestic pubic the fact that the goods have been exported below its cost price.

(7) A counter-trade transaction provides some slight additional certainty of exports in an uncertain world.

(8) Counter-trade permits price discrimination among customers by allowing concealed discounting in recession period without openly breaking the price maintenance provisions of the organisation. It happened when OPEC countries sold their oil to other countries through would counter-trade transactions at concealed discount.

(9) Exporters in underdeveloped countries and communist countries feel that they can flourish markets for their own products at the expense of others expertise if the importer

(counter purchaser) of their products offers them products which have not been developed in their countries before.

Thus, there are many sound reasons why counter-trade has got momentum in the last decide.

Drawbacks of Counter-trade

Counter-trade transactions are often extremely complex and difficult as compared to simple export-import trade for cash. This is the reason why the counter-trade transactions are less preferred because it requires planning and commitment unheard of in the traditional cash-for-goods methods of international trade. There are a number of drawbacks or pitfalls. Some of them may be summarised as follows:

(1) Export sales linked to counter-trade require careful planning to ensure that the imported products will be of good quality, easily disposable, delivered on schedule and reasonably priced to take account of the additional marketing costs that may be involved. But in most cases, when a company exports goods to a country on counter-trade, it must accept goods that the country cannot or would not try to sell them otherwise in the world market. To unload these goods, the company usually has to cut prices. Since it cannot affort to absorb all losses, it may paid the price of goods it sells to counter-trade customers.

(2) In the ideal counter-trade deal, an exporter has to prepare a list of items that can be sold easily in the international/internal markets or pass along to established customers.

(3) It is somewhat costly as the manufacturing firms have to set up subsidiaries to handle counter-trade arrangement or to employ services of experts in this line. Experts are sometimes required in this field.

(4) Counter-trade is full of risks because everything is uncertain in a counter-trade arrangement. Risks increase as the arrangement is extended over several years. It involves political and economic risks.

Change in political scene of the country and consequent changes in policies of the Government may block the substantial money. Where a large sale of plant, equipment or technology is involved, a potential change in the political and national security considerations, adds to the uncertainty. When counter-trade is in buy back form, exporters may have to obtain bridging finance for themselves or provide it to foreign buyers. This increases the financial costs of the counter-trade transactions.

Counter-trade transactions are time-consuming to conclude as they are extended over several years and due to the complexities involved, only 5 to 10 per cent deals are materialised.

The existing international trade law, the GATT, has no provision dealing specifically with counter-trade practices. Many of its restrictive and discriminatory features may be considered as undesirable under IMF policies. The main objective behind these transactions was to enter the weak market and reluctance to openly cut their prices. The current craze is only temporary.

India through State Trading Corporation has entered not a number of 'link deals' with Poland, Bulgaria, Yugoslavia, Tanzania and Malaysia involving imports of cement, newsprint and palm oil against the supply of a number of items such as engineering goods, leather, tobacco and other manufactured products.

MEANING OF DIRECT EXPORTING

Direct exporting means exporting the goods by the exporter firm itself without taking help of middlemen. In it the manufacturer takes upon himself the task of managing the export sales. The exporter supervises every step in the export of goods. He shoulders the entire responsibility for the operations and bears all risk. This means his greater involvement in the export business. To quote Vern Terpestra "The advantages of directness are not only greater sales, also greater control, better market information and development of in-house expertise in international marketing. The costs of going direct are high because the direct exporter bears them alone."

Functions Required in Direct Exporting

(i) Engaging in the direction and supervision of export including the development of export policy.

(ii) The adaptation of the product for export, including export packing.

(iii) Selling, including such functions as advertising, sales promotion, sales training, translation service. etc.

(iv) Transportation of the product, including documentation for shipment, rail and ocean shipping, insurance and other related matters.

(v) Credit and terms of payment.

(vi) Financing, including exchange, invoicing and collections.

Advantages of Direct Exporting

(i) **Better knowledge of customers' Demands.** In such a case the manufacturer is in direct touch with the importers and thereby attains better understanding and knowledge of the requirements. This leads to better adaptability.

(ii) **Better Returns on Exports.** In the absence of middlemen, the manufacturer enjoys full returns on the sales of his goods in foreign market.

(iii) **Complete Control.** The manufacturer has comprehensive control over the prices to be charged for his product.

(iv) **Better Appreciation of Market Conditions.** Through direct exporting, the manufacturer has a better appreciation of marketing opportunities and trends, competitors, product acceptance and other important factors.

(v) **Better Goodwill.** Through direct exporting, the goodwill so earned is likely to remain an asset of the manufacturer and not to anybody else.

(vi) Permanency. In the absence of middlemen, the manufacturer is assured of permanency in the business of exports he takes complete responsibility of his own export trade.

(vii) Short Chain of Distribution. The chain of distribution is shortened in direct exporting because some of the middlemen are eliminated completely. It may result in early delivery of goods at lower prices to the foreign consumers.

(viii) Only Choice for Certain Products. The direct exporting is necessary in the following cases and there is no other alternative to get success:

(a) In respect of commodities which use a highly technical sales organisation and aftersale services;

(b) When middlemen are disinclined towards accepting all the risks of export trade;

(c) When exporter desires a direct flow of information which may be integrated into practices with a view to adapting production according to marketing conditions;

(d) When importer or buyer in foreign country wants direct contact with manufacturer or where middlemen builds a barrier between the two parties;

(e) When complex international situation, with its multiplicity of exchange regulations and tariffs, has increased the cost of exporting; and

(f) Where aftersale services are required.

(ix) Greater Dedication by Own Staff. In direct exporting all the export operations are conducted by manufacturer's own staff. As their own prosperity depends upon the success of export trade. They work with greater dedication. There are more specific advantages to have their own staff for this purpose:

(a) The employees have more knowledge about the company's products than an agent or distributor;

(b) They can be compensated in accordance with the long-term overall interests of the whole enterprise and of the employees, and

(c) They can be trained in company's specific sales methods and techniques;

(d) They serve as a better source of information about the product acceptance and other market conditions. Such information shall be more reliable.

Thus, direct exporting is more advantageous than the indirect exporting provided the firm is financially sound to organise the direct exporting.

Disadvantages of Direct Exporting

(i) **Large Financial Resources Needed.** The process of direct exporting requires large funds to support the cost of selling, the extension of credits, and financing.

(ii) **Managerial Ability.** Direct exporting, requires the managerial ability will aware about foreign markets, their needs, process of documentation, shipping, financing and language etc., can only involved succeed in direct export trade.

(iii) **It is Risky.** In direct exporting the risk involved in export trade such as of credits, financing, collection, rejected merchandise, are borne by the manufacturer.

(iv) **Increased Distribution Costs.** The distribution costs in maintaining suitable channel of distribution incurs huge costs which has the bearing on price of the commodity.

(v) **Other Limitations:**

(a) It frequently involves the maintenance of stocks in overseas depots which is, at best, an expensive operation.

(b) The manufacturer is frequently called upon to supply service direct from the factory—another expensive undertaking.

(c) It involves greater initial outlay before profits begin to flow in.

In short, this type of exporting is not suitable to small exporting firms which cannot arrange adequate finances for export or undertake to bear the risks involved, or manage it competently. This system is more favourable to large firms.

FORMS OF ORGANISATION IN FOREIGN MARKETS

(1) Establishment of Branches and/or Plants. The company may decide to have its own branch or plant in a foreign market. If the firm has a branch abroad, it might be able to obtain complete knowledge of the market. The branch may be able to provide aftersales service facilities in a more effective manner. It may also hold goods as ready stocks to provide off-the-shelf delivery to the buyers. It will also act as a showroom for company's products. If a company has a branch in a foreign market, it adds to the company's prestige, both in India and in the foreign market concerned. Again, a sales branch can be effective in countering a competitor's campaign.

Foreign branches could be established to take care of regional requirements. For example, a pharmaceutical company in India has established a branch at Lagos to look after the requirements of Ghana, Ivory Coast and Cameroon besides Nigeria. Its office at Singapore caters to the requirements of Asian countries, South Korea, Taiwan and Hong Kong.

Establishment of a branch would necessarily involve a lot of expenditure. In fact, the company has to choose between efficiency and high overheads. The volume of business, however, provides the real answer to this question. Of course, establishment of a branch abroad is conditioned by the regulations of the importing country.

If the volume of business so justifies, a company may decide to have a plant in the foreign country either for assembly or for assembly and manufacturing both. There are many advantages of foreign manufacturing:

(a) Savings in transport costs,

(b) Overcoming tariff and non-tariff barriers,

(c) Contribution to the national aspirations of the importing country, and

(d) Availability of cheaper raw materials and/or labour.

(2) Licensing Arrangements. The company may enter into an agreement with a firm in the importing country whereby it permits the latter to manufacture goods in the former's brand name in exchange of a royalty. Thus, the exporting company allows the company in the importing country the use of its brand name, patent rights, trade marks and copy copyrights and provides the necessary know-how for it. In many cases, this is the only way to overcome tariff barriers and import restrictions. There is practically in investment on the part of the exporting company. Moreover, there is no risk of nationalisation. But there are two problems :

(a) Quality control may be difficult to achieve; and

(b) The importing company may decide to compete with the exporting company in third markets.

The latter danger is very often sought to be controlled by putting restrictions on exports in the licensing agreement itself.

(3) Joint Ventures. Joint Ventures are a *via* media between the establishment of a plant abroad and the licensing arrangement. In joint ventures, the exporting company has some investment and a voice in its management too. The exporting company has the advantages of:

(a) Higher returns than royalties, and

(b) Greater control on production and marketing.

But it does involve greater investment of capital and higher risks. However, the risk of nationalisation is much less because of the investment of national party.

(4) Appointment of Exclusive Agents. This is the most widely used method. It is the simplest and the least expensive. An agent is the sole representative of the manufacturer in the importing country. He may, however, handle non-competing lines. He does not operate on his own account and gets a commission for his services.

Advantages

(a) This system is the simplest and the least expensive because one has full control, over the prices of the products.

(b) The distribution expenses are the least because, one is not to appoint the salesmen in the importing country.

(c) Overhead expenses are the least and the transportation cost internal and external, is reduced to the minimum because the goods are exported in response to a number of orders.

(d) Aftersale services wherever required, may be provided by the exporter easily through the agent.

Disadvantages

(a) As the exclusive agent is the sole representative of the exporter be cannot appoint another agent in the region agreed upon.

(b) The business of the exporter depends very much on the goodwill of the agent in that country. If his image is not good, it affects the exporter's business adversely.

(c) The agent once appointed cannot be removed easily though he does not share or undertake the risks in the business.

This system is suitable to technical industrial products, the per unit price of which is very high or where after sale service is required.

(5) Distributors. A distributor is the sole importer of the manufacturer's products. He usually operates on his own account. He may also own wholesale and retail outlets. He provides repair and service facilities as well.

Advantages

(a) The manufacturer is free from the marketing activities in the foreign market.

(b) He has control over the prices and the facilities provided to the customers under the agreement. However, full control in foreign markets is not possible. Facilities given different to distributors in the same country may differ.

(c) This system is most suitable where demonstration of the working of the product before sale is required such as television, refrigerators, washing machines, motor cars, scooters etc.

Conceptually, direct exporting can be segregated into various forms, depending on the international character of the company. This is shown in the following chart:

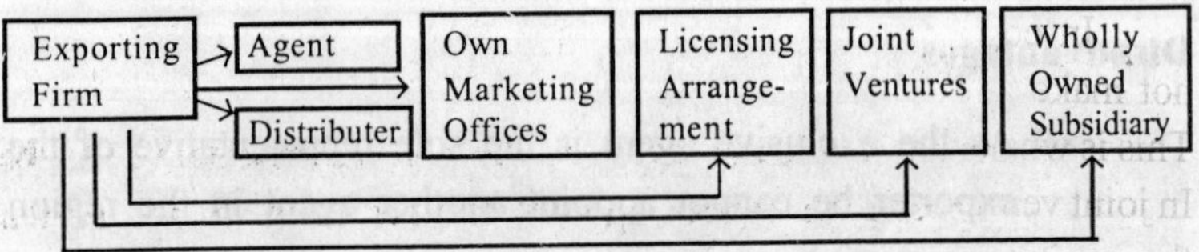

The first stage for a company going international directly is to appoint either an agent or a distributor in the target market. Once the market has proved its long-term potential, the company may decide to go to the second stage in terms of having its own marketing network in that market. The third stage is reached when the exporting firm decides to have his merchandise locally produced. But the manufacturing will be made not by the company but by a local firm with whom it may sign a licensing agreement. A licensing agreement may provide for a transfer of processes or know-how from the exporting company to the local firm or the right to use its brand names and trade marks by the local unit. The area within which such rights can be executed will be specified in the licensing agreement. In return, the exporting company will get paid by the local firm on the basis of a predetermined formula.

(6) Appointment of Export Salesmen. They represent the exporter in foreign countries and sell goods on his behalf. They get a fixed salary or a fixed percentage on sales as commission from the exporter. These salesmen may be the sole salesmen of the exporter or may sell goods for a number of parties.

Export salesmen may be travelling salesmen or resident salesmen. While the travelling salesmen travel in the specified areas, the residential salesmen do not travel from one place to another. They work permanently at one place.

Advantages

(a) They find the potentials of the markets, collect information and communicate it to the exporter.

(b) They report to the producer of the markets from time to time and carry out the orders and directions given to them by the exporters.

In concluding licensing agreements, the home company will not make any financial commitment in terms of equity investment. This is what distinguishes joint ventures from licensing arrangements. In joint ventures, the home company and the local firm jointly provide the equity capital of the company which is set up to take over the production and marketing function. Depending on the legislation as may be in force in the target country on foreign investment, the home company can have either majority or minority participation.

The basic advantage of joint ventures is that the home company can start local manufacturing and can control its operations substantially without incurring very large financial outlays. The basic problem relates to the fact that the management power and responsibilities will have to be shared and, therefore, unless there is unanimity on basic policies and issues, the company cannot be run efficiently.

The problem relating to the division of power does into arise when home company sets up its wholly owned subsidiary. This is a distinct advantage. The disadvantage is that the home company will have to bear the entire financial burden of setting up the unit. Moreover, in many countries, wholly foreign-owned companies are not allowed, at least in certain specified industrial sectors. Such legislation may limit the option of a company to set up its own foreign operations.

SELECTING AN AGENT IN FOREIGN MARKETS

Care should be taking in selecting an agent in the foreign market by the exporter keeping in mind the various characteristics of the product consumers who use it and the market conditions in that country.

Legal Procedures

It is better to have a written agency contract between the two parties incorporating all the essential dauses which may affect the principal agent relationship taking into account the legal provisions of the two countries regarding agency. Legal advice must be sought before entering into an agreement in respect of the following:

(i) Language and style of the agreement should be very clear or not confusing:

(ii) It should not violate the provision of national or intemational laws prevalent in the two countries.

(iii) Jurisdiction of court in case of any dispute should be defined in advance.

Points of Consideration in Selection

(i) Licensed Person. It should be considered the law of if the importing country specifies the nature of the agent who may act in the field. In such cases only licensed or recognised person and no other can be appointed as an agent.

(ii) Wide Network. The agent should have a wide network in major commercial centres of the country. If his activities are limited to a particular market, the exporter will have to appoint different agents for different centres to widen the scope of business.

(iii) Full Knowledge. The agent must have full knowledge of the market of the product. He must be a person who deals in the product line.

(iv) Financially Sound. The agent must be financially sound so that he may be able to provide many other facilities which may be required in the business such as warehousing, aftersale service, repaid and service centres etc.

(v) High Contacts. It should have contacts with the important persons in the business and should be in a position to safeguard the interest of the firm.

(vi) Qualified Staff. The agency must have specialised and qualified sales staff competent to handle sales of sophisticated product which are technical and required demonstration.

(vii) Standing. The exporting firm should also consider the standing of the agent in the market and in the product line. He should also inquire into other accounts that he is presently handling, and the total turnover of the agent as per account.

(viii) Undertaking Additional Functions. Though an agent is not responsible for any function except to procure order he may perform certain other functions if asked for. The exporter must also consider what functions in addition to those referred in the agency contract can he undertaken in case of need. Such acts may be credit guarantees, information of credit accounts, advertising and other functions on behalf of the principal etc. If an agent can undertake additional functions it may be of advantage to the exporting firm in case of emergency.

A firm may maintain agency relations for long, if the above points are taken into account in selecting an agent in foreign markets.

INDIRECT EXPORTING

Indirect export means export through middlemen. When an exporter allows an intermediary in his own country to perform certain important marketing function in relation to exporting the product, it is indirect exporting. It is almost equivalent to domestic sales. The company, under this system, sells its products in its own country to another party which will undertake the responsibility of exporting the same to other countries. In this way, the exporter losses, to a limited extent, his control over certain marketing operations.

If a manufacturer has once adopted the indirect method of exporting it is not necessary always to export indirectly through middlemen nor does it preclude the manufacturer from selling a part of his production directly. The actual method that is adopted depends on the volume of business and the manufacturer's decision often changes in obedience to the different conditions of the sales.

Advantages of Indirect Exporting

(i) Free from Botheration. The merchant exporter of the middlemen takes care of all the botherations involved such as documentation, shipping arrangements, financial, political and credit risks, procuring licences from Government department etc. and assumes all sales in foreign markets. Therefore, the producer exporter is free from all legal and procedural formalities which are necessary for making exports.

(ii) No Need for Export Organisation. In direct export, the company need not establish its own channel for distribution of its export trade without investing its capital funds because the middlemen purchase in cash from the company and the even sometime offer advance for producing goods for exports. Thus, the firm's capital is not tied up.

(iii) A Boon to New Entrants. As the new entrants in export field are new and know nothing about export and problems involved in it, they sell their products to the merchant exporter who knows everything is export trade and all about different export who markets gradually, the new entests gain experience and become fully aware of the procedures, formalities and problems of export trade.

(iv) Economy. After the producer sells the product to the middlemen, he free from all worries of selling the product in foreign markets. He saves a lot of money because he is not required to conduct market surveys; set up his own distribution channel, carry out programmes for advertising and other promotional activities and provide after sale services etc.

(v) Concentration on Production. Indirect exporting enables the manufacturer exporters to concentrate on production problems, leaving the question of foreign selling to the sales specialists of export markets/houses.

(vi) Market Information. Merchant exporters are experienced persons having full knowledge of various markets and marketing conditions. They are the best source of information to the exporter-producers about foreign markets and the demand of the product therein. The producers can adapt their products on the basis of such authentic information and improve their profitability.

(vii) Building Trade. Indirect export affords a means of building up a quick volume of trade, because the middlemen know where and how to get rapid international distribution. By selling the goods in different markets of the world the merchant exporter helps the exporter to produce more.

(viii) Sales Opportunities. The merchant exporters may provide sales opportunities in otherwise out of way markets.

(ix) Large Orders by Middlemen. Middlemen are mostly well reputed firms, who obtain large orders from the importers of different countries. The producer firm gains out of his goodwill provided the quality is good.

Disadvantages of Indirect Exporting

(i) Ignorant and Dependent. As the middlemen perform all the functions of export trading, the manufacturer exporter, remains ignorant of export markets and marketing operations even after years of exporting and continuous to be totally dependent on middlemen.

(ii) No Scope for Product Development. As the middlemen sell products in which they are interested, and the firm remains ignorant of the market there is no scope for product development. So also, long-term development of the market is not possible. As the firm is not in direct touch with the customers of foreign markets, it cannot play their product.

(iii) Inappropriate in Certain Cases. Indirect exporting is inappropriate in following cases:

(a) Where the products are either highly specialised or custom built, overseas importers like to deal directly with the manufacturer or his representative.

(b) Direct involvement of exporter is called (or where aftersale services or warehousing facilities are required.

(c) Where the unit value is much higher or it is an industrial product, the importers ask for full satisfaction abut the quality of the product.

(iv) Availability of Middlemen. As export merchants may not be available for all markets, the distribution problems remain unresolved.

(v) Commission to Middlemen. As the middlemen, engaged in export trade, charge commission for their services, it increases the cost of the product to the ultimate users and reduces and profitability rate to the manufacturer. The seller does not have any control over prices.

(vi) No Efforts to Promote Exporter's Product. An export commission house primarily represents the foreign customers as a buying representative and purchases goods only for foreign importers. It is not interested in any particular manufacturer. Therefore, it cannot be expected to do much to promote the sales of the manufacturer.

(vii) No Obligation to any Manufacturer. The export merchants generally concentrate on products which offer them the greatest profit. They buy products in the cheapest market, sell them in the best market and feel no particular obligation to any manufacturer. They oblige only those manufacturers who offer them higher commission. In this race small manufacturers product may be ignored.

(viii) No Stability of Business. Built up by indirect methods the stability of any export business, cannot be assured. The middlemen control the outlets and may, at any time, shift their clientele to competing lines.

EXPORT CREDIT GUARANTEE CORPORATION (ECGC)

Establishment

In India Export Credit Guarantee Corporation (ECGC) was established in 1954. The export Risk insurance Cooperation (ERIC) was merged in it. ECGC is under the administrative control of the Ministry of Commerce. The Head Office is in Bombay and regional offices are at Calcutta, Madras, Delhi and Bombay. Wholly owned by the Government of India it works On 'no profit no loss' basis.

The risk element in the export business is greater than the risk involved in domestic trade because the two parties of the export contract belong to different countries. The export contract involves a number of complications economic, legal, political and social. For minimising the risk element in export business and to facilitate the flow of finance from banks and other institutions to exporters there is an Export Credit Guarantee Corporation (ECGC).

Functions of the Corporation

The main functions of the corporation are:

(i) By issuing suitable policies, it insures exporters against the attendant risks of export operations.

(ii) It provides financial guarantees to banks and exporters for exports against deferred credit payment terms.

(iii) Any other activity assigned to it by the Government of India from time to time.

Insurance Policies Issued by ECGC

The ECGC has issued the following two types of policies:

(i) Standard Policies, and

(ii) Special Policies.

(i) Standard Policies. Standard policies are issued by the ECGC to exporters to protect them against the risks of international trading especially those relating to losses in exports on deferred terms of payment. There are three types of standard policies:

(a) ***Specific Shipment Policy (Political Risk).*** This policy covers the risks caused by the political reasons such as importer's Government action to block or delay payment, war, revolution or civil disturbance, cancellation of import licence, demurrage or addition handling charges due to delay, and any other causes of low occurring outside India.

(b) ***Specific Shipment Policy (Comprehensive Risks).*** Such policy covers both the political and commercial risks involved in export transactions. The policy covers the commercial risks caused to the exporter by the insolvency of the buyer, delay in payments for more than 4 months, non-acceptance of goods not due to exporter's default.

(c) ***Contract Policy.*** Contract policy covers the additional risks due to cancellation of export licence or imposition of new export restrictions in India. The above two specific policies cover risks from the time the goods are shipped but the contract policy covers the risks from the data of contract.

The extent of coverage of financial losses (on account of political or commercial risks) under the ECGC standard policy is 90% of the losses.

(ii) Special Policies. Special policies, besides the risks covered under standard policies, are issued by the ECGC to cover the risks as desired by the exporters to meet their needs in export transactions.

To suit the various needs of the exporters, the ECGC has devised the following policies:

(a) Construction works policy covers the risks of non-payment of contract price to the contractor by the foreign contractee.

(b) Policy for consignment export covers the loss on consignment transactions.

(c) Services policy covers the risks of non-payment for services rendered aboard. Policy covers only technical and professional services.

(d) Manufacturer's credit insurance policy covers 80% of the risks due to default on insolvency on the part of the exporter.

(e) Exporter's credit insurance policy. This policy covers 50% of losses arising out of default or insolvency of manufacturers.

(f) Market development policies cover losses on market development on 50 : 50 basis if market surveys are done by an independent agency .

Financial Guarantees

Exporters require adequate financial support from bank to carry out their export contracts effectively. ECGC's guarantees to the bank protect the latter from losses on their lending to exporters.

The beneficiaries under the guarantees given by ECGC are not the banks alone but the exporters as well. These guarantees have been designed to encourage banks to give liberal credit and other facilities connected with exports, both at pre-shipment and post-shipment stages.

Five guarantees have been evolved for this purpose:

(a) Packing Credit Guarantee;

(b) Post-shipment Export Credit Guarantee;

(c) Export Finance Guarantee;

(d) Export Produftion Finance Guarantee;

(e) Export Performance Guarantee; and

(f) Export Finance (Overseas Lending) Guarantees.

These guarantees give protection to the bank against losses due to non-payment by an experter arising from his insolvency or default. ECGC pays the bank three-fourths of the loss in the case of Export Finance Guarantee, Post-shipment Export Credit Guarantee and Export Performance Guarantee and two-thirds of the loss in the case of the rest.

The Corporation agrees to pay 75 per cent of the loss to banks which offer to cover all their pre-shipment accounts under a whole turnover Packing Credit Guarantee.

Again, ECGC agrees to pay, in special cases, 80 per cent of the loss in respect of advances made under the Post-Shipment Export Credit Guarantee against shipments of engineering and metallurgical items of the value of Rs. 2 crores or more under a single contract. In the case of Export Performance Guarantee, higher cover of 90 per cent of loss is available on payment of proportionately higher premium.

Policies Issued by the ECGC

The main functions of ECGC are to issue suitable policies to exporters to cover the various risks attached to export trade and to provide guarantee is to commercial banks for the risks inherent in the export credit advanced by them to exporters. Apart from this the ECGC may come forward with the new schemes to suit the Indian exporters.

The ECGC has issued two types of Insurance Policies:

(i) Standard Policies, and

(ii) Specific or Special Policies.

Special Schemes

In the past few years ECGC has brought forward following progressive schemes to encourage exports:

(i) Overseas Investment Insurance. The involvement of exporters in capital participation in overseas projects has assumed importance with the increasing exports of goods and turnkey projects from India. ECGC has evolved a scheme to provide cover for such investments.

(ii) Exchange Fluctuations Risk Cover Schemes. Recently, the ECGC has evolved two new schemes to provide greater protection to exporter of capital goods and turnkey projects against the risk of fluctuation in foreign currency.

(a) Exchange Fluctuation Risks (Bid) Scheme. It gives protection in respects of bids tendered in approved foreign currencies between the date of bid and the date of contract. If the contract is won, the ECGC refunds 75% of the premium.

(b) The Exchange Fluctuation Risks (Contract) Cover. If the contract is won, the exporter will be required to obtain this order for eligible deferred receivables. In that event he will be allowed in terms of this scheme to have the rate of exchange prevailing as on the date of bid if it is more advantages than the rate of exchange on the date of the contract.

Special Schemes for Small Scale Exporters

For small scale industries the ECGC provides a higher percentage of cover and makes procedural relaxations in matters like settlement of claims, sanction of credit limit, etc. The scheme applies to exporters whose annual export turnover is not more than Rs. 10 lakhs.

Evaluation

By providing covers for the various risks to exporters and providing guarantees to banks advancing money for various purposes to exporters against the probable risks involved in such transactions, ECGC has done a valuable service in the export trade. Certain special schemes have also been evolved by the ECGC for the greater interest of exporters and export trade.

The Covers Issued by ECGC

(i) Standard Policies issued to exporters to protect them against payment risks involved in exports on short-term credit.

(ii) Specific Policies designed to protect Indian firms against payment risk involved in *(a)* exports on deferred terms of payment, *(b)* services rendered to foreign parties, and *(c)* construction works and turnkey projects undertaken abroad.

(iii) Financial guarantees issued to banks in India to protect them from risks of loss involved in their extending financial support to exporters at the post shipment as well as pre-shipment stages.

(iv) Special schemes, *viz.* Transfer Guarantee meant to protect banks which add confirmation to Letters of Credit opened by foreign banks, Insurance cover for Buyers Credit, cover for Buyers Credit, Lines of Credit, Overseas Investment insurance and Change Fluctuation Risk Insurance.

Standard Policies

(1) Shipments (Comprehensive Risks) Policy. This is to cover both commercial and political risks from the date of shipment.

(2) Shipment (Political Risks) Policy. This is to cover both risks from the date of shipment.

(3) Contracts (Comprehensive Risks) Policy. This is cover both commercial and political risks from the date of contract.

(4) Contracts (Political Risks) Policy. This is to cover only political risks from the date of contract.

The Shipment (comprehensive Risks) Policy is the one ideally suited to cover risks in respect of goods exported on short-term credit. It covers both political and commercial risks from the date of shipment. Risk of pre-shipment losses due to frustration of export contracts is nil or very low since goods exported on short-term credit are raw materials, primary goods, consumer goods or consumer durable which can be resold easily. Contract policies, which cover risks from the date of contract are issued only in special cases when goods to be exported are manufactured to the non-standard specifications of a buyer.

Shipments to associate or to agents and those against letter of credit can be covered for only political risks by suitable endorsements to the Shipment Comprehensive Risks Policy. Premium is charged on such shipment at lower rates.

Risks Covered Under Standard Policies

Under its policies intended to protect the exporters against overseas credit risks, ECGC bears the main brunt of the risk and pays the exporter 90 per cent of his low on account of 'commercial' and 'political' risks.

Commercial Risks

(a) The insolvency of the buyer;

(b) The buyer's protracted default to pay (within 4 months of due date) for goods accepted by him; and

(c) In some special circumstances specified in the policy, buyer's failure to accept the goods, when such non-acceptance is not due to the exporter's actions.

Political Risks

(a) Restriction on remittances in the buyer's country or any Government action which may block or delay payment to the exporter;

(b) War, revolution or civil disturbances in the buyer's country;

(c) New import licensing restrictions or cancellation of a valid import licence in the buyer's country;

(d) Additional handling, transport or insurance charges due to interruption or diversion of voyage which cannot be recovered from the buyer;

(e) Cancellation of export licence or imposition of new export licensing restrictions in India (under contracts policy); and

(f) Any other cause of loss occurring outside India, not normally insured by commercial insurers, and beyond the control of the exporter or of the buyer.

Risks not Covered

The Standard policies do not cover losses due to the following risks:

(a) Commercial disputes raised by the buyer, unless the exporter obtains a decree from a competent court of law in the buyer's country in his favour;

(b) Causes inherent in the nature of the goods;

(c) Insolvency or default of any agent of the exporter or the collecting banks;

(d) Buyer's failure to obtain necessary import or exchange authorisation from authorities in his country;

(e) Loss or damage to goods which can be covered by commercial insurers;

(f) Exchange fluctuations.

Specific Policies

Contracts for export of capital goods or projects for construction works and for rendering services abroad are insured by ECGC on a case to case basis under specific policies. Special mention may be made of the services policy to protect Indian firms against payment for their services and the construction works policy to cover all payments that fall due to a contractor under a composite contract for execution of civil engineering works which may involve provision of services as well as supply of materials.

All contracts for export on deferred payment terms exceeding Rs. 1 crores in value and all contracts for turn-key projects and construction works abroad require prior clearance of the Working Group consisting of representatives from Reserve Bank of India, EXIM Bank and ECGC. Applications for this purpose are to be sent to EXIM Bank through the exporter's bank. An 'in principle' clearance at the Working Group enables the exporters to get necessary facilities from the institutions concerned.

Forms the Specific Policy for Supply Contracts

It may take any of the following four forms:

(a) Specific Shipments (Comprehensive Risks) Policy to cover both commercial and political risks at the post-shipment stage;

(b) Specific Shipment (Political Risks) Policy to cover only political risks at the post-shipment stage in cases where the buyer is an overseas Government, or payments are guaranteed by a Government or by banks, or are made to associates;

(c) Specific Contracts (Comprehensive Risks) Policy;

(d) Specific Contracts (Political Risk) Policy.

Contracts Policy provides cover from the date of contract. Losses that may be sustained by an exporter at the pre-shipment stage due to frustration of contract are covered under this policy in addition to the cover provided by the Shipment Policy.

ECGC's Special Policies

An exporter sometime needs coverage of risks connected with various export transactions. The ECGC has devised the following special policies to suit the various needs of the exporters:

(1) Construction Works Policy. A contract for construction work comprises not only the supply of the material required but also the provision of services as well as the execution of civil engineering works connected with the completion of the contract. The ECGC's constructions works policy provides cover for all payments that fall due to the contractor under this contract.

The policy covers contract entered into with various Government or contracts with other bodies where payments are guaranteed by an overseas Government. In such contracts, supplies from third countries shall be limited to 15% of the value of the total supplies.

The policy is issued to cover the specific contract and it take effect from the date of the contract. The risk coverage is usually comprehensive in nature. Cover can also be provided for the contractor's equipment such as cranes, bulldozers and trucks used for constructions against risk like confiscation, by a suitable endorsement on the policy.

(2) Policy for Consignment Exports. The ECGC covers exports made on consignment basis. A special endorsement for the purpose may have to be obtained by the exporter on the standard specific shipment policy. The cover obtained would provide for political risks from the date of shipment and risks from the date of sale of overseas stock to the buyer, subject to the terms and conditions of policy.

(3) Services Policy. A services policy of the ECGC is designed to protect Indian exporters against the risk of non-payment for services rendered to foreign parties. Under this policy, technical and professional services are covered. The services policies are availed of for the coverage of both political and commercial risks.

(4) Manufacturer's Credit Insurance Policies. This insurance cover is given to a manufacturer to export his goods through an exporter or an export house. Exporters normally obtain credit from the manufacturer while they offer credit to the buyer. Under the manufacturer's credit insurance policy, the manufacturer is protected against default or insolvency on the part of the exporter. The extent of coverage is 80% of the manufacturer's loss.

(5) Exporter's Credit Insurance Policy. Sometimes exporters offer credit to a manufacture for the procuring and manufacturing of export goods. The ECGC's Exporter's Credit Insurance Policy covers losses arising out of default or insolvency on the part of the manufacturer. The extent of coverage is 50% of the total loss to the exporter.

(6) Market Development Policies. Often, an exporter has to undertake detailed market surveys to assess market potential and devise strategies for marketing a product. Besides, several publicity measures are also undertaken for the development of the overseas market. If such expenses are not recovered in terms of the prospects revealed by the survey, the ECGC shares the loss with the exporter on a 50:50 basis, provided that the surveys are undertaken by an approved and independent agency.

FINANCIAL GUARANTEES

In view of the peculiar nature of, and the risks connected with the export financing, the ECGC has designed a number of financial guarantees to the commercial banks to extend credit to exporters. The guarantees are given only to commercial banks to provide liberal credit for exporters to export both at pre-shipment and post shipment stages.

Six guarantees have been evolved for the purpose.

(a) Packing Credit Guarantee.

(b) Post-shipment Export Credit Guarantee.

(c) Export Finance Guarantee.

(d) Export Production Finance Guarantee.

(e) Export Performance Guarantee.

(f) Transfer Guarantee.

For guarantees under (b), (c) and (e) the cover is three fourth of the loss and for others, it is two-thirds of the loss.

The ECGC indemnifies the financing bank to the extent of $66\frac{2}{3}\%$ of the loss and 75% of the loss respectively on premium charges varying between 3 paise and 7.5 paise per Rs. 100/- per-month.

In the case of a small-scale merchant exporter whose turn-over does at exceed Rs. 2 lakhs, the ECGC idemnifies the bank upto 90% of the loss.

(b) Post Shipment Export Credit Guarantee. The commercial banks extend post-shipment credit to exporters by purchasing, negotiating and discounting their export bills. Against this credit, banks are eligible to obtain a cover from the ECGC which protects them against defaults or insolvency of the exporters. The standard or specific policies, however, provide the financial risks to the exporter but they do not provide for loss substained by him or account of his own default or disputes between him and the buyer. To cover these risks and secure the advances, banks ask the ECGC for post-shipment credit guarantee. Normally, the bank is covered to the extent of 75% of the loss on this account.

(c) Export Finance Guarantee. Reclamation of incentives, such as cash assistance and duty drawback may take some time after the completion of exports. Banks extend advances to exports against these receivables to help them finance their export operations. Such advances may be given up to a maximum of 50% FOB value or the actual amount of receivables, whichever is less. The ECGC's export finance guarantee scheme indemnifies the bank against losses incurred by it on its advances exporters owing to their default or insolvency. The extent of coverage is 75% of the losses incurred.

(d) Export Production Finance Guarantee. Usually goods eligible for incentives do not fetch the price equal to what could be received in domestic markets. Until the exporter receives full FOB value from the buyer and amount of assistance from the Government, he does not get full domestic value of his product. As because the assistance from Government in the form of cash assistance and Duty Drawback takes time, the ECGC guarantees the loan advancing banks to the extent of 66.67% of loss owing to insolvency or default of the exporter for the loan advanced by the bank upto 50% over and above the FOB value at the pre-shipment and post-shipment stages.

(e) Export Performance Guarantee. An exporter-negotiating exports on deferred terms of payment may need to arrange for bank guarantees for the following purposes:

(i) ***Bid Bond.*** The foreign buyer may require Bid Bond when an exporter wants to quote for a tender. It is guarantee certifying the genuineness of the offer submitted by the buyer.

(ii) ***Advance Payment Guarantee.*** After the exporter secures the bid, the buyer may pay the exporter a percentage of the value of the contract as an advance against the bank guarantee.

(iii) ***Bank Guarantee for Payment of Retention Money.*** In order to ensure the performance, the buyer may retain percentage of the contract value as retention money and agree to release it to the exporter against a bank guarantee.

(iv) ***Bank Guarantee for Performance of the Contract by the Exporter.*** This guarantee is required by the buyer when the contract is awarded to the exporter.

(v) ***Bank Guarantee lor Loans of Foreign Exchange.*** It may be necessary for an exporter to raise funds in foreign currency to finance his operations in connection with an export project. In these cases, the financing institutions abroad may need a bank guarantee to be furnished by the exporter.

The exporter approaches the bank for these guarantees. To cover the risks involved in such transactions, the bank obtains a counter guarantee from the ECGC under the latter's Performance Guarantee Scheme.

The proposals for these guarantees may be made by the bank to the ECGC, qn the basis of which, ECGC counter guarantee will be made available.

The ECGC identifies the bank upto 662/3% of the total loss in the case of bid bonds and 75% of the loss in the case of the other guarantees required by the exporter.

(f) Transfer Guarantees. Sometimes an exporter may ask his own bank in India to confirm a foreign letter of credit. When the bank confirms the letter, it binds itself to honour the drafts drawn by the beneficiary if they are in accordance with the letter of credit. The confirming bank may run the risk of the foreign bank not reimbursing the Indian bank, especially in the event of certain political situations such as war, civil war, transfer delays, moratorium etc. To protect these banks against these risks that may delay or prevent the transfer of funds to bank in India. The ECGC has devised the Transfer Guarantee Scheme which safeguards the banks in India against such types of risks.

In the last few years ECGC, has brought forward many progressive schemes and policies to encouraged exports, and cover the risks of the exporters and the financial institutions. However, the exporters should not forget the cardinal principle of making their own comprehensive commercial evaluation of the buyer, his previous record and antecedents before they embark on credit or insurance cover.

❑

6

Legal Dimensions of International Marketing

CONFLICT OF LAWS

One of the distinctive features of international marketing is that exporters have to deal with different legal systems. An Indian manufacturer selling his products domestically knows that he and his customer are governed by Indian laws and subject to the jurisdiction of India's Courts. But an Indian exporter selling his products to an importer, say, in the USA, must contend with the fact that US laws may well have some influence either on the contractual terms to be agreed upon between him and the importer, or on the settlement of dispute, if any, arising out of the contract. This is what is known, technically, as the conflict of laws which can be settled in advance by incorporating specific provisions in the contract as to the proper law governing the contract and jurisdiction.

Further, because the buyer and the seller are at great geographical distance from each other, many intermediaries like shipping, airlines, insurance companies and banks are involved, and trade terms and usages differ across the countries, it is advisable for the exporters to enter into written export contracts, incorporating all the necessary details.

Written Vs. Constructed Contracts

Though as a rule all large export orders, including those for long-term supply contracts and project exports, are invariably quoted on the basis of detailed documentation and written agreements signed by both the parties are entered into, a fairly large part of India's exports is carried out without the backing of written export contracts. This is especially true in the case of export of products like handicrafts, garments, jewellery, etc. It does not mean that because there is no written contract, there is no contract at all. There has to be a contract if exports are to be made. There exists, in such cases, what is known as a 'constructed contract'. A constructed contract is one where the existence of a contract can be inferred from relevant documents, *viz.*, telex messages, proforma commercial invoice or letter of credit. The exporters must, however, make sure that all the information on which agreement is required are available on any or all of these documents.

Export contracts are private contracts and the State does not interfere in the conclusion of such contracts provided the subject-matter is not malafide. But all private contracts must be concluded in such a way that no provisions of the public laws are violated. The Government of India has promulgated various laws governing the conduct of export-import business in India. The terms of export contract must be consistent with the provisions of such enactments.

Export/Import Contract: The Boundary Relationships

The major laws which have to be kept in mind while entering into export contracts are:

(1) Foreign Trade Development and Regulation Act, 1992. This Act has replaced the Export Import (Control) Act 1947. However, all orders made under the latter Act shall continue to be in force if these are not inconsistent with the provisions of the FT (D&R) Act, 1992.

Under this Act, a Code No., once granted, can be suspended or cancelled if a person has made exports or imports in a manner gravely prejudicial to the trade relations of India with any foreign country or to the interests of other persons engaged in import or export or has brought disrepute to the credit of the goods of the country.

Under the authority of this Act, the office of Director General, Foreign Trade, brings out the export-import policy and lays down the procedures. The policy determines, among other things', whether export of a product is banned, whether the export of the product is subject to quota restrietions or licensing arrangements, whether export of a product is canalised through a Government undertaking and whether there is any floor price regulation regarding that product. If an exporter wants to enter into an export contract for a product for which there is a floor price provision, he must make sure that the price he is quoting is not lower than the floor price as fixed by the Government. Or, if the product under consideration is subject to quota restrictions, the exporter should sign a contract which would specify that the performance of the contract will be subject to the availability of the quota from the concerned government department, with a view to ensuring that he will not be sued for non-performance of the contract by the im porter in case he cannot export because the quota is not made available by the government department.

(2) Foreign Exchange Regulations Act, 1973. Section 18 of FERA provides that for all cash exports, the foreign exchange proceeds from exports must be brought back to India within 180 days. The exporter, therefore, cannot enter into an export contract with an overseas importer under which he extends credit for more than 180 days, except where exports are made on deferred payment terms or on consignment basis. The Foreign Exchange Manual which is issued under the FERA by the Reserve Bank of India provides that an exporter normally cannot pay more than 12.5 per cent to his agent abroad for the services provided by him. The exporter, therefore, cannot enter into an agreement under which he commits himself to pay an agency commission of more than 12.5 per cent unless he has obtained prior permission from the Reserve Bank of India to that effect.

(3) Preshipment Inspection and Quality Control Act, 1963. In order to protect the image of the country as an exporter the Government of India has under this Act provided that items which are subject to this Act cannot be exported unless a designated agency certifies that the quality of the products being exported is as per the standards laid down. The standard being asked for by the importer may be higher but not lower than the standards as applicable under the Act. Even if an importer does not ask for quality certificate, it is obligatory on the part of the exporter to secure this certificate from the concerned agencies.

(4) Customs Act, 1962. The Customs Department is vested with the task of carrying out physical as well as documentary check on all goods crossing the Indian customs frontier. All export consignments will be checked by the customs authorities at port or airport with a view to ascertaining that the goods being shipped are? those which are declared in the documents and that no under/overinvoicing is involved. The authority to check the export-import consignments is given under the Customs Act.

(5) International Commercial Practices. Apart from the Indian laws, there are certain international commercial practices which also may have a bearing on export-import contracts. Two documents prepared by the International Chamber of Commerce, Paris, are widely used in international business. These are (1) Uniform Customs and Practice for Documentary Credits (UCP), 1993 and INCO Terms, 1990. The UCP is a document which is used by banks in the negotiation of export-import documents. INCO Terms define the various trade terms like FOB, C&F, CIF, etc. and codify the respective rights and obligations of the two parties under various contract terms.

Types of Legal Issues

An international marketer has to face a number of legal issues in implementation of the corporate export marketing plan. The basic legai issues can broadly be classified into:

(a) those relating to export-import contracts;

(b) those relating to the relationships between the exporter and agents/distributors;

(c) those relating to products, *viz.*, trade marks, patents, product liability and promotion;

(d) those relating to credit contracts (Letters of Credit).

A brief discussion of each of these legal issues is given below.

A. Elements of Export Contract

The elements of an export contract vary depending upon the nature of the product being exported. There are, however, some elements which are almosts universal in their application. These elements are:

(1) The parties;

(2) The description of product;

(3) Quality;

(4) Price per unit;

(5) Total value;

(6) Currency;

(7) Tax and charges;

(8) Packing;

(9) Marking and labelling;

(10) Mode of transport;

(11) Delivery: place and schedule;

(12) Insurance;

(13) Inspection;

(14) Documentation;

(15) Mode of payment;

(16) Credit period, if any;

(17) Warranties;

(18) Passing of risk;

(19) Passing of property;

(20) Availability/non-availability of export-import licences;

(21) Force Majeure;

(22) Settlement of disputes;

(23) Proper Law of the contract;

(24) Jurisdiction.

FOB/CIF Contracts

Various types of export price quotations are used in international marketing. Fifteen terms have been codified by the International Chamber of Commeree. Most important among them are f.o.b., c.& f. and c.i.f. When the price quotation is made on f.o.b. basis, the corresponding export sales contract will be an f.o.b. contract. Similarly, the c.i.f. quotation will result in a c.i.f. contract. Under the relevant export sales contract, the exporter and importer have certain rights and duties. The International Chamber of Commerce has delineated the rights and responsibilities of the exporters and importers in their publication 'INCO' Terms'. A brief description of the respective rights and obligations under various contractual terms is given below:

F.O.R. (named port of shipment) Contract

Duties of the exporter will include *inter alia*:

(a) Supply the contracted goods in conformity with the contract of sale and deliver the goods on board the vessel named by the buyer at the named port of shipment;

(b) Bear all costs and risks of the goods until such time as they shall have effectively passed the ship's rail; and

(c) Provide at his own expense the customary clean documents in proof of the delivery of the goods.

Duties of the importer will include *inter alia*:

(a) Reserve the necessary shipping space and give due notice of the Sale to the exporter; and

(b) Bear all costs and risks of the goods from the time when they shall have effectively passed ihe ship's rail and pay the price as provided in the contract.

C.I.F. (named port of destination) Contract

Duties of the exporter will include *inter alia*:

(a) Supply the goods in conformity with the Contract of sale, arrange at his own expense for the shipping space by the usual route and pay freight charges for the carriage of goods;

(b) Obtain at his own risk and expense all documentation regarding government authorisation necessary for the export of goods;

(c) Load the goods at his own expense on board the vessel at the port of shipment and procure at his own cost in a transferable form a policy of marine insurance for a value equivalent to c.i.f. plus 10 per cent; and

(d) Bear all risks until the goods shall have effectively crossed the ship's rail and furnish to the buyer a clean negotiable bill of lading.

Duties of the importer will include *inter alia*:

(a) Accept the documents when tendered by the exporter, if these are in conformity with the contract of sale and pay the price;

(b) Receive the goods at the port of destination and bear all costs except freight and marine insurance incurred in respect of the cardage of the goods; and

(e) Bear all risks of the goods from the time they shall have effectively passed the ship's rail at the port of shipment.

The details of the responsibilities and the expenses to be incurred in connection with the carrying out of those responsibilities by the two parties under various contractual terms are indicated in Table 1. A model contract form is given in the Annexure to this Chapter.

Table 1: Distribution of Responsibilities between the Exporter and the Importer under Various Contract Terms

	Ex. Works	*FAS Port of Export*	*FOB Vessel Port of Export*	*C & F Port of Import*	*FIF Port of Import*	*Delivered Duty Paid*
(1)	*(2)*	*(3)*	*(4)*	*(5)*	*(6)*	*(7)*
Seller's Plant	CXO					
Provide Invoice and Packing list	CS	CS	CS	CS	CS	CS
Provide Certificate of Origin	CS	CS	CS	CS	CS	CS
Load on to Carrier		CS	CS	CS	CS	CS
Provide and Pay Inland Transport/ Insurance Costs		CS	CS	CS	CS	CS
Pay for Demurrage		CS	CS	CS	CS	CS
Obtain Export Documents		CS	CS	CS	CS	CS
Deliver to Port		CS	CS	CS	CS	CS
Unload at Port		CS	CS	CS	CS	CS
Pay Port Dues		CSXO	CS	CS	CS	CS
Give Notice of Name of Vessel				CS	CS	CS
Give Notice of Sailing Date				CS	CS	CS
Give Notice of Loading Berth				CS	CS	CS
Give Notice of Required Delivery Time				CS	CS	CS
Load on Ship			CSXO	CSX	CSX	CSX
Pay Loading Charges			CS	CS	CS	CS
Provide Bill of Lading/Airway Bill			CS	CSO	CSO	CS
Provide Insurance					CS	CS
Pay Cost of Ocean/Airshipment				CS	CS	CS
Unload at Port of Import						CS

Contd.

(1)	*(2)*	*(3)*	*(4)*	*(5)*	*(6)*	*(7)*
Pay Unloading Charges						CS
Pay Port Dues						CS
Pay Customs Duties and Taxes						CS
Pay Demurrage Costs at Port						CS
Provide Import Documentation						CS
Pay Inland Transport/Insurance Costs						CS
Receive at Importer's Warehouse						CS
Unload from Carrier						CSO

C = Exporter's expenses.

S = Exporter's responsibility.

X = Point where importer assumes risk.

Blank Space = Importer's responsibility and expense.

O = Point where importer takes ownership, unless otherwise provided in the Contract.

B. Export Agency Agreement

Agency agreement is a legal document, which establishes commercial relationship between the principal and the agent. It incorporates the conditions mutually agreed upon by the concerned parties for the conduct of business. When negotiating an agency agreement, the Indian firm should be careful on certain points. These are:

Parties to the Contract. The identity of the parties must be made explicit; especially whether the agency is assignable or not, should be made clear.

Contracted Territory. The territory for which the sole agency is being granted is to be explicitly mentioned.

Contractual Products. The agreement should indicate specific products for which the agency is being concluded. If products are not specifically mentioned, this implies that the agent is working for the entire product range, both present and future, of the firm which will be very unsatisfactory from the standpoint of the exporter.

Customers. Generally, the agent may be required to contact all potential customers. But in some cases the principal may like to reserve the right to himself to contact directly some specific group of buyers. If so, this is to be mentioned in the contract.

International Buying Groups' operations are becoming increasingly important. The principal, therefore, may like to reserve the right to negotiate directly with such buying groups in his own country for orders, which ultimately will be executed in the agent's territory. Whether the agent will be eligible to commission on such sales should be made explicit in the agreement.

Acceptance or Rejection of Orders. The principal may also like to reserve the right to accept or reject any order secured by the agent. This may be specially important when credit terms are involved and the principal is not sure of the creditworthiness of the buyer. Reservation of this right also will have to be mentioned in the agreement.

Payment of Commission. Payment of commission is the crucial clause of the agreement. First, the rate at which the commission will be paid has to be indicated. Secondly, since commission payable is calculated on percentage basis, the base for such calculation is to be determined. Thirdly, the time when the commission becomes payable should also be indicated. Legally speaking, commission becomes due when the principal accepts the order. But there is a time gap between the acceptance of the order and the receipt of the payment. Many uncertainties are involved within this time gap. The exporter may make the shipment but the overseas buyer may default. The result will be the same in either case, because the principal will not get the payment while the commission has already fallen due. To avoid such problems, it should be made clear that the commission will be paid on the basis of the invoice value and will become payable only on realization. The provision, in fact, is necessary also in view of the RBI regulations.

Settlement of Disputes. With a clearly drafted agency agreement, there should normally be no reason for disputes to arise.

But in case disputes do arise, the mechanism for settling such disputes should be agreed upon in advance by both the parties and indicated in the agency agreement. Referring the disputes to arbitration is the best procedure. Care, however should be taken as to the venue and the proper law of the agreement. The Indian firm may attempt to get a place in India as venue and Indian law as the proper law. In case it is not acceptable to the agent, there are two possibilities of compromise, *viz.*, *(a)* that the venue will be in a third country, or *(b)* that the venue will be the place of the defendant.

Renewal and Termination. The agreement should in itself also provide for the renewal or termination procedure. If the agent is sound, obviously no principal will think of terminating the agreement. The problem of termination arises only when the agent is not effective. In the civil law countries, termination may pose financial problems to the principal because of compensation to be paid to the agent. The proposed EEC Directive on Agency Laws will make the situation even more critical. It, however, appears that if there is a minimum turnover clause in the agreement and the agent fails to reach the pre-determined level, this can be taken as a valid ground for termination and hence no terminal compensation becomes payable. Therefore, it may be in the interest of the principal to insist on a minimum turnover clause in the agreement.

Agency Agreement Vs. Distribution Agreement

It may be worthwhile to compare an agency agreement with a distribution agreement. A distribution agreement is one which is signed by the Indian exporter with a distributor abroad. The basic distinction between an agency agreement and a distribution agreement relates to the title of the goods. Under an agency agreement, the agent is responsible only for the procurement of orders. Subsequently, there is a direct contractual relationship between the exporter and the party placing the order. Title of the goods, even when stocked at the agent's premises, remains with the principal. So does the risk.

Under a distribution agreement, on the other hand, the contractual relationship is only between the principal and the distributor. But there is no subsequent contract between the principal and the ultimate buyers. The distributor purchases the goods from the principal on his own account and, therefore, both risk and title to the goods pass on to the distributor.

Similarly, credit risks are to be borne by the principal in the case of an agency agreement, unless *del credere* terms are involved, while in the case of distribution agreement credit risks will be borne by the distributor. Further, in the case of an agent, the principal may be subject to third party liability because of any action on the part of the agent taken during the course of business. However, when a distributor is appointed, such third party liability does not go back to the principal. Liabilities on account of product warranties, of course, will remain with the principal even when a distribution agreement has been concluded.

It is, therefore, clear that the extent of legal liabilities under an agency agreement tends to be higher than under a distribution agreement. But this has to be viewed against the relative disadvantages in terms of marketing factors, which is implicit in a distribution agreement. When a distributor is appointed, he operates as an independent organization buying and selling on his own account. Therefore, the control of the principal on the distributor cannot be foolproof. Under an agency agreement, on the other hand, the agent is always under the direct control of the principal and, therefore, the latter can effectively manage the marketing operations in the way he likes. Moreover, it is more difficult to get a distributor than a good agent.

C. Laws Relating to Products

Trade Marks

Trade marks are words or designs or combination of these. The words may be manufactured words, *i.e.*, words which do not exist in any language but have been invented specifically for the purpose of trade mark, *viz.*, XEROX or KODAK. Trade marks are expected to perform many marketing functions. Some of these are:

(a) to enhance or create distinctiveness;

(b) to help identifying the product;

(c) to lead to easier recognition of the product;

(d) to symbolise the quality of the product; and

(e) to stimulate the desire to buy.

Protection of Trade Marks

A manufacturer can apply for registration of his trade mark to the registering authority of the country where he is exporting or wants to export. Certain names cannot be registered. Names, surnames, geographical place names, descriptive words or numerals are generally not allowed to be registered. Before registering a trade mark, the registering authority will conduct a check whether this or a similar trade mark has already been registered. If no evidence of such a trade mark is found, the trade mark being applied for will be published in the official journal of the registering authority. Anybody can raise objections to the granting of registration within a specified period after the publication. If the ground for objections, if any, is found to be not in order, the registration is given. This is more or less the practice followed in most countries, though there are minor variations. An exporter has to assign the task of trade marks registration to attorney firms which are specialised in such matters.

Product Liability

Product liability is the result of increased consumerism and, therefore, is most prevalent as a legal concept in the U.S.A But it is becoming quite common in the EEC and even in countries like Singapore, Mexico, ete. Product liability can be defined as the responsibility borne by the manufacturers, distributors and retailers for any consequential injuries/damages from products they make or sell.

There are three recognised bases of product liability:

(a) Negligence on the part of the manufacturer/seller. The manufacturer must exercise reasonable care in designing and manufacturing the product.

(b) The principle of strict liability. This is a principle established by the US Supreme Court in 1953 which set the principle that the aggrieved party need not prove negligence on the part of the manufacturer but hold him strictly liable for any injury resulting from a defective product, irrespective of whether he was negligent or not.

(c) Under some contracts of sale, there are express warranties; there are also implied warranties that of merchantability.

Legal action may be brought against any/every party involved in the manufacture and distribution of the product. A foreign supplier may plead that the foreign courts do not have jurisdiction over him. Even if he is successful in that attempt, he would incur the cost of legal proceedings; or if his distributor gets penalised, he will stop purchasing from him subsequently. So either way, the exporter will lose if his product is found to cause injury and liable for damages.

The exporter must, therefore, study the relevant laws and regulations of the country and make sure that his products will not be affected by them or carry out necessary modifications of his products to meet the requirements of the law. He should also take product liability insurance.

Laws Relating to Packaging and Promotion

Most countries have laid down detailed rules regarding the packaging of many items, especially foodstuffs, toiletries and pharmaceuticals. Information to be given on the product package is listed out in these rules, which generally include chemical composition of the product, net weight, date of manufacture and date of expiry. If there are special precautions to be taken while using the product, that also must be clearly indicated. These rules vary from country to country and product to product.

Similarly, many countries have laws regarding product advertising. Unsubstantiated claim for the product made in the advertisement may make the manufacturer subject to legal action. There are advertising industry associations in many countries which voluntarily have laid down code of conduct for industry members. An exporter who wants to promote his product will have to consider these codes.

D. Laws Relating to Letters of Credit

The exporter wants to ensure that he is paid for his merchandise before the possession and title to the merchandise pass to the importer. This is sought to be achieved through the intermediary of the bank which opens a letter of credit on behalf of the importer, naming the exporter as the beneficiary. The mechanism of letters of credit has been explained in the chapter on Export Finance.

A letter of credit represents a contractual relationship between the opening bank and the beneficiary, *viz.*, the exporter. The bank in fact makes a commitment under the L/C that it would make, payment of the agreed sum, as indicated in the L/C, subject to the condition that all documents as asked for are submitted to the bank and on scrutiny, found to be in order. Opening and negotiation of the letters of credit are governed by the International Chamber, of Commerce Brochure No. 500, entitled "Uniform Customs & Practice for Documentary Credits", commonly known as UCP.

Even though an LIC represents a contract, which is based on a sale/purchase contract, the credit transaction is supposed to be independent of the physical transaction of the goods. UCP General Provisions and Definitions Article 3 provides:

"Credits, by their nature, are separate transactions from the sales or other contracts on which they may be based and banks are in no way Concerned with or bound by such contracts."

Parties to the Letter of Credit

A number of parties are involved in the international trade transactions involving the use of letters of credit:

(a) There is first a contractual relationship between the importer and the exporter, evidenced by the sales contract.

(b) There is a banker-customer relationship between the applicant of credit. *viz.*, the importer, and the opening bank. An identical relationship exists between the beneficiary, *viz.*, the exporter and the negotiating/advising bank.

(c) The third relationship is between the two banks, where the negotiating bank is performing as a special agent of the opening bank.

(d) The fourth relationship is between the beneficiary and the opening bank which is that of a credit contract.

Doctrine of Strict Compliance

Since the banks have to make payments only on the basis of documents presented to them, this doctrine has come to be developed. Under this doctrine, the bank has the right to reject any document which is not in strict conformity with what is asked for in the letter of credit. There is no minor or major discrepancy in documents. Any discrepancy makes the document liable for non-acceptance.

In Equitable Trust Co. of New York vs. Dawson Partners Ltd., the defendants bought Vanilla beans from Jakarta. They had asked the bank to open a confirmed letter of credit in favour of the seller and to make payment on the presentation of certain documents including a certificate of quality signed by experts. The seller submitted a certificate signed by an expert. The Bank made the payment but the buyer refused to accept the documents. The Court held. that the bank was not entitled to reimbursement. It was held that:

> "It is both common ground and common sense in such a transaction that the accepting bank can only claim indemnity if the conditions on which it is authorised to acceptance in the matter ofthe accompanying documents are strictly observed. There is no room for documents which are almost the same or which will do just as well."

The same principle has recently been reconfirmed by the Supreme Court of India in United Commercial Bank vs. Bank of India and Others.

METHODS OF DISPUTE SETTLEMENT

Arbitration Vs. Litigation

There are two well-recognised methods for settlement of disputes, *i.e.*, litigation and arbitration. Litigation is not suitable for settlement of trade disputes as it is beset with inordinate delays, high costs and uncertainty of the final decision. The basic limitations of litigation are:

(1) Court Process is Proverbially Slow, Time-consuming and Formalistic. It easily takes a few years for settlement of a dispute in a court of law.

(2) Avoidable Necessity of Expert Witnesses and other Evidence. A judge howsoever expert or eminent in the field of law, cannot be expected and is not well-versed in the practices, procedures and customs of various lines of trade particularly the international trade. When a commercial dispute is tried in a court of law, the trade practices and procedures have to be proved before the court by expert witnesses having knowledge and experience on such matters.

(3) Inconvenience to the Parties. The time and date of hearings in a court of law are not exactly convenient or suitable to the litigants. Sometimes one has to wait from morning till evening before his case is called; may be only to learn that the case is adjourned.

(4) Adverse Public Image. The court proceedings are open to the public and judgements of superior courts are also published. This is not suitable particularly for businessmen as it may expose their internal and private affairs and trade secrets and bring unnecessary notoriety and loss of goodwill and reputation.

(5) Bitterness and Disruption of Trade Relationships. Acrimony and bitterness usually accompany litigation and irrespective of which party wins, many times it results into a breach or disruption of the long standing trade relationships between the parties.

(6) Different Laws and Procedures. In international trade transactions, the traders have to deal with parties from different foreign countries whose laws and procedures are not familiar to them. International trade laws and procednres are rather complicated and beset with uncertainties. Litigation in foreign courts is, therefore, even more difficult than in domestic courts.

The basic advantages of arbitration are:

(1) Quickness. Arbitration is much quicker than litigation. It can be completed as quickly as the parties want it, depending on the circumstances and the nature of the particular case. Under the Arbitration Act, the arbitrators have to make the award within four months from the date of entering on the reference. Usually an arbitration case may be settled between four months to one year.

(2) Inexpensiveness. The costs and expenses in arbitration are also much less than in litigation. Apart from the arbitration fees which usually are around 2 per cent of the claim value or less in institutional arbitration, the other incidental expenses are rather moderate and low.

(3) Promotes Goodwill. Arbitration is a process of goodwill and it helps promote friendly trade relations between the parties. The arbitrator is a person chosen by the parties themselves on the basis of their faith and confidence in him.

(4) Sound and Cogent Decision. In arbitration it is possible to choose a person having knowledge and experience in the particular line of trade to which the dispute relates, thereby avoiding the necessity of expert witnesses for educating the judge or for proving trade customs and practices.

(5) Privacy. Arbitration proceedings are not open to public and arbitrators' decisions are not published in law reports like the court decisions. Therefore, arbitration preserves the privacy and trade secrets of the parties.

International Arbitration

In the case of international transactions, arbitration becomes international when at least one of the parties involved is resident or domiciled outside India or the subject-matter of the dispute is abroad. The law applicable to an arbitration proceeding may be the Indian law or a foreign law, depending on the terms of the contract and the rules of conflict of laws.

In the case of international transactions, arbitration can take place either in the exporter's or importer's country. It is, therefore, necessary to have a legal system for the recognition and enforcement or arbitral award given in another country. The International "New York Convention" on Recognition and Enforcement of Foreign Arbitral Awards, 1957 has been ratified by 109 countries which recognise and enforce arbitral awards given in the countries which are signatories to this Convention.

Law for Enforcement of Foreign Awards in India. Countries which are parties to any of the International Conventions have to pass implementing legislation giving effect to the respective Conventions. India, which is a party to the 1927 Geneva and the 1958 New York Convention, has enacted the Arbitration (Protocol and Convention) Act, 1937 and the Foreign Awards (Recognition and Enforcement) Act, 1961, respectively, giving effect to the two Conventions. The provisions of the two Acts are made applicable to foreign awards made in such countries as are notified by the government from time to time in the Official Gazette under the respective Acts.

Prior to 1996, statutory provisions on arbitration were contained in three different enactments, *viz.*, the Arbitration Act, 1940, the Arbitratior, (Protocol and Convention) Act, 1937 and Foreign Awards (Recognition and Enforcement) Act, 1960. The Arbitration Act laid down the framework within which domestic arbitration was carried in India while the other two Acts dealt with foreign awards. The Arbitration and Conciliation Act, 1996 has repealed the earlier Acts. The new Act has strengthened and clarified the provisions relating to international commercial arbitration.

Procedure for Enforcement in India. Any person interested in a foreign award may apply in writing to any court having jurisdiction over the subject matter of the award praying that the award be filed in the court. The application shall be numbered and registered in the court as a suit between applicant as plaintiff and the other parties as defendants. The Court shall direct notice to be given to the parties requiring them to show cause why the award should not be filed. Thereupon, the court on being satisfied that the foreign award is enforceable under the Act shall pronounce judgement according to the award. Upon the judgement so pronounced, a decree shall follow and no appeal shall lie from such decree except in so far as the decree is in excess of or not in accordance with the award.

Enforcement of Indian Awards in Foreign Countries. It is understood that awards made in India will be similarly enforceable in foreign countries which are parties to any of the international conventions relating to the enforcement of foreign awards, according to the provisions of the respective conventions. However, enforcement of awards in countries which do not adhere to either the 1937 or the 1961 Convention or other similar international regulations is somewhat more difficult. The enforcement of awards in such other countries would largely depend on principles of private international law and might meet with considerable difficulties.

❑

7

Procedure and Documents for Export

PROCEDURE FOR REGISTRATION AS AN EXPORTER

Unlike domestic business, an exporter is required to get his business registered with various Government agencies. The following are some of the main steps that on exporter has to follow:

(1) To Decide the Nature of Business. Exporters generally start their business on a small scale like sole proprietorship or partnership. This is because there is lot of uncretainty in export business. Export is also a risky business. When the business earns profit, the size of the business is increased and the business is converted into private limited company and later joint stock company. When the scale of operation is changed simultaneously the resources and inputs into the business must change.

(2) To Open a Bank Account. The exporter should be extremely careful in the selection of a bank. He should open a current account in such a bank which would support him in business. As far as possible, he should open an account in a bank which is authorised to deal in foreign exchange. The exporter must maintain cordial relations with his banker. A good bank is the most dependable support to the exporter.

(3) To Fix Credit Limit. The exporter must apply to the bank and get pre-shipment and post-shipment credit limit fixed. This will enable the exporter to know how much capital he should raise from other source and what value of orders he should entertain.

(4) To Obtain FAX Facility. Communication through FAX has become very common and popular. It is the fastest means of communicating and sending documents to the business counterparts. In case of established exporters they can own FAX facility but a newcomer can settle for FAX facility provided by FAX agents.

(5) To Obtain Income Tax Number. The exporter must possess income tax number from Income-tax authorities. A newcomer in export business will initially get a temporary number from the income tax department. Late, after the business is settled the department issues a permanent number.

(6) To Obtain Code Number. Every exporter is required to obtain a code number from RBI. The exporter must quote income-tax number allotted to him by the income tax authorities on the CNX form which is used for obtaining code number. The exporter must collect two copies of code number application form from the Exchange Control Department (Exports) of RBI. In a sealed envelop the exporter is required to put two copies of CNX form, a copy of income tax number certificate and a confidential report about the financial standing from the bank and forward it to RBI. After checking the relevant documents, the officials will send a copy of CNX form to the exporter with a code number written on the back page. The exporter must make use of this code number while corresponding with RBI. As per the Exim Policy (1992-97) exporters are required to obtain Import-Export Code (IEC) number. The exporter is required to apply to Chief Controller of Imports and Exports to obtain IEC code number. This will entitle to import or export any item of non-prohibited goods. This code number is made compulsory now. It is not applicable for export of services like consultancy or construction contracts.

(7) To Apply for Exemption from Sales Tax. The goods meant for exports are eligible for exemption from both state and central sales taxes. The export firm should be registered with sales tax authorities and follow the necessary procedure laid down by them. In the State of Maharashtra the exporters are required to use Form No. 14.

(8) To Register with ECGC. Export Credit and Guarantee Corporation (ECGC) which is a division of Ministry of Commerce provides credit insurance to exporters against commercial and political risks involved while collecting payments from abroad. By filling up a proposal form, the exporter must apply to the nearest office of ECGC. This form should be accompanied by a confidential bank report, a prescribed amount of fee and a detailed report about the business. The ECGC policy helps to overcome the non-payment risks from the foreign buyers. A policy with ECGC also helps to get liberal credit from the bank. This is because ECGC gives various kinds of pre-shipment and post-shipment financial guarantees to the bank on behalf of the exporter.

(9) To Register with Export Promotion Council. There are different export promotion Councils for different types of business like Engineering Export Promotion Council, Chemical Export Promotion Council, Textile Export Promotion Council etc. The council issues three forms *viz.*:

(a) Application for Registration,

(b) Application for Membership, and

(c) Registration cum Membership Certificate.

After filling up these forms, the exporter will submit the same with prescribed fee and necessary discounts to the export promotion council. After verifying the documents, the council will return a copy of Registration cum Membership Certificate to the exporter. With the Receipt of this certificate, the exporter will now be known as "Registered Exporter". A registered exporter becomes eligible to get export incentives and benefits offered by the Ministry of Commerce. A registered exporter receives ocean of literature pertaining to export business from the council. At the same time, the council can also guide the exporter regarding market information.

In case the export unit is to be located in Export Processing Zone (EPZ) or as Export Orient Unit (EOU); the exporters are advised to follow the instructions provided in the Handbook of Procedures (1992-97).

(10) To Become Member of Chamber of Commerce and Productivity Councils. The exporter must take up the membership of local chamber of commerce, productivity council and any other trade promotion organisation recognised by the Ministry of Commerce. These bodies often provide the much needed recommendations on behalf of exporters to the Government The Chamber of Commerce is the most representative body of business community. It is authorised to issue an important document known as "Certificate of Origin" to the members. Bodies like National Productivity Council (NPC) and Bombay Productivity Council help exporters to improve the quality and control the cost of production. They also provide short-term training courses for exporters.

(11) To Become Member of IIFT. Indian Institute of Foreign Trade (IIFT) provides invaluable source of information regarding markets and products having export potential. IIFT is an autonomous body. It conducts residential, short-term and long-term training programmes for exporters. It is advisable to take membership of IIFT, when the business is well established.

EXPORT DOCUMENTATION

Documents in export trade play a very significant role from the very beginning when an exporter gets an order from a foreign buyer to the final stage when the exporter seeks cash assistance and other incentives offered by the Government. Documentation facilitates the smooth flow of physical goods and payments there of across national frontiers. At every step during exporting, one or the other document is required. The exporter cannot move any further without documents.

Export transaction requires many documents to be submitted to various authorities. The two board groups of documents are commercial documents and regulatory documents.

Letter of Credit is an important document of authority for payment given by the importer to the exporter through bank channel. After defining letter of credit, we would discuss the parties involved in the letter of credit and the contents of letter of credit.

Various stages are involved in receiving the payment of exports with the help of letter of credit. We would discuss each of these stages in brief.

Depending upon the nature of transaction and credit, the letter of credit is issued in different forms. We would discuss the different forms or types of letters of credit.

Export transaction requires many documents to be submitted to various authorities. Exporter has to take special care in the preparation of these documents. From October 1, 1991 the new standardised documents have come into effect in India. They are called Aligned Documents prepared under the Aligned Documentation System, which are based on United Nations layout.

Types of Export Documents

Broadly export documents can be classified into two categories:

(i) Commercial documents

(ii) Regulatory documents.

(1) Commercial Documents. These documents physically effect transfer of goods and their title from exporter to importer, and help in realising export proceeds:

Commercial documents are classified into two categories:

(a) Principal documents.

(b) Auxiliary documents.

Principal Documents. The principal documents are:

(a) Commercial invoice.

(b) Packing list.

(c) Bill of Lading.

(d) Combined transport document.

(e) Certificate of inspection/Quality control.

(f) Insurance Certificate or Insurance policy if there is CIF contract.

(g) Certificate of origin.

(h) Bill of Exchange and Shipment advise.

Auxiliary Documents. Auxiliary documents are those which are not in the category of principal documents, as:

(a) Proforma invoice.

(b) Intimation for inspection.

(c) Shipping instructions.

(d) Insurance declaration.

(e) Shipping order.

(f) Mate's receipt.

(g) Application for certificate of origin.

(h) Letter to the bank for collection/Negotiable documents.

(2) Regulatory Documents. Regulatory documents are those documents, which are prescribed by the Government regulations. Their complain is compulsory. These documents are:

(a) Gate Pass I/Gate Pass II which are called GP-VGP-II. These documents are prescribed by the Central Excise authorities.

(b) AR4/AR4A Form, prescribed by Central Excise Authorities.

(c) Shipping Bill Bill of Export, prescribed by Customs Authorities prescribing dutiable, duty free and goods under DBK claim.

(d) Export application/Dock challan, prescribed by Port Trust.

(e) Receipt for payment of port charges.

(f) Vehicle ticket.

(g) Exchange control declaration *i.e.*, GR form /PP form prescribed by Reserve Bank of India.

(h) Freight Payment Certificate.

(i) Insurance Premium Payment Certificate.

Whether commercial or regulatory, all these documents can be again classified on the bases of their needs and requirement, as:

(i) Documents Related to Goods:

(a) Invoice.

(b) Packing list/Note.

(c) Certificate of origin (COO).

(ii) Documents Related to Shipment:

(a) Mate Receipt.

(b) Shipping Bill.

(c) Cart Ticket.

(d) Certificate of Measurement.

(e) Bill of Lading.

(f) Airway Bill (AWB).

(g) Form B-X, for export by post.

(iii) Pocuments Related to Payments:

(a) Letter of Credit (L/C).

(b) Bill of Exchange (B/Ex).

(c) Trust Receipt.

(d) Letter of Hypothecation.

(e) Bank Certificate of Payment.

(iv) Documents related to Inspection: Certificate of Inspection.

(v) Document related to excisable goods:

(a) GP forms.

(b) Form C.

(c) AR-4/AR-4A form.

(vi) Documents related to Foreign Exchange Regulations:

(a) GR forms.

(b) PP forms.

(c) VP/COD forms.

(d) CNX forms.

On the basis of the functions to be proformed, export documents can be classified under four categories:

(1) Trade Documents. These include commercial invoices, bill of exchange, bills of lading, latters of credit, marine insurance policy and certificates, etc.

(2) Regulatory Documents. These are the documents which are required for complying with the rules and regulations governing export trade transactions such as foreign exchange regulations, customs formalities, export inspection, etc.

(3) Export Assistance Documents. These are the documents which are required for claiming assistance under the various export assistance measures as may be in operation from time to time. Presently, these refer to import replenishment licences, cash compensatory support scheme, drawback of Central excise and customs duties and packing credit facilities.

(4) Foreign Documentation. These are the documents which are required by the importer in order to satisfy the requirements of his Government. These include certificate of origin, consular invoice, quality control certificate, etc.

SIGNIFICANCE OF EXPORT DOCUMENTS

Export documentation is the use of various documents in the export trade. Several documents encompass the entire gamut of export from the stage when the exporter receives an export order upto the final stage when he gets the refund of duty and the cash assistance and other incentives offered by the Government.

Export Documents serve two purpose namely,

(i) Regulation of trade, and

(ii) Facilitation of export operation.

A number of documents are used in export trade. It facilitate the flow of goods and payments thereof across the national boundaries.

1. Regulation of Trade

(i) G-R- Form. An exporter has to follow provision for regulating the imports and exports, imposed by the Government of importing countries as well as of exporting country. Various documents are used to satisfy these regulation provisions. For example, in India, one of the important documents required is GR-I form under Foreign Exchange Regulation Act 1973 in which the exporter submits an undertaking that all foreign exchange earned by him by exporting the goods will be handed over to Reserve Bank of India. Thus an export cannot be made unless the exporter submits the GR-I form. The exporter has to obtain the following other documents imposed by the Government of India the regulate to export trade.

(ii) Export Licence. An export license has to be obtained for controlled commodities.

(iii) Inspection Certificate. Indian Government has enacted pre-shipment and quality control inspection of a number of export goods, in order to build up an image of Indian goods abroad. The exporter has to obtain an inspection certificate.

A number of Importing countries require a host of documents to meet the regulatory provisions the important among which are the following:

(iv) Consular Invoice. Some countries require that their missions in the exporting countries should certify the goods being exported and give consult invoice certificate.

(v) Certificate of Origin. Some countries, especially the commonwealth countries and advanced countries of the world which have offered concessions under the Generalised System of Preferences (GSP), require that the exporter must submit a certificate of origin.

To summarise, an exporter has to submit GR-I form, export licence, inspection certificate, consular invoice and certificate of origin. These are regulatory documents.

2. Facilitation of Operations. Export documents are required for operational purpose. The customs authorities are entrusted with the responsibility of verifying that all the requirements of the regulations in force in the country have been complied with by the exporter. The Government has devised the following documents to facilitate this task of verification.

(i) The Shipping Bill. The customs authorities negotiate the shipping bill and without it no shipping company accepts the cargo. Bill invoices and packing lists are to be submitted along with shipping bills.

(ii) Airways Bill. In the case of shipment by air, the document in place of Bill of Lading is known as Airways Bill.

(iii) Bill of Lading. Bill of lading is the acknowledgement by the shipping company that the goods to be exported have been shipped on Board.

(iv) Marine Insurance Policy. It is taken by the exporter to cover the risks to his goods in the transit.

(v) Other Documents. These cover various provisions such as floor price regulations, permission from the STC for the export of canalised goods. Measurement and weightment regulation etc. are to be obtained be the exporter.

(vi) Export Assistance Schemes. The exporter applies to various authorities, for the assistance like import replenishment licence, duty drawback and cash assistance schemes etc. in case of the goods exported.

Thus from the stage he files the contract for exporting the goods to the last stage when he actually exports them a number of documents are required to be obtained by an exporter.

A number of documents which are used in India durin export transactions are current and usually acceptable in international trade all over the world. We are discussion hereunder the significance, and particulars of some important documents. The documents, we are taking up are:

(i) Commercial Invoice. This is the basic document in an export transaction. It contains all the information which is required for the preparation of all other documents. It is, thus, a document of contents. It gives the description of the goods, Customs Co-operation Council Nomenclature (CCCN), price, charges, the terms of shipment and the marks and numbers on the packages containing the merchandise. The date, name and address of both buyer and seller, name of shipping vessel and the port of debarkation should also be included. There is no standard form a commercial invoice. The exporter has to design his own form. Some countries, however, prescribe their own forms. In such causes, the exporter has necessarily to use the form prescribed by the importing country.

The description of the merchandise in the commercial invoice must correspond exactly to the description in the letter of credit. Unless the letter of credit specially states otherwise, a generic description of merchandise is usually acceptable in the other documents. It is preferable, however, that merchandise description in all documents corresponds exactly to the description in the letter of credit. Marks and numbers on the commercial invoice, insurance documents, bills of lading, and packing lists must correspond.

(a) Combined Certificate of Origin and Value. It is required by the commonwealth countries.

(b) Consular Invoice. It is required by Philippines. It is to be certified by the authorised consular invoice mission of the importing country in the exporting country. It may be obtained by paying prescribed fee.

(c) Legalised Invoice. Some countries including Mexico require legalised invoices which is not very much different from consular invoice as far as the aim of exporting country is concerned. However, there is no prescribed form for obtaining the legalised invoice.

(d) Customs Invoice. Countries including USA and Canada require customs invoice for their customs valuation. The exporter has to submit the invoice in the prescribed form in such cases. On the basis of price charged as per agreement, the commercial invoice may be of the following types:

(i) EO. a. invoice,

(ii) C&F invoice,

(iii) Ex-ship price,

(iv) France invoice.

(e) Proforma Invoice. A temporary commercial invoice prepared and sent by an exporter to the importer, it contains almost the same particulars as commercial or final invoice. Its purpose is to help the importer *(a)* in getting an import licence in his own country, if the import of such commodities requires that and *(b)* in opening the letter of credit in favour of the exporter in his own country. The exporter should cultivate a habit of sending a proforma invoice, even if it is not demanded.

(ii) GR Form. This form has been prescribed by the Reserve Bank of India to ensure that the foreign exchange receipts in respect of exports are repatriated to India. This has to be prepared in duplicate. Both the copies have to be submitted to the customs authorities at the port of shipment. Customs authorities will certify the value declared by the exporter on both the copies of the GR form and will also record the assessed values. They will retain the original to be sent to the Reserve Bank of India (RBI) directly. They will return the duplicate copy which is submitted to the negotiating bank along with other documents after shipment of the goods. The negotiating bank sends the duplicate copy to the RBI after the export proceeds have been realised.

When the exporter wants to retain the proceeds of his exports with agents or branches abroad or to make other approved types of payments abroad, he has to seek the permission of the RBI. For this purpose, he has to submit GR-3 form. This is prepared in triplicate. The original is submitted to the customs authorities who send it to the RBI directly. The duplicate and triplicate copies are to be dealt with in accordance with the procedure laid down by the RBI. Export by 'parcel post', other than 'value payable,' are to be declared on PP form. Export under 'value payable' or 'cash on delivery' have to be declared on VP/COD form.

(iii) Letter of Credit. Popularly known as L/C, letter of credit is the most important form in the export trade. It is a promise made by the overseas importer through his banker where the letter of credit is opened by him, to the exporter through his banker to pay the shipment of goods. The exporter examines the terms and conditions of the L/C to ensure *(a)* that he can meet them, and *(b)* that they confirm to the basic contract entered into with the importer followings three types of letter of credit.

(a) ***Irrevocable and Revocable.*** If L/C is irrevocable, the importer cannot revoke it once it is opened with the bank in his country. On the country the revocable L/C can be revoked by the importer at any time.

(b) ***With or without Recourse L/C.*** In the case of with recourse letter of credit, if the buyer fails to pay the bank after a specified period, the bank can have recourse on the exporter. The exporter makes himself liable on the bill when he negotiates. His liability ends if the bill is paid by the drawer. In without recourse.

(c) ***Confirmed and Unconfirmed.*** In the case of a confirmed L/C the payment of foreign exchange is confirmed by the bank in exporter's country preferably exporter's bank. It confirms that the payment will be received in foreign exchange within specified period and will be handed over to RBI. If there is no confirmation by the local bank on L/C, it is unconfirmed L/C. The exporter should insist on confirmed L/C.

(iv) Bill of Exchange. When a draft is drawn on a foreign bank, it is known as a foreign draft or bill of exchange. A bill of exchange, is, thus, a means of collecting payment from the foreign buyer through the banking channel. It is also a method of extending credit. It has two main functions. If the bill of exchange is payable at sight, it becomes a demand for payment and a receipt for payment made. If the bill of exchange is payable at some future date after sight, it is demand for payment by the exporter, a promise of payment by the importer, and a receipt for payment after such payment has been made.

(a) ***Clean Bill of Exchange.*** This B/E does not accompany any other document. If it is on sight, the importer makes the payment of the bills as soon as it is presented before him by banker. It is a demand for payment and a receipt for the payment made. If the bill is payable at a future date after sight, it is demand for payment by the exporter and a promise to pay the amount by the importer, along with a receipt for payment after the payment has been made.

(b) ***Documentary Bill of Exchange.*** It accompanies other documents of title of goods such as bill of lading, insurance policy, invoice etc. and is presented before the importer through the bank. If bill is payable on sight, the banker will hand over the document attached to the importer as soon as he makes the payment of the bill. If the bill is payable on some future date, the banker will hand over the documents to the importer as soon as he assigns his acceptance. Thus the documentary bill may be D/P bill (Documents against payment bill) or D/A (documents against Acceptance). Under documentary credit the bill of exchange must be drawn strictly in accordance with the terms of credit.

(v) Shipping Bill. This is a custom document. There are three types of shipping bills, namely:

(a) Shipping Bill for Free Goods;

(b) Dutiable Shipping Bill, and

(c) Drawback Shipping Bill.

The shipping bill must be prepared according to the category of the export goods.

(vi) Certificate of Origin. As the name implies, this certificate is the document which certifies the place of origin of the merchandise. It is required by commonwealth countries and also by those developed countries which have offered concessions to the developing countries under the Generalised System of preferences (GSP). It can be obtained by the authorised agencies. To issue certificates of origin the Government of India has authorised the Federation of Indian Chamber of Commerce and Industry (RCCI), the Export Promotion Council (EPCs) and various other trade association.

(vii) Marine Insurance Policy. A basic instrument in marine insurance, it is a contract, a legal document between the policy holder and the insurance company. It can be produced in the court of law in case of any claim. It is generally taken at the time when the goods are ready for shipment, unless otherwise advised by the importer. It would be for CIF Value (Cost, insurance and Freight) plus 10 per cent to cover expenses. It can be used as a collateral security by the exporter when he wants advance against his bank credit.

(viii) Bill of Lading. Bill of Lading (B/L) is a document which is issued by the shipping company acknowledging that the goods mentioned therein have been shipped on board the ship and an undertaking that the goods in like order and condition as received will be delivered to the consignee, provided that the freight specified therein has been duly paid. The Bill of Lading has the following main functions:

(a) It is a document of title to the goods shipped;

(b) It is a receipt for goods; and

(c) It is an evidence of the contract of affreightment.

When the export contract is c.i.f., the exporter makes payment of the freight and gets 'freight paid' bill of lading. On the other hand, if the contract is f.o.b, the freight has to be paid by the importer. In that case, the shipping company will issue a 'freight collect' bill of lading. The bill of lading should give the details about the exporter, carrying vessel, goods shipped, port of shipment, destination, consignee and the party to be notified on arrival of the goods at destination. B/Ls are made in sets, usually of two or three originals, anyone of which gives title to the goods.

A shipped or on board bill acknowledges that the goods have been loaded on board. A received for shipment bill confirms that the shipping company or its agent merely has the goods in custody for shipment. It may be converted to a shipped bill by a suitable annotation by the carrier after the goods have been loaded on board. With the growth of container transport and inland collecting debts, the received for shipment B/L has become much more widely used.

A clean B/L is one which bears no superimposed closure or statement declaring of a defective condition of goods or of the packaging or of some other aspect of the consignment.

Where there is no direct shipping link between the buyer's port and the seller's port, arrangements have to be made for the goods to be transferred to a second ship at another port. In such cases it is necessary for the exporter to obtain a through B/L covering the whole voyage. The through B/L will also be issued where different modes of transport are used.

Airway Bill. Air transport is widely used for moving valuables on urgently required goods. The document of transport used is an airway bill (air consignment note). It is non-negotiable; so it does not carry the same validity as a bill of lading for sea transport.

Combined Transport Document is a document of carriage relating to multi-modal transport. Almost every consignment has to be transported by more than one means of transport, particularly since the advent of container transport. The combined transport or through container document allows for this, covering the movement of goods from start to finish.

(ix) Charter Party. Where the quantity of goods to be shipped is very large, the exporter may contract to hire the whole or a substantial part of the ship for the purpose of exporting the goods to a particular port of destination. The agreement entered into between the exporter and the owner of the ship is known as 'Charter Party', which is "an agreement by which a ship owner agrees to place an entire ship, or a part of it, at the disposal of a merchant for the conveyance of goods binding the shipowner to transport them to a particular place, for a sum of money which the merchant undertakes to pay for the carriage". It may be for a specific voyage charger party. It may be for a specific period of time irrespective of voyage undertaken known as final charger party.

COMMON DEFECTS IN DOCUMENTATION

The bank making payment on behalf of its foreign correspondent must verify that all documents and drafts conform precisely to the terms and conditions of the letter of credit. The requirements of credit cannot be waived or altered by the paying bank without specific authority from the issuing bank. To avoid payment delays, the beneficiary should prepare and examine all documents carefully before presenting them to the paying bank.

Paying banks find that the following discrepancies between the documents and the letter of credit occur most frequently:

(a) Drafts are presented after letter of credit has expired or after time for shipment has expired;

(b) Invoice value or draft exceeds amount available under letter of credit;

(c) Amount of insurance coverage is inadequate or coverage does not include risks required by letter of credit;

(d) Insurance document is not endorsed and/or countersigned;

(e) Charge included in the invoice are not authorised in the letter of credit;

(f) Bills of lading are not "clean"—that is, they bear notations that qualify good order and condition of merchandise or its packing;

(g) Bills of lading are not marked "on board" when so required by letter of credit;

(h) Date of insurance policy or certificate is latter than the date on bills of lading;

(i) "On board" endorsement or changes on bills of lading are not signed by carrier or its agent or initialled by party who signed bills of lading;

(j) "On board" endorsement is not dated;

(k) Bills of lading are not endorsed;

(l) Bills of lading are made out "to order" (shipper's order blank endorsed) where letter of credit stipulates "straight" (direct to consignee) bills of lading or *vice versa*. (In fact, it is better for the exporter to prepare 'to order' B/L, as this will keep the goods in the custody of the bank. In cases of straight B/L the title of the goods passes automatically to the named consignee);

(m) Bills of lading are not marked "freight prepaid" when freight charges are included in invoice;

(n) Bills of lading to not indicate "frieght prepared" as stipulated in the letter of credit;

(o) Descriptions, marks, and numbers of merchandise are not same on all documents presented or are not as required by letter of credit;

(p) Not all documents required by letter of credit are presented;

(q) Invoice states "used", "second hand" or "rebuilt" merchandise when such condition is not authorised by letter of credit;

(r) Invoice does not specify shipment terms (C. & F., C.I.F., F.O.B., etc.) as stated in letter of credit;

(s) Invoice is not signed as latter of credit requires.

PROCESSING OF AN EXPORT ORDER

Why is an Export Order processed?

An export order has to be processed to meet the requirements of materials required by the importers. The export order must be processed as expeditiously as possible so that the buyers can receive the materials on time, as per their delivery schedules and also conforming to the specifications stipulated by them.

Parties, Acts and Publications Involved

The most important Acts/Publications which must be consulted by an exporter in connection with the processing of an export order are: Foreign Trade (Development and Regulation) Act, 1992; Customs Act, 1962; Carriage of Goods by Sea Act, 1924; Foreign Exchange Regulations Act, 1973; Schedule of Charges of Goods in respect of the Port of Shipment; Handbook of Export Promotion; and Export-Import Policy and Handbook of Procedures (1997-2002). The main parties which are involved in this processing are: the exporter, the foreign buyer, the negotiating bank, the shipping company, the insurance company, the Reserve Bank of India, Director General of Foreign Trade, the Collector of Customs, the Port Commissioners, and the Clearing & Forwarding Agents.

Before we discuss the various stages involved in the processing of an export order, we will discuss some of the important steps required to enable a businessman to undertake export business which are: *(i)* Registration with Export Promotion Councils, etc., and *(ii)* Obtaining the Importer/Exporter Code Number.

Registration. An exporter should get himself registered by making an application on the prescribed form with an Export Promotion Council related to his main product line of export. If there is no EPC, registration may be done with the Regional Licensing Authority concerned. Some of the important registering authorities are Export Promotion Councils, Commodity Boards, the Marine Products and Agricultural and Processed Food Products Export Development Authorities, Jute Commissioner, Khadi and Village Industries Commission, State Directors of Industries, Development Commissioners of Foreign Trade Zones/Export Processing Zones, and the Federation of Indian Export Organisations. Once an exporter has been registered, the registration shall remain valid for 5 years. Registered exporters have to submit quarterly, reports about exports made by them.

Importer/Exporter Code Number. Every person importing or exporting goods is required to obtain an Importer/Exporter Code Number from the Regional Licensing Authority concerned. Customs authorities shall not allow clearance of goods to an importer or exporter who does not possess a valid Importer-Exporter Code Number. Application for allotment of Importer/ Exporter Code Number should be made in duplicate, in the prescribed form to the regional import trade control licensing authority concerned. Code Number allotted to a person is valid for import/export of any commodity by that person. It is compulsory for the importer/exporter to quote his Code Number in the relevant Bill of Entry/Shipping Bill.

First Stage

The exporter should scrutinise the export order with reference to the terms and conditions of the contract. This is the most crucial stage. All subsequent actions and reactions will depend on the terms and conditions of the export contract. It should be ensured that the contract has been entered into in accordance with the prevalent export promotion policies of the country and the foreign exchange regulations. The export order must specify the mode of payment in unmistakable terms such as Letter of Credit, Documents on Payment, Documents against Acceptance, etc. The best mode of payment is through an irrevocable and confirmed letter of credit. The essential terms and conditions of the export order must tally with those of the L/C The specifications stipulated by the importer in the export order and the L/C such as delivery schedule, packing, inspection, marking, etc., must be strictly adhered to. The documents required by the foreign buyer must be prepared and submitted to the negotiating bank in the exact specified form and manner. The most important documents which are usually demanded by the importer are: *(1)* Bill of Exchange, *(2)* Commercial Invoice, *(3)* On-board Clean Bill of Lading, *(4)* Marine Insurance Policy, *(5)* Packing List, and *(6)* Certificate of Origin. The export order should be confirmed by the exporter only after the terms and conditions of the L/C have been found to be in order.

Second Stage

As soon as the export order has, been confirmed, preparations for the despatch of goods are started. A 'delivery note' (in duplicate) is sent to the works Manager or the Factory Manager. This note should contain (he description of the goods as has been given in the export order, along with a copy of the instructions given by the importer. The date by which the goods must be manufactured, the date by which the necessary formalities must be completed, the requisite time margins to be given and the shipment must be clearly intimated to the Works Manager. Nothing should be left to the discretion of the Works Manager. This is what the manufacturer-exporter has to do. A merchant-exporter has either to obtain the required goods from the market or has to get them manufactured from other manufacturers. The specifications and instructions to be intimated to the supplier of export goods shall, however, remain the same.

Third Stage

As soon as the goods have been manufactured or procured, the following procedures are to be followed:

(1) The clearance of the Excise Authorities has to be obtained. This can be done in two ways. The first way is to make payment of the excise duty at the time of removing the export consignment from the factory and file a claim for rebate of duty after exportation of goods. The second way is to secure clearance under Bond. This involves entering into a bond under such terms and conditions as the Collectol of Customs may decide. When the export goods are removed from the factory, a debit entry for excise duty is made in the Bond Account of the exporter. This obligation is discharged after exportation of the goods. The exporter has to prepare two important documents: AR-4 form and invoice/challan in lieu of Gate Pass. If the exporter so wishes, the Central Excise Officer can make physical verification at the factory and seal the packages. For this purpose, a prescribed supervision fee has to be paid.

AR-4 form is to be prepared in sixtuplicate. These are presented to the Range Superintendent, Central Excise, who after necessary formalities signs all the copies. The original, duplicate and sixtuplicate copies are given back to the exporter; the triplicate copy is sent to the Maritime Commissioner or Asstt. Commissioner incharge of refund, etc.; the fourth copy is sent to the Chief Accounts Office and the remaining copy is kept by the office of the Range Superintendent.

(2) The other authority which is to be approached immediately at this stage is the Export Inspection Agency for conducting quality control and preshipment inspection. An Inspector is deputed by the Inspection Agency to inspect the export consignment. If the goods conform to the prescribed specifications, an inspection certificate is issued.

(3) If the goods are despatched to the port of shipment by railway, Railway Receipt is obtained.

Fourth Stage

After the goods have been despatched to the port town, the Works Manager sends a 'despatch advice' to the Export Department. Soon after, an application is sent to the insurance company for marine insurance cover. The insurance policy is obtained in duplicate.

At this stage all formalities in relation to floor price regulations, canaligation, certificate of origin, ECGC cover and consular invoice, wherever necessary, should be completed. Thereafter the Export Department sends the following documents to its clearing and forwarding agents, along with detalled instructions: *(1)* Commercial Invoice showing the details and value of goods specifiying f.o.b. or c.i.f. or c.&f. price, as the case may be, and the market/real value (usually two copies); *(2)* Original export Order; *(3)* Original Letter of Credit; *(4)* GR form original, showing the I.E.C. Code No. allotted by the D.G.F.T; *(5)* AR-4 Form (original and duplicate copies); *(6)* Invoice/Challan in lieu of Excise Gate Pass (original); *(7)* Packing and Weight Lists; *(8)* Certificate of Inspection; *(9)* Declaration Form in triplicate; *(10)* Consular Invoice, where necessary; *(11)* Export Licence, where necessary; *(12)* Endor sements regarding floor price, canalization, etc where necessary; *(13)* Purchase Memo; and *(14)* Railway receipt.

Fifth Stage

The clearing and forwarding agent takes delivery of the consignment from the railways and arranges its storage in the warehouse. Thereafter he prepares the requisite copies of the shipping bill. The most important particular which are to be filled in the shipping bill are: *(1)* Consignee's name and address; *(2)* Vessel's name; *(3)* Rotation number allotted by the Customs to the vessel; *(4)* Agent's name; *(5)* Colour; *(6)* Port of discharge; *(7)* Final destination; *(8)* Exporter's name and address; *(9)* Number of packages; *(10)* Marks rind numbers; *(11)* Gross, net and tare weight; *(12)* Description; *(13)* f.o.b. value; *(14)* Country of origin; *(15)* Code Number of the goods; *(16)* Number and date of the Exchange Control GR Form; *(17)* AR-4 number and date, where necessary; and *(18)* Export Licence number, where necessary. There are there types of shipping bills, namely, *(i)* Shipping Bill for "free" goods; *(ii)* "Dutiable" Shipping Bill; and *(iii)* "Drawback" Shipping Bill. The Shipping Bill must be prepared according to the category of the export goods. The Shipping Bill with requisite number of copies (usually five copies) is submitted to the Export Department of the

Customs House along with documents from serial No. (1) to serial No. (13) specified in the fourth stage.

The Shipping Bill for "Free" goods is processed in the following manner: *(1)* Deposit in Box; *(2)* Dealt with by Receiving Clerk; *(3)* Dealt with by Noting Clerk; *(4)* Dealt with by Distributing Clerk; *(5)* Checked and passed by appraiser; *(6)* Okayed by Principal Appraiser; *(7)* finally initialled by Assistant Commissioner of Customs, where necessary; *(8)* Checked and initiallec: by Pass Examiner and Shipping Bill number is put down; *(9)* GR form detached; and *(10)* Returned to the clearing and forwarding agent by the Distributing Clerk. In the case of the processing of "Dutiable/Drawback" Shipping Bill, apart from the first seven steps mentioned above, the following additional steps are taken: *(1)* Pass Examiner; *(2)* Duty Calculator; *(3)* Accounts Clerk dealing with Deposit Account or Cash; and *(4)* Cashier for Duty Receipt. In case Drawback is involved, the Shipping Bill would also require to be passed by the Drawback Appraiser, with an endorsement on the duplicate Shipping Bill or original where necessary, for holding the drawback examination of the export goods in the docks.

Sixth Stage

After the Shipping Bill has been passed by the Customs, the clearing and forwarding agent presents the Port Trust Copy of the Shipping Bill to the Shed Superintendent of the Port Trust and obtains carting order for bringing the export cargo in the iransit shed for physical examination. Thereafter, in the case of Shed cargo, the Dock Challan is prepared. Where the ship loads overside, the dock charges are indicated on the Shipping Bill itself and, therefore, no separate Dock Challan is prepared. The following details are given in the Dock Challan: *(1)* Consignee's name and address; *(2)* Vessel's name; *(3)* Port of destination; *(4)* Exporter's name; *(5)* Marks and Number of packages (these must be the same as given in the Shipping Bill); *(6)* Gross weight; *(7)* Measurement in cubic metres or weight in metric tons; *(8)* Port charges payable; and *(9)* Other details, as required.

The Dock Challan is processed in the following manner: *(1)* Place in Receiving Box; *(2)* The clerk calculates and checks the Port Commissioner's shipping charges; *(3)* Deposit with Cash Clerk; *(4)* Sheet Writer; *(5)* Distributing Clerk releases the Dock Challan to the clearing and forwarding agent after debiting the exporter's account with the Port Commissioners, if maintained, or after collection of charges in cash or by Banker's cheque.

Seventh Stage

The passed Shipping Bill including the Dock Challan, where submitted, Cart Ticket or Boat Note, in case of Overside cargo, are carried by the Authorised Licensed Sircar accompanying the goods for making the cargo ready for shipment after finally being passed by the Port Commissioners and the customs shed staff. For Shed Cargo in dock, the following steps are taken: *(1)* Gate Warder checks documents, registers and permits entry of cargo into dock; *(2)* Export Shed Writer accepts Dock Challan and Cart Ticket; *(3)* Receiving Clerk issues unloading slip for cargo from lorry after checking its condition; *(4)* The Supercargo arranges unloading cargo from lorry; *(5)* The Writer registers Dock Challan in manifest and sends it to the Customs Preventive Officer for endorsement; *(6)* The Preventive Officer examines and checks the contents, weight, etc., of the goods and if, in order, makes an endorsement "Let Ship" on the duplicate copy of the Shipping Bill, and the Dock Challan is finally signed by the Customs Divisional Officer; *(7)* The Port Commissioner writes in Shed register the details and releases the Dock Challan; and *(8)* The Supercargo takes over control of the cargo for shipment. In case of Overside cargo, the cargo is lightered to the ship accompanied by a Boat Note and the Shipping Bill. The Boat Note and the Shipping Bill are then registered with the customs for which a pass is issued.

Eighth Stage

The Ship's Export Clerk calls for cargo from shed or boat and after loading prepares the Mate's Receipt. The Mate's Receipt is signed by ther ship's Captain or his agent. It is then delivered to the Port Commissioner's Shed. The Clearing and Forwarding Agent pays the port charges and takes delivery of the Mate's Receipt. In the case of Overside Shipment, the Mate's receipt is directly given to the Clearing and Forwarding Agent. It is then presented to the Preventive Officer for certifying the fact of shipment on all copies of the Shipping Bill, original, duplicate and sixtuplicate copy of AR-4 form, and all other documents which need post-shipment endorsement from the Preventive officer. The Mate's Receipt is presented to the Shipping Company and, requisite number of copies of the Bill of Lading (usually two negotiaple and about a dozen non-negotiable copies) are obtained by the clearing and for warding agent.

Ninth Stage

The clearing and forwarding agent forwards the following documents to the exporter: *(1)* Full set of Bill of lading; Clean, on Board, together with the required number of non-negotiable copies; *(2)* Export Promotion copy of the Shipping Bill; *(3)* Copies of Customs-attested Invoice; *(4)* AR-4 form (duplicate copy); *(5)* Original Export Order; *(6)* Original Letter of Credit; and *(7)* Railway Concession form, duly attested by the Customs.

Tenth Stage

As soon as the exporter receives the above documents from the clearing and forwarding agent he completes the remaining formalities. The exporter files a claim with the Maritime Commissioner of Central Excise or Asstt. Commissioner in the Port town for rebate of Central Excise duty or for getting credit in the bond account, as the case may be. Side by side, shipment advice is sent to the importer. The following documents are forwarded along with the shipment advice: *(1)* A non-negotiable copy of the Bill of Lading, *(2)* Customs Invoice, *(3)* Commercial Invoice, and *(4)* Packing List.

Eleventh Stage

The following documents are presented to the negotiating bank: *(1)* GR form (duplicate copy), *(2)* Bill of Exchange, First and Second of Exchange, *(3)* Full set of Clean-on-board Bill of Lading (all negotiable copies) and one non-negotiable copy, *(4)* Original Letter of

Credit, *(5)* Commercial Invoice (two copies), *(6)* Customs invoices, where necessary, *(7)* Certificate of origin (two copies), *(8)* Packing list (four copies), *(9)* Marine Insurance Policy (two copies), *(10)* Bank Certificate in the prescribed form (two copies), *(11)* Additional copies of the Commercial invoice to be certified by the bank and returned to the exporter, and *(12)* Consular Invoice, where necessary.

Twelfth Stage

The processing at the negotiating bank is done in the following manner: All the documents are scrutinised with reference to the terms and conditions of the original Letter of Credit. Thereafter, a set of the following documents is transmitted to the banker of the importer by the first air mail followed by a second set of these documents by the second air mail to ensure that in case the first set is lost, the importer can take delivery of the consignment on the basis of the second set of documents: *(1)* Bill of Exchange, *(2)* Negotiable Bill of Lading, *(3)* Commercial Invoice, *(4)* Customs Invoice, *(5)* Insurance Policy, *(6)* Certificate of Origin, *(7)* Consular Invoice, where necessary, and *(8)* Packing List. The negotiating bank transmits the duplicate copy of the GR form to the Exchange Control Department of the Reserve Bank of India.

The original copy of the Bank Certificate, along with attested copies of the Commercial Invoice, is returned to the exporter: The duplicate copy of the Bank Certificate is forwarded to the office of the Director General of Foreign Trade in the area.

The exporter is paid the value of the export consigment against the above mentioned documents.

STAGES INVOLVED IN RECEIVING THE PAYMENT OF EXPORTS

The mechanism procedure followed for the purpose of letter of credit is given as under:

(1) Request for Opening L/C. Importer makes request to his banker for opening 1etter of credit In favour of exporter. Importer may pay to his bank the entire money in advance or request it to open L/C against his current account. Application in prescribed form is made to this effect by importer to his bank.

(2) Signing Contract. Importer then makes agreement with his bank for reimbursent of money which is payable to exporter. The contract so made is signed by him over the security as demanded by the bank.

(3) Produce Exchange Control Copy of Import Licence. The importer has produce to the bank the valid import licence for this purpose. This copy of import licence is called Exchange Control Copy of Import Licence. Bank demands it to avoid any exchange problem.

(4) Scrutiny of the Importer's Proposal. The bank of the importer then proceeds to scrutinise the proposal of letter of credit. In the scrutiny process the bank lays emphasis upon the following aspects:

(a) Credit standing of the importer.

(b) Amount of credit involved in the letter of credit.

(c) Type of import contract, whether FOB or CIP etc.

(d) Whether it is forward exchange contract or spot exchange contract.

(e) Type of credit and nature of drawing.

(f) Report about the beneficiary *i.e.*, exporter.

(g) Nature of goods to be imported by the importer.

(h) Margin money deposit required if any.

(i) Import trade and exchange control provision.

(5) Opening the Letter of Credit. Upon scrutiny, if every think is found satisfactory the opening bank contact the negotiating bank (exporter's bank) for advice and confirmation of transaction. If the opening bank is satisfied the letter of credit is opened in favour of exporter and forwards it to the negotiating bank with a request to inform about it to the beneficiary.

(6) Receipt of Letter of Credit by Exporter and Confirmation. On the intimation of negotiating bank the exporter receives the letter of credit in his possession. He goes through the terms and conditions contained in it. Exporter compares this letter of credit and conditions there in with the terms of his export contract. Any discrepancy found in it is referred back to the opening bank. When from both the side things are finally settled the exporter sends his confirmation to importer through the banking channel.

(7) Shipment of goods and drawing of Bill of Exchange. When letter of credit is confirmed from both the sides, the exporter arranges for the goods and makes their shipment. He follows the terms and conditions contained in the letter of credit while making shipment of goods. A full set of export documents along with the bill of exchange drawn upon importer is presented to the negotiating bank. The negotiating bank sends these documents to the opening bank for onward transfer to the importer, after due scrutiny of all documents.

(8) Realisation of Export Proceeds. After the shipment of goods and on the stipulated date the opening bank (issuing bank) reimburses all money of letter of credit to the negotiating bank which has been already paid by it to the exporter.

(9) Presentation of Documents to Importer. The issuing (opening) bank finally hands over all relevant documents of the transaction to the importer against the trust receipt of title to goods and debits his current account for the corresponding amount. The parties get discharged when importer reimburses the money to the opening bank.

BANKING PROCEDURE OF NEGOTIATION

After the goods have been physically loaded on board the ship, the exporter should arrange to obtain his payment for the exports made by submitting relevant documents to the bank and obtain payment, the process being called 'negotiating the documents' through the bank.

(i) Bills of Lading—three negotiable copies and as many non-negotiable copies, as required.

(ii) Bill of Exchange.

(iii) Certificate of origin.

(iv) Marine Insurance Policy in duplicate.

(v) Letter of Credit in original.

(vi) GR-l form, duplicate.

(i) Bill of Lading. It is the most important negotiable document in the entire process of exporting because it carries with it legal title to the goods shipped on board the vessel indicated therein. It is a receipt given by the shipping company for the goods loaded on a particular ship. It contains a broad description of the goods, the quantity of goods, the total number of packages, gross and net weight, the port of shipment, the port of discharge, the name of the ship, and the amount of freight paid. Its significant details are the number, the date of the bill of lading and the freight paid. As the date of the shipment of goods, it should be within the validity date given in the documentary letter of credit.

No adverse entry about the apparent condition of goods is made a in a clean bill of lading. When an adverse comment does appear on it, it is termed as a classed bill of lading. A classed bill of lading is normally not accepted by the foreign buyer, unless the letter of credit specifically permits the acceptance of such a bill. The exporter should endeavour to negotiate documents with a clean bill of landing, otherwise the buyer has the right to refuse acceptance of goods because they do not conform to the conditions of the letter of credit. A bill of lading is transferable when a suitable endorsement is made on it. The exporter should take due care while preparing it. The two most widely used endorsements are the following:

(a) "To order and endorsed in blank." Since it is endorsed in blank, any individual who gains possession of it can get delivery.

(b) "Endorsed to the order of". When it is endorsed to the order of a person, bank or a company, only the party indicated in the endorsement can get delivery of goods. The endorsee can further re-endorse the bill of lading in favour of another party, who can then take delivery of goods. If the bill of lading is made out in the name of the buyer or the foreign bank opening the credit as a consignee, either the buyer or the foreign bank, as the case may be, can take delivery of the goods.

A bill of lading issued after the goods are loaded on the vessel is called an "on board bill of lading." A buyer usually asks for a full set of "clean shipped" or "on board" bill of lading as part of the negotiable documents required by him. The letter of credit would specify what constitutes the full set of bill of lading.

(ii) Commercial Invoice. A commercial invoice is a document prepared by the exporter giving details of goods shipped, their brief description, the shipping marks, the unit and total FOB, C&F, or CIF value as the case may be, depending on the (L.C.) contract, the number and date of the bill of lading as well as the name of the ship carrying the cargo. The description of the cargo mentioned in the invoice should be on the same lines as found in the letter of credit. The invoice should be made out in the name of buyer or the consignee mentioned in the letter of credit.

(iii) Certificate of Origin. A certificate of origin states the country in which products under export were originally produced/ manufactured. The goods produced in a particularly country attract preferential tariff rates in the foreign market at the time of importation. Or goods produced in a particular country are banned for import in the foreign market. The certificate of origin helps the buyer in adhering to the import regulations of the country. Some of the foreign markets may accept the certificate of origin issued by a

Chamber of Commerce of an exporting country. Others require these certificates to be legalised by their own respective consulates. An exporter submits a copy of the commercial invoice to the Chamber of Commerce, together with the nominal fee prescribed by the Chamber. The Chamber issues a certificate of origin. The certificate of origin issued by the Chamber of Commerce is submitted to the Consulate of the concerned foreign country, which makes its endorsement on the certificate.

Special certificates of origin are applicable for available of concessions under Generalised System of Preferences in which the certificate of origin in the specified form usually in triplicate, is obtained from anyone of the following agencies:

(a) Export Inspection Council and its agencies.

(b) Chief Controller of Imports and Exports.

(c) The Central Silk Board, The Coir Board, The All-India Handicrafts Board and the Textile Committee are also authorised to issue certificates of origin for the products under their purview.

(iv) Marine Insurance Policy. Where the contract with the foreign buyer is on CI (Cost and Insurance) or CIF (Cost, Insurance and freight) basis, the responsibility for taking insurance cover against all risks of damage to or loss of goods during the sea voyage is that of the exporter an application received from him describing the goods loaded as well as the value of the goods for which the insurance is required, the insurance company issues a policy in the name of the exporter and endorsed in blank. The premium charged by the insurance company would depend on the total value for which the goods are insured, the type of ship as also its age, and the port of discharge of the cargo as evidenced in the bill of lading. The premium rate when goods are loaded on deck of the ship is higher than when they are loaded in the hold of the ship, for the risks involved and the chances of damage to the cargo are more when these are loaded on deck of the ship.

The insurance policy issued by the insurance company should carry the name of the vessel and the description of goods, corresponding to those found in the bill of lading. It comes into effect only after the date of the bill of lading.

As a specialised subject Marine Insurance covers many types of risks. The insurance cover differs from material to material and also depends upon the risks involved. The exporter should consult the insurer before taking out a suitable policy.

(v) Letter of Credit. A complete set of negotiable documents is presented to the negotiating bank through whom the documentary letter of credit has been advised. If the exporter has complied with all the terms and conditions of the letter of credit while submitting his documents to the negotiating bank, the documents are deemed to be clean. The letter of credit opened by the buyer through his bank authorises drawing a bill of exchange against which payment will be made by the opening bank on behalf of the buyer, provided the terms and conditions specified in the letter of credit are complied with. A bill of exchange is a draft by the negotiating bank on the opening bank or the buyer as the case may be. It is an instrument of payment which is negotiable. The drafts drawn are of two types, *(a)* Sight Draft, *(b)* Usance Draft.

(a) Sight Draft. If the letter of credit stipulates payment at sight, the exporter draws a "sight draft" on the buyer or his bank. When sight drafts are drawn by the exporter, he expects the buyer to arrange for payment immediately on presentation of the draft. Until payment for the draft is made, shipping documents will not be handed over to the buyer to enable him to clear the goods.

(b) Usance Draft. When the exporter has offered credit terms for payment, a "usance draft" is drawn by the negotiating bank of the exporter for payment after a specified period. The buyer on whom the draft is drawn retires the draft after 30 days, 60 days, or 90 days as agreed between him and the exporter at the time of concluding the contract.

The letter of credit opened by the buyer will clearly specify the credit period which has been agreed upon. It would mention that the draft should be drawn for 30, 60 or 90 days, as the case may be.

For a credit period beyond 180 days, the exporter has to obtain the prior permission of the exchange control authorities in India. The bill of exchange drawn should correspond to the conditions stipulated in the letter of credit.

The letter of credit would specify the details of the despatch of documents. The negotiating bank of the exporter would accordingly mail the complete set of documents. Usually, a set of documents is transmitted to the banker of the buyer specified in the letter of credit by the first available air mail, followed by a second set by the next available air mail. If the first set is lost, the buyer or his bank may take possession of the goods on the basis of the second copy. The process of negotiation is completed with the despatch of documents by the exporter's banker.

(vi) GR-l form. Besides the negotiation of the documents, the banker has to perform other formalities. As part of the negotiable set of documents, the exporter has submitted the duplicate copy of the GR-l form. After negotiations are complete, and payment is physically received by the bank, the duplicate copy of the GR-l form is sent to the RBI after due checks.

LETTER OF CREDIT

Letter of Credit is a document of authority for payment of guarantee for payment given by importer to exporter through banking channel. Importer's bank undertakes guarantees for payment on behalf of the importer.

Letter of Credit is a document of credit. International Chamber of Commerce (ICC) has defined it a banker's documentary credit. Since letter of credit is a document of credit issued by bank, its definition is applicable to letter of credit, which runs as follows:

Banker's Documentary Credit is "an arrangement, however, named or described, whereby a bank (issuing bank), acting at the request and in accordance with the instructions of a customer (the applicant to the credit), is to make payment to or to the order of the third party (the beneficiary) or is to pay, accept or negotiate bills of exchange (drafts) drawn by the beneficiary, or authorised such payments to be made or such drafts to be paid, accepted or negotiated, by another bank, against stipulated documents and compliance with stipulated terms and conditions."

—International Chamber of Commerce

The Documentary Credit is defined under Article 2, of the uniform Customs and Practices for Documentary Credit (UCP), as:

The Documentary Credit (S) and Stand-by letter (S) referred to as credit means, "any arrangement however named or described, whereby a bank (the issuing bank), acting at the request and on the instructions of a customer (the applicant for the credit):

(i) Is to make a payment to or to the order of a third party (the beneficiary), drawn by the beneficiary.

Or

(ii) Authorises another bank to effect such payment or to pay, accept or negotiate such bills of exchange (drafts), against stipulated documents, provided that the term and conditions of the credit's are complied with."

- Article 2, Uniform Customs And Practices for Documentary Credit

Hence, the letter of credit makes sure that all import-trade regulations of the importer have been fulfilled and their will be no payment problem for the exchange control authorities.

Parties. There are four parties involved in the letter of credit:

(a) Opener. Importer opens L/C. Therefore importer is opener.

(b) Beneficiary. Exporter is beneficiary because he gets the payment there of. But any other can be beneficiary.

(e) Opening Bank. The bank of importer (opener) is the opening bank.

(d) Negotiating Bank. The bank of exporter is the negotiating bank because` this bank negotiates documents on behalf of the exporter, with the opening bank.

These parties enjoy their rights and hold certain responsibilities which are under given in the "uniform customs and practices for documentary credit" Articles 15-20.

Conditions. (Contents of Letter of Credit) The letter of credit lays down certain conditions as given under:

(a) Date of bill and date of shipment of goods must be shown clearly.

(b) Name of Vessels (ship) approved by party for shipment along with the approved flag on the ship must be there.

(c) It should contain packing standards and the conditions thereof.

(d) It should also contain the marketing specification as done on the package.

If these conditions are not fulfilled by the shipper (exporter), the importer may reject the goods and consequently refuse payment of goods.

Types Letter of Credit

Depending upon the nature of transaction and credit, the letter of credit is issued on different forms. Therefore, the letter of credit is of different types:

(i) Documentary Letter of Credit. This letter of credit specifies the various documents which are required to be supplied by the exporter to the importer. That is why it is called documentary letter of credit.

Following documents are normally specified by letter of credit to be supplied by the exporter:

(a) Commercial invoice.

(b) Bill of Lading.

(c) Insurance Policy.

(d) Consular Invoice.

(e) Certificate of Origin.

(f) GSP Certificate.

(g) Certificate of quality analysis.

(h) Packing list.

(i) Document of title to goods.

(j) Bill of exchange/draft.

The payment is made by the negotiating bank to exporter against this letter of credit when a full set of these documents is handed over by the exporter.

(ii) Revocable and Irrevocable Letter of Credit. The nature of recoverable letter of credit is that it can be withdrawn by the opener (importer) or opening bank (Importer's bank) at any time. For withdrawal pre-consent of exporter is not taken nor the notice to this effect is given to him. This letter of credit therefore does not sufficiently protect exporter for getting his payment. If exporter makes shipment of goods on the strength of this letter of credit, he does it on his own risk. This type of letter of credit is not very common. The irrevocable letter of credit is just opposite of revocable letter.

The irrevocable letter of credit can not be withdrawn without prior permission and intimation of exporter. It indeed is the definite guarantee given by opening bank to exporter ensuring payment of exports. However, conditions stipulated in the letter of credit have to be fulfilled by the exporter. Exporter usually insists upon irrevocable letter of credit because it protects the exporter.

(iii) Clean Letter of Credit. As the name suggests this letter of credit does not contain any condition as regards making the payment. It also does not contain any condition for acceptance of bill of exchange drawn by exporter upon the importer. The negotiating bank finds convenient to get reimbursed from the opening bank. This does not put any condition upon exporter to get the payment from the bank. It is therefore clean in the sense that there is no condition for payment to be made.

(iv) Assignable/Non-assignable Letter of Credit. Assignable means transferable. Non-assignable means non-transferable.

A letter of credit which can be easily transferred by exporter with its rights in favour of any person, is called assignable letter of credit. Exporter may assign this letter of credit to any person.

On the other hand non-assignable letter of credit can not be transferred in favour of any person. Only the beneficiary, whose name is given in the letter alone can get the payment. Such person is exporter only. Bank does not make payment to any other party except one whose name is stated therein.

(v) Revolving Letter of Credit. When the export transaction between the same parties is of regular and continuous feature, this letter of credit is used. Provision is made to make available the credit against one and the same letter of credit, for all subsequent export transactions. There is no need to open a separate letter of credit for every export transaction again and again.

(vi) Confirmed Letter of Credit. When the opening bank (importer's bank) is stranger bank to exporter, this letter of credit may be insisted upon. The opening bank therefore appoints a bank in the exporter's country which is known to exporter. Through such bank the confirmation of credit is made by opening bank. Exporter can draw the bill of exchange upon such confirming bank. Exporter thereby doubly confirmed; firstly by the opening bank and secondly by the confirming bank. It is a fool proof arrangement of payment of export. Any letter of credit which provides such arrangement is called confirmed letter of credit. However, this letter of credit is normally avoided because the opening bank will have to pay the commission to the confirming bank. Unless it is very necessary exporter should not insist upon the confirmed letter of credit.

(vii) With or Without Recourse Letter of Credit. In case of the with recourse letter of credit paying bank can hold responsible to the exporter for recovery of payment if importer does not reimburse it to the paying bank. Exporter, then, will have to refund all money he received along with interest to paying bank under such eventuality. Without recourse letter of credit does not have the provision to hold the exporter responsible if importer does not reimburse to the paying bank. In such eventuality the paying (opening) bank has the recourse to importer only. In other words, in the event of default made by importer to make repayment to paying bank only the importer will be held responsible, not the exporter.

(viii) Back to Back Letter of Credit. Merchant exporter has to purchase goods from the manufacturer for export purpose. Exporter may request opening bank to open the letter of credit in favour of such manufacturers or supplier. This is in fact a secondary credit. Instead of making payment to exporter the manufacturer or supplier gets directly the money from importer. This facilitates exporter to get goods for export on credit basis. Such an arrangement of payment made by a letter of credit is called back to back letter of credit. However, banks are not happy about his arrangement. They are reluctant to open this type of letter of credit. If the opening bank agrees for such letter of credit then the original letter of credit issued in favour of export is retained by the opening bank.

(ix) Red Clause and the Green Clause Letter of Credit. Under the red clause letter of credit, exporter can get advance money from the negotiating bank. This letter of credit is an authority given to negotiating bank to extent credit and lend advance money to exporter. Opening bank takes responsibility of risk likely to arise due to non-submission of documents or non-execution of export order by the exporters. This letter is typed or printed in red; therefore it is called red clause letter of credit.

Green clause letter of credit provides arrangement for storage of goods at the port. Pre-shipment finance as well as storage facility both the available to exporter under this letter of credit. For such a letter of credit in India, prior permission of Government is required.

(x) Restricted Letter of Credit. Sometimes the importer may insist upon shipping document to be negotiated (transferred) through a specified bank only. Any letter of credit making such restriction (condition) is called restricted letter of credit. Negotiating bank (exporter's bank) normally does not encourage this letter of credit. Banks does not give credit or advance money to exporter if the letter of credit restricts documents to be routed through a specified bank only.

(xi) Travelling Letter of Credit. This letter of credit enables exporter to travel abroad and draw the money specified from the bank. All banks honour all the cheques or bills drawn upon. Exporter gets more facility and advantages than what traveller cheques offer.

(xii) Omnibus Letter of Credit. Only reputed exporters are entitled to get this letter of credit. This letter of credit allows exporter to draw the money from bank in lump sum against the security of general lien on goods.

(a) Commercial invoice and its importance.

(b) Consular invoice.

(c) Shipping Bill.

(d) Bills of lading and its types.

(e) Mate's Receipts.

(A) COMMERCIAL INVOICE AND ITS IMPORTANCE

This is a Basic Export Document. It contains all the information, which is required for the preparation of all other documents. It is the exporter's bill for goods. There is no standard form for such invoice, but it can be designed as per the requirements of the exporter. However, if any information to be included as per the special requirement of the importer, it must be complied with. Many countries like Canada, USA etc., require special type of invoice.

The commercial invoice should contain:

(a) The name and address of the exporter.

(b) The name and address of importer.

(c) The description of goods, like quality, quantity, weight, etc.

(d) The value of goods, less discounts, if any.

(e) Terms and conditions of sale.

(f) The signature of the exporter.

(g) The net amount payable by the importer.

Other details of shipment to be included as:

(a) Name of the ship.

(b) L/C number.

(c) Import-Export licence number of the exporter.

(d) Bill of Lading number.

(e) Packaging specifications.

(f) Shipping Bill number and date.

(g) Shipping terms and conditions.

(h) Identification marks on the package.

(i) Freight charges.

(j) Marine Insurance premium.

(k) Any other details, if required.

Combined Certificate of Origin and Value

This certificate is required by Commonwealth Countries. This certificate is printed in a special way by the Commonwealth countries.

This certificate should contain special details as to the origin and value of goods, whioh are useful for determining import duty. All other details are generally the same as that of Commercial Invoice, such as name of the exporter and importer, quality and quantity of goods, etc.

(i) Custom Invoice. This is required by countries like Canada, USA, for imposing preferential tariff rates.

(ii) Legalised Invoice. This is required by certain Latin American countries like Mexico. It is just like consular invoice, which requires certification from Consulate or authorised mission, stationed in the exporter's country.

Importance of Commercial Invoice

The commercial invoice is important both to the exporter and to the importer.

(i) Importance to the Exporter:

(a) It is the exporter's bill which the importer has to pay. It enables the exporter to collect payment from the importer.

(b) The exporter needs to submit copies of commercial invoice to a number of authorities' such as export inspection agency, excise authorities customs authorities, negotiating bank, etc.

(c) It helps the exporter or his agent to prepare other documents based on the commercial invoice, such as shipping bill.

(d) It can act as a documentary proof in case of disputes between the exporter and importer regarding the amount payable by the importer and such other aspects.

(ii) Importance to the Importer:

(a) It helps the importer to pay customs duty.

(b) It helps to know the exact amount that is to be paid to the exporter.

(c) It may be required to obtain loan from the bank against the import of goods.

(d) Certain types of invoices such as custom invoice helps the importer to obtain preferential tariff rates.

(B) CONSULAR INVOICE

Certain countries like Philippines, Australia, New Zealand, etc., require that the goods imported in their country should be certified by the Consulate of their country stationed in the exporter's country. The exporter has to pay a certain fee to obtain this certificate/invoice. Such charges/fees vary from country to country. This invoice facilitates prompt clearance of goods from the customs authorities in the importing country.

Normally, it is necessary to convince the customs authorities of the importing country that the description and value of goods as shown in the exporter's invoice is one and the same as that compared to imported goods. At times, customs authorities, on suspicion may desire to open the packages and check the goods for the purpose of calculating duties payable to customs. If this is done a considerable delay takes place in clearing the goods and the importer may be put to hardships. To avoid all this problem both to the customs authorities and to the importer, a consular invoice is obtained, which is issued by the Consulate of the importing country stationed in India.

It is generally prepared in three copies. One copy is retained by the Consulate office for reference, the second copy is sent to the customs authorities of the importing country and the third copy is given to the exporter to forward the same through his bankers to the importer along with other documents.

Importance of Consular Invoice to the Exporter

(a) Once the invoice is signed by the consulate of the importing country, the exporter is reasonably assured that there are no import restrictions placed on his exports in the importing country, and that there will be no problem in realisation of foreign exchange or export proceeds.

(b) It ensures prompt clearance of goods from his customs for the purpose of loading on the ship.

Importance of Consular Invoice to the Importer

(a) It enables him to get prompt delivery of goods from the customs.

(b) The customs normally do not open the packages, thereby, saving a lot of efforts on the part of the importer.

Importance of Consular Invoice to the Customs

(a) The customs of the exporting country can easily clear the goods.

(b) The customs of the importing country can easily calculate the import duties without checking or opening the packages.

(C) SHIPPING BILL

This is the main document required by Custom authorities for granting permission for shipment of goods. It is only after the shipping bill is stamped by the customs, the cargo is allowed to be carted to the docks. The shipping bill is generally prepared in five copies:

(a) Customs Copy,

(b) Drawback Copy,

(c) Export Promotion Copy,

(d) Port Trust Copy, and

(e) Exporter's Copy.

The shipping bill contains description of goods and other particulars such as:

(a) Name and address of the exporter.

(b) Number and description of packages.

(c) Quantity, weight and value of goods.

(d) Name of vessel in which goods are to be shipped.

(e) Country of Destination.

(f) Total amount of duty.

(g) Port at which goods to be discharged.

(h) Any other details, if applicable.

Types. Generally there are five types of Shipping Bills:

(a) Free Shipping Bill

(b) Dutiable Shipping Bill

(c) Drawback Shipping Bill

(d) Shipping Bill for Shipment Ex-Bond

(e) Coastal Shipping Bill.

(a) Free Shipping Bill. It is used in case of goods which neither attract any export duty nor entitled for duty drawback. It is printed on white paper.

(b) Dutiable Shipping Bill. It is used in case of goods which attract export duty and it may or may not be entitled for duty drawback. It is printed on yellow paper.

(c) Shipping Bill for Shipment Ex-Bond. It is used in case of imported goods for re-export and which are kept in-bond. It is printed on yellow paper.

(d) Drawback Shipping Bill. This is used in case of DBK or when refund of duties is allowed on the goods exporter. Generally it is printed on green paper, but when DBK claim is to be paid to a bank, then yellow paper may be used.

(e) Coastal Shipping Bill. It is used in case of shipment which are moved from one port to another by sea in India. It is not an export document.

Generally, the format of shipping bill in case of export by air and by sea is more or less the same, except colour of the form may be different.

Importance of Shipping Bill

The shipping bill is an important export documents. Without the shipping bill, it is not possible to export the goods. The importance of shipping bill can be stated as follows:

(a) It is an important document required by the custom authorities for clearance of goods. The customs authorities endorse the duplicate copy of shipping bill with "Let Export Order" and "Let Ship Order"

(b) Shipping bill endorsed by the customs enables the exporter to obtain export incentives, such as excise refund and duty drawback.

(c) It helps to load the goods on the ship. The customs preventive officer hands over the duplicate copy of the shipping to the agent of the shipping company who gives permission to load the goods on the ship.

(D) BILL OF LADING AND ITS TYPES

A bill of lading is a document issued by the shipping company upon shipment of the goods. It is a contract between the shipper (exporter) and the shipping company for the carriage of goods to the port of destination. It is a document title to goods and as such required by the importer to clear the goods at the port of destination.

A bill of Lading normally contains the following details:

(a) The name of the shipping company.

(b) The name and address of the shipper/exporter.

(c) The name and address of the importer/agent.

(d) The name of the ship.

(e) Voyage number and date.

(f) The name of the ports of shipment and discharge.

(g) Quality, quantity, marks and other description.

(h) The number of packages.

(i) Whether freight paid or payable.

(j) The number of originals issued.

(k) The date of loading of goods on the ship.

(l) The signature of the issuing authority.

BL is usually made out in signed set of 2 originals, anyone of which can give title to goods. The shipping company also issues non-negotiable (unsigned) copies which are not documents title to goods but are normally used for record purpose.

The reverse side of BL bears the terms and conditions of the contract of carriage. The clauses on most BLs are more or less similar. A BL should be clean *i.e.*, it should not contain any adverse remarks by the shipping company as to the quality and condition of goods.

The goods can be consigned to order which means the importer can authorise someone else to collect the goods on his behalf. In this case, the BL will endorsed, normally on the reverse side, by the exporter. If the importer/consignee is named, the goods will only be realised to him, unless he transfers his right by endorsement (the bill of lading must however provide for such endorsement).

Types of Bill of Lading

(a) Clean BL. This type of BL do not contain any adverse remarks as to the condition and quality of goods. A clean BL is always insisted by the importer.

(b) Claused BL. Such BL contains an adverse entry by the shipping company, such as, "TWO CASES DAMAGED'.

(c) Stale BL. If the BL is presented to the bank for negotiations after many days from its issued it is called as Stale BL. As far as possible BL must be presented to the banks as soon as possible, otherwise it will create undue difficulties to the importer as well as to the exporter.

(d) Freight Paid BL. When freight is paid by the shipper, then this type of BL issued with the words 'freight paid'.

(e) Freight Collect BL. When the shipper does not pay freight, such bill will indicate that "freight is to be collected from the importer".

(f) To Order BL. In this type, the BL is issued to the order of a certain person.

(g) Straight BL. In this importer/consignee/agent is named in the BL, it is called straight BL.

(h) On Board & Received BL. The BL can be either the shipped/ board or received for shipment depending upon whether the goods are loaded on board the ship or received by the shipping company for storing.

(i) Container BL. This BL is issued, by the container shipping lines when the cargo is transported from an inland place of the shipper to the final place of its arrival.

Importance of Bill of Lading to the Exporter

(a) It acts as a proof that the goods have been loaded on the ship.

(b) It helps him to send a shipment advice to the importer.

(c) If any damage to the goods take place in transit, he can hold the shipping company responsible for the same, if such damage is caused due to the negligence of the crew of the vessel.

(d) A copy of bil of lading is required to be attached to the application for claiming incentives such as DBK.

(e) Under the CIF contract, it enables him to pay the exact amount of freight to the shipping company.

Importance to the Importer

(a) It is a document title of goods, as such he can claim the possession of goods from his customs.

(b) It enables him to pay proper freight amount under FOB contract.

Importance to the Shipping Company

(a) It helps the shipping company to collect the freight from the shipper or the importer.

(b) It safeguards the interest of the shipping company against wrong claims by the exporter or importer in respect of damage to goods prior to loading of goods because any such damage is reflected in the Bill of Lading.

(E) MATE'S RECEIPT

The mate's receipt is issued by the mate (assistant to the captain of the ship) after the cargo is loaded on the ship. It is an acknowledgement that the goods have been received on the board the ship. It contains information relating to:

(a) Description of packages.

(b) Condition of goods/packages loaded on the vessel.

(c) Name of the vessel.

(d) Date of loading.

(e) Port of loading.

(f) Port of delivery.

(g) Name and address of the shipper (exporter).

(h) Name and address of the importer/consignee.

(i) Other required details.

Types. The Mate's Receipt can be qualified, or clean. If there are any adverse remarks by the mate of the ship as to the quality or condition of the cargo then such mate's receipt is known as qualified mate's receipt. If there are no adverse remarks on the receipt, then such receipt is called as clean mate's receipt. As far as possible the exporter should get clean mate's receipt.

Procedure to Obtain Mate's Receipt

After loading of the goods on board the vessel, the mate of the ship issues an acknowledgement giving details and condition of the goods loaded on the ship. This acknowledgement is called Mate's receipt.

The mate's receipt is then sent to the port trust office. The C&F agent pays the port trust dues and collects the mate's receipt. The mate's receipt is then shown to the Customs Preventive Officer. The customs preventive officer certifies the fact of shipment on the relevant documents.

The mate's receipt is then sent to the shipping company and copies of bill of lading are obtained. It. is to be noted that mate's receipt is just an acknowledgement and not a document title to goods.

Importance of Mate's Receipt

The main importance of mate's receipt is that it serves as an acknowledgement of the goods loaded on the ship. After loading, the goods remain in the custody of the captain/mate of the ship.

PROCESSING OF AN EXPORT ORDER

The procedural aspects of our export operations are quite for a midable, and a student, or for that matter even an experienced exporter, is over whellmed by the magnitude of procedural requirements at every stage of export execution-right from the time an export order is obtained until the realisation of export proceeds and the benefits thereof.

The treatment of procedures, right from the receipt of a confirmed order until the realisation of export proceeds and export benefits is based on the personal and practical experience of an exporter. Following are the relevant procedures involved in an export operation with reference various phases of export :

1. Offer and Receipt of Confirmed Orders. The proposal submitted by an exporter is referred to as the 'OFFER', when accepted by the foreign boyer, it becomes an order.

The offer made by the exporter is usually in the form of a 'proforma invoice' which is just a document indicating the exporter's intention to sell, and is usually addressed to the prospective buyer. It would include the following:

(i) **The Consignee or the Buyer.** The complete name and address of the buyers should be clearly indicated. The consignee may be individual, a limited company, a corporation or a Government department.

In the case of a Government department, it is essential address the communication, by the designation of the official concerned, such as the Permanent Secretary, Public Works Department, Ministry of Public Works and Road Maintenance.

(ii) **Description of Goods.** The proforma invoice should carry a brief description of the goods, indicating important technical specifications and physical features which makes the identification of the product easy. A separate sheet giving these should be appended as a part of the proforma invoice where detailed technical specifications are called for.

(iii) **Price.** The proforma invoice should indicate the unit and total prices of the product in internationally accepted or mutually agreed currency. It should indicate the total quantity of the products offered. In case of certain products for which quantity discounts are given the invoice should clearly indicate the quantum of discount for a specific volume. Hence, the maximum quantity should be made clear to which the invoice is applicable.

The basis of price indicated in the proforma should be FOB, C&F or CIF or any other internationally accepted term. It should be acceptable to the buyer. Often, the proforma invoice is submitted in response to a tender enquiry or other enquiries where the basis acceptable is clearly mentioned.

(iv) Conditions of Sale. The profonna invoice submitted entails legal obligations on the part of the exporter to supply the product to the buyer, if the invoice is being accepted by him. Following conditions of sale and other factors qualifying it should be clearly spelt out:

(a) Validity. The proforma invoice submitted should indicate the period for which it is valid for acceptance. The buyer has the right to accept the proforma invoice anytime within the validity period while the exporter has to fulfil his obligations. The exporter should evaluate the various problems which may arise, such an increase in the price of his product, internal transport, shipping charges, freight and such other variables, and be reasonably confident that he will be able to fulfil his obligations.

In case of tenders, the validity period is stipulated by the buyer. In other cases, a period has to be given which is consistent with the product concerned and with the international practice.

(b) Exaltation Clause. This is normally included when the delivery is to be effected over a prolonged period, or in cases where certain elements of cost are known to be variable. In the former cases, the escalation in prices asked for is given in the form of the increase in the cost of raw materials or wages; or by means of a flat increase in the percentage value of FOB on supplies made after a particular period (say, an increase of 2.5% of the FOB value of the price indicated on supplies made six months after the date of the proforma invoice, and an increase of 5% of FOB value on all supplies made 12 months after the date of the invoice). In the latter case, it is stated that certain elements of cost would be charged on an actual basis. A typical example is the increase in shipping freight which cannot be determined earlier. Hence, it is normally included in the proforma, as given below:

(c) ***Delivery Schedule.*** The delivery schedule given in the proforma invoice should be realistic. In cases where CIF quotations are given, the legal obligation is on the part of the exporter to make the goods available at the port of destination as per the delivery schedule indicated. Due to the vagaries in shipping, many of the exporters take the precaution of indicating clearly in the proforma invoice the clause, "subject to the availability of shipping space."

(d) ***Inspection.*** Where inspection of goods is required, it is necessary to specify in the proforma invoice the authority which would conduct the inspection, as also the nature of inspection. Normally, export goods are offered for inspection before shipment. Hence the terms of reference for inspection should be made clear in the offer itself.

(e) ***Force Majeure Clause.*** A detailed commercial clause in a proforma invoice comes to the rescue of the exporter when he is prevented from fulfilling his contracts because of development such as war, riots and other cases which are beyond his control.

(f) ***Payment Terms.*** The mode of payment, such as Letter of Credit and the various clauses there in required by the exporter, should be clearly stated.

(v) **Other Obligations.** Other obligations agreed to by the exporter in the proforma invoice the following:

(a) ***Alter Sales Service.*** Assistance would be rendered to the buyer in the form of after-sales service by the exporter or his agent.

(b) ***Spare Parts.*** Agreeing to make available spare parts for sale for the equipment supplied for a certain period of time, especially in cases where the products can go out of production due to the introduction of new/improved products.

(c) ***Warranty.*** Warrant for the equipment supplied, taking full responsibility for any manufacturing defect of equipment or part thereof, and free replacement thereof during the specified warranty period.

(vi) Confirmed Order. When the proforma invoice is accepted by the buyer, it becomes a confirmed order. Normally, the duplicate copy of the proforma invoice is duly signed by the buyer, accepting the conditions therein and returning it to the exporter, who insists on the establishment of the documentary letter of credit, so that the buyer's' commitment is complete. Experienced exporters treat an export order as confirmed only after the letter of credit is established.

In some cases the buyer may accept the proforma invoice and confirm the order by a letter. Orders of high value, as well as orders from public sector and Government organisations, are in the form of a contract specifying the obligations of both the parties. The proforma invoice and confirmed order are important basic documents in the execution of an export order/contract.

2. Producing the Goods. The next step in the processing of an export order is to make arrangements for the items to be produced at the factory of the exporter or to be obtained from a supplier. This step covers all the operations from the time an agent for production is placed, till it reaches the export warehouse.

An exporter may be the export department of a manufacturing concern, or one, who has different sources of supplies developed with supporting manufacturers. If it is a department of a manufacturing concern, an internal indent is raised on the producing division, which indicates the quantity, the complete specifications of the item to be produced as well as the delivery dates by which the goods should be ready at the factory/warehouse of the exporter.

(i) Sales Tax Exemption. An exporter within production facilities of his own, raises a formal purchase order on a supporting manufacturer, which would indicate the quantity and description of the items, delivery date, the payment terms and the other obligations of the supplier in connection with the purchase order. Purchase from such suppliers for domestic sales, may attract sales tax. However, in the case of export, the transaction will be exempt from sales tax, provided that suitable evidence of export is produced against such purchase. In the state of Mahrarshtra, a provision is available for non-payment of sales tax if the exporter/shipper produces "Form 14". The declaration made by the exporter in this form indicates that whatever he has purchased for export has been exported, as a whole, in the same condition in which he has purchased it. This provision is of great help to the exporting community, for it encourages more exports from this State by established exporters.

(ii) Excise Duty Rebate. A levy imposed by the Government of India on all excisable items as specified by it, Excise duty is usually collected at sources, *i.e.*, at the manufacturing state. As soon as the manufactured products are ready for despatch from the factor they attract the levy. The products can be removed from the factory premises only after the excise is paid. However, products meant for export are exempted from the imposition of excise duty. Excisable goods are exported either under a claim of rebate of duty paid or under a bond without payment of duty. The rebate is made under Rule 12 of the Central Excise Rules, 1944. When an excise duty is paid, an exporter submits to the Superintendent of Central Excise of the locality the following documents for the purpose or claiming rebate.

(a) Gate Pass-GP-1;

(b) AR-4 Form

Three copies of GP-1, together with five copies of AR-4, are forwarded to Central Excise authorities. The GP-1 and AR-4, give the description of a product and indicate its quantity as well as the value and the excise duty payable on it. On its basis on official of the Central Excise visits the factory and inspects the packed goods to find out whether they are according to the details mentioned in the AR-4 form. After he is satisfied, he certifies the GP-1 and AR-4 form and retains them to the manufacturer. The third copy of the AR-4 form is sent to the Maritime Collector of Central Excise in charge of the port specified in the AR-4 form. The fourth copy is retained by the Central Excise, and the fifth copy by the exporter. At the time of export, the exporter gets a suitable endorsement on the original and duplicate copy of the AR-4 form from a Preventive Officer of the Customs Department at the port. An application in the specified form, attaching the endorsed copy of the AR-4 form and bill of lading, is made to the Government for the necessary refund.

As against the about procedure, finished products meant for export can be cleared from the factory under an excise bond without payment of an excise duty whatsoever. For this purpose, the exporter has to execute with the Excise Authorities a bond, which is usually backed by a bank guarantee from the company for a specified amount. As this amounts to a "running bond account", the bond is arranged for a suitably large value with the approval of the excise authorities so that a number of export consignment may be exported under the bond without interruption.

(iii) Pre-shipment Inspection of Export Cargo. The Government of India has introduced a compulsory pre-shipment inspection for selected items of export to ensure that the products to be exported conform to high quality standards. This scheme is administered by the Export Inspection Council (EIC), with the emphasis on quality control rather than on inspection for export.

The exporter makes an application in the prescribed form to the Export Inspection Agency, enclosing the following documents.

(a) Copy of the commercial invoice.

(b) A crossed cheque or demand draft for the necessary fee in favour of the EIA, or the Bank Passbook showing the necessary deposit in favour of the EIA.

(c) A copy of the export contract.

(d) A declaration of the importer's technical specifications of quality and/or a sample approved by the importer in support of the declaration of specifications.

The application must be submitted well in advance of the expected date of shipment. After processing the application, the EIA fixes the date of inspection. An Inspector of the Agency visits the factory for the purpose of inspection of the consignment. He carries out inspection on a sampling basis. Facilities for conducting a text may be provided to the inspector if he makes a request for them. Where such facilities are not available, tests are conducted at independent laboratories and the results evaluated. If the inspector is satisfied with the results, the samples are repacked and the entire consignment marked and sealed in the presence of the inspector. The inspector makes a report to the Deputy Director who, in turn, issues an Inspection Certificate in triplicate to the exporter. The consignment is now ready to be moved to the exporter's warehouse or to the port area for shipment.

The Export-Inspection Council recognises the manufacturing unit as an "export-worthy unit", if it is a manufacturer exporter or a manufacturer whose products are regularly exported. In this case the question of issuing an inspection certificate by the concerned Export Inspection Agency is reduced to a mere submission of an application on the part of exporter. Many exporters are following this system of obtaining recognitions of export-worthiness from the EIC for their manufacturing units.

For this purpose, the procedure adopted by the EIC involves periodical and rigorous checks of the process of manufacturing during the various stages of production. It also requires a check of the process control and quality control system adopted by the unit itself which ensures that the unit is adequately supported with facilities for the enforcement of the quality control standards required by the BC. In'this respect the inspection checks are conducted by a panel of experts. Once the Council is satisfied with the findings of the inspection checks, the export-worthy status is granted to the unit. The working of the unit is periodically monitored to ensure that quality standards do not go down.

In order to obtain an inspection certificate, a manufacturer-exporter has to submit his application in the prescribed form together with the following:

(i) A crossed cheque or a draft or a bank passbook showing the necessary deposit in favour of the EIA for the necessary fee.

(ii) Commercial invoice.

(iii) The importer's technical specifications.

In addition, there will be a declaration by the exporter stating that the products are manufactured according to the levels and quality control stipulated by the EIC.

The application is submitted to the EIA, which examines it and issues a certificate of inspection in triplicate, the original for the customs, the duplicate for the overseas buyer, if required, and the triplicate is retained by the exporter for his record.

Some years ago, a committee was appointed under the DGTD to review export inspection problems, which has since come up with a progressive recommendation that, where export units have the necessary quality control facilities, a "Self-certificate" procedure may be adopted so that these export units are authorised to issue their own Inspection certificates and are held responsible for the same.

3. Shipment. Shipment is the more popular method of despatching goods to an export buyer than despatch by air as the freight charges for shipping are very much less than those of air freight. The physical size of products, sometimes, constraints the exporter to despatch them by air, especially when these are heavy machinery or engineering goods.

"Shipment" covers all the procedural aspects from the time the product meant for export leaves the export warehouse, till it is loaded on board the ship and the relevant documents for such loading are collected from the shipping company. As the type of work involved is somewhat specialised, it is usually performed by the exporter's clearing and forwarding agents, who are speclalised personnel arranging for the completion of all the formalities connected with the shipment of goods. The exporter arranges for a complete set of shipping documents to be passed on to the forwarding agent, as soon as the export goods reach the warehouse. These documents include:

(a) AR-4 form in original and duplicate.

(b) Proform invoice (in duplicate) and packing list, where necessary;

(c) GR-l form (duplicate).

(d) Letter of credit covering the export order, together with the export contract or order in original.

(e) Certificate of inspection where necessary.

(f) Form of declaration (duplicate), and

(g) Shipping bill (five copies)

(i) AR-4 Form. When the goods are despatched from the factory, the original copy of the gate pass, as well as the original and duplicate copy of the AR-4 form, are sent to the exporter, who passes them on to the forwarding agent along with other shipping documents, so that the necessary endorsements on them may be obtained from the relevant authorities at the time of shipment to enable the exporter to obtain a rebate on duty or obtain credit in his running excise bond account.

(ii) Proforma Invoice and Packing List. Along with the invoice an exporter furnishes a packing slip listing the items packed in the consignment, together with the price of each consignment listed in the packing slip.

(iii) GR-l Form. It is an exchange control document required by the RBI. As per the exchange control regulations, an exporter has to realise the proceeds of the goods he has exported within 180 days from the date of their shipment from India. The GR-l form procedure applies to exports made to all countries outside India, excluding Nepal and Bhutan. The GR-l form is identified by the number in the left hand top corner and the date. To be submitted in duplicate along with other shipping documents, if it should indicate the exact quantity and description of an item planned to be exported and the value thereof. The quantity and value corresponds with those mentioned in the confirmed order received from the importer. The other important details to be furnished in the GR-l form are the name of the exporter, the importer, the currency in which the payment is expected to be received, the country of destination, and a declaration of the commission/discount payable. The customs authorities, after scrutinising the GR-l form retain the original copy and forward it to RBI. The duplicate is returned to the exporter, to enable him to submit the same to RBI through the negotiating bank, through which payment is to be received.

(iv) Shipping Bill. It is the main document required by the customs authorities for the purpose of granting permission for shipment.

(v) Export Licence. The Government of India regulations require that for certain categories of export products before shipment an export licence be obtained from the licencing authority who is usually the Joint Chief Controller of Imports & Exports (JCCI&E). One complete set of shipping documents with the prescribed application form is submitted to the JCCI&E which scrutinises the application with reference to quantity, value and description of goods in all the documents. In case of items with floor prices, the authorities check whether the price to be realised as indicated in the document is in line with the minimum floor price fixed by the Government. If they are satisfied, the JCCI&E grants the licence for the export of goods by a suitable endorsement on all the copies of the shipping bill.

As the Government of India has delicensed a number of products, in the last few years, the need of approaching the licensing authorities arises only for a few product.

(vi) Customs Clearance. No cargo meant for export can be loaded on a ship unless the customs authorities at the port accord their formal approval called the export licence. A complete set of shipping documents, including five copies of the shipping bill "under claim of drawback," is submitted by the exporter to the customs house concerned. An officer of the Customs Department of the rank of an appraiser, scrutinises the complete set of documents to determine the following:

(a) Whether the description, quantity and value indicated in the shipping bill for which permission is sought for export, correspond with those mentioned in the contract entered into with the buyer, and whether they are authenticated in the letter of credit received from the buyer.

(b) Whether the prices are correct.

(c) Whether the formalities relating to exchange control, quality control, inspection and licensing have been complied with, wherever applicable.

The customs check the details in the GR-l form, including its number and date and the entry thereof in the other documents. The original copy of the GR-l form is retained by the customs and later forwarded after recording the same in their register. The original copy of the shipping bill, together with a copy of the proforma invoice, is retained by the customs. After an examination of the documents and an appraisement of the value, the customs appraiser makes an endorsement on the duplicate copy of the shipping bill, giving directions to the dock appraiser about the extent of physical examination to be conducted at the docks. The entire set of shipping documents-except the original GR-l form, the original shipping bill and a copy of the proforma invoice is returned to the exporter's forwarding agent for further processing. Customs clearance for the export of products mentioned in the shipping bill is deemed to have been obtained with the endorsement on the duplicate copy of the shipping bill by the export department of the customs house.

(vii) Carting Order. Now the export cargo lying in the warehouse of the exporter has to be moved inside the port area and subsequently loaded on board the assigned ship. For this purpose the forwarding agent has to obtain permission from the Port Trust authorities to allow him to physically move the goods inside the port area. The permission is called the carting order where loading has to be carried out. The Shed Superintended issues this carting order after verifying the endorsement of the steamer agent on the port trust copy of the shipping bill, as also the endorsement of the customs house on its duplicate copy. With this permission, the export cargo mentioned in the shipping bill is physically moved into the appropriate shed of the Port.

(viii) Customs Examination of Cargo at Docs. The remaining copies of the entire set of shipping documents consisting of the duplicate, triplicate and export promotion copies of the shipping bill, the proform invoice with the packing list, the original and duplicate of AR-4 form and the inspection certificate is presented to the custom appraisers connected with the shed. The customs examination at the docks needs to verify whether the goods packed and kept ready for shipment are the same as those mentioned in the shipping bill. The customs appraiser, may physically examine the goods packed inside the cases and satisfy himself before making his endorsement on the shipping bill, thus certifying that the goods have been examined. Once this endorsement has been obtained on the duplicate copy of the shipping bill the goods are deemed to be "out of charge" of the customs.

(ix) Let Ship. The let ship order constitutes an authorisation by the customs to the shipping company to accept the cargo on board the vessel. The preventive officer of the Customs Department supervises the loading of the cargo on board the vessel nominated for its export. Before the goods are loaded on to the ship, permission for loading called the "Let Ship Order" has to be obtained by the exporter's forwarding agent from the Preventive Officer. It is given as an endorsement on the duplicate copy of the shipping bill and then handed over to the agent of the cargo.

(x) Mate Receipt. After the goods are loaded on board the vessel, the Captain or master of the ship furnishes to the Port Superintendent in charge of the shed a document called the "Mate Receipt" which certifies loading of the cargo on board the vessel and contains other details, such as a brief description of the cargo, the number of packages, the shipping marks, the name of the vessel, the date of issue, and a comment by the Master of the vessel on the condition of the cargo at the time of its receipt on board the vessel. Damages to packing or improve packing are mentioned in the mate receipt. As such remarks on the bill of lading may not be acceptable to the buyer, the exporter tries to obtain a clean Mate Receipt, *i.e.*, one without any adverse comment on the condition of the cargo at the time of shipment, by ensuring that no damage occurs at the time of loading.

(xi) Port Trust Dues. The bill of lading frum the shipping agency gives the exporter a title to the goods shipped on the vessel. It is given by the shipping agent only after the mate receipt is presented to him by the exporter or his forwarding agent, who arranges to pay the port charges and collects the mate receipt surrendered to the port authorities by the master of the vessel. The mate receipt is furnished to the Preventive Officer, who records the certificate of shipment on the duplicate and export promotion copies of the shipping bill, as also on the original and duplicate copies of AR-4 forms. The drwback copy and the export promotion copy of the shipping bill together with the duplicate copy of the AR-4 are given back to the exporter's forwarding agent.

(xii) Bill of Lading. The exporter's forwarding agent surrenders the mate receipt collected from the port trust office to the agent of the shipping company and collects copies of the bills of lading.

The exporter's forwarding agent returns to the exporter the following documents at the end of this process:

(a) A copy of the invoice duly attested by the customs;

(b) Drawback copy of the shipping bill;

(c) Export promotion copy of the shipping bill;

(d) The original letter of credit and the customers order or contract;

(e) A full set of "clean on board" bill of lading, together with non-negotiable copies, as required by the exporter;

(f) A duplicate copy of the AR-4 form.

Shipping is the more popular method of despatching goods to an export buyer than despatch by air. The freight charges for shipping a cargo are very much less than these of air freight. Moreover, the physical size of products, sometimes, constraints the exporter to despatch them by air, especially when these products are heavy machinery or engineering goods.

The clearing and forwarding agents are specialised personnel who arrange for the completion of all the formalities connected with the shipment of goods. As soon as the export goods reach the warehouse, the exporter arranges for a complete set of shipping documents to be passed on to the forwarding agent. These comprise:

(a) AR-4 form in original and duplicate;

(b) Proforma invoice (in duplicate) and packing list;

(c) GR form (in duplicate);

(d) Letter of credit;

(e) Commercial Invoice;

(f) Form of declaration (in triplicate);

(g) Shipping bill (five copies);

(h) Inspection Certificate;

(i) Copy of Export Contract/L.C./Export Order;

(j) Copy of registration certificate from the canalised agency.

When the goods are despatched from the factory, the original copy of the gate pass, as well as original and duplicate copy of the AR-4 form, are sent to the exporter, who passes them on to the forwarding agent along with other shipping documents, so that the necessary endorsement may be obtained on them from the relevant authorities at the time of shipment to enable exporter to obtain a rebate on duty.

GR-1 form is an exchange control document required by the RBI. As per the exchange control regulations, an exporter has to realise the proceeds of the goods he has exporter within 18 days from the date of their shipment from India. In order to ensure that the RBI has introduced the GR-1 procedure. The GR-1 procedure applies to exports made to all territories outside India, excluding Pakistan, Afghanistan, Nepal and Bhutan.

Shipping Bill

A shipping bill is the main document required by the customs authorities for the purpose of granting permission for shipment.

A drawback shipping bill is prepared in five copies. It contains the name of the exporter or the shipper, his address, the Code No., the description and quantity of goods to be shipped, the value of goods, the number of packages and the marketings on them, the amount of drawback claimed, the port of destination, the name of the ship together with the name of the agent, etc. The five copies include the customs and statistical copy, the port trust copy, the drawback copy and the export promotion copy. The port trust copy is utilised for the purpose of claiming incentives such as cash compensatory support and import replenishment licences.

Export Licence

The Government of India regulations require that an export licence be obtained for certain categories of export products before shipment is made. The licence has to be obtained from the licencing is authority who is usually the Joint Chief Controller of Imports & Exports (JCCI&E). One complete set of shipping documents with the prescribed application form is submitted to the JCCI&E for the grant of an export licence.

Customs Clearance

According to prevailing customs regulations, no cargo meant for export can be loaded on a ship unless the customs authorities at the port accord their formal approval. After obtaining the export licence, where necessary, a complete set of shipping documents, including five copies of the shipping bill "under claim of drawback," is submitted by the exporter to the customs house concerned.

The customs also check the details in the GR-l form, including its number and date and the entry thereof in the other documents. The original copy of the GR-l form is retained by the customs and later, after recording the same in their register, forward it to the RBI. The original copy of the shipping bill, together with a copy of the proforma invoice, is retained by the customs.

Carting Order

The export cargo lying in the warehouse of the exporter has now to be moved inside the port area and subsequently loaded on board the assigned ship. The forwarding agent, for this purpose, has to obtain permission from the Port Trust authorities to allow him to physically move the goods inside the port area. This permission, which is given by the Superintendent of the Port Trust in change of the shed where loading has to be carried out is called the carting order.

Customs Examination of Cargo at Docks

The remaining copies of the entire set of shipping documents—mainly consisting of the duplicate, triplicate and export promotion copies of the shipping bill, the proforma invoice with the packing list, the original and duplicate of AR-4 form and the inspection certificate is presented to the custom appraiser connected with the shed. The main purpose of the customs examination at the docks is to verify whether the goods packed and kept ready for shipment are the same as those mentioned in the shipping bill.

Let Ship

The preventive officer of the Customs Department supervises the loading of the cargo on board the vessel nominated for its export. Before the goods are loaded on to the ship, permission for loading has to be obtained by the exporter's forwarding agent from the preventive Officer. This permission is called the "Let Ship Order".

Mate Receipt

As soon as the goods are loaded on board the vessel, the Captain or Master of the ship furnishes a document called the "Mate Receipt" to the Port Superintendent in charge of the shed. It is a document certifying loading of the cargo on board the vessel and contains other details, such as a brief description of the cargo, the number of packages, the shipping marks, the name of the vessel, and the date of issue. The mate receipt also contains a comment by the master of the vessel on the condition of the cargo at the time of its receipt on board the vessel.

Port Trust Dues

An exporter has to obtain the bill of lading from the shipping agent which gives him a title to the goods shipped on the vessel. This is given by the shipping agent only after the mate receipt is presented to him by the exporter or his forwarding agent, who arranges to pay the port charges and collects the mate receipt surrendered to the port authorities by the Master of the vessel.

Bill of Lading

The exporter's forwarding agent surrenders the mate receipt collected from the port trust office to the agent of the shipping company and collects copies of the bills of lading.

Thus, at the end of this process, the forwarding agent returns the following documents to the exporter:

(a) A copy of the invoice duly attested by the customs.

(b) An export promotion copy of the shipping bill.

(c) A full set of clean bill of lading together with non-negotiable copies as required by the exporter.

(d) The original letter of credit and the customer's order of contract; and

(e) A duplicate copy of the AR-4 form.

At the end of the customs procedure, the exporter is left with the following documents:

(a) A copy of invoice duly attested by the customs authorities.

(b) Export promotion copy of the shipping bill.

(c) A full set of 'Clean or Board' bill of lading with non-negotiable copies.

(d) The original L/C and the export contract.

(e) Duplicate copy of AR-4/AR-4A form.

REALISATION OF EXPORT INCENTIVES OFFERED BY THE GOVERNMENT OF INDIA

Exporters can claim the completion of shipment of goods. The procedure to claim important incentives is stated as under:

1. To Claim CCS. The procedures to claim Cash Compensatory Support CCS is as follows:

(i) ***To Whom to Apply.*** Application for CCS should be sent to the regional licensing (Disbursement) authority, within a prescribed time limit.

(ii) ***When to Apply.*** Application should be made within a period of 3 months from the date of shipment period. Applications received later than 6 months without sufficient reasonable cause shall stand rejected.

(iii) Documents Required.

(a) A copy of commercial invoice, attested by bank.

(b) Bank certificate, evidencing export,

(c) Copy of shipping Bill, certified by customs, and

(d) Any other document, if required.

The GOI has also Simplified Payment Scheme (SPS) to claim CCS. Only those exporters enrolled under SPS can apply under SPS.

Cheques for CCS are issued in the name of exporter's bank, bank credits the registered same to exporter's account.

2. To Claim DBK. The procedure to claim DBK is as follows:

(i) ***To Whom to Apply.*** The applications is to be submitted to the nearest Customs House. The data submitted by exporters is verified by customs officer.

(ii) ***When to Apply.*** Exporters should apply within 60 days after the customs officer has given 'Let Export Order'.

(iii) Documents required to be submitted with DBK claim application.

Following documents are to be submitted:

(a) Shipping Bill copy (Drawback Copy).

(b) Copy of Commercial Invoice, certified by bank.

(c) Copy of B/L.

(d) Copy of brand rate letter where drawback claim is against a brand rate.

(e) Any other relevant document.

Claims if found admissible, shall be sanctioned and cheques are issued to the exporter.

The GOI has introduced simplified procedure of disbursement, for sanctioning claims with in 24 hours.

3. To Claim REP Licence. The following is the procedure to claim REP licence:

(i) ***To Whom to Apply.*** Application for claiming REP against exports affected can be filed with the regional licensing authority.

(ii) ***When to Apply.*** Application for claiming REP must be submitted within a period of 3 months from the date of export. Applications submitted later than 6 months are considered, subject to cut in REP licences.

(iii) ***Documents Required:***

(a) Statement of exports.

(b) Bank Certificate.

(c) List of items imported.

(d) Copy of the Shipping bill.

(e) Copy of commercial Invoice, certified by bank.

After verification of the REP application, the licensing authority issues REP Licence to the exporter, which can be freely transferable.

4. To Claim IPRS. The following is the procedure to claim IPRS:

(i) ***To Whom to Apply.*** The application for IPRS is to be submitted to the Engineering Export Promotion Council (EEPC) in triplicate.

(ii) ***When to Apply.*** Application for a particular month of exports should be submitted within six months from the date of exports, otherwise, it will be subject to cuts, of 10%, 30% and 50% for delays upto 12, 18 and 24 months. Application received after 24 months are rejected.

(iii) ***Documents Required***

(a) Photocopy of RCMC, issued by EEPC-Statement of exports,

(b) Commercial invoice, attested by bank,

(c) Statement of usage, and wastage of raw materials, if required,

(d) Any other relevant document.

On examination of the application, the EEPC sends two sets of application to the licensing authority. The licensing authority issues a payment authority to EEPC on one application set. The EEPC then issues a cheque in favour of exporter.

5. To claim Central Excise Rebate. The following is the procedure to claim central excise rebate:

(i) To Whom to Apply. Apply to Maritime collector of central Excise in Form "C" in triplicate.

(ii) When to Apply. Within a period of six months from the date of exports.

(iii) Document Required.

(a) Application in Form "C" in triplicate.

(b) Duplicate copy of AR-4/AR-4A, endorsed by preventive officer.

(c) Copy of Bill of Lading.

(d) Original Copy of Gate Pass.

If application is found in order, the Central Excise authorities sanction the refund to the exporter. If the goods are exported under 'Bond' then the Bond is discharged.

The exporter can also claim other incentives, such as Octori refund, rail freight rebate etc. The exporter should approach the concerned authorities, with required documents, to claim such incentives.

❒

8

International Marketing Mix

The first stage in international marketing is to identify the right market where the exporter can sell his product profitably because one market differs from another and a person cannot sell his product in all the markets of the world. So, he has to segment them in such a way that he may be able to meet the requirements of the market. It requires concerted efforts, otherwise the firm will not succeed in marketing the right product in the right market. It costs lot of time and money to find out a suitable market and to avoid waste of limited resources, time and efforts. It may also minimise the business risks and make success sure. It is, therefore, better to concentrate on a few fruitful markets rather than to spread too thinly. As soon as the exporting firm establishes itself in one or some select markets, it can move on to other market taking detailed survey of the new markets, So, initially it is better to approach a limited number of customers in a market and then approach a large number of foreign customers in other markets of the same foreign country. For all exporter, it would be advisable to carry himself on to similar other markets having gained the experience.

CLASSIFICATION OF WORLD MARKETS

Before making an entry into the world market, a firm has to identify those markets in which it can sell its products easily. One market differs from another but still in one respect or the other, they can be grouped in different segments. It is important for the firm entering the world market to segment them in such a way that it is able to effectively meet their requirements. The problem of segmentation does not arise if the firm is exporting or is planning to export its products to a single country. But when it is exporting or is planning to export to more than one country, the problem does arise. The question is then very much pertinent how a firm should segment its market on the international plane.

The world markets can be classified on different bases, *viz.*, *(1)* Industrial development of the countries, *(2)* Population, *(3)* Gross National Product, *(4)* other characteristics.

1. Classification on the Basis or Industrial Development. This basis is very frequently used in segmenting the world markets by the international agencies. On this basis, markets can be divided in four distinct segments, *viz.*, industrially devdoped economeis, more developed developing economics, raw materials exporting economies and subsistence economies.

A. Industrially Developed Economies. Industrially developed countries provide a large market as they have no or little import restrictions. These countries lay more emphasis on the production of more sophisticated products and therefore insist more and more on research and development. Therefore, they like to import goods of simpler technology and simpler manufactures. They provide ample opportunities for the marketing of the following types of products:

(a) Labour intensive products like electronics and light engineering goods because these countries have an acute shortage or labour.

(b) Spares and components and raw materials to field their industries as they are not rich in agricultural raw materials.

(c) Decorative articles and craft articles because of their affluence.

(d) Anti-pollution equipment and those articles whose production has been banned for risks of pollution because they are very particular about preventing pollution.

As these countries have modern technology they are willing to provide technology to set up production and processing facilities in developing countries.

B. More Developed Developing Economies. This category would include countries like India, Brazil, Mexico, Hong Kong etc. These countries are striving to update these technologies for current range of manufactures and therefore have much scope for absorbing modern technology in their efforts to set up new manufacturing units. They are also interested in setting up joint ventures in other less developed countries. India, for example, has entered into contracts with some developed countries of the world like Japan and USSR to import modern industrial technology and also set up joint ventures in Nepal. Bhutau and other less developed countries.

C. Raw Materials Exporting Economies. This category includes countries like those in Gulf area and many countries in Africa and Latin America. Such countries export raw materials and purchase everything like food, consumer durables, transport equipments, service facilities etc.

Their foreign earnings are quite uncertain because of large fluctuations in their export prices. They are not able to produce much for their requirements and import almost anything. They are also interested in importing turnkey projects. Changes in these countries take place rather slowly and, therefore, the level of sophistication in products required by these countries is much less than that required by developed countries.

D. Subsistence Economies. This type of economy is found in the least developed countries. They almost produce nothing and depend very much on the imports. They need:

(a) equipment to exploit their untapped resources,

(b) infrastructural facilities like railways, roads, building, transport equipments, power generation equipments, transmission line tower etc.

(c) turnkey projects like housing, schools, hospitals etc.

As there countries lack infrastructure's, the most developed countries do not offer lalest technology and therefore there is much scope for the developing countries like India to export their products in these countries. New industries can be set up in these countries.

2. Other Bases of Division of World Markets. The segmentation of world market can also be done on some other bases:

A. On the Basis of Population. The population can be another criterion for division of markets. The higher the population of a country the bigger is the market. It is, therefore, worthwhile to assess the potentiality of the market keeping in view the size of the market. When analysing the population, it is necessary tc look at—*(i)* age groups and sex, *(ii)* social class, *(iii)* educational background, *(iv)* number of households, *(v)* geographic concentration and differences, and *(iv)* the rate of change in each of the above characteristic.

B. On the Basis of Gross National Product. Gross National Product (GNP) and its rate of growth as also the standard of living of its population may provide another basis for classification of countries and the markets can be segmented and classified on their GNP basis. The big industrialised nations having larger GNP like the USA, West European countries Japan, Australia and Canada are the best markets. for consumer goods and consumer durables. Even though these countries produce these manufactures but stills the rich prefer to purchase the imported items because most of the people in the country are wealthy enough to be able to buy imported products. This classification, however, is not much different from the classification done on the basis of economies given earlier because the industrially-developed countries occupy top positions in GNP as well. The least developed countries occupy the positions at the other end, Markets can be classified here also on the basis of economies.

C. Other Bases. (1) The size of population related to the income per head of a country's inhabitants is one of the most important criteria it deciding the respective values of the markets and it would be desirable to devote a lot of time to study this aspect.

(2) Big countries may have different market characteristics in different parts of the country. For example the USA may be divided into four different parts, *viz.*, New England, South Mid. West and West. What may be sold in one part of the country, may not necessarily be sold in another part of the country. On the other hand, there may be different countries in the continent. Their market characteristics may be more or less similar.

(3) Some other variables like socio-economic variables, cultural groupings and other behavioural patterns as reflected in usage rate consumer motive and the adoption process. Apart from these, a firm may choose othei variables also for segmenting the market.

However, before a firm determines whether a particular segmentation strategy is worthwhile, it must consider the following three points:

(1) The size of each segment under consideration must be measurable which means that the sufficient data are available about the segment in question. In case the necessary information is not available or it is too costly to collect then it is not worthwhile to adopt such strategy as optimisation of resources is lost.

(2) The segment selected must be such that it can yield adequate returns. In other words, it must be substantial enough to be profitable.

(3) Lastly, the firm must make sure that the segment selected must be accessible in an effective manner. In other words, market. ing institutions like channels of distribution and promotional media must exist in the proposed segment so that the consumer may be contacted with least efforts. It would be futile to select a segment where retail distribution system is not organised.

Thus, a firm that wants to make entry in the world market should first classify the market taking the product characteristics in mind on either of the basis given above considering the profitability of the product, accessibility to the market and the availability of information relating to the segment.

SHORT-LISTING OF FOREIGN MARKETS

A preliminary survey of different markets of the world may reveal that there are ample opportunities for export in a number of countries but taking into account the various constraints, it is not possible for a firm to do business in all these markets. It has to pick put a few possible markets out of the total markets surveyed. A preliminary study may help in avoiding the markets which are obviously impossible or less likely ones in comparison to other. There are many free sources of information available to an exporter to help the do so.

Criteria for Eliminating the Markets

The following are some of the points which may serve as the criteria for eliminating the obviously impossible or difficult-to-enter territories from an Indian exporter's point of view:

(1) If the Government of India has imposed an embargo on export to some countries, as for example South West Africa and South Africa, the export to those countries will be impossible.

(2) There may be some commodities, the export of which are restricted or prohibited either completely or only to some countries. In India the exports of antiques and art products as also strategic materials to enemy countries are prohibited.

(3) In some cases cost of product adaptation may be so high that an exporter may not afford it.

(4) In compatibility of technical standards may eliminate some markets.

(5) If some countries impose formidable tariff barriers which may make the product too costly in the concerned country, it is not possible to export such commodities to such countries.

(6) Some importing countries may impose embargoes or quotas on the import of certain specific products from some specific countries or a group of countries. For example, developed countries

have imposed restrictions on the imports of cotton textiles and readymade garments from underdeveloped countries.

(7) In some cases, shipping costs may be far too high. Therefore, trade with far-off countries is difficult.

(8) Where the competition is quite severe and it may not be easy to enter the market or it may not be profitable to sell the product in such markets without much costs.

(9) There may be some non-tariff barriers which may make the export of some commodities to some countries virtually impossible or difficult.

(10) In case of technically sophisticated products, too much promotional expenditure may have to be spent, such as on preparing sales literature and catalogues in many languages. Also after sale service and maintenance of stocks of spare parts may be difficult.

Market Entry Conditions

In previous lines, it has been discussed that there are some markets which should be avoided. On the other hand if there are certain preferences available to India, such markets may be more attractive than and should be preferred to others. The various types of preferences available to Indian exporters are discussed as follows:

1. The Generalised System of Preferences. Under the generalised system of preferences (GSP), the developed countries allow the imports from developing countries like India either duty free or at concessional rates. It has naturally helped India's exports. asp make the imports cheap in comparison to products coming from countries which are not entitled for GSP and in this way it increases the competitive strength of the product. To take advantage of GSP, an exporter must know: *(i)* whether his product is covered by GSP, *(ii)* the preference margin enjoyed by his product, *(iii)* quotas for the import in that country, if any, and *(iii)* procedural formation on this point may be gathered from the Indian Institute of Foreign Trade. Trade Development Authority, the Ministry of Commerce, and Export Promotion Councils.

2. Exchange of Preferences Among Developing Countries. 16 developing countries, including India. have been exchanging preferences among themselves under 1972 agreements. These countries are Brazil, Chile, South Korea, Spain, Mexico, Pakistan, Philippines, Tunisia, Turkey, Uruguay, Yugoslavia, Israel, Egypt, Paraguay, Bangladesh and India. India is also a beneficiary of Bangkok or agreement where developing countries of ESCAP are extending-preferences to each other on 93 products. The exporter must be aware of the products covered by these preferences. Their information is also available from the same organisations mentioned above.

3. Import Promotion Centres in Some Countries. Some countries have established import promotion centres to promote imports from developing countries and to provide assistance to their exporters. A directory of such import promotion centres (IPC) has been compiled by the International Trade Centre, UNCTAD/GATT and can be obtained from them on request. The countries where such centres have been established are Australia, Austria, Belgium, Canada, Czechoslovakia, Denmark, Finland, France, GDR, Federal Republic of Germany, Hungary, Israel, Italy, Japan, Netherland, New Zealand, Norway, Poland, Romania, Sweden, Switzerland. USSR, U.K. and Yugoslavia.

These centres provide advice and information almost of every type necessary for the promotion of import from the developing countries. The U.K. Import Promotion Centre, apart from general information, also: *(i)* acts for the European Community or all matters relating to the visit of missions sponsored by E.C. Commission to the U.K., and *(ii)* gives assistance to overseas companies seeking a U.K. joint venture partner. In most cases, these services are provided free of charge.

4. Other Advantages. An Indian exporter should also examine whether India has got any particular advantage in the market. Such advantages may be: *(a)* proximity, *(b)* trade dominated by persons of Indian origin, *(c)* existence of shipping facilities, *(d)* political relations, if they are not good, business may get setback even if the terms offered are more attractive, *(e)* existence of rupee payment agreements.

Thus, after carrying out market surveys, some markets where entry is impossible or difficult, they should be rejected outrightly and in other cases where some additional preferences are available, those markets should-be favourably considered.

Sources of Information Available to Exporters

There are many sources of information available to Indian exporters to help them. Such sources are:

(1) Export promotion councils, the Trade Development Authority, and various chambers of commerce.

(2) United Nations publish detailed international trade statistics which can help the exporters in locating the market for their products.

(3) Libraries maintained by foreign embassies in India provide a number of references to assist exporters.

(4) Export Import Bank can provide information about assistance provided by the bank to Indian exporters and foreign importers of Indian goods.

(5) Commercial banks and the Export Credit Guarantee corporation of India can provide information about the foreign exchange and payment conditions in different countries and also the credit ratings and risks.

(6) Reserve Bank of India publish the 'Reserve -Bank of India Bulletin' incorporating the policies regarding exchange control regulations and other credit information.

Analysis of the Information

The information available to an Indian exporter must be analysed. in such a manner that it will reduce the possible markets to probable or more likely markets. The process of analysis would be as follows:

1. The exporters must examine first the India's export statistics which are officially published in the 'Monthly Statistics Relating to

India's Foreign Trade'. This analysis would enable the exporter to find out the markets of the similar products and the rate of growth of exporters. In doing so, data for a period of three to five years should be collected to find out the long-term trend of the markets.

2. The next step is the examination of import statistics of the different countries. It will enable him to know the relative size of the various markets. A careful analysis would reveal the quantity of imports, main rivals and the nature of imports trend whether they are increasing, decreasing or static of different markets. Always expanding market should be selected because further sales in these markets would be possible without much affecting the competitors and would make the market task easier. This statistics may be available in foreign embassies or consulates in India and chambers of commerce. In addition OECD World Trade Statistics and United Nations International Trade Statistics also provide these data.

3. Examination of reports of research studies made by the Indian Institute of Foreign Trade, Trade Development Authority and Export Promotion Councils may reveal vuious markets and the products covered by them.

4. Examination of the above two statistics may give an idea of the possible unit value realisation as also the price paid for imports in foreign countries from different sources.

5. Talks to some experienced exporters of allied products (because a competitor would avoid disclosing the facts), contacting trade associations and chamber of commerce would help in appraising the markets. Export promotion councils also assist the new exporters in finding out new markets by providing necessary details about each of them.

6. The Economic Times, a daily, publishes supplements covering one particular country and other articles and research papers prepared by its Research Bureau giving lot of information useful to markets. Some journals like the Commerce/Eastern Economic also conduct valuable researches from time to time.

7. Commercial banks provide valuable information about the payment position and exchange control regulations in different countries. They also provide necessary information about the export credit available to Indian exporters and about the various risk covers provided by the ECGC.

8. Freight forwarders may supply the necessary information relating to availability of shipping services as also the freight charges to different countries. Underwriters may provide the details about marine insurance.

9. India's commercial representatives abroad may also help in collecting the valuable information regarding health, sanitary and other regulations like marketing, labelling, packaging etc. and in the selection of agents. The Indian embassies abroad may give the exporters as much information as possible along with the published material, if any, supporting the claims, if they would like to contact them.

Having collected the information from the various sources government and otherwise the exporter should start processing and analysing the information in respect of each prospective market to make a final decision.

As soon as the exporter locates the probable markets for his product, it might be better, and useful for him to have a visit to those markets and see at first hand what each market has to offer. The visits should be arranged at appropriate times preferably when a trade fair is on so that he may have an idea of what is available in the market concerned and other necessary marketing information such as competitors, price, strength and weaknesses of the competing products. He must also take the precaution that the man visiting a foreign market must know his product well.

Again, it would be advisable to the exporter to test the market carefully to minimise the risks before mounting any export offensive. It would be useful to find out the market segment which offers the best potential.

It might be stressed again that it would be better to concentrate on a few markets which would be in the manageable limits of the exporter. It would be necessary to review from time to time the export markets and to reassess their characteristics and potentials.

The product is meant for consumers for whom it is produced and therefore it must be to their satisfaction. To make the product to the satisfaction of consumers, product planning is necessary.

PRODUCT POLICY

The product is meant for consumers for whom it is produced and therefore it must be to their satisfaction. To make the product to the satisfaction of consumers, product planning is necessary.

Consumers will buy only what suits them, and not what the company is manufacturing or presenting. The product planning is, therefore, of special importance in foreign markets to get the success. Taking the special view of the level of competition in world markets, an exporting firm must develop the product what the prospects in the foreign markets need. Each foreign market is different. What is acceptable in U.K. may not be acceptable in USA or Federal Republic of Germany. Choices or tastes may differ. Thus export markets need a different approach to product planning. In general the 'product' being offered to foreign customers must have something special, either in terms of attraction or advantage what will motivate them to opt for this in preference to others. This is the crux of the product planning for exporters.

Here, it is important to understand the meaning of 'product" and 'product type'. 'Product type' is the aggregate of various 'products' performing the same type of function or giving the same type of satisfaction. 'Product', on the other hand, satisfies the interest of a specific segment of the consumers. For example, car is a 'product type' but a specific brand of car, say 'Toyota car' is a product. Here, we are discussing the product and not the product type. Likewise, a new product does not mean a new product type but a product that differs in only a limited number of ways from the established product is a new product.

Product Adaptation Strategy

Product adaptation may be used as a strategy in selling the product in the foreign market which is dominated by the competitors. As we know that a product may be in different stages of its life cycle in different markets, the firm may now face the difficult choice of choosing a product adaptation strategy so that it may successfully be sold in overseas markets. A slightly modified product may have a better chance of success in getting a hold in the market than a product which is similar to the existing product in all essential aspects. The modification in the product may serve as the 'selling points'. The process may also result in cost reduction and then it will be an additional advantage.

Warren Keegan has outlined five alternative adaptation strategies which a firm may use for selling the product in different foreign markets. These strategies are:

(l) Strategy One-One Product, One Message—World-Wide. This strategy may be known as product extension strategy. Under this strategy, firms extending their operations to foreign markets sell the same product, with the same advertising and promotional themes and appeals which they are using in the home market. Coca cola used this alternative successfully. It uses the same drink and uses the same advertising and promotional themes overall the world as it uses in USA. The advantage of this strategy is cost saving due to economies of scale and elimination of research and development costs. Promotion and packaging costs are also lower.

This strategy does not work in situations where foreign consumers' perception of a product is different or the tastes and preferences differ from that of the domestic consumers. In these situation, the marketer should try to adjust or use new product strategy but only after surveying the markets.

(2) Strategy Two—Same Product—Modified Communication. This strategy is used when the product is almost the same which the exporters sell in the domestic market but the communication message or promotional themes and appeals differ in different markets according to the needs it serves to the people in different markets, *i.e.*, different propositions are used in different markets for selling the same product. For example, Indian bicycles in the USA and other western countries are advertised abroad for the pleasure they give rather than for their transportation qualities because bicycles are used there only for fun and pleasure. When the approach of product satisfying the different needs is pursued a product transformation occurs and, therefore, it may be called a product transformation strategy.

It is also a low cost strategy. Since originally the product is the same, costs associated with R&D, manufacturing set-up, inventory and tooling are avoided. The additional cost is only or reformulating the communications around the newly-identified product function.

(3) Strategy Three—Product Adaptation—Commuication Extension. The third strategy is to adapt the product to suit the foreign market conditions but to extend the same communication message as developed in their home markess. The strategy assumes that the product will serve almost the same purpose in foreign markets as it serves in the domestic market. But the use conditions are changed. Therefore the promotional appeal differs. This strategy is used mainly by detergent manufacturers. They change the formula to suit the local water conditions or weather conditions but the theme for advertising is the same.

This strategy is economical because the promotional strategy is the same but additional cost are involved in extra engineering and production changes.

(4) Strategy Five—Product Innovation. This strategy is quite different from the other four discussed above. The above strategies are effective in international marketing only when prospective customers in foreign markets have purchasing power to buy the product offered by the firm. But in developing countries markets where people do not have much purchasing power, a low cost product which they can purchase needs to be developed. The firm must follow the strategy to develop a new product specially to suit their need at a price which the prospects can afford. Extensive research is required to follow the strategy and, therefore, it is the costliest strategy but if the costs of product development are not excessive, this strategy can be highly rewarding in international marketing because the pay offs under this strategy are the, highest.

(5) Strategy Four—Dual Adaptation. As we observed that conditions in foreign markets differ significantly and ideally the marketer should adapt his marketing strategy to suit these conditions. The present strategy is based on this assumption. Under this approach, the marketer should adapt the product and the communication both to suit the local markets and to increase the product acceptability. In effect, it is the combination of the second and third alternatives. The example of this strategy is provided by garment manufacturers who design their product differently for different foreign markets and adapt their communication accordingly. In essence, this strategy is based on differentiation approach and hence all benefits and limitations of that approach hold good here also.

Choosing the Correct Strategy

It is apparent that a firm has many alternative adaptation strategies to serve to the foreign markets. Which one should be chosen as the correct and most suitable strategy is the main problem of the firm before entering the foreign market. In doing so, the following factors should be considered:

(1) Firm's Objectives. The main consideration in selecting a strategy is the firm's objectives. If a firm follows profit maximisation as its objective, the best strategy for it would be product extension strategy, *i.e.*, the same product with the same communication appeals may be sold in the foreign countries. It involves no expense and gains all economies of scale. But it should be viewed in relation to the other factors listed here.

(2) Product-Market Analysis. The firm should also establish the product-market relationship of the firm's product. The firm must consider the various issues relevant in relation to the product of the firm such as who uses the product, when it is used, for what purpose it is used and how it is used. Does the product require power sources, linkage to other systems, maintenance, preparation style, matching etc.? Mandatory adaptation situations purchasing power of its prospective customers and the price of the product should also be favoured while deciding the strategy. Thus various, factors deciding the nature of the demand of the product should be analysed in depth before selecting the product adaptation strategy. In the light of these factors the firm should answer the question whether the needs of the individual markets are so different as to necessitate differentiation in the product.

(3) Company Resources. While selecting the product strategy, the firm must keep in mind its own resources—financial as well as non-financial. Product adaptation involves costs. It may be lucrative to differentiate the product from one market to another, but the cost involvement may be beyond what its financial resources can permit. In such situations, it is not advisable for the first to adopt the strategy which required excessive costs involvement. A strategy which does not involve costs, such as product and communication extension strategy may be followed in such circumstances.

(4) Packaging. Another important factor to be borne in mind while deciding on the strategy for the different foreign markets is the product package. The product may be differentiated in different markets only by the size, design, colour and the language on the package. Besides, other factors like the climate of the importing country, length of distribution climate, transport hazards, mandatory provisions, customs requirements etc. should also be considered in packaging.

In essence, a product adaptation strategy may be selected taking into account the various essential factors as given above. As we know, the product has different stages of life cycle in different markets, the different strategies for different markets may be adopted for the product because the product needs different types of adaptation in different stages.

STANDARDISATION

It is an important part of the marketing process to determine the shape or form of the product in which it should be put on the market. It is the problem of establishing, maintaining standards and providing confirmity to them. 'Standards' play an important part in securing efficiency and economy.

Standards are ideal or model products which provide a basis of composition with identical products. Standards convey an idea of uniformity and identity in respect of quality or quantity or some other matters. Thus "Standard is a measure that is generally accepted as having a fixed value." (Ouddy and Ravzan). The measure may be in units of intrinsic qualities or characteristics of the product or service. A standard is determined as a result of the scientific study of the essential qualities or characteristics that must be present in a product.

Advantages of Standardisation

There are certain clear-cut advantages of standardisation of products in foreign market. Terpstra has identified six factors which may favour international product standardisation.

1. Economies in Scale of Production. The most importtant argument in favour of international standardisation is that it will extend the markets. If one standard version of a product is sold in all the areas, naturally it will have a larger demand and consequently larger production runs. The firm, thus, will be able to achieve the large-scale economies, resulting in lower costs of production and distribution, and bringing the break-even point lower.

2. Economies in Marketing. Standardisation brings economies in marketing as well. When the same product is launched in different markets, various economies can be achieved in terms of producing advertising, sales, literature, inventory management and aftersale service requirements. Again, it has not to alter its marketing mix in different environments to suit the local requirements. It may lead to an increase in sales. Significant economies may be obtained in the areas of product packaging and advertising.

3. Economies in Product Research and Development. Due to large-scale economies, a firm earns larger profits. It can flow be able to spend more on research and development to improve the quality of the product so that it may introduce a new product havıng larger adaptability. The costs incurred in product research and development may be recovered earlier from the entire sale. The per unit cost of research and expenditure will be lower. Thus standardisation brings down the cost of product research and development.

4. Consumer Mobility. Today's consumer is more mobile as he travels all over the world. Transcontinental travels has now become fairly common. If he gets a product in the same style and fashion in foreign markets that he gets in his home country, he becomes more loyal to such a firm than to a firm which differentiates its product from country to country.

5. Image. Standardisation projects an image of the product or of the country in the minds of consumers. When the name of a product or country is associated with the high standard of quality in the minds of the consumer, the same product in a foreign country manufactured by the same producer or in the same country may enjoy a psychological premium in the minds of the consumers in the foreign markets. This image projected by the sale of standardised product all over the world will increase the sales of the product.

6. Consistency in Dealing with Customers. Standardisation affords an opportunity to the firm to achieve consistency in its dealings with customers. It is generally felt that consistency in product styles, in sales and customer service, in brand names and packages is a powerful tool for increasing sales. Thus consistency projects an image of the characteristics of the minds of the consumers and they recognise it as they know it.

7. Impact of Technology. Industrial products generally tend to have standard specifications. If one product is popular in one country due to its standardised specifications/technology, it may be demanded by the customers and dealers in other countries. An important reason for the dealers asking for the standardisation appears to be their desire to offer the same level of service to their customers all over the world. They do not require much adaptation for foreign markets unless climatic and similar considerations call for it.

Apart from the above six factors described by Terpstra there are certain other advantages of standardisation.

8. Significant Control. Significant control over the operation of the company in the world market is yet another factor that contributes to the firm's desire to adopt a standardisation strategy. Different standards for different markets may make the control over the operation of associates difficult. It may lead to a state of anarchy in its pricing policy and the distribution system.

Despite the benefits of standardisation in the international markets stated above, this strategy suffers from certain serious limitations. Let us see what they are.

Limitations of Standardisation

The various limitations of standardisation are:

1. Physical Environment. One of serious limitations of standardisation arises from the differences among national markets on account of their physical environment like climate, country's topography, and resources position. These differences in physical environment demand that the firm must differentiate its standardisation strategy in each market. For example, climatic conditions may severely restrict the use of a product in a particular form. The form of the product will have to be chauged if that particular market is to be served.

2. Technological and Legal Factors. There are certain technological and legal factors that restrict the use of standardisation strategy all over the world markets. They have no option with the exporting firm except to product adaptation. For example, if a company wants to export electrical goods to Japan, these will have to be of 110 volts and not 220 volts. Similarly, for export of food items, the health regulations as imposed by the importing countries must be adhered to. Where the company has a choice, it will be a matter of relative costs and benefits of the alternate strategies of uniformity and adaptation.

3. Buyer's Choice. Where goods are to be exported according to the specifications spelt out by the buyer (importer) the exporter has no choice except to export the goods as per specifications.

4. Other Factors. Besides, differences arising out of the stages of economic and industrial development, culture, competitive practices existence of absence of marketing institutions, stage of product life cycle in each market also restrict the use of standardisation strategy in all the foreign markets.

Thus, there are factors which initiate a firm to adopt standardisation strategy because of its cost-saving characteristics that affords several potential benefits in production and distribution of the product. There are, on the other hand, several other factors that restrict the use of this strategy and support the use of differentiated marketing strategy that allows the firm to mould its product, price, promotion and distribution to suit the local requirements. This, undoubtedly, may lead to an increase in sales but at a higher cost and may even lead to fragmentation of the entire market into several small submarkets and total dilution of the parent company's control over its associates in the international markets.

The above two strategies of standardisation are two extremes of the problem as two market's can never be identical or quite different in all the terms. Thus, a better strategy to use is a concentrated marketing strategy. In this straiegy, various countries which are similar in their basic characteristics are clustered in pairs. Although it is not possible to cluster them completely, as no two countries are exactly similar. It is possible to accept minor differences and pair them. This strategy is developed by Simon Majaro and presupposes that every market has one single market, which it considers as the basic bench mark territory. This bench mark territory should be strongest one and neither too small nor too big. The objective of this approach is to identify, in a somewhat qualitative manner, the degree to which other foreign markets come close to the bench mark territory.

CONCEPT OF PRODUCT LIFE CYCLE

All products have certain length of life during which they pass through certain identifiable stages. As soon as a product is introduced in the market, its life begins, then it goes through a period during which its market grows rapidly, eventually it reaches at maturity and then stands saturated. Afterwards its market declines and finally its life comes to an end.

Product development and adaptation are not static concepts. They are dynamic because the market (especially global market) itself is evolving overtime. Due to this continuous evolution, products tend to become obsolete with the passage of time. Market for a product remains saturated over a time horizon and unless a new product designs and substantially improved versions are developed sales and profitability will decline considerably with the passage of time. For example, when the market of black and white TV became saturated, a new version-colour TV was introduced and the market revived.

Conceptually, a product passes through four important stages of its life cycle : *(i)* Market development, *(ii)* Market growth. *(iii)* Market maturity, and *(iv)* Market decline.

During its market development stage, the product is introduced for the first time in the market and it struggles for its acceptability among the potential buyers. Heavy promotional expenditure is made to make the product popular, gradually, sales pick up but the profits are not much due to heavy promotional efforts. During the growth stage, the market acceptability is attained and sales pick up rapidly consequently the profits also go up because of *(i)* large-scale production economies, and *(ii)* low cost of distribution and selling expenses. Gradually high profits attract the competitors to enter the field.

In the third stage, the maturity stage, the product tends to approach the saturation level and the rate of growth slacks down. Hence, profitability rate also shows a downward trend. In its final stage of market decline, the consumers lose interest in the product because of new and developed products enter the market. Sales of the product decline precariously.

It is not necessary that all products pass through this cycle of product life. Staple items are classic examples which do not conform to this theory. Almost all semi-durable and durable consumer items and almost all fashion items tend to pass through this cycle of stages.

This cycle of a product can be depicted in the following: diagramme.

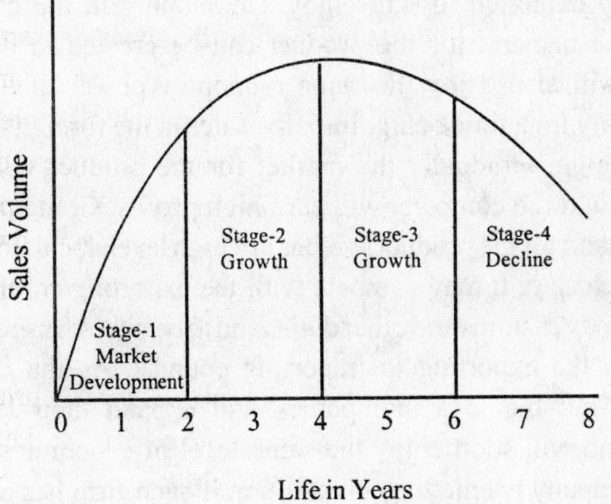

Fig. Product Life Cycle

Implications of Product Life Cycle Theory

There are following implications of the product life cycle theory in the marketing field:

(1) Sure of Success. Almost every product passes through, the various stages of the life cycle. A company which has come out with a new product can be sure of enjoying the market success, and the monopoly situation only for a short while. As the product becomes popular and acceptable among customers, other competitors, sometimes with improved designs and lower price, will join. As more and more competitors join the race, the products move towards an end. It may be possible that the growth stage for the industry as a whole extends over a sufficiently long period while it is shorter for an individual concern. Moreover, the first and innovating company will have to share the market with an increasing number of competitors.

(2) Implications in International Marketing. The concept of product life cycle call be extended to the international marketing also. A firm tends to produce what is needed by the consumers. If the company is popular with the domestic consumers, the products manufactured by it may soon become popular and will satisfy the felt need of the domestic consumers. When a new product is first commercially exploited, it will enjoy a monopoly in the domestic market. If the demand for the product can be created in overseas markets, it will also enjoy the same monopoly power in overseas market but only for a time being. Initially, sales in the foreign markets may not be high. Gradually the market for the product will grow substantially and the company will earn high profits. Gradually over time, the demand for the product reaches at a high level, local firms will start manufacturing. It may compete with the exporting company as it will have to pay customs and other duties and to bear the transportation charges from the exporting to importing country. As the demand increases further the local companies will expand their level of production and will soon enjoy the same level of economies as the exporting company is enjoying. In addition if such firm has an edge over the exporting company in relation to some other elements of costs such as low labour costs etc., they may soon be able to compete in the third countries or even in that country itself where the domestic operations of the innovating company are based. Therefore, a product starling with a monopoly advantage may end up where it is replaced with imports from a foreign country. For example, U.S.A. once used to export large number of bicycles, now it is one of the largest importers because of labour cost economies in the importing countries.

One more important implication of product life cycle in the international marketing is that one can discern different life cycle patterns in different parts of the world because firms do not look to overseas markets unless their sales and profits show a downward trend in the domestic market. In other words, firms jump to international markets only when the competitive structure of the local market hits them 'below the belt'. It means when one product is in the maturity or declining stage in the local market it may be in the innovation of market development (Ist Stage) stage in country A and in the growth stage in country B.

Companies Product Planning and Product Life Cycle

International prcduct life cycle has important implications for a company's product planning. At the outset, the analysis shows the product lines where the established manufacturers have loosened their hold, *i.e.*, they are in third or in fourth stage due to the pressure of international competition. The stage in which the product is placed is, therefore, indicative of the extent of competition that might be expected. The product life cycle will show whether the market is expanding or declining and therefore may help in determining the time for export production.

The pricing policy of a firm as an element of marketing mix should also be determined taking into account the product life cycle. Finally, the product life cycle plays an important role in developing new end, uses of the product through research and development. Jute industry in India is a glaring example of such development. The industry in India is in a declining stage and, the only way to accelerate it is to innovate new products and new end-uses. The addition of new end-uses has revived the industry to a great extent. New developments such as developing packaging materials, decorative articles and materials for specialised end-uses are taking place in the industry.

Thus companies plan it product taking into account the stages of life cycle of the product of other competitors and its own. Various policies are also subject to review of the life cycle of the product such as price policy, production policy, advertising and distribution policy, transportation policy etc. It should also be borne in mind that a product only successfully developed and launched, has no guarantee that it would always be successful and profitable unless steps are taken to review periodically and upgrade the product itself and its presentation. What is important is the continuous innovation and development and keep the pro. duct alive.

MARKING AND LABELLING

Marking and labelling means stencilling those words and letters which are to be used for consignment. Generally importer gives his initials as shipping marks. Other informations which generally find place on the package are point of despatch, port of destination, order number and case or box number, weight or measurement of the package. Gross weight and net weight should be shown separately. The shipping marks shown on the consignment for export on each bundle or box at the outer space, so that they may be seen even from a distance. In case, there is no instructions from the importer, exporter can use his own shipping marks.

It is also usual to have, as a part of marking, a simple design such as a circle, a diamond, a square, a triangle, a star of any other pattern which can be easily reproduced by stencilling. There must be some identical marking on the packages related to one buyer so that they can, be identified easily at the time when the buyer takes delivery. Following are some examples of marking and labelling:

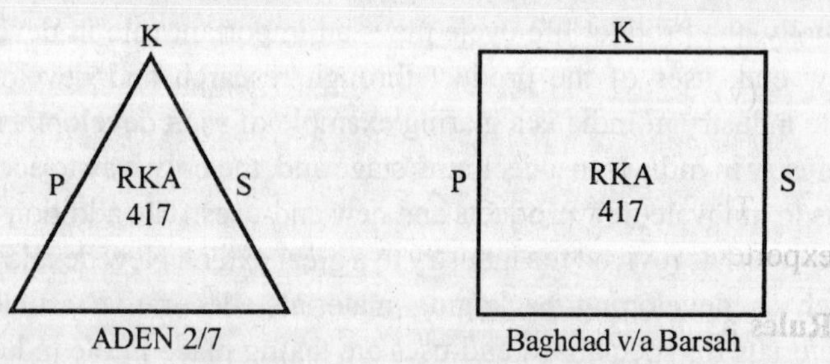

Inside the pattern will be one, two or three latters (probably the customer's initials) and underneath these letters the buyer's order number. On the top or at the sides outside the pattern, there may be two or three other letters, representing the exporter's initials. Below the pattern will be the name of the destination port at which the buyer will take the delivery. If the goods are to be transhipped in route, the name of the final port of destination will be followed by the words, '*via....*'.

The transhipment port should be filled in the banks space. Some shipping companies demand that the cases should be marked with bands of different colours for different ports so that these cases may be easily identified by illiterate workers at the time of unloadmg them.

Why Marking or Labelling

Marking or Labelling on the packages are necessary because of the following reasons:

(i) Case marking facilitates identification of packages by the buyer at the time of delivery at the destination port.

(ii) Shipping companies generally insist on such markings.

(iii) It avoids mix of goods with similar consignments at the time of loading and unloading by the illiterate porters at different ports in route to distination.

(iv) There are some legal provisions of the customs authorities regarding marking in India and importing countries which are to be fulfilled in order to avoid heavy penalties. Weights and measures, contents and country of origin should be painted on the package legibly. Custom regulations of foreign countries must he strictly enforced.

(v) The contents of the package may be known without removing the outer packing case and unpacking the goods.

Thus marking on cases or packages meant for shipment aids the exporters, importers, shipping companies and the custom authorities.

Rules as to Marking and Labelling

The international cargo handing coordination association has following recommendations for the marking of goods carried by sea-going vessels:

(i) The marks should appear in a certain order. Essential data should be placed in oblong frames with lines 1.5 centimetres thick and subsidiary information should be placed in another type of frame.

(ii) Declarations on large package should be placed on a two contiguous sides and for consignments bound together on a pallet, also on the top. Handling instructions should be given on all the four sides. Smaller packages, such as goods in sacks, should be marked on two opposite sides.

(iii) Only fast dyes should be used for lettering. Essential data should be in black and subsidiary data in a less conspicuous colour. Red and orange lettering should be reserved for dangerous goods only. For foods packed in sacks, only harmless dyes should be used so that they cannot affect the goods inside.

(iv) Letter should be at least 7.5 centimetres high for essential data and 3.5 centimetres for subsidiary data. If the package is too small, letters may be given in the same proportion.

(v) Stick on labels should only be used on individual packages or parcels and all old labels and marks should be removed.

(vi) The surface to be marked should be smooth and clean.

(vii) Markings should be made by stencil or by branding or by pencil or brush without stencil but it should be legible to prevent confusion.

(viii) The figures should indicate the total number of packages making up the consignments and the consecutive number of the individual package.

Thus these recommendations should be taken into account while marking the packages for shipment.

Requirements of Interested Parties for Marking

Marking and labelling starts as soon as the shipment has been properly packed to meet the reguirements of three interested parties: *(a)* Consignee, who may be either an importer, or his representative, or his customer; *(b)* Shipping agencies; and *(c)* Customs officers. The requirements of these parties regarding marking and labelling are as under:

(a) Consignee's or Importer's Requirements. For the purpose of aiding the importer and his agents in handling in accordance with the best commercial practices, a scientific marking policy should be adopted. The additional marks on each package, other than those for transportation and customs purposes are aimed at: *(i)* enabling the particular shipment to be readily recognised and singled out from the many others arriving at a busy dock; *(ii)* knowing the contents of the package without unpacking the goods; *(iii)* facilitating, forwarding and distribution.

(b) Shipping Agency's Requirements. A shipping company will not accept the cargo, offered to it for shipment unless it is legibly marked and all old symbols and markings are effaced completely. The markings should denote a symbol or pattern port of destination etc. clearly. Marking may be stencilled or printed in any other method which may be durable and legible.

(c) Customs Requirements. The customs regulations of foreign countries, if any, pertaining to the labelling of various kinds of imported goods must be detailed, definite and strictly be enforced. Generally, the customs regulations require that the packages must bear the gross and net weights of the packages for duty purposes, and the country of origin, on the outside. Markings, of course, must not injure the merchandise. When marking or labelling is required, the words must appear in a conspicuous place and be of permanent nature. Heavy fines have been provided for the violation of such provisions and if the violation is suspected to be fraudulent, the fines and penalties are much heavier, customs regulations of foreign countries are also frequently strict in so far as the labelling of individual package is concerned.

Thus, marking and labelling should be in such a way that it fulfils the requirements of all the three interested parties, *i.e.*, importer, customs anthorities and the shipping company. It is in the interest of exporters and the shipping company. It is in the interest of exporters as well because he can avoid any unnecessary hardship, delay and expense by observing the necessary requirement.

PRODUCT PACKAGING

Packaging may be an art or science concerned with the development and use of materials, methods and equipments for applying a product to a container or *vice versa* designed to protect throughout the various stages of distribution. Thus a package is a container or a wrapper of a product in which it is wrapped of packed so that it may safely reach the consumers without losing its utility.

The terms 'Packaging' and 'Packing' are generally being used interchangeably. Traditionally 'Packaging' refers to the unit of retail or consumer container and 'Packing' to transport container. Consumer packaging has import marketing implications while transport containers are more important from logistics point of view.

A good package is the representation of the artistic combination of the designer's creative skill and the product, marketing and sales knowledge of the manufacturer's management team. The development of packaging is the sum total of the talents of the designer, the researcher, the techincian, the advertising man, the marketing expert, the sales department and the top management. William J. Stauton has defined the term as "Packaging may be defined as the general group of activities in product planning which involves designing and producing the container or wrapper for a product". Thus packaging is a brand activity that requirer careful consideration by the management. It includes activitiess for the development of container or wrapper.

Important Aspects of Packaging

In developing the marketing plan for a product, in international market, packaging is an important element. Packaging should be viewed from its promotional and protectional aspects.

(1) Promotional aspect of Packaging. Packaging of a product plays an importart role in promoting the product in the international markets. With the advent of self-service starts and super markets, the package of a product serves as a 'silent sales man'. It is capable of performing many of the salesman's tasks. When there is no salesman to promote the product in the stores, the package as kept on the shelf must attract the attention of the consumer, describe the product's and producer's features, project the confidence and make a favourable overall impression. Good packaging thus leads to improved consumer acceptance because it carries and projects various qualities of the product as well as the manufacturer.

Good packaging must reinforce the integrated marketing concept. Brand names occupy a dominant role in marketing which is popularised through advertisement. But the reminding of brand names and making brands acceptable to customers are achieved through proper packaging. Packaging must, therefore, support and reinforce the brand identity the company is trying to build. In this way, good packaging creates demand for the product and brings large-scale production and distribution gains.

(2) Protectional Aspect of Packaging. The second important aspect of packaging is its protectional aspect which it provides to the product, cosumer packaging intends to offer better convenience to consumers in use and in storage. It protects the product from:

(a) Pilferage and adulteration. It cannot be adulterated with any other product unless repacked.

(b) Product loss. Oil, petroleum products etc. are lost if remain exposed.

(c) Contamination by dirt or dust, *e.g.*, clothing, food products.

(d) Moisture gain or loss, *e.g.*, cement or sugar,

(e) Chemical change.

(f) Insect attack, *e.g.*, moth in woollen garments.

It has been estimated that good packaging increases the unit value realisation approximately three times if we are able to develop and bring about retail packs for a large number of exportable items. It also increases the popularity of the product.

(3) Transport Packaging Protection during Transit. The basic function of transport packaging in international marketing is to ensure that the goods will reach safely in the hands of consumers. To ensure the goods is no excuse for not bothering for damages or pilferage in transit. Good packaging is essential irrespective of the fact whether the goods are insured or not. Improvements in packaging are needed to avoid transit losses due to environmental hazards, *i.e.*, climate, moisture, etc. and to achieve greater speed in handling and deliveries. The materials used in packaging should be such that protect the goods from the ill-effects of moisture, gas, light, air, etc. so that goods may preserve its attributes, shape, weight, stability, fragility, rigidity, surface finish and durability etc. Thus packaging plays an important role in the storage, preservation, protection and distribution.

The type of packaging which ensures that the goods will be delivered in a good condition to the foreign buyer will vary depending upon the various factors such as *(a)* the product, *(b)* the poor of destination, *(c)* the length of the journey. *(d)* the climate of the place of delivery and place of destination, *(e)* eat and measure to which the goods are subjected during the voyage, *(f)* the loss of the importing and exporting countries regarding packaging of goods, *(g)* mode of handling the goods etc. In many cases, the packaging conditions are specified in the contract itself and therefore the exporter should not be bothered about. He must adhere to the conditions laid down in the contract. Even when the importer has not laid down any condition as to packaging, it is the prime duty of the export to provide transport packaging of the type which may ensure the safe arrival of the shipment in merchandise condition and must adhere to the above factors.

(4) Legal Provisions. The mandatory provisions as to packaging of the goods imported also have important bearing on the packaging of goods. Most developed countries have enacted comprehensive legislation on the type of containers, both bulk and consumer especially for food items. For example, exports of food products to the USA must conform in all respects to the provisions of the U.S. Foods and Drugs Act. Similarly, Australia bans the imports of any packing material containing vegetable matter in order to check insect contamination of the country's wood resources Large consignments of Indian goods were repacked at the Australian Port of entry at the exporters' cost. In 1978, the USA directed that all Indian export consignments in wooden packings be first fumigated before they are unloaded at U.S. ports.

The laws of the importing countries may also specify the labelling requirements to be shown on the packages imported. However, these rules may vary from country to country. These rules require the following information to be shown in the label:

(i) name and address of the manufacturer/importer;

(ii) clear description of the product's composition;

(iii) net weight or volumetric measurement;

(iv) duration of the product's life;

(v) storage conditions required after the package has been opened ;

(vi) manufacturer's instructions for use or preparation, if any.

Factors to be considered for Package Designing

In packaging, designing is the most important element to be considered. In designing a package, the following factors should be considered:

(1) Language. The language in which the package is printed should he the local one so that its contents call easily be read and understood by the consumers of the target market. If it is not so, the objective of package is itself lost and it will not perform the promotional function what is expected from it.

(2) Package Size. The size of the package should be determined only on finding out the buying characteristics of the buyers. Size and frequency of consumption, storing capacity of consumers and the nature of product would be the probable factors to decide the buying characteristics. If the buyers shop the product regularly or they do not possess storing capacity such as freezers etc., the size of packages will have to be smaller.

(3) Container. Some markets, especially developed countries, generally prefer disposable containers. Especially recently because of preoccupation regarding environmental pollution, the regulatory agencies sometimes insist that containers should be made of materials which will not have undesirable environmental effects. In the developing countries, however, reusable containers are preferred because of their storing utilities.

(4) Colour. Consumers may have colour preferences but they vary from country to country. The packagers must know about the preferred colour while designing the package. For example, green is supposed to be favoured colour in Islamic countries. Greeks like both white and blue but these are considered to be colours of mourning and sorrow in the Far East.

(5) Climate. Climatic conditions also affect the type of packaging. A country with a hot humid climate will have a different type of packaging, especially for eatables and perishable items, than what is required in a country having cold climate. The package must be made of materials which may protect the contents from the climate of the importing country.

(6) Length of Distribution Channel. Length of distribution channel, *i.e.*. time taken between production and final consumption has an important bearing on deciding upon the packaging. The longer is the time, the greater is the necessity of providing better and stronger packaging.

(7) Accepted Norms. If the buyers in a specific foreign market are accustomed to purchase the product in a specific form or shape, it will be better to pack the product only in that form or shape because it will be readily acceptable. The exporter may feel difficulty in selling out the product if he changes the shape or form of packaging. For example if people in a market prefer shaving cream in tube, it will not be easier for an exporter to sell the product in jars.

The above factors may require different packaging in different markets. But, like adaptation, the management should first explore the possibilities of the same packciging in different markets, essentially to save the costs. Only when it becomes absolutely necessary to differentiate, it should be resorted to.

❒

9

Pricing and Distribution Strategy for Export

Pricing decisions plays a significant role in the marketing of any product in the export market. Unfortunately, no simple mathematical formula is available for an international marketer in arriving at the right pricing decision. No doubt, as in the domestic market, the interaction of market forces like demand and supply affect the price at which the product can be sold. Besides, developing countries like ours are eager to improve their share of the total international trade. However, most of the products manufactured by them especially in the non-traditional category, do not have the sophistication of those manufactured in developed countries in technical specifications and range. The most attractive feature of the products of developing countries is the competitive nature of their prices *vis-a-vis* the prices of similar products manufactured by the advanced countries. It is in this context that pricing policies have more relevance in international marketing than in the domestic market.

The manufacturing cost of a product plays an important role in determining its final selling price in the export market. After all, a company or a corporation is in business to earn a reasonable profit, and therefore would, as far as possible, endeavour to recover at least the costs incurred by it in manufacturing and marketing its product. It is possible that, under certain circumstances, business organisations may decide to sell their products at price lower than the cost prices. But they would do so with the definite objective of gaining a foothold in a new market, or of sustaining their own market participation for a short while till prices pick up.

Pricing is a very critical decision in international marketing management because it is a major factor influencing a firm's total revenue from exports and its profitability. There is no science mathematical formula or a hard and fast rule that can be applied in pricing a product correctly. No doubt, as in the domestic market, the interaction of market force like demand and supply affect the price at which the product can be sold in the international market. Besides, several other factors economic, social, political marketing conditions, product attributes—influence the decision especially in international marketing.

Objectives of Export Pricing

The various pricing objectives are as follows:

(i) Survival. An exporter faces competition not only from his fellow exporters but also from other countries exporters. In such competitive markets, one of the marketing tools which can make the exporter survive in the competition is pricing. Making price competitive, thereby earning less profit in order to survive, could be one of the objectives of pricing. Keeping prices competitive and maintaining low prices is a short-term objective, as every exporter aims at increasing profits at a later stage.

(ii) Maximum Sales Growth. As an exporter survives the competition, the objective shifts to having maximum sales growth. Depending upon competition and sensitivity of market to price, the final pricing decision needs to be taken. There are two alternatives available for this purpose.

(a) Setting lower prices to overseas buyers leads to higher sales volume, thereby earning more profits. For this purpose, market should be highly price sensitive. Such low prices discourage competition thereby further increasing sales.

(b) Setting higher prices to indicate superior quality of the product. Such indication leads consumers to rate products higher compared to that of competitors. Due to this perception, sales volume of the product increases.

(iii) Maximum Current Profit. An exporter may determine his objective of securing maximum profits. A price which would generate such a profit is to be established. For this purpose it is necessary to have complete information of cost and demand. A price which can generate maximum cash flows or a higher rate of return is determined. But this objective is more of a short term nature and bases its performance on profits which may turnout to be dangerous in export markets.

(iv) To Establish Leadership. Another objective behind pricing is to establish not only a superior quality image but also emphasise on leadership or number one position in the export markets. By charging a higher price and making a noticeable difference in the price as compared to that of competitors this objective can be fulfilled.

Importance of Export Pricing

Price is one of the important elements in marketing mix. Pricing is the most important and delicate area of export marketing. It is rightly treated as an important factor in successful export strategy. The importance of export pricing is as listed below:

(a) Consumers are extremely sensitive about quality and price. If price is not set properly, success of the firm comes in danger.

(b) The volume of sale and market demand depends on pricing policy.

(c) Competitive capacity in foreign market depends on the price fixed.

(d) It decides the success and failure of export efforts.

(e) One of the important components in marketing mix.

(f) Helps in capturing foreign market.

(g) Builds goodwill in the market.

(h) Enables to achieve objectives of the firm.

(i) Develops brand image and product differentiation.

(k) Increases/affects profitability of the firm.

(l) Pricing helps in penetration of market by keeping them low initially and gradually raising them.

(m) Sometimes price becomes a promotional tool which can be emphasised on promotional campaign of the exporter.

(n) Pricing not only helps in increasing profit and raising revenue but also in enhancing market share of that product.

(p) Pricing helps by having good profitability to undertake diversification, research and development, etc.

PRICE AND NON-PRICE FACTORS

In an international market, prices are fixed taking into account price factors and non-price factors.

PRICE FACTORS IN PRICING DECISIONS

Pricing is like a tripod. Costs, demand and competition are its three factors. It is not possible to say that one or another of these factors determines price. The significance of these factors in pricing is as follows:

(1) Role of Costs

It is a popular fallacy to believe that price depends upon costs. However, it is true that the price cannot be fixed below cost for long. Costs determine the floor price below which an exporter may not agree to sell the goods. But while an increase in costs may justify the increase in prices yet it may not be possible to do so because of the marketing conditions of demand and supply. On the contrary it is possible that any increase in demand may lead to an increase in price without an increase in costs.

(a) **Cost-Price Relationship.** The cost-price relationship does not support the claim that costs determine the price. Some times the prevalent price may determine the cost that may be increased. The manufacturer exporter cuts the costs according to the prices current in the market. The product is tailored according to the needs of the target consumers and their capacity to pay for it. Hence declining costs often result in better quality at the same price and raising costs lead to deterioration in quality.

(b) **Difference in Costs of Producers.** The costs do not determine the price because costs of each producer differ substantially due to different internal and external factors while the prices of their products are close to one another. The price must also vary substantially. A firm would suffer a loss if costs are to determine the price.

(ii) Demand

(a) **Adaptation.** Another leg of the tripod demand determines the prices in the international markets. Demand in international markets is also affected by a number of factors which are different from those operating in domestic market. Customs and tastes of foreign customers may differ widely which the product must be adopted to the needs of the foreign customers. Then higher price may be fixed for the product as compared to competitors. In this way demand of the product depends upon how the product has been adopted by the supplier.

(b) **Elasticity.** If the demand of the product is elastic, a reduction in price may increase the sales volume. On the other hand, higher price may be fixed if the demand is inelastic and the supply is limited.

(iii) Competition

Competition in the target foreign market increases the elasticity of demand as it would have been otherwise. Sometimes may be so severe that the exporter has no other option except to follow the market leader.

(a) **Brand Type Competition.** Competition may be either brand type or functional type. Brand type refers to competition amongst brands of a product which aim at satisfying the same need.

(b) Functional Competition. It means the type of competition where the manufacturer tries to differentiate the function of the product from its competitors. This he may do either by altering its packages or by adding attributes to the product. Both these types of competition have pressure on the company's pricing decisions.

(c) Discouraging Competition. Sometimes a company determines a price of the product with a specific objective of discouraging competitors from entering a given foreign market.

NON-PRICE FACTORS IN PRICING DECISIONS

Following non-pricing factors play important roles in creating demand in foreign countries:

(1) Confidence. Sometimes the importers of developed countries do not have much confidence in the quality of products manufactured in developing countries. Thus Indians and exporters of other developing countries find their products at a lower price than that of their competitors. Though the quality was comparable Indians had to sell their storage batteries 10 per cent lower in Saudi Arabia than U.S. and European batteries. Thus fixing lower price is inevitable to make our product acceptable in foreign markets.

(2) Brand Image. If products are well-differentiated and have a brand image in the minds of foreign customers, their manufacturers may charge higher prices for their products. Brand names like Bata, GKW, Dunlop, HMT, Lucas, etc., which have already earned a good brand image are able to sell their products at higher price.

(3) Frequency of Purchase. If consumers purchase the goods very often as in the case of non-durable consumer items, they think of the price. On the other hand price is not important if the item is durable consumer item, products having snob value or gift item. If a particular product appeals, the people are willing to pay very high price. Thus durable consumer items, artistic items or gift items are sold at much higher prices.

(4) Close Association of Price and Quality. There is a close association between the price and the quality of the product. It is generally believed that lower priced goods do not carry adequate value while the higher priced goods carry a much greater conviction about quality. In periods of inflationary price rise, a reduction in price may lead to a reduction in demand because it has an adverse reaction on the consumers. Unless there are chances to increase sales by reducing the price, reduction in prices or fixing a low price for the product in comparison to others is not regarded a good strategy.

(5) Comprehensive Knowledge of the Product. In industrial goods, the importer has a good knowledge of the quality of brands available in the world market. Therefore besides quality, he considers other factors like technical soundness of the product, steady availability at reasonable price and comprehensive after sale service offered by the manufacturer. Price is not the indicator of quality alone. It is a composite of all other related factors.

(6) Before and After Sales Service. Before and after sales services count much more than a lower price in case of valuable industrial and engineering products.

(a) ***Before Sale Service.*** In the case of engineering goods before sale, service covers:

i. Advising the importer about the relative suitability of competing products, and

ii. Demonstrating the use of his product.

(b) ***After sale Service.*** After sale service in case of sale of engineering goods and durable consumer goods includes:

i. Rectification genuine technical fault in the product,

ii. Educating the users on the proper use of the product and providing training for its proper maintenance,

iii. Free service during warranty period, and

iv. Ensuring supply of spare parts and components after the warranty period.

Price may be fixed comparatively higher if these services are under taken by the exporter in the foreign markets.

(7) Continuity of Supply. In foreign trade if regular supplies of the product or ancillary products are not maintained, the country may lose the markets. Developing countries substitute for a number of exporter products due to their failure to maintain regular supplies. However an uninterrupted supply of the product may assure better prices.

(8) Prompt Deliveries. Prompt deliveries attract the foreign buyers to pay more. Most of the developing countries fail on this point. Delayed deliveries have affected India's exports to Sri Lanka, Burma and Arab countries. While foreign importers want deliveries within three months from the date of order, Indian exporters of machine tools do not deliver the goods before 6 months. Studies made about generalised system of preferences reveal that the reliability of product quality and delivery dates are more important factors than price.

(9) Supply of Complete Range of Product. Sometime the price of the product depends upon the fact that the producer (exporter) is in a position to supply complete range and in large quantities of the products. Here also, Indian exporters fail to come up to expectations. In developing countries, the exporters do not supply the products in huge quantities because of lack of resources. One manufacturer in developing countries does not manufacture the complete range of products but produces only one or two items of the range. For example, cycle manufacturers in India do not produce a complete cycle but only its components.

(10) Settlement of Claims. The exporter and importer are not close to each other in foreign trade. Often they even do not know each other. The importer does not hesitate to pay higher price if there is an arrangement between them for prompt acceptance and settlement of claims.

(11) Terms of Credit. In exports of capital goods such as machinery and equipment, availability of finance and terms of credit are the determining factors. Developed countries dominate in this respect. They supply goods on credit while exporters from developing countries, including India, can not do so because of their limited resources. In India, the Export Import Bank of India offer such credit to importers and the ECGC also offer guarantee cover for the credit given to importers.

Thus there are a number of non-price factors which help to maintain the differential prices in the international markets. However, their influence varies from product to product and market to market. The price factors, such as cost, demand and competition affect the prices and play important though limited roles in determining the price strategy. Taking advantage of these non-price factors would also involve some costs though the returns are likely to cost be higher than costs if proper efforts are made. Thus, in comparison to cost factors non-price factors are more influential in pricing.

METHODS OF COSTING

There are various methods of costing in exports. Main methods are:

(i) Job or Batch Costing. This method is adopted, in a factory undertaking a large number of jobs according to customer specifications. Each individual job or batch of jobs is taken separately for costing purposes. It may be a large job or a small job; an individual order or a number of small orders treated as a batch. It may even be a stock order for stock replenishments for one's own use. In each case, a cost account is opened for the particular job or batch and all the appropriate expenditure is charged to it. The actual time spent by workers on the job, as recorded on time sheets, or job cards, indicates the direct labour element of the job. Direct materials are taken into cost as per the priced requisitions from the stores; which parts brought from sub-contractors and any work subscontracted, are directly allocated as a simple percentage of the labour cost or time, as a machine-hour rate, as a percentage of the material cost or according to some other appropriate method, devised by each unit, considering investment in plant and machinery, etc.

(2) Process Costing. Process costing is normally applied in any industry or a factory, where the final product has passed through several distinct stages of manufacture (processes). It is common in industries such as textile manufacturing units in which the basic raw materials like wool, cotton, asbestos, and man made fabrics undergo such processes as according, dyeing, spinning and waving before emerging as the finished product; or in continuous industries, *e.g.*, the manufacture of gas, chemicals, glass and paper industries. In process costing, it is customary to ascertain the cost of operating each process to which all expenditure incurred is charged. When the process or a particular operation which is complete, the partially completed product passes to a process cost account, from which it is requisitioned for the next process; or it becomes the raw material of the next processes, and is then charged to that process account. Three special problems arise from process costing. Firstly, in the manufacture of main product, certain by-products may be unavoidably obtained. Secondly, wastage is inevitable but it should be kept as near as possible to the theoretical minimum, and Thirdly, the main product of the one firm may be the by-product of another firm that may be available be in the open market, at a lower price than the cost of producing it in one's own factory.

(3) Standard Costing. Standard costing is a method by which actual costs are compared with targeted or estimated costs. Standard costs have been defined as the value of work which it is estimated, should be provided in a given period of time. It provides a method of analysing the deviations from the forecast and measures the costs of these deviations in terms of money. It is genetally applied in repetitive industries where a large range of products are produced with relatively few operations. It is also applicable to jobs or batch productions, which are based on standard processes or standard operations, for which standard operation times, etc. can be pre-set.

METHODS OF PRICING

The export price structure, like the domestic price structure, begins on the factory floor. But there is no similarity in the costs included in the two strictures. The pricing of the products for domestic and export purposes shall be calculated in a somewhat different manner. The export price structure is the basis of all export price quotations, discount and commissions. There are various methods of pricing the product in the foreign markets. The methods may be grouped into two *i.e.*, cost oriented export pricing methods and market-oriented export pricing methods.

The pricing of the products for domestic and for the markets abroad is calculated in a somewhat different way. The price structure for export is the basis of all export price quotations, discount and commissions. The various methods of pricing the product in the foreign markets are grouped into following two methods:

(i) Cost oriented export pricing methods,

(ii) Market oriented export pricing methods.

These are being explained below:

COST-ORIENTED EXPORT PRICING METHODS

These are based on costs incurred in the production of the articles. As total costs include fixed costs and variable costs, export pricing may be based on full cost (fixed and variable) or only on variable costs. A reasonable profit will be added to the base cost to arrive at the export pricing. Thus cost-oriented export pricing methods may be:

(i) Full cost or total cost method, and

(ii) Variable cost or marginal cost method.

I. Full Cost or Total cost Method

This method is also known as cost-plus method and it is the most common method. Under this method for arriving at the export pricing, the total cost of production of the article is considered. In addition to the fixed and variable costs incurred in the production of the item, all direct and indirect expenses needed for the export of the product including cost on transportation, freight, customs duties, risk. To this a reasonable profit allowance is added to the cost. From this amount the value of all assistance received from any source is deducted. Given below are the various elements of the total cost:

(i) Direct Cost. It includes variable and other costs directly related to exports:

(a) ***Variable Costs.*** It includes expenditure on Direct materials, direct labour, variable production overheads, variable administrative overheads.

(b) ***Other Costs Directly Related to Exports.*** These are in addition to the variable costs. This include:

Selling costs advertising support to importers in the foreign market. Costs on Special packing, labelling, Commission to overseas agent, Export credit insurance, Bank charges, Inland freight, Forward charges, Inland insurance, Port charges, Duties on Exports of the product, expenditure on Warehousing at port, Documentation and incidental, expenditure therein, Interest on funds involved or cost of deferred credit Cost of after sale service, including free supply of spare parts, consular fees. Preshipment inspection and loss due to rejection of product.

(ii) Fixed Costs. It includes overheads on production and Administration Publicity and advertising, Travel abroad, After sale service. From this amount following are deducted:

(a) Compensatory assistance,

(b) Duty drawback,

(c) Import replenishment benefits,

(d) Expenditure on Freight and Insurance.

Merits of this Approach

(a) Its main advantage is that through this method exporter becomes aware of the full cost in marketing the product in a market abroad.

(b) It is a very simple method.

Disadvantages

When smaller number of units are to be exported it would be difficult for the exporter to supply the product at the same price because of its high cost of production per unit due to fixed costs. This method is justified only when the cost of information about demand and the administrative cost of applying a demand based pricing policy exceed the profit contribution arrived at by when this approach is applied.

II. Marginal Cost Pricing

In this method the price is determined on the basis of variable cost or direct cost, while fixed cost element in the total cost of production is totally ignored. The firm is concerned here only with the marginal incremental cost of producing the goods which are sold in foreign markets. Now, the fixed cost remains fixed up to a certain level of output irrespective of the volume of output. On the other hand, variable costs vary in proportion to the volume of production. Thus, the variable or direct or marginal costs set the price after output at break-even point (BEP).

This method is based on the following assumptions:

(i) The export sales are bonus sales and any return over the variable costs contributes to the net profit.

(ii) The firm has been producing the goods for home consumption and the fixed costs have already been meet or in other words, breakeven point has been achieved. Thus, if the manufacturers are able to realise the direct costs, including those involved in export operations specifically, they would not affect the profitability of their firms. However, the profitability of firms should be assessed with reference to marginal cost which should normally constitute the basis for export pricing. Direct costs and other elements in calculating price will remain the same.

Advantages

(i) No Overhead Costs. Export sales are additional sales. Hence these should not be burdened with overhead costs which are ordinarily met from the domestic trade.

(ii) Firms from Developing Countries. This approach is advocated for firms from developing countries who are not well-known in foreign markets as compared to their competitors from developed countries. Therefore, lower prices based on variable costs may help them enter a market. Price may be used as a technique for securing market acceptance for products newly introduced into the market.

(iii) Large Market. Since the buyers of products from developing countries are usually in countries with low national income, it is advisable for the firm to serve a large segment of the market at low prices. Low prices may serve to widen and create markets. In such countries price is still the decisive factor and quality is comparatively less important.

Disadvantages of Marginal Cost Pricing

(i) Attracts Anti-Dumping Process. Developing countries might be charged of dumping their products in foreign markets because they would be selling their products below net prices and attract antidumping provisions which take away their competitive advantage.

(ii) Cut-throat Competition. The use of this approach may give rise to cut-throat competition among exporting firms from developing countries resulting in loss in valuable foreign exchange to the exporting countries.

(iii) Marginal Cost Pricing is not Advisable in the Following Cases:

(a) If the importers are regularly purchasing the product at a low price, it will be difficult for exporters to increase the price of the commodities later on. It may lose their market.

(b) This policy is not useful or of limited use to industries which are mainly dependent upon export markets and where over-heads or fixed costs are insignificant.

Circumstances of Feasibility

(i) Large Domestic Market. There must be a large domestic market of the product so that the overheads may be charged from products manufactured for domestic market.

(ii) Higher Prices in Home Market. The home market has a capacity to bear the higher prices.

(iii) Mass Production. Mass production techniques must have been adopted so that the gap between the full and marginal costs may be reduced.

(iv) No Overhead Costs. Additional production for exports is possible without increasing overhead costs and within permissible production capacity.

Market-oriented Export Pricing

Both the above approaches are based on cost considerations only. The costs are, no doubt, important but the competitive prices should also be considered before fixing the export price, competitive prices mean the prices that are charged by the competitions for the same product or for the substitute of the product in the target market. Once this price level is established, the base price, or what the buyer can afford, should be determined.

The base price can be determined by following the three basic steps:

(i) First, relevant demand schedules (quantities to be bought) at various prices should be estimated over the planning period;

(ii) Then, relevant costs (total and incremental) of production and marketing costs should be estimated to achieve the target sales volume as per demand schedules prepared; and

(iii) Lastly, the price that offers the highest profit contribution, *i.e.*, sales revenues minus all fixed and variable costs.

The final determination of base price should be made after considering all other elements of marketing mix within these elements, the nature and length of channel of distribution is the most important factor affecting the final cost of the product. Besides, product adaptation costs should also be considered in fixing the base price.

The above three steps; though appear to be very simple, but it is not so because there are various other factors that should be looked into. The most appropriate method to estimate the demand of the product shall be the judgemental analysis of company and trade executives. One other way may be the extrapolation of demand estimates for target markets from actual sales in identical markets in terms of basic factors.

The following chart gives the nature of analysis for market-oriented export pricing:

Analysis for Market-oriented Export Pricing

Market Price

Less –	Retail Margin on selling price	—
	Cost to the Retailer	—
Less –	Wholesaler's mark up to his cost	—
	Cost of the wholesaler	—
Less –	Importer's mark up to his cost	—
	Cost to the Importer	—

Less –	Import Duty	—
	Landed Price	—
Less –	Freight and insurance charges	—
	f.o.b. realisation of the exporter	—

Having found out what the market can bear, the firm has to determine whether it can sell the product at that price profitably or not by working back from the market price as shown above.

This analysis gives an idea of the upper limit of what the firm can charge. The cost analysis discussed earlier gives the lower limit of what a firm can charge. The price of the product in the foreign market may be then fixed between these two limits,. As the firm gathers experience, it would be able to set the price that gives the highest profitability. However, in many cases, it happens that the market realisation is very low. In such circumstances, the exporter may compare his f.o.b. realisation (under market-oriented export pricing) with the direct cost or full cost as calculated under cost-oriented export pricing. He can then determine whether he should export the goods or not. He can decide to export the goods even at a loss if he thinks that market prospectus are better in future and the loss is only a short-term phenomenon and he feels a better realisation in future.

Whatever be the price determined by the firm for its product, it must consider the prices and non-price factors before taking a final decision.

VARIOUS TYPES OF PRICES QUOTED IN INTERNATIONAL MARKETING

A 'Quotation' also known as "an export offer" is the basis of any exports transaction. The Quotation, may be made in any of the following four ways; in the international market.

(i) A Preform Invoice. A proforma invoice is prepared at request of the importer by the exporter indicating the price, other charges as per terms of contract during shipment. It is to be noted that performa invoice is needed for the importer to obtain the import licence or for the allotment of foreign exchange, and thus it should, be very accurate and clear.

(ii) Public Global Tender. The offer may be made in response to a public global tender advertised by importer. Such offers should cover all the conditions of the tender and listing out the price and other charges as freight, insurance etc. It should also include escalation clause.

(iii) Letter Indicating the Price. An offer can be given in the form of a letter mentioning the price, terms of payment and the delivery period.

(iv) Printed Price List. Where the goods have a standard export price, an offer may by made in this form. The other terms and conditions either may be printed in the price list or may be mentioned in an attached letter.

Base of Export Price Quotation

The terms given by INCOTERMS are about uniform export terms for delivery. These terms are used all over the world, and indicate the followings:

(i) The charge and expenses to be paid by the seller.

(ii) The place of delivery of goods.

(iii) The 'point in time' expressing the transfer of the good and their transit risks.

Export price quotations are made according to the above terms. Following are the most common types of Price Quotations:

(i) Ex-works Quotations. Under this type of quotation, packing costs are borne by the exporter and the delivery is taken from the works or a warehouse of the exporter. Therefore, other expenses and transit risks are borne by the importer. Ex-works price quotations are not commonly used in international marketing. But the products which are heavy and therefore, shipping freight and transportation charges cannot be worked out in advance, this type of quotations are usually accepted.

(ii) F.A.S. (Free Alongside Ship) Price. Under this type of quotations the exporter bears all the expenses upto putting the goods alongside the ship. But the expenses on putting them on the ship is the buyer's responsibility. In cases where shipping companies accept goods on stream for transportation and where goods are moved by barges to side of vessel, this type quotation also includes barge charges. In such cases, the goods and the transit risks are transferred when ship is able to accept load.

(iii) C&F (Cost and Freight) Price. Under this types of quotation, all obligations and expenses incurred in F.O.B. pricing, as well the ocean freight is to paid by the exporter.

(iv) F.O.B. (Free on Board) Price. One of the most common terms used in export pricing, FOB mean that the exporter is responsible for putting the goods on board of the ship. Delivery of goods occurs as soon as the goods are loaded on the ship and there after the goods and the transit risks are transferred when the goods are taken to ship's rail.

(v) C.I.F. (Cost and Insurance and Freight) Price. It implies that all the costs as in C&F case, together with the marine insurance are included in the quotation and therefore are paid by the exporter. In other words it includes F.O.B. price freight insurance charges.

(vi) Franco Price. This type of price quotation includes all costs up to godown or warehouse of the importer. Thus, all the expenses upto the importer's godown abroad are borne by the exporter. In this case property in goods and all risks is transferred when the delivery is made to the importer at his godown.

(vii) Ex-ship Price. This rype of quotation comprises all the costs will the goods reach at the importer's port. And as soon as the goods are off loaded at importers port, the property in goods and all risks are transferred.

So, there are various alternative types of Quotations. The price quoted in any of these ways, will also decide the point where the risks and the property in goods will be transferred.

FACTORS AFFECTING EXPORT PRICE QUOTATIONS

The base price explains the amount and degree of the expenses and the risks to be borne by the exporter. In addition to this there are other conditions which the buyer prefers to be included in the contract to be discharged by the exporter, and these conditions of the contract relating to any export transaction may affect the price calculation of a manufacturer exporter to a great extent. It all becomes more strong when the merchandise is the capital goods involving installation, performance guarantees, supply of spare parts etc. Given below is the implications of such conditions and their effect on price calculation by the exporter:

(i) Exchange Rate Variation. The risk arising out of the rate variations of different currencies is always there. It may bring a sharp decline in the payments for export in terms of rupees. There are following three possible ways to set rid off this risk:

(a) It can be done through quoting the prices in Indian rupees, because if it is done so, the realisation to the exporter will in no way, be affected by the variations in exchange rate.

(b) But in case the buyer insists on quoting the price in his country's currency then the problem can be solved by adding a clause to the effect that the quotation is based on present exchange parity and any change thereafter will be on importers, account.

(c) By taking a forward exchange cover with the ECGC to cover the risk the problem can be solved. But this method attracts an extra expenditure.

(ii) Packing of Consignment for Export. Packing of the goods for exports is the responsibility of the exporter to ensure that it protects the goods in transit against all kinds of perils during the shipment. It is also a practice that importer specify the packing requirements either "as an element of marketing mix or under the law of the country". Thus, in order to avoid any problem the exporter must provide adequate packing to protect the goods during voyage and where over necessary it should be done as per specifications of the buyer. In both the cases, the required cost of packing should be included in the export price quotations.

(iii) Guarantees. The exporter extends guarantee warrantee to the buyers and inserts a guarantee clause in the export contract. It is generally adopted as a comitment of marketing strategy . . durable consumer goods. The importer may require rigid guarantee/warrantee provisions it may exert upon the exporter as extra costs.

(iv) Spare Parts. A contract relating to export of machinery and equipment or capital goods, there is a provision for supply of spare parts which requires special consideration particularly when there is a big supply. The common practice adopted in such cases are to 'under change' on the main equipment and 'overload' on the supply of spare parts. The practicability of this technique depends upon the market conditions as well as the technical characteristics of the item. In case long-term supply of spare parts is to be done following two points must be considered in addition to the above :

(a) For the price to be charged for spare parts, some criterian should be arrived at, in consultation with the buyer. In this regard the supply at current market price may be considered as one of the reasonable solutions to this problem.

(b) Expected costs of manufacturing as well as keeping the inventory of spare parts must be continuously estimated before forwarding the quotation.

(v) Price Variation Formula. In the cases of long term supply contracts or project exports, since the total time taken between the offer and the execution of the contract is fairly long, and during this period there may be an escalation of price. It is not easy to estimate the escalation at the time of making a contract. At the same time a conservative estimate may cause rise in the prices so much that hardly any chance of winning the contract. To solve these problems, it is advisable to the exporter to insist on inclusion of an escalation clause in the contract according to the formula agreed upon between the two parties. But this problem does not end here; because the importer may be unwilling to accept the price escalation clause and stress up on a fixed price through out the contract. In case the formula is agreed upon, precaution should be taken to define following three points as clearly as possible :

(a) The cost elements to be comprised under the formula ;

(b) Extent of increase in cost above which the formula will apply;

(c) The documents to be submitted for proving the claim about change in costs.

The formula states, in general, that the buyer will not share the burden due to change in the fixed cost elements nor he be told to contribute more towards more profitability of the seller. This can be done so when only cost changes on account of labour and raw materials will be shared as per formula agreed between parties.

(vi) Change in Specifications. In addition to the prices escalation formula, the contract must also comprise for additional payment for covering increased cost is to be increased at particular instance of the buyer after the contract has been solemnised. Thus, any change in specification of the item will be at the cost of the buyer. It is essential it the buyer reserves the right of change in specification at a later date. The exporter should, therefore, quote the price subject to change when the importer requests change in the scope and quality of the products contracted for. In such cases the exporter will be duly compensated for the changes required thereafter.

(vii) Penalty/liquidated Damages Provision. Nearly every contract includes such a clause to bind the supplier to the terms of contract. The big contracts, after provide penalty usually on a fixed percentage basis of either the total value of the contract or the part of the contract which remains incomplete is more favourable to the supplier. When the exporter is not fully confident of his capability of satisfying the conditions and contract and can anticipate about the penalty clauses, reasonable provisions if possible should be made in the price quotation prepared by the exporter.

These are the factors which affect the price to be quoted, the exporter should consider them while preparing an export price quotation.

EXPORT PRICING STRATEGY

Export price strategy depends upon three main factors, *viz.*, the characteristics of the product and the nature of its demand, the philosophy of the management and the market characteristics. But it will be useful to keep the following points in view while quoting prices for export markets:

A single set of prices would not suit all markets. There are various reasons which might make prices different for different markets, *viz.*, political influence, buying capacity, financial and import facilities and total market turnover. Therefore, prices will often have to be different for each market in order to make the local price of the product competitive. An example can be provided by the printing of books published in the USA in Asia to be sold at lower price in the developing countries of Asia. Thus margins of profit may vary from market to market. However, there is nothing wrong in making higher margins in some export markets and lower ones in the others provided there is an overall profit in export business. Europeans and Japanese do it more often than Americans.

Factors Affecting Pricing Strategies

(i) Characteristics of the Product and the Nature of its Demand. It is a major factor in fixing the price of the product at a particular time. Improvement in quality of the product and product adaptation according to the changing competitive conditions in the foreign market should be taken as a continuous process. Elasticity of demand also influences the price. If the demand of a product is inelastic, the price reduction will not help increase the revenue. Higher prices may be fixed, taking in view the competitive position in the market. If, the product is highly elastic, the sales revenue can be appreciably increased by slightly reducing the price. Pricing strategy means whether to fix higher price or a lower price as compared to the competitor's prices. It very much depends upon the elasticity of demand and the competitive position.

(ii) The Philosophy of the Management. The philosophy means the objectives of the management in exporting goods. The main objective of the management of every concern is to maximise profits. As there is an adverse relationship between the price and the demand, the management can earn more profit at increased revenue by reducing the price if the demand is more elastic. On the other hand, if the objective of the management is to export a committed value of merchandise, the price may be even lower than the marginal cost. If a new product is introduced in a competitive market, the management, may sell it even below cost. Discounts may be increased or prices may be reduced in order to bar the new entrants in the market. Thus, the strategy of pricing depends upon the philosophy of management.

(iii) Market Characteristics. Market characteristics include the number of competitors, the degree of competition, supply position, quality of the product, substitutes available in the market etc. These also determine the pricing strategy of the firm.

Various Price Strategies

The export price quotations can not be the same for all the markets as prices may differ from market to market due to political influence, buying capacity, financial and import facilities, total market turnover and other pricing and non-pricing factors etc. The profitability may be different in different markets. However, there is nothing wrong in making higher margins in small export markets and lower ones in the others provided there is an overall profit in export business.

Thus, different strategies may be used in different markets. While in some markets, prices may be higher, in others, they may be around the cost price and still others, they may be even less than cost price. The following pricing strategies are used in the export market:

(i) Market Penetration Strategy. Generally the exporter offers a very low introductory price to speed up his sales and, therefore, widens the market base. It aims at capturing the market. This strategy is necessary for establishing one's product in the market, if the quality of the product has to be provide before its wide acceptance.

(ii) Probe Pricing Strategy. Fixing low price for its product may have an adverse effect on the image of the firm and of the product. If it is lower than the price of competitors or it is reduced subsequently, it may raise doubts in the minds of the buyer about the quality of the product.

Sufficiently higher prices may be quoted on the first few offers. When no information is available on the extent of competition or the likely preferences of the buyers, no business is really expected except feedback information. The prices may be adjusted accordingly. This is called probe pricing, *i.e.*, fixing high prices only to probe the export markets.

(iii) Skim-the Cream Pricing Strategy. Under this strategy a very high introductory price is fixed to skim the cream of demand at the very outset. This policy is useful when there is no competition in the market. Such prices continue to be high till the competitors begin to enter the foreign market, after it the exporter reduces the price.

(iv) Follow the Leader Pricing Strategy. In a competitive market or where adequate market information is not available, it may be useful to follow the leader in the market. Comparing its product with that of the leader, the exporter may fix the price of his product. In such cases, the price of the product is lower than that of the leader's product. However, this strategy has no rational or scientific base for fixing the price.

(v) Differential Trade Margins Strategy. Variations in trade margins may be adopted by the exporter as the pricing strategy in the foreign market. This allows following types of discounts on the list price.

(a) ***Quantity Discounts.*** These encourage to procure huge orders. It may be based on the rupee value or on the quantity purchased or the size of packages purchased.

(b) ***Special Discounts.*** These may be allowed while introducing the product. These are given on all purchases.

(c) ***Cash Discount.*** It attracts promp' payments. It ensures quick playback.

(d) ***Seasonal Discount.*** It aims at shifting the storing function in the channel. The approach is 'buy sooner or more'.

(e) ***Trade Discount.*** It is a reduction in list price given to channel members in anticipation of a job they are going to perform.

(vi) Standard Export Pricing Strategy. Sometimes the exporter quotes the standard price or list price, *i.e.*, one price for all, though there may be some margins for negotiations in many markets, especially in underdeveloped countries. In such cases, fixed prices may serve only as starting point for negotiation. It is desirable to keep a certain margin for negotiations. This strategy is generally adopted in case of export of capital equipment, *i.e.*, plant and machinery.

(vii) Cheaper Price for Original Equipments and Higher Price for Spare Parts. In some cases, it might be useful to quote lower prices for the original equipment and higher prices for the spare and replacement parts to be exported later on when required. This strategy is useful where standard spare parts can be supplied only by the supplier of original equipment. It could be used for tractors, telephone equipment and railway equipment.

Different pricing strategies may be adopted in different markets taking into account the level of competition, the marketing characteristic and the philosophy of the management. Profitability cannot be ignored in the long run, exports may be continued in the short run, even below the marginal cost.

DISTRIBUTION LOGISTICS FOR EXPORTS

The route through which goods reach from manufacturer to buyer is called a channel of distributions. According to William J. Staution "A channel of distribution (sometimes called a trade channel) for a product is the route taken by the title to the goods as they move from the producer to the ultimate customer or industrial user." In the opinion of Phillip Kotler "Every producer seeks to link together the set of marketing intermediaries that best fulfil the firm's objectives. This set of marketing intermediaries is called the marketing channel, also trade channel or channel of distribution."

Distribution is the entire function of goods into the hands of consumers. The term channel denotes the middlemen engaged in passing on the goods from the place of production to the place of consumption. Channel is the route through which goods move from the place of production to the place of consumption (chain of middlemen). The channels of distribution are the means employed by manufacturers and sellers to let their products move to the market and into the hands of users. The management decides the channel distribution it wants to employ. A channel of distribution includes the original producer at the one end, the final buyer at the other end, and the middlemen between the two *i.e.*, wholesalers or retailers. The term 'middlemen' refers to those institutions or individuals in the channel which take title to the goods and negotiate and sell the goods a broker or an agent. There are a number of middlemen in the foreign trade. There is a diversity of channels of distribution in the international market. While one particular channel may be used to distribute a specific product in one country, another channel may be used in another country for the same product. Thus, there may be a long channel of distribution in one country and a short channel in another.

MAJOR CHANNELS OF DISTRIBUTION IN EXPORT MARKETS

No uniformity can be traced in the channels that may be employed by the producing units and its structure and composition depends upon the

(i) Nature of product, and

(ii) The producing unit strategy.

The channel may vary even if the product is the same in case the strategy of the producer differs. In general the channel of distribution of a consumer product is longer than that used in an industrial product because of their nature. The channel of distribution of a consumer product is generally longer than that used in an insutrail product.

I. Channel for Consumer Goods

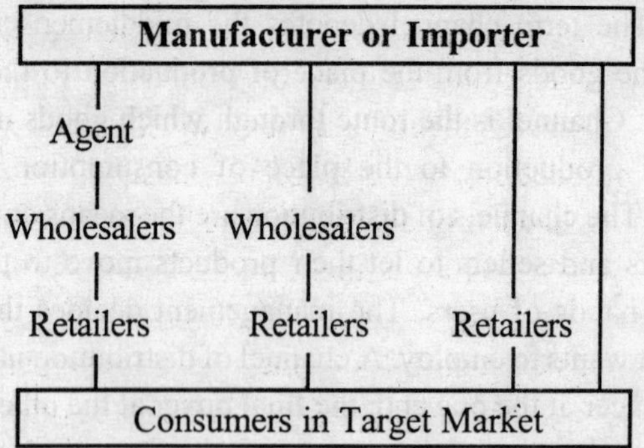

II. Alternative Channel

In target market there are four possible alternative channels avialable:

(i) The Product, May or may not Appoint the Agents for Marketing Consumer Goods. It is up to the producer, he may or may not appoint the agents for marketing consumer goods. Appointing an agent is though essential where the producer cannot invest the money needed in the development of a sales force of his own. In case he decides to appoint agents, he approaches wholesalers and retailers only through agent and the channel in this case becomes.

Manufacturer or Importer → Agent → Wholesalers → Retailers → Consumers.

(ii) Direct Touch with Wholeseller. When agents are not appointed, then the producer gets directly in touch with the wholesalers who deal with the retailers. The channel then becomes:

Producer/Importer → Wholesaler → Retailers → Consumers.

(iii) Direct Contact with Retailers. If the producer/the chief importer establishes his own sales force, he need not appoint wholesalers. He then directly contacts the retailers through his sales own force and thus the channel becomes:

Producer/Chief Importer → Retailers → Consumers.

(iv) Direct Sale to the Consumer. In case when producer directly sells to the consumers; but this method is not advisable to sell consumer goods in foreign markets. However, recently even in foreign markets, selling through post is gaining momentum.

III. Channels of Distribution for Industrial Goods

(i) Direct Sale to Buyers. The items having small number of potential buyers; the producer may sell directly to them. In case the market is large and the users are few, the more proper and better approach is to use his own sales force to contact the consumer.

(ii) Agent-cum Distributer. When the number of buyers is large and the market area is small, or the nature of product requires extensive support system *i.e.*, demonstration in the user's premises, the producer may take the help of agent-cum-distributor or one of the two. The causes for doing so, is that the local dealer is more aware of his country's envirɔnment and customers' needs and not the sales staff of the exporting firm.

Thus, the producer of industrial products may choose alternative channels given in the following figure:

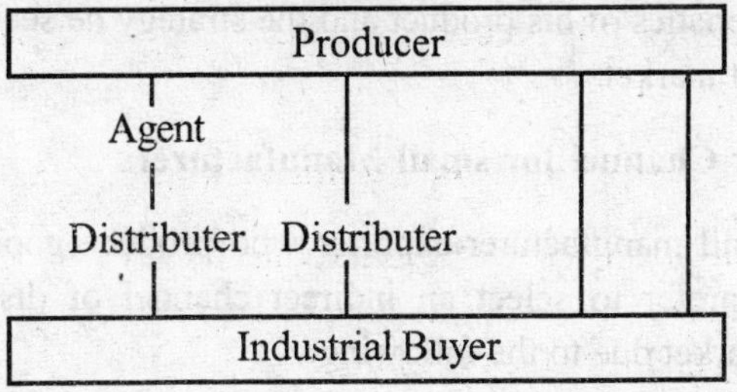

IV. Linking the Domestic and Overseas Channel

Two different aspects are to be considered while planning the export channel:

(i) The marketing channel that is available in the target overseas markets; and

(ii) The most appropriate channel to link the domestic operations to the overseas channels.

The principal forms of penetrating exports markets are selling to local export house or buying organisations for indirect exporting and appointing agent or distributors for direct exporting. If these forms are combined with the domestic channel of distribution in the importing country, the export distribution channel can be identified as follows:

Indirect Exporting

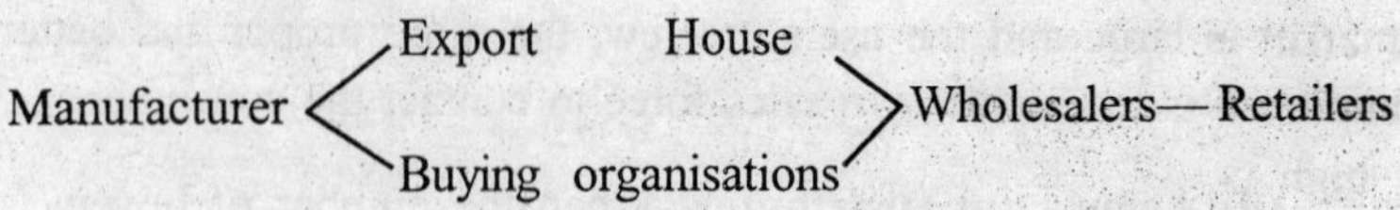

Direct Exporting

The above figure is illustrative of consumer goods. The channel will be shorter in case of industrial products. The first task of the producer exporter is to find out the possible distribution channel through which he may reach the target consumers keeping in view the characteristics of his product and the strategy he seeks to follow in the target market.

V. Indirect Channel for small Manufacturers

A small manufacturer-exporter who produce goods on small scale will prefer to select an indirect channel of distribution in overseas market due to the following:

(i) The Cost Element. As small scale manufacturer cannot establish its own channel in the foreign markets because of its high cost in proportionate to level of production he will sell his exportable surpuls to the agent or export house engaged in the export business and available in domestic market. This will free him from all worries of export trade. He gets necessary feedback information from these agents/export house who also provide many other facilities such as financing their trade.

(ii) Purchase of a Set. Customers of certain range of products generally purchase a set of complementary products rather than one. Therefore, a small manufacturer who produces only one item of the set, cannot sell the product directly in foreign markets. He sells his products to such distributors who deal in a complete line of the product.

(iii) Inability to Compete. In the foreign market a small manufacturer cannot compete against the big manufacturers due to his high cost of production and distribution. The export houses/ agents sell the goods in markets were the demand of such goods in increasing so as to fetch a fair price of the product. A small manufacturer cannot contact the wholesalers or importers in foreign markets. He is not aware of the demand and supply position of different markets where he can sell his product profitably. He therefore does not bother about direct exporting and goes for indirect exporting channel of distribution which is more suitable to him.

FACTORS TO SELECT THE BEST CHANNEL

The best channel decision is one that works best in the marketing strategy selected by the company. The channel should be an ideal one that could meet the customers' needs and preference. In choosing the channel, the producer always have to struggle with what is ideal and what is available. What is available cannot be said ideal or what seems ideal cannot be engaged. There are various factors that put limitations on the ideal choice, hence every producer has to select a channel that is less than ideal. Ideally every company wants to select the lowest cost channel, but the lowest cost channel is not necessarily be the best of the product. Thus, the producer is not free to select any channel, he likes but his decision is influenced by several factors.

The factors that influence the channel choice of a manufacturer, may be classified as factors relating to:

(1) Product Characteristics

The product characteristics are the most important in following channel decision. The marketing executive must study the attributes of the product in selection of channel.

(a) Perishability. The more perishable the product, the shorter should be the channel. Dairy, bakery products, fruits and sea foods etc. must reach the consumers as soon as possible after their production. Therefore they require more direct marketing to consumers due to dangers associated with their repeated handling and delays.

(b) Unit Value. Products whose unit selling price is high as compared to its cost like cut-diamonds, are often sold directly through company's sales force. A high unit cost and value is invariably associated with complexity. This can be done effectively by the company's own sales force. On the other hand, if the unit value is low as in case of items of daily consumption, the channel of distribution may be long while their turnover is high, because they are frequently purchased by the consumers.

(c) Weight and Bulk. Bulky or large size products are usually sold directly by the company to the consumer due to transportation difficulty. The channel may be long if products can be handled and transported easily.

(d) Complexity of Product. Technologically complex and specialised products are usually sold direct as they need demonstration and explanation about it working. Examples of such products are Computers, industrial products etc. On the other hand, the products of non-technical nature may be distributed through a long channel.

(e) Standardisation. Standardised products are those each unit of which is similar in colour, weight, size, quality etc. These should have indirect and lengthy channel of distribution because they are sold extensively and by brand. As against this, products which are not standardised and are produced on order, have direct selling.

(2) Market Characteris

The following market a or consumer or supply characteristics influence the channel decision:

(a) Number of Purchasers. In general, it may be observed that the larger the number of customers, the greater the need for channel agents regardless of the stage of market development. For example, if a company sells an industrial machinery only to twenty leading firms in a given foreign market, there is hardly a need for the middlemen and the firm can undertake the supply of such machinery through its own salesman. But, on the other hand, if the company produces and sells mass consumption items like soap, garment etc., it should select the longer chain of middlemen to distribute the item more effectively and at lower cost.

(b) Size and Number of Orders. Where customers make frequent and regular purchases in small quantity, lengthier marketing channels may be indicated. The producer may like to sell to wholesalers. If the size of orders from the customers is large and not frequently purchased such as durable consumer goods or high unit value products, the smaller channel may be required.

(c) Geographical Distribution. If customers of the product is widely dispersed geographically, long channels may be required to avoid delay in supplying the goods. Conversely, if customers are geographically concentrated, it is easy to approach them and a shorter channel or the direct selling may suffice.

(d) Customer's Buying Habits. Customer's buying habits also affect the channel decision. If customers in a particular market, expect credit facility, desire to purchase all necessaries at one place or desires for the personal services of the salesmen, the channel may be lengthier or shorter depends upon the capacity of providing those facilities for meeting out the needs of the customers. If producer can provide those facilities the channel will be shorter, otherwise lengthier.

(e) Buyer of the Product. The channel decision also depends upon who buys the product? In some countries, Government departments buy commodities often in large quantities and on a long term basis for their use. It is direct selling. If goods are purchased by the central or state buying agencies such as State Trading Corporation and Export Promotion Councils etc. which may supply the imported goods to wholesalers or industrial users, the channel may employ wholesaler retailers or only retailers. Some large retailers or distributors in foreign countries prefer to purchases direct from the producers, the channel may include one or two middlemen.

(3) Middlemen Factors

The choice of channel also depend upon the strength and weaknesses of various types of middlemen performing various functions. Their behavioural differences, product lines they deal in, the number, location and size of the middlemen also affect the design of the channel. The following are some considerable factors :

(a) Services Provided by Middlemen. Services provided by the middlemen may affect the channel choice. The middlemen who agree to provide the services which the company requires to provide to customers, may be appointed otherwise company will made it own arrangement for the sale of the product.

(b) Attitude of middlemen. The middlemen's attitude towards company's policies affect the channel decision. The middlemen are notoriously known for maximising their profits rather than that of the manufacturer. If the company allows them to fix the prices of the product, they will happily agree to sell the product of the company. If the company wants to follow the Resale Price Maintenance Policy, the choice is limited. Moreover; if the middlemen trust on the higher profits, they will select the product line and brand which sells most. A new entrant in the field will find it difficult to sell his product unless he shares the marketing expenses.

(c) Availability of Middlemen. The kind of specialists, the marketing manager would like to use may not even be available or willing to cooperate, especially if the company is a late entrant in the field and his competitors have already tied up the middlemen perhaps as part of a selective or exclusive distribution policy. Thus, in a foreign market, if the desired channel does not exist or it may belong to a competitor, it is then imperative for the firm to collect all the necessary information on the distribution pattern in a given foreign market. Only then should a decision be taken on the channel choice.

(d) Cost of Channel Usage. The cost of performing marketing functions at each level of distribution and the overall cost of performing total marketing task have an important bearing on the choice of channel. The relative cost of different marketing channels and the cash flow effectiveness of channel under consideration should be closely examined. Here the firm should keep in mind the initial expenditure which are non-recurring in nature. It should also study the recurring elements like the cost of staffing and training personnel. The channels including direct channel which ensures efficient distribution at least expenses and which secures the desired volume of sales should be chosen.

(e) Sale Volume Potential. In selecting a channel, the middlemen's potentiality to reach the maximum number of buyers should be probed into through special marketing surveys or other channels suitable adjustments for the strengths and weaknesses of competition should also be made. If the channel can reach the targeted sale volume, it may be selected. Keeping in mind that no single channel will be capable of realising targeted sales potential, a combined potential of two or there possible channel should be estimated.

(f) Contract with Middlemen. The international marketer must apply his legal brains to chalk out the contract with middlemen in the given foreign market. The reason for doing so is that if any aspect of agreement is overlooked by the firm, it may cause not only embarrassment and harassment to the firm but may also lead to the hostility of the distributors against the firm. It may also lead to a loss of face in the market. Sometimes, the host Government also adopt a hostile attitude towards such firms. To avoid a legal fight, the agency regulations should be studied in details. If the regulations do not coincide with the firm's objectives, the firm should take up the distribution task.

(4) Company or Enterprise Factors

The choice of channel is also influenced by company's characteristics such as its financial position, size, etc. The following factors are important:

(a) Financial Resources of Company. The financial strength of the company determines which marketing tasks, it can handle efficiently and which ones are to be delegated to the middlemen. A financially weak company may engage a financially strong intermediary so that it may push its sales well. Though it is not in the interest of the company in the long run. A company having good financial position, on the other hand, will establish its own selling and distribution set up on overseas market to avoid overdependence on middlemen taking all other factors into consideration.

(b) Product-Mix. If the product-mix of a company is wide enough, it can deal with it customers directly by establishing its branch offices in overseas markets. A fresh expansion of plant capacity may require more aggressive channel to find a place in the market. A well established product of mass consumption require a long channel. Similarly, consistency in the company's product mix ensures homogeneity of its marketing channel.

(c) Size of the Company. A large company already marketing a wide range of products may be in a good position to take up an additional product of the same time and handle it the same way, usually directly. It need not think again on the choice of the channel. A smaller firm, on the other hand, will find it difficult to engage the same channels because of the attitude of the middlemen and its own financial constraints.

(d) Marketing Policies. The company's marketing policies such as speedy delivery, after sale services, heavy advertising, uniform retail pricing also influence the channel decision. If company is of the view that the intermediaries can provide the services to customers according to company's marketing policies, it can delegate its selling activity to middlemen otherwise, it may engage itself indirect selling.

(e) Attitude of Company Executives. The attitude of company executives may have preferences or prejudices for a particular channel in a particular overseas market. Their attitude may be the result of their experience of working with certain types of middlemen.

(5) Environmental Factors

Another major constraints in the channel design is the general characteristics of the total environment of the foreign market. This factor includes the economic social and political environment of the country and varies from country to country. The foreign marketer should try to establish similarities in the foreign markets. These includes:

(a) Economic Conditions. When economic conditions in a country are depressed, the producer prefer a shorter channel to cut costs. If there is multipoint tax on sales, the line should be shorter to avoid the tax-burden on the consumers and they prefer to sell direct to retailers or consumers. If there are no such economic constraints, the channel may be longer.

(b) Legal Restrictions. If there is any legal restriction of any selling activity in the host country, the producer must have to adhere such provisions. For example, any activity not allowed under MRTP Act (Any activity which may have the effect of unreasonably preventing or lessening competition is not permissible) cannot be permitted to be undertaken. In case of controlled items, the channel should be strictly according to government policy of the host country.

(c) Social and Ethical Considerations. Social and ethical considerations such as distribution of goods through black marketing involves questions of ethics and are injurious to society.

Thus, the above factors influence the channel decision of the company and the manufacturer not always enjoys a complete freedom in selecting an ideal channel. He is to consider various financial, ethical, legal, marketing and product considerations before reaching a final decision. In taking decision, he must think over the cost and control aspect of the channel. This means what would be the level of control of the firm over the functioning of channel Would it be able to satisfy the customers and the company's objectives in the minimum cost? The choice will be best if the answer of the above questions is in positive.

APPROACHES TO CHANNEL STRATEGY

These approaches are:

(i) Gravity Approach,

(ii) Push Approach;

(iii) Pull Approach.

These are explained below:

(i) Gravity Approach. It is essentially a passive approach because under it the sell is in touch with an intermediary and seller his whole production to him. The intermediaries look after the distribution process in the export markets. The final consumers are not aware of the producer of the goods used by them because the manufacturer does not creates his own organisation in export market.

(ii) Push Approach. It is quite opposite to the gravity approach. Here it is thought that the exporter should establish his own distribution channel and assume complete control over it to use it as an instrument of promotion. For this the exporter, should make effective planning, establish organisation and have effective control over it.

(iii) Pull Approach. This approach relies much upon the intensive promotional campaigns as advertising, personal selling to develop brand loyalty among consumers in the market. The manufacturer is not much concerned about the channel because through advertising and publicity he creates demand and thus the consumers create a pressure on the distribution outlets to keep his product. The channel members always try to keep the product in their outlets to serve the consumer best. Thus, the manufacturer does not sets up his own to sell his product and forces the channel members to contact the manufacturer for the distribution of the product.

DISTRIBUTION LOGISTICS FOR EXPORTS

Logistics of distribution is an aspect of distribution decision. It involves the consideration of cost of transportation and warehousing of products during the course of exportation. Transportation and warehousing should be considered well in advance even at the time of selection of export markets. The distribution system has to perform two basic functions *(i)* to generate demand for the product and *(ii)* to make sure that the demand so created is matched by adequate and timely supply. Along with all other members of the channel the exporter should perform the dual functions. To achieve this objective he will require a logistics plan by considering the following points:

(a) Alternative Modes of Transport. What are the alternative modes of transport *viz.*, rail, road or ship available for transporting the goods from the point of production to the point of consumption?

(b) Optimal Mode. Which mode is optimal from the point of view of the distribution costs?

(c) Warehousing. Is there any need for warehousing arrangements keeping in view the product and the marketing characteristics.

Problem of Transportation

The above mentioned first two points in the logistics plan relate to transportation. These should be considered even at the time of the selection of export markets. The firm should examine whether a particular mode of transport is the best taking into account the nature of product and availability for carrying its goods to a given foreign market. Non-availability of the required mode of transport to a target market may outweight all other advantages that an exporter may have. For example, as the exporters of fruits, vegetables and sea-foods require shipping space with registration facility therefore unless the potential markets are served by shipping lines having refrigeration facilities, export of such items cannot be undertaken.

Another aspect of the problem of logistics planning is that the importing and exporting countries may not be connected with each other directly by shipping or air services and transportation of goods will involve transhipment from an intermediate point. This may involve delay in delivery of good apart from involving higher costs and uncertainties regarding the safety of cargo. Any delay may prove fatal for logistic planning. Hence, export shipment may have to be planned much in advance to coordinate the schedule of the on-going vessel from the port of shipment to the transhipment point and from there to the port of final delivery.

The selection of the appropriate mode of transport *i.e.*, air, ship or land along with its cost to the total distribution costs should be calculated and compared with the costs of other transportation modes available. This cost may vary from mode to mode, product to product and market to market.

Surface v/s Air Transport

The choice regarding modes of transport in relation to export marketing revolves around the appropriateness of transporting goods by ship or by air. Assuming that both types of transport systems are available to the shipper, the choice should depend on the estimates he makes as to the total costs of distribution by ship and by air. It is found that the important elements of costs behave in the following fashion for ocean and air transport:

Cost Element	*Air Transport*	*Surface Transport*
Freight	High	Low
Depot costs	Low	High
Fixed inventory	Low	High
Packaging	Low	High
Insurance	Low	High

From the above statement, it is seen that only freight element is higher for air transport, but for all other cost elements, it has an edge over surface transport. Therefore, it is perfectly possible that taking into account all the elements relating to distribution, transport by air may turn out to be a cheaper alternative to surface transport.

For deciding the mode of transport, nature of product is a consideration. If the product is highly perishable and cannot survive the sea voyage, air transport is the only solution. Cargoes of high value but low volume are eminently suitable for transport by air as the freight cost is fairly low. Bulky items, however, may be transported only by sea.

Availability of time for making the goods available in the markets is also worth consideration. Goods can be transported only by air if time is very short. Air transport may be used in emergency.

The criteria to decide the mode of transport are cost, speed, frequency, reliability, safety and appropriateness with regard to the nature of product. Air transport cannot be recommended for bulky items since lifting capacity of aircraft puts restrictions on the physical dimension of cargo. Air transport suffers from the handicap that the direct variable transportation cost happens to be highest of all mode of transport. Air transport scores over sea transport with respect to all other factors *i.e.*, speed, frequency, reliability and safety.

While analysing total distribution cost system it is necessary to distinguish between the fixed and variable costs. In total distribution costs, transportation, packing and receiving and shipping costs are variable costs. On the other hand administration, warehousing, inventory carrying costs and order processing costs may be termed as fixed costs. In a study carried out in the USA, it has been observed that the ratio of fixed and variable costs is 49.1 and 50.9 per cent. This proportion may vary from product to product. Variable distribution cost in air transport is however, much higher than the sea transport. In sea transport the fixed cost element is higher.

Advantages of Air Transport

Basically, there are 10 reasons which can make the total distribution costs cheaper through the use of air transport, at least for certain categories of merchandise. The reasons are:

(i) Low inventory carrying costs.

(ii) Decreased capital costs of goods in transit.

(iii) Less packing lowers cost and reduces chargeable weight.

(iv) Related surface transport costs are reduced.

(v) The loss due to rough handling and pilferage is reduced to the minimum.

(vi) Breakage is negligible.

(vii) Deterioration is avoided.

(viii) Obsolescence is eliminated.

(ix) Insurance premium is reduced.

(x) Costs related to administration, ordering, etc., are minimised.

Indian exporters have started moving some items by air to foreign markets. About 30 per cent of India's total exports are now moving by air. Principal items that are being exporter by air are cut and polished diamonds, gems and jewellery, garments, finished leather and precious metals. All these products satisfy the criterion of high-value and low volume and, therefore, it becomes profitable to export such goods by air.

Problem of Warehousing

Another factor in the physical distribution is warehousing and due to following reasons need for warehousing in a corporate unit may originate.

(i) Seasonability. There are certain commodities that are produced in a particular season but they are sold throughout the year.

(ii) Variation in Demand. When the demand is felt in a particular season for example demand for sugar around the festivals is higher and thus stock is maintained to meet such additional demand.

(iii) Impact of Speculation. An enterprise maintain a large inventory of items of which prices fluctuate because of speculative tendencies.

(iv) Product Conditioning. There are certain products about which to attain the required level of quality it is stored for instance rice is stored to add something to its quality over a certain period of time.

Importance of Warehousing Operations in Export Marketing

Warehousing operations enjoy special importance in international marketing due to the following reasons:

(i) Break Bulk Operations. These are the operations in which the exporter ships in goods in bulk quantity and thereafter repack them into small consignments as per orders received from individual customers. This system is economical particularly when individual orders are too small to fulfil the minimum space stipulation of shipping company and such cases the exporter has to pay minimum freight even if minimum space is not needed.

(ii) Timely Supply. In practice many distributors etc., in Western Europe and the USA keep low level of inventory and expect that deliveries whenever needed would be made at a very short notice. To meet the requirements, in such countries, it is necessary to store products to make timely supply at a very short notice. This is particularly necessary in case of spare part of engineering products.

(iii) Reassembly Operations. These operations are especially for engineering goods and other items. With the view to save shipping space many items are exported in Completely Knocked Down (CKD) condition. There are some countries that insist that the goods must be imported in this condition and where CKD shipment are carried out the warehousing facility is needed by the exporter in importing country to reassemble the product.

(iv) Meeting Quota Requirements. There are some countries that impose quota limitation on the import of some selected products for instance textile or footwear on global basis, and executed on first come-first served basis. With the view to meet the quota requirement of the importing country, it is necessary for the exporter to consign the goods well ahead of time. It is one of the common ways to win the quota regulations.

Costs of Warehousing

As the maintenance of warehouse in international marketing, is important and imperative in certain circumstances, the exporter must think over its cost. The exporter should make the use of warehousing facilities on a selective basis as warehousing involves additional costs which make the product in competitive in foreign markets. The costs involved in warehousing can be classified under the following three heads:

(i) Cost for Space. As an alternative to arrange for warehousing space a firm may decide to set up its own warehousing facilities abroad. In this case, there will be fixed costs that is, investment in creating warehousing facilities. Another alternative is the national rent for the space *i.e.*, the amount which can be fetched if the space is let out to some other persons. One has to book the warehousing firms. Such firms charge rent on the basis of the value of goods warehoused.

(ii) Cost of Inventory Handling. The good are exported on the consignment basis for the purpose of warehousing. The capital remains blocked until the goods are sold. If the turnover rate is slow and the rate of interest is high, the cost of inventory holding may be quite significant. Thus cost of inventory holding should be borne in mind. If goods are exported on letter of credit basis there is no question of cost of inventory holding because the exporter gets immediate payment and no capital is blocked.

(iii) Handling and other Incidental Charges. A number of handling operations are involved as and when the sales materialise such as the goods have to be off loaded from the ship, transported to the warehouse, stored, and finally disposed off to the users. Several documents required for these handling operations also involved Costs which should also be borne in mind.

To conclude, the physical distribution of goods involves two important costs transportation cast and warehousing cost. As these costs form a substantial part of the total costs, the management should make an endeavour to pull dawn these costs to the minimum level. These should be managed effectively by the exporter so that his product may be competitive in foreign markets.

❒

10

Joint Ventures and Turnkey Projects

JOINT VENTURE

In international market a joint venture is created when a foreign company joins hands with the local company having a local interest in that country and they own some type of business operation. The two companies in Joint Venture may have together sense of cooperation, sharing of ownership and control in an economic enterprise, licensing agreements, contract manufacturing and management contracts.

Joint venture may achieve the dual purpose to propel the economy forward and limit the extent of region participation, management and control in a developing country like India.

Ways to Initiate Joint Venture

(i) A new business enterprise may be created in partnership sharing profits and management.

(ii) The foreign company may invest in the existing local company.

(iii) A local company may invest and acquire interest in an existirg foreign company.

In whatever form in which it is created, the central theme of joint venture is the sharing of ownership and management control.

Joint Ventures in Home Country

Joint venture is a partnership having two sides-technical and emotional. On the technical side, the partners share contributions, profits etc. On the emotional side, there is a feeling of cooperative efforts. A joint venture may be established in home country in collaboration with a foreign firm or the local firm may join a foreign firm. Both ways its basic concept is of sharing ownership management and control. Whether a joint venture should be established in home country or in foreign country depends on economy and many other considerations.

Reasons for Joint Venture Abroad

(i) To utilise the special privileges and influence of the local partner.

(ii) To reduce the risks involved in the venture caused by economic and political circumstances of the capital importing country by sharing it with the local partners.

(iii) To make use of production facilities, sales network and indigenous capital available in the local country.

(iv) To enjoy the special tax benefits of the capital importing country.

Reasons for Joint Venture in Home Country

(i) To expand foreign manufacturing and service activities equipped with a modern techniques.

(ii) To develop a source of supply of required raw materials.

(iii) To ensure Government participation in joint ventures with a view to increase the rate of economic development.

(iv) To integrate the joint venture activity and the normal activity of the local partners (supplier-customers relationship) for the advantage of both the local company and foreign company.

(v) To acquire means by which an international marketer is able to penetrate an overseas market.

Advantages of Joint Ventures

In a joint venture programme the investing firm can expect to establish a firm footing in the foreign country. In India, some firms have decided to invest abroad owing to severe curbs on the expansion of large houses under the Industries (Development and Regulation) Act, and the MRTP Act. But Indian's have been attracted by the schemes of tax holiday, export incentives, guarantees against expropriation, freedom to remit profits and repatriate capital and in many cases protective tariffs.

Joint ventures increase exports of capital goods, spare parts and components from the investing country. In fact, joint ventures help in projecting a country's image abroad as a supplier of capital goods and technology. It also leads to greater employment in the industrial sector. The country benefits from greater inflow of foreign exchange in the form of dividends, royalties and technical know how fees.

In India, the Export-Import Bank of India (EXIM) provides overseas investment finance to enable Indians to finance equity contribution in a joint venture. In addition, the Export Credit Guarantee Corporation provides insurance cover for overseas investment made by them.

(1) To Enter into More Overseas Markets. The joint venture approach enables the company to enter more overseas markets with a limited capital and manpower resources than would be otherwise possible.

(2) Minimisation of Risk. Risk is minimised as the management skills and experience of a local partner facilities easier adaptation to the particular changes of an unfamiliar business environment. The risk of adverse action by the local Government is reduced because the local interest is involved in joint venture. The risk is minimum in those ventures where the local partner is some agency of the Government.

(3) High Morale. The morale of labour is high because of the local ownership. Local participation in ownership can have a favourable effect on the morale of labour.

(4) Good Public Relations. As the joint venture is looked upon with more favour by nationalistic consumers the sale and profits of the joint venture may be greater.

Disadvantages of Joint Ventures

(1) Lower Profits. As all profits and prosperity are shared with the partners, the amount of resources and profits potential for the company are reduced.

(2) Potential Disagreement. As is usual, after sometimes potential disagreement begins to creep in between partners.

(3) Operations Substantially Affected. When a party enters into joint venture, its operations in other foreign markets may be substantially affected. This problem may be peculiar when the party wants to operate in or to create a joint venture in third market where the joint venture has been selling its products. By creating a new venture in the third market the international marketer because a competitor of the joint venture in which, he is a partner. Thus competing with one-self is a very ridiculous situation. As this policy has not yet been accepted by many companies in foreign countries its activities in foreign countries are restricted.

(4) Complications. Joint venture may complicate long term international manufacturing and marketing policies of companies that are either multinational in character or tend to become multinational. This is particularly true when the management and control of a joint venture is in the hands of local partners.

(5) Changes Factors of Success. Where a foreign company buys into an existing local enterprise, a serious problem may arise. Often, a joint ownership does not work out satisfactorily because unknowingly it changes the combination of attributes which were responsibles for its success before the foreign company entered in the picture. Hence, differences creep in very soon.

When Joint ventures may be appropriate:

(i) When a company lacks resources to expand its international operations.

(ii) When a company wants to enter an overseas market where wholly owned activities are prohibited.

(iii) When the company wants to utilise the market position or the management skill of the local partner.

(iv) When complete control over the project is not necessary for the success of venture, only part control may suffice.

Before entering into a joint venture agreement, a local firm must consider its own interest in the long run and also the country's interest. The success of joint venture depends upon a good partner. It is better to find all possible areas of disagreement and specifically provide for them in the joint venture agreement.

India's joint venture proposals are appreciated by developing countries generally because intermediate labour-intensive technology developed by India is more suited to their requirements.

Developing countries generally welcome India's joint ventures because intermediate labour-intensive technology developed by India is more suited to their requirements and they can adopt it directly without any or with slight modifications. Moreover, most developing countries, because of their limited home market, may not be able to afford large-scale capital-intensive technology provided by developed countries and thus prefer the medium-scale technology developed by India. Finally, host countries perceive little threat from Indian joint ventures to their political or economic independence.

Factors Determining the Selection of a Country

Following are the factors that must be considered in this regard:

(i) About Market for the Concern Product. This includes size, growth, existing competition whether local or foreign.

(ii) Government Regulations. This includes, Tax concessions and incentives, price controls, local requirements, export obligations, extent of equality holding permitted, degree as well as nature of protection, profit and capital repatriation.

(iii) Economic Stability. This includes, the management—economic and fiscal policies-growth rate of the economy, inflation, trade balance, balance of its indebtness.

(iv) Political Stability. This includes : Sound political institutions, mechanism for orderly transfer of power, acceptance of the obligations of the previous Government, political relations with India.

Some factors which could be considered for selection of a country for the establishment of joint ventures are given below:

(i) Market for the product concerned:

(a) Size of the market;

(b) Market growth;

(c) Existing competition-local and foreign.

(ii) Government regulations:

(a) Tax concessions and incentives;

(b) Price controls-their severity;

(c) Local content requirements;

(d) Export obligations;

(e) Extent of equity holding permitted;

(f) Degree and nature of protection;

(g) Repatriation of profits and capital.

(iii) Economic stability:

(a) The economy and its management—economic and fiscal policies growth rate;

(b) Degree of inflation;

(c) Trade balance, balance of payments and balance of its indebtedness;

(d) Import and debt service cover.

(iv) Political stability:

(a) Sound political institutions;

(b) Mechanism for orderly transfer of power;

(c) Acceptance of the obligations of the previous Government;

(d) Political relations with India.

Guidelines for Joint Ventures

In order to avoid substantial transfer of capital from India and to link joint ventures with the promotion of exports of capital equipment and technology, the Government of India has framed certain guidelines which have the following main features:

(a) Indian participation abroad should ordinarily be through a corporate entity in India having at its command necessary manufacturing experience and technical competence;

(b) Participation by Indian companies should be in accordance with the rules and regulations of the host country; and

(c) Mode of participation in the equity share capital should normally be through export of capital equipment and technology but cash remittances will be permitted in deserving cases depending upon the merits of each case.

There were 208 effective Indian joint ventures abroad at the end of December 1985, out of which 156 were in production or operation and 52 were in various stages of implementation.

Extent and Pattern of Indian Participation

According to data, in about 85 per cent of the joint ventures, the partners held only a minority of shares, this owing to the guidelines regulating participation. However, the present guidelines are flexible to accommodate majority participation when permitted by the host countries.

Indian investment (in equity capital) in the 154 joint ventures in operation in 1984 was mainly effected through exports of capital equipment. In addition to these, by the capitalisation of know how etc., (6.7 per cent), cash remittance (8.9 per cent), issue of bonus shares (18.9 per cent and loans, adjustment of future profits, capitalisation of preliminary expenses, etc., was 2.0 per cent.

The total Indian equity in 156 joint ventures reported to be in operation on December 31, 1985 was about Rs. 94 crores.

Country Coverage

Indian joint ventures, currently in operation, are dispersed over 30 countries. Over 80 per cent of them are concentrated in 10 countries Malaysia (25), Singapore and Sri Lanka (16 each), Indonesia and Nigeria (12 each), Thailand (10), USA, UK, and UAE (9 each) and Kenya (7).

The other countries where Indian joint ventures are in operation are : Mauritius, Saudi Arabia, West Germany, the Philippines, Oman, Hong Kong, Nepal, Bangladesh, Switzerland, Kuwait, Bahrain, Australia, Fiji, Tonga, Uganda, Bostwana, France and the Netherlands.

There is a heavy concentration of investment in South East Asian countries (64.5 per cent) followed by Africa (28.7 per cent). This heavy concentration in South East Asian countries and Africa is declining and the share of South Asia, West Asia and the developed countries of Europe, America and Australia is increasing in the joint ventures under implementation.

Product Mix

The product mix of these joint ventures is varied and includes diesel engines, paints and varnishes, bottling and packing, corrugated sheets, spinning mills, automobiles and ancillary products, viscose staple fibre, iron pipe fitting, oilseeds crushing, steel furniture, paper, bulk antibiotics, sugar mills, textiles, pharmaceuticals, electrical, cement products, readymade garments, cycles and vanaspati. While most of the Indian joint ventures in developing countries are in the field of manufacturing, in developed countries they are mainly in the area of service ventures like hotels, restaurants, food processing, construction, consultancy, etc., with a few exceptions like the asbestos cement project in the United Kingdom and the tufted carpet yarn plant in Ireland.

Benefits Received by India

The benefits that have accrued to India by the establishment of joint ventures till March, 1985 amounted to Rs. 9.31 crores by way of dividends, Rs. 29.64 crores by way of fee for technical know-how, engineering services, management and consultancy, selling agency commission, etc., and Rs. 147.91 crores by way of additional exports over and above exports towards equity which amounted to Rs. 62 crores.

PERFORMANCE OF INDIAN JOINT VENTURES ABROAD

Size of Investment

In about 85 per cent of the joint ventures, Indian partners held only minority shares because the old guide-lines governing Indian joint ventures abroad stipulated only minority participation. The present guide-lines are flexible and allow majority participation if the host country does not object to it.

The average size of Indian participation in term of equity capital employment was about Rs. 1.05 crores but about 55 per cent of units had an equity capital Rs. 30 lakhs or less. The average size of joint ventures under implementation in terms of equity capital was Rs. 2.3 crores, indicating that the more recent joint ventures were relatively larger.

Countries Covered

Indian joint ventures currently in operation are dispersed over 28 countries. In 1984, 82 per cent of them were concentrated in 10 countries-Malaysia (26), Singapore (19), Indonesia (12), the USA (12), UAE, Thialand, and the UK (9 each), Sri Lanka (10), Nigeria

(13), and Kenya (8). The other countries are—Mauritius, Saudi Arabia and West Germany (3 each), the Philippines, Oman and Hong Kong (2 each), Nepal, Bangladesh, Switzerland, Kuwait, Bahrain, Australia, Fiji, Tonga, Uganda, Bostwana, France and the Netherlands (one each).

There was heavy concentrations of investment in South East Asian countries (64.5 per cent) followed by Africa (28.7 per cent). Now the share of these country is declining while of South Asia, West Asia and the developed countries of Europe, America and Australia is increasing in joint ventures under implementation.

Product Mix

The product mix of Indian joint ventures is varied. It includes diesel engines, paint and varnishes, corrugated sheet, automobiles and ancillary products, cements, sugar, textile, pipe fittings, oil-seed crushing, pharmaceutical, steel furniture, paper, readymade garments, cycles etc. Most of the joint ventures in developing countries are in the field of manufacturing. In developed countries they are mainly in the area of service ventures like hotels, restaurants, food processing, construction, consultancy etc. with a few exceptions.

Problems faced by Indian Joint Ventures

(i) In ability to gauge the market prospects.

(ii) Failure to select the right partners.

(iii) Subsequent backing out of the local partners and non-approval of the technology sought to be supplied, by Indian partners.

(iv) Relentless price competition.

The basic cause of the failure of Indian joint venture was the lack of adjustment in the new marketing environment because they were habituated to a sheltered market in India. Many units found it difficult to survive in the face of relentless price competition.

Most of the problems could have been avoided if the entrepreneurs had thought seriously before entering into joint ventures agreements. There was information gap and the Indian entrepreneurs did not have enough information about many countries. Fortunately, the rate of mortality has come down in recent years. This could be due to greater care exercised in the scrutiny of the proposals by the Government.

According to Mr. M.K. Raju, poor performance of Indian joint ventures is due to:

(a) Poor project management;

(b) Poor operations control; and

(c) A lack of commitment.

Poor project management has led to cost escalation in the range of 40 to 100 per cent. Poor production control has led to poor quality, lack of cost consciousness and irregular deliveries. Mr. Raju's study identified some other problems:

(d) Insistence on using 'scaled down' duplication of Indian plants back home in order to use Indian equipment and little regard to scale factor;

(e) The prohibition of cash remittance from India to joint ventures thus artificially restricting the growth of some Indian ventures, and in availability of Indian joint ventures to control any of the critical variables such as-price, product, leadership, distribution channel or manufacturing cost.

Suggestions for Improvement

(i) Export Agencies. An export agency should be set up to disseminate information about business opportunities in other countries.

(ii) Better Study. The entrepreneur who is going to collaborate should make accurate feasibility studies, undertake market surveys and prepare their own project reports and not mainly depend upon the information supplied by other agencies.

(iii) Consortium of Banks. A consortium of Indian banks should be formed to ease the cash starvation problem of Indian joint ventures.

(iv) Flexibility. More flexibility should be afforded to Indian entrepreneurs to specify appropriate equipment and scale of operations rather then insisting on Indian equipment. Insistence on Indian equipment adversely affects India's image as the host countries feel that the main motive behind setting up joint ventures is only to find sales avenues for Indian capital goods and equipment.

(v) Buy Back Arrangements. Indian industrialists should be prepared to enter into buy back arrangements from joint ventures in countries with limited home market like Sri Lanka.

Though the position of Indian joint ventures is not satisfactory but much progress is expected in the near future as is clear from the decline in mortality rate in recent years. The Government should be cautious in approving the proposals for joint ventures so that they can survive in the changing marketing environments in foreign markets.

MOTIVATING FACTORS FOR JOINT VENTURES

A developing country like India, requires:

(i) To propel the economy forward, and

(ii) To limit the foreign participation, management and control.

This dual objective may be achieved by encouraging the establishment of joint ventures abroad with local partners.

In late fifties India took initiate in setting up joint ventures. India set up a textile mill in Ethiopia in 1957 in its first joint venture attempts. Since then India took active part in the economic development of many other foreign countries by establishing joint ventures. Following are the motivating factors in setting up joint ventures abroad:

(i) Severe Curbs on Expansion. As the Government of India has imposed severe curbs on the expansion of large industrial houses under the Industries (Development and Regulation) Act and the MRTP Act, many Indian firms, decided to invest abroad because they had little scope for expanding their business and industrial activities in India.

(ii) Attractive Incentives by Developing Countries. Many less developed countries welcome long term investments in the form of capital or know-how by offering attractive incentive in the form of tax concessions, investment guarantees, export incentives, freedom to remit profits and repatriate capital and in many cases protective tariff. In this way developing countries offer many attractive possibilities for joint venture for India which lured most of the Indian firms. In this regard India has to meet a stiff competition in those markets from developed countries though this should be taken as a challenge not an obstacle.

(iii) Improving India's Image Abroad. Joint ventures helped in projecting India's image abroad as a supplier of capital goods, technology etc. They gave improved India's export trade of capital goods, spare parts and components. India has now a name in the exports of technical know-how and consultancy services through joint ventures. Indian joint ventures have helped in the utilisation of ideal capacity in the capital goods industrial sector and thus reducing costs in general in several countries. India has emerged as a leader among the developing countries through joint ventures.

(iv) Labour Intensive Technology. Most developing countries welcome India's joint ventures because intermediate labour intensive technology developed by her is most suited to their requirements and may be adopted without or with slight modifications. As many developing countries do not encourage large scale capital intensive technology from developed countries due to their limited home market, they prefer medium scale technology developed by India.

(v) Fulfilling the Government's Aim. By setting up joint ventures in these countries Indian has actively participated in the economic development of many developing countries. She has developed capital goods and industries. She has served as an expert in providing technical know-how and consultancy services. She is not only interested in exporting the goods for consumption to these countries but also in furthering their industrialisation programme through pooling resources for joint individual members. These have led to greater employment opportunities in the industries concerned. India also gains greater foreign exchange earnings in the form of dividends, royalties, and technical know-how. India's aim is achieving collective self-reliance and mutual cooperation among developing countries.

(vi) Neutralising Adverse Cost Effect. According to the MacDougal Committee the differential rates between Indian and international price for non-traditional goods was 25 to 30 per cent. If it set up in foreign country near the market and near the sources of raw materials, a joint venture would give a fillip where there is solid domestic demand.

Some motivating factors have initiated the Indian industries to set up joint ventures in collaboration with some foreign firm in their home country. Some Indian firms have set up joint ventures in a third country in collaboration with foreign firms.

Indian Government Guide-lines for Joint Ventures

(i) Through Corporate Entity. It should be through a corporate entity in India that should have necessary manufacturing experience and technical competence at its command.

(ii) According to Rules. Participation by Indian companies should be in accordance with the rules and regulations of the country where the project is to be located. Association of local parties, local development banks and financial institutions should be encouraged to the maximum extent.

(iii) Condition of Participation. Mode of participation in the equity share capital should be through export of new indigenous capital equipment and plant and machinery required for joint venture. However, participation in one or more of the following ways, may also be considered:

(a) Export of know-how.

(b) Capitalisation of service fees, royalty and other payments.

(c) Raising of foreign exchange loans abroad.

(d) Grant of loans by Indian participating companies to the joint venture units.

(e) Cash remittance on consideration of fields of collaboration.

(iv) Requests for Contribution to right Issues/additional Equity in the Joint Ventures Project. These will be considered on the basis of past performance of the project and other financial details. Such contribution shall be through exports of machinery/equipment but exports of components and raw materials will be allowed on merit of each case.

(v) Technical and Financial Viability. Schemes for industrial and manufacturing joint ventures should be technically and financially viable. These should be supported by a detailed project report alongwith cash flow statement and profitability projections. Similar scheme for commercial/trading/service venture should be supported by feasibility studies and projections.

TURNKEY PROJECTS

India's export trade structure has recently been changed to a great extent. Till recently, India had been an exporter of traditional items which were mainly raw materials but now India has emerged as a major exporter of non-traditional items including, capital equipment and other sophisticated items and projects and, consultancy services:

Project and consultancy export-which is the subject matter of this chapter-includes four types of exports of services namely, *(i)* turnkey projects involving rendering of services in erection and Commisioning of plant and supervision thereof along with the supply of plant and equipment, *(ii)* engineering services only (not involving any supply of equipment); (iii) consultancy services which may include feasibility studies, projects reports, design preparation, advice etc. and (iv) civil construction contracts.

India has performed well in this sector and there are good prospects for its improvement in near future.

PROJECT EXPORT

For the purpose of project assistance, project exports are defined as:

(i) Turnkey projects, namely, projects which involve the rendering of services like design, civil construction, erection and commissioning of plants or supervision thereof, along with the, supply of equipment.

(ii) Engineering services contracts, involving the supply of services alone such as design, erection, commissioning or supervision of erection and commissioning. This does not involve supply of equipment.

(iii) Consultancy services contracts, include the preparation of feasibility studies, project reports, preparation of design and advice to the project authority on specifications for plant and equipment, preparation of tender documments evaluation of tenders and purchase of plant and equipment.

(iv) Civil Construction contracts, with or without preparation of designs or drawings for the civil work to be undertaken.

The above categories are not to be treated as mutually exclusive. A project contract include supply, of services or equipment coming under more than one of the categories.

Performance in the Field of Project Export

India has achieved a moderate success during the last decade in the export of capital goods projects and civil engineering jobs.

In the field of exports of capital goods and turnkey projects. India has performed well. Between 1973-74 and 1980-81, the exports have increased from Rs. 64.04 crores to Rs. 371 crores showing an increase of about 480 per cent during the period. It was about 40 per cent of the total engineering exports during 1980-81.

The performance in construction contracts is, however much spectacular. The Middle East countries such as Iraq and Libya emerged as very important markets for infrastructural projects due to their oil revenue.

The report of Task Force on Project Exports has revealed that international bids submitted by the Indian companies have recorded a very substantial increase both in terms of value and number during 1975-76 to 1980-81. The number of bids cleared by IDBI working group stood at 318 for a total value of Rs. 7545 during 1980-81 as against 875 bids during 1975-76, for a total value of Rs. 873 crores. The trend is definitely very encouraging but the disconcerting fact is that the number of countries where the Indian firms have submitted their bids have declined substantially. The number of countries was 48 in 1976-77 and 52 in 1977-78 which had come down to 40 during 1980-81. However, it may be an indication that Indian exports might be pursuing a policy of selectivity as far as their target markets were concerned. The maximum bids were for construction contracts. In fact only a few product categories namely, power generation equipment, transmission line towers, railway wagons, buses and other vehicles, apart from civil construction account for about 90 per cent of the total bids in terms of value 22 per cent of the total bids submitted were for power generation equipment and transmission line towers taken together.

The bulk of the projects in power sectors have been financed by the international financial institutions such as Asian Development Bank, World Bank etc. India's share in ADB projects was only 5 per cent in 1980 and in World Bank Projects, India's share had been estimated at about $ 400 m out of total World Bank disbursement of $ 5 billion. Moreover bulk of the amount was earned from World Bank enanced projects in India.

Prospects for India's Project Esports

As we have pointed out above that the construction contracts were secured by Indian entrepreneurs in Middle East countries, mainly in Iraq and Libya due to their oil revenue, were the highest in

1980 and later, the share was reduced subsequently. The main reason for this decline is the recent decline of oil prices in international markets. The continued war between Iraq and Iran also has adversely affected India's project exports prospects in Middle East countries. However, there is good opportunities for projects exports in countries which are less affected by the decline in oil revenue like S. Arabia, Kuwait, Quatar, Abu Dhabi, Libya and Egypt.

The Task Force on Project Exports appointed by the Government of India in its report has pointed out that there are good prospects for project exports in neighbouring countries like Bangla Desh, Burma, Pakistan, Afghanistan, and Nepal. They offer good opportunities to Indian firms to participate in their economic developmental programmes. The sector in which India has developed expertise of international standards and can exploit overseas market opportunities are civil engineering, power systems, industrial plants, chemicals, petro-chemicals and pharmaceutical industries and transportation.

The Task Force has estimated the target that India should achieve by 1990 as follows:

Construction contracts	Rs. 10,000 crores
Capital goods and Turnkey projects:	
(a) Cash	Rs. 1,500 crores
(6) Deferred Payments	Rs. 3,000 crores
(c) Service contracts	Rs. .1,400 crores
Total	Rs. 15,900 crores

India has recently become the member of African Development Bank as well. India is now eligible to participate in those tenders for projects financed by African Development Bank. India has also approached EEC that India should also be given participation in projects financed by European Development Fund in African. Carribbean and Pacific countries. Indian firms are already eligible to participate in projects financed by European, Investment Bank.

Problems and Help of ECGC in Turnkey Projects

Despite good prospects, the Indian firms face a number of problems in the field of project exports in overseas markets. The following problems which are generally faced by them in participating in the international tenders may present a view of difficulties.

(1) The first and the foremost problem is delay in securing tender documents. The time lag between the floatation of tenders and their submission is about 2—3 months. A major part of the time is lost in transmission of tender documents that results in reduction of time for analysing the tender documents and developing a strategy for proper bidding. However, the Engineering Export Promotion Council publishes Project Export News' on a bi-monthly basis and the World Bank the 'Development Forum—Business Edition.' The interested parties serious in project exports may subscribe to these journals.

(2) Another problem is the role of consultants in drawing up the tender documents. Sometimes, the tender documents are designed in such a way so as to favour a particular country by incorporating some specific standards or clauses which Indian firms fail to honour and they feel themselves discriminated. Indian consultancy firm should, therefore, be given all possible assistance to gain a foothold in the fiercely competitive market.

(3) The third difficulty is that the already established firms in the international markets get the contract on the basis of their image. It particularly happens when large amount and high technology are involved. Many Indian firms have not so far reached at that stage when they can compete successfully with their rivals—the multinational corporations. It is a fact that many Indian firms which have subsequently proved their ability started as a sub-contractor under some foreign prims contractor. The work being done by the Engineering Export Promotion Council in the development of sub-contracting business has already started bearing fruits.

(4) The another problem in the field with the Indian firms is that they are unable to other liberal credit terms as are offered by many

other foreign firms. Since our major markets are developing countries which are always under foreign exchange crisis, the attraction of liberal credit affects their decision in awarding the contract.

(5) Finally, but not the least importantly, is the problem related to agency commission. The agents play very important role in project exports. Effective, good, active and influential agents are not in abundance in a country and, therefore, to attract them, adequate agency commission has to be paid. The present rates should be revised, at least on a selective basis.

The Government has set up a Working Group of financial institutions streamlining the process of obtaining clearance from various Government departments. The Working Group considers all important aspects of the bids such as deferred payment terms, agency commission, setting up of offices at the project site, capability of project exporter etc., with a view to eliminating chances of failure of a project that may bring a disrepute to the country. The exporter has to submit the project cost estimates and cash flow statement to enable the Group to take a decision on the profitability of the project.

Help by ECGC

The main function of ECGC is to cover risks in the international trade by issuing various types of insurance policies. Besides covering the risks under standard policies, the ECGC has devised some special policies to suit the various needs of the exporters. The ECGC also provides guarantees for the various risks involved in the international trade.

In the case of project exports, the ECGC has devised the following policies and guarantee schemes.

Policies for the Purpose

(1) Construction Works Policy. The ECGC Construction Works Policy provides cover for all risks for all payments that fall due to the contractor under construction contract for the supply of materials required and the services as well as the execution of the contract. The policy covers all those contracts which are entered into with the foreign Governments and where payments are guaranteed by an overseas Government. In such contracts, supplies from third countries shall be limited to 15 per cent. Covers under the policy may also be provided to the contractor's equipment such as cranes, bulldozers, and trucks used for construction against risk like confiscation etc. by a suitable endorsement on the policy.

(2) Services Policy. Another policy to provide help to project exporter is Services Policy under which the ECGC covers risks against non-payment for services rendered to foreign parties. Under this policy, only technical and professional services are covered against political and commercial risks.

Guarantees Provided by ECGC

The ECGC provides guarantees under Export Performance Guarantee Scheme for the bids made and awarded to Indian firms at various stages as under:

(1) Bid Bond. The genuineness of the offer submitted by an Indian firm may be guaranteed by the ECGC if required by the buyer when the exporter wants to quote for a tender.

(2) Advance Payment Guarantee. After the exporter secures the bid, the buyer may pay the exporter a percentage of the value of contract as an advance against the bank guarantee.

(3) Guarantee for Retention Money. In order to ensure due performance of the contract, the buyer may retain a percentage of the contract value as retention money and agree to release it to the exporter against a bank guarantee. The ECGC undertakes any loss on account of retention money.

(4) Bank Guarantee for the Performance of the Contract. This guarantee will be required when the contract is awarded to the exporter.

(5) Bank Guarantee for Loans Raised in foreign Exchange. If it is necessary for the Indian firm to raise foreign loans to finance its operations in connection with an export project, the ECGC may provide a guarantee required by the financial institution of the country where loans are raised.

The above guarantees are provided by the banks against which they obtain a counter guarantee from the ECGC under the contractors' 'Performance Guarantee Scheme'. The ECGC indemnifies the banks upto 2/3rd of the total loss in the case of bid bonds and 75% of the loss in the case of other guarantees required by the exporter.

The ECGC thus provides a wide coverage against the risks involved in the project exports.

MARKETING VARIABLES IN PROJECT EXPORTS

The following marketing variables should be taken into account while considering a proposal for project export:

(1) Though price factor is an important factor in project export too, yet the non-price factors such as product characteristics, reputation of the firm (seller), location of production, and credit terms etc. are more important.

(2) In many of the developing countries, the importer/buyer do not prepare detailed plans and specifications on their own. Bidders submit their own planning studies and specifications hoping that these would be able to introduce specifications to their own advantage if the contract is awarded or will obtain preferential treatment in the award of the contract. The project exporter must take note of it.

(3) In spite of the talks on unbundling of the technology package, the trend is towards more comprehensive deals including training maintanance, and infrastructure development. This has resulted in bids being submitted by a consortia of companies even from different countries.

(4) Governments of foreign countries are also reluctant to buy projects from those exporters who have not been successful to sell to its own Government. When the U.S. Defence Department bought aircraft from General Dynamics instead of Northrop, it was effectively

out of the competition for sales to Belgium, Denmark and the Netherlands.

(5) In the high technology sector, the primary basis of competitive advantage is the product characteristics. A contract awards by a respected government can influence the decision of other buyers.

(6) One selling method in project export may be to bring the Government purchasers into contact with satisfied customers so that they may be satisfied with the operation of the system by talking to the existing satisfied users.

(7) Although sale of high technology items depend on/personal selling, during the bidding process, many firms, undertake image advertising. It is doubtful whether this advertising can easily overcome the negative reputation. So, personal selling should be preferred at this stage.

(8) Agents are very active and used intensively for the sale of this type of products apart from serving as conduits for payments to Government officials. They also advise the principals of coming projects and contracts so that they can send their own staff to determine the desirability of going ahead for them. This function is important because the cost of preparing a bid for a large contract may be more than a few million dollars.

(9) Financial arrangements are extremely important for sales to developing and the centrally planned economies. Most industrial countries offer financial arrangements to promote exports of their firms. Additionally, they participate in international lending institutions which increase the borrowing capacities of the shortage economies.

(10) A popular way for the promotion of project exports is, organising fairs and exhibition. The show in fairs and exhibition may prepare a ground for a large contract.

(11) For sale to Eastern European countries, many companies have taken recourse to enter into a number of barter type arrangements

such as direct barter, switch trading, offset trade and co-production schemes etc.

These variables affect the marketing strategy of the project exporters and they should consider them seriously and adopt the strategy which is necessary in that country before bidding for the project.

CONSULTANCY EXPORTS

Consultancy export is a new-dimension in the foreign trade of India. India has just entered the area of consultancy exports Until recently, developed countries dominated the world market in regard to exports of consultancy services. India has over 200 consultancy and design organisations. These services earned foreign exchange worth Rs. 18 crores during 1980-81 as against only Rs. one crores in 1974-75. The Task Force estimated that India would earn about Rs. 200 crores by the end of 1990.

Consultancy services contracts are part of project export contracts and include the preparation of feasibility studies, project reports, preparation of designs and advice to the project authority on specifications for plant and equipment, preparation of tender documents, evaluation of tenders and purchase of plant and equipment. Thus, consultancy exports have a bright future.

Facilities extended by the Government of India

With a view to promote consultancy exports, the Government of India has extendad a number of facilities to exporters of such services. Some of these are:

(1) R.B.I. will provided blanket foreign exchange facility for undertaking tours abroad to those consultancy export firms which have earned not less than Rs. 5 lakhs in the previous year.

(2) R.B.I. grants permission to open site offices abroad based on the past performance and future potential.

(3) R.B.I. has advised the commercial banks to advance credits to consultancy organisations at lower interest for their export activities.

(4) Deferred credit facilities in respect of the service portion of the turnkey project subject to a maximum of 20 per cent of the total value may be extended.

(5) Under MDA assistance, a consultancy firm which has prepared a project report free of cost at its own initiative, will get reimbursement upto 60 per cent of the total expenditure incurred.

(6) If a consultancy, design or engineering firm which itself is not an actual user is awarded a contract for technical services abroad for which it requires imported raw materials, it can apply, for the necessary imports. Public sector undertakings are also provided such facilities. Consultancy firms can also apply for design, drawing office equipment, instruments etc. for actual use. The value of these licences in limited to 10 per cent of foreign exchange earned by the consultancy firm.

Thus, the Central Government has extended so many facilities to consultancy firms in order to streamline consultancy service exports. It is expected that consultancy exports will grow rapidly in the near future.

❐

11

Export Promotion

According to William J. Stanton, "Promotion is an exercise in information, persuasion and influence."

According to Philip Kotler, "Promotion encompasses all the tools in the marketing mix whose major role is persuasive communication."

Thus promotion includes providing information about the product persuing and influencing the target consumers to buy the product. The various activities that help easy sale of goods are commonly known as 'promotion activities' or promotional mix. These include all those activities which are undertaken to promote the sale of products ultimately.

Scope of Promotion

Promotion includes providing information about the attribution of the products and communicating messages aimed at satisfying its shareholders, government dealers and the like. In the marketing mix marketing communication is as important as other elements. In the broad sense of the term marketing communication mix includes all the four marketing P's Product, Promotion, Packaging and Price. Product's design, colour, packaging and price, all communicate something. As soon as the company decides to enter the market, all marketing mix elements reinforce the decisions or the position. In the narrow sense of the term marketing communication refers to the marketing tools which are normally classified under 'promotion', one of the four P's they are called 'promotools' and include various forms of 'advertising', sales presentations and demonstrations, point of purchase displays, sales aids (catalogue, literature, coupons, free samples) and publicity programmes.

Objectives of Sales Promotion Activities

(i) To Provide Information. The promotion communicates what is required to be communicated to various sections of the trade *i.e.*, customers, government, shareholders and dealers etc. it informs the customers and dealers all about the product *i.e.*, attributes, colour, size, design, uses, price, packaging etc. It is necessary while introducing the product to the market and thereafter, if there is any change in these elements, through various promotion tools *i.e.*, advertising, salesmanship, publicity, point of purchase etc. In the international situation it plays more significant role because the buyers in the foreign markets may be unaware of the product. Even if they are aware, their tradition and culture may prevent them from using it unless it is adapted to suit them and such changes are communicated to them effectively.

(ii) To Increase Sales. Promotional campaign or communication mix seeks to increase the company's sales by changing the elasticity of demand of the product through various techniques *i.e.*, distributing samples, or free gifts, purchase premiums, coupons etc. activities make the product popular and increase the demand.

(iii) To Reduce Seasonal Decline. Some products are used in a particular season. Promotional activities help maintaining the sales of the product in slack season when demand is little. Customers and middlemen are offered attractive discounts and free gifts. Other sale techniques are used to the customers to purchase the product even in the off season. The practice of offering off-season discount is in vogue in almost all countries of the world.

(iv) To Keep Memory Alive. Sales promotion keeps and memory of the product alive in the minds of the customers. Besides advertisement promotional activities help achieve this objective. It is required at all stages of product life cycles.

(v) To Develop Preferences and Convictions of Buyers. Sales promotion efforts are necessary to create awareness in the beginning, later on it seeks to develop brand image and product preferences among the buyers so that they may switch over to the company's product. To aquire conviction on conviction of buyers, promotion efforts of the company must include the act of convincing the buyer about the quality of the product. It should be adapted to their needs and requirements.

Importance of Promotional Activities

(i) Sale of Goods in Imperfect Markets. Under imperfect conditions there is severe competition in market and the selling of the product is not possible only on the basis of price differentiation or product attributes unless necessary information about the differences in the characteristics and the uses of the products of various competitors in the market are brought to the knowledge of the target consumers. This may be done by promotion activities through demonstration or comparative advertisement. If they are convinced by the arguments advanced by the company, the customers may stick or switch over to the brand of the company's produce. Thus promotion is necessary for selling the product successfully.

(ii) Bridging the Gulf between Manufactures and Consumers. Mass selling is impossible without promotional activities as the market has so widened at present that it has crossed the geographical boundaries. The distance between manufactures and consumers has increased, beyond imagination. The manufacture now cannot contact the consumers directly to get them acquainted with the product. Hence promotion is necessary particularly in foreign trade to bridge the gulf between manufactures and consumers.

(iii) Promotion War. Competition is a must in imperfect markets. If one competitor increases his promotional spendings and adopts aggressive strategy to oust the other competitors and capture the market, the other competitors must adopt similar promotional strategy to oust others or to survive in the market. Thus leads to promotion war which cannot be fought without promotional activities.

(iv) Increased Standard of Living. Sales promotion is always the result of large scale production. This however could be achieved only with the appropriate methods of large scale selling. Large scale selling is possible only with the help of promotional activities. The standard of living of the people becomes better because better quality of goods are available at cheaper rates due to large scale production and competitive saturation.

(v) Increased Trade Pressures. The growth of large scale retailers, super markets, chain stores etc. has brought greater pressure on manufacturers for support and allowance due to increase in the profitability of the manufactures. This pressure is even greater in export trade because the exporter is to a greater extent dependent on middlemen's services. As selling through ones own sales establishment is not easy, many manufactures resort to sales promotion activities to aid the retailers.

(vi) More Employment Opportunities. Promotional activities increase employment. They require a large number of salesmen who are specialists in the field.

Production is increased to meet the exportable surplus which increases the employment of opportunities in production and selling activities in domestic as well as in foreign markets.

(vii) Product Acceptance. Most of the sales promotion devices such as contests, premium coupons etc. increase product acceptance among prospective buyers faster than any other promotion method.

(viii) Effective Sales Support. Sales promotion policies supplement the efforts of personal and non-personal salesmanships (advertising). Good sales promotion materials make the salesman's efforts more productive. Promotion activities reduce their time spent in prospecting and the turn-downs.

(ix) Encouraging Middlemen. Promotion activities such as credit facilities, higher trade and cash discount, free gifts etc. encourage middlemen-wholesalers, retailers, agents or distributors to purchase more and more stock of the manufacturer's purchase. The middlemen sell the product in preference if they get higher profits or other facilities. Thus promotional activities encourage the middlemen to push the product.

Today the promotional activities have become part and parcel of marketing mix. Every manufacturer takes resort to such activities. In this world of mass production and competition promotional activities are necessary to survive in the market especially in foreign market. No product can reach the consumers unless it is promoted effectively in domestic as well as in overseas markets.

EXPORT PROMOTION MEASURES

(i) Supply of Raw Materials

(a) The raw materials used in an industry may be imported or indigenous, which means that they are produced in the country. The principle involved in this is that the necessary import licence will be made available to an industry for the import of raw materials necessary for export production. These are issued to the manufacturers of export products directly, or through their export houses.

(b) Similarly, export industries, engaged in the production of engineering goods, are assured of supplies of specified indigenous raw materials. An allotment can be made after export, when the necessary documents are produced. It can also be obtained in advance, provided that the demand is based on specific export orders.

(ii) Exemption from Custom Duty

Another export measure, to assist the manufacturers is the provision, whereby an exporter need not pay customs duty on imports made against an advance licence. There is a list of 148 items (published in Import Policy Book) for which exporters can obtain advance licences and import the items without the payment of customs duty. There is a detailed drill to be observed procedure-wise. This step helps the exporter not to lock up considerable amounts of money by way of duty. Previously, fhe exporter had to pay customs duty on imports made and later daim it back from Government by a procedure referred to as drawback of duty".

(iii) International Price Reimbursement Scheme (IPRS)

This scheme is introduced with a view to make available to exporters raw materials, at international prices. Where the quantity of raw material used is of a substantial order, and is worth importing directly, the exporter can use the mechanism of advanced licence, or pass book scheme, to enable him to import without paying the custom duties, and utilise it in the export production.

(iv) Cash Compensatory Support

This is referred also as Cash Assistance. This is one export promotion measure which, though often referred to by many is least understood.

In India, industries have to pay a variety of taxes and duties-taxes on raw materials as well as bought out components. Also, there are supplier of sub-assemblies, etc., who in turn pay taxes on their purchase.

Consequently, the end product in its cost structure contains a huge tax incidence. Also, there are taxes and duties on electricity, water, fuels used and on other consumable items, which amount to a sizeable quantum.

(v) Drawback of Duties

In the manufacture of industrial products especially, the manufacturer has to purchase raw materials and also their components. On such purchases he has to pay customs duty on imported items and excise duty on a large number of indigenous purchases. These taxes go towards the building up of the prices of his products.

The 'Scheme of Drawback of Duties' enables the manufacturer to get a refund of these duties.

Drawback is composed of the elements of customs and excise duties paid on materials utilised in the manufacture of the exported products.

(vi) Marketing Development Fund

The Government of India has been undertaking a large number of measures to improve the country's export trade. In an effort to have a common source to help implementation of the measures, the

Marketing Development Fund (in short, MDF) was created in 1963-64. The fund is utilised mainly for the development of market for Indian products abroad, for compensatory support for export commodities and for other export promotion efforts.

(vii) Excise Exemption Facilities

Various goods, either in the finished form or as they are being used in the manufacture of certain products, are liable to payment of excise duty under the Excise & Salt Act, 1944.

Goods exported out of the country are, however, given the facility of obtaining a refund of such payments, which may be had either after paying the duty or by exporting under bond.

Most of the firms prefer executing a bond with the Excise Authorities, so that goods may be cleared without payment of duty, thus avoiding a lock-up of funds.

(viii) Fiscal Benefit

In order to promote exports and enable the exporters to plough back into the export trade their profits for higher exports, the government has exempted the export profits from tax, under 80 HHC provision of the income-tax act.

In case of an exporter who is engaged in the sale of goods both in the export and domestic markets, the proportion of profits is taken in the same ratio as the export, turnover to the total turnover.

(ix) Finance Facilities

Another export promotion feature is credit facilities made available to exporters for purchase, manufacture and packaging prior to shipment, as also post-shipment credit facilities. Medium and long-term credits are also made available for the sale of capital equipment.

Export credit is provided by commercial banks which, in turn, are refinanced by the Reserve Bank of India or the Exim Bank of India. The scheme of assistance was formalised in 1968. According to this scheme, the Bank enters into participation arrangement with approved commercial banks for providing assistance to exporters in the form of credit for pre-shipment and post-shipment requirements, performance bonds for tenders, financial guarantees, etc. The refinance is provided to commercial banks at a concessional rate.

(x) Export Training

Apart from the courses/training conducted inside the country by the Indian Institute of Foreign Trade and other bodies, there are also training facilities abroad.

Many developed countries like Germany, Australia and France conduct export development courses for the export executives of developing countries. These courses give an opportunity for the trainees to know the export promotion procedures and technique adopted by these countries and other regulations relating to the their imports. The selection for admission to these courses is normally by a committee comprising IIFT, the host country and the Ministry of Commerce, afrer due advertisement in national paper. Preference for admission to these courses is given to middle management executives.

(xi) Bilateral Agreement

Since independence, India has entered into trade agreements with many countries. These agreements are bilateral in the sense that they are between two parties, but do not necessary commit each party to export or import specific quantities of commodities covered by the agreements. In some cases, a ceiling for certain commodity heads is given. This ceiling is based upon the country's ability to supply and also on the balance of trade between the two countries.

These trade agreements also provide for certain arrangements in respect of mode of payment for imports. In some cases, the mode of payment is in Indian Rupees, which are called "Rupee Payment Agreements". There is always some misunderstanding about the implications or payment when mentioned in Indian Rupees. All payments made to foreign countries in Indian Rupees are, in the final analysis, payments in foreign exchange. Even when Rupees are not directly converted into a foreign currency, they are utilised by the foreign buyer for financing export from India or for availing of services in India, for both of which he would have normally remitted foreign exchange. In other words, in all such cases, the foreign exchange that would otherwise have been earned by exports or services, is lost' to the country. Thus, though at first the transaction takes place in Indian Rupees, the final result is that India pays for the goods and services supplied by the foreign party in foreign exchange.

Factors that Affect the Promotion Decisions

Before taking a decision on its promotion strategy for foreign markets, a firm has to consider a large number of factors. Some of them are:

1. Corporate Objectives. The objectives of the firm affect the promotion decision to a great extent. A firm may have different objectives in different foreign markets or different firms may have different strategy in the same market. Firm's level of commitment to international operations will determined its promotion strategy. The objective of the firm in international marketing may be to create its image on a long term basis or it may be to maximise its cash resources or profitability in a short time and then withdraw itself from the market. A firm may want to sell its product only to a few customers whereas another firm would like to reach to the masses. The promotion strategy would be different in each case. A firm's promotion strategy wanting to sell only to a few customers will be quite different from a firm wanting to sell its product to the masses or to develop its own image in the market. Thus corporate objective shall determine the promotion strategy of a firm. It is so why different firms use different strategies in their international operations.

2. Nature of the Product or Services Offered. The nature of the product or the services offered by the firm is another factor that will determine the promotion strategy of a firm. Certain products are standardised and their promotional themes are also standardised. In such cases standardised promotional strategy can be used throughout the world. For example soft drinks like coca cola, satisfy the same basic need-thirst of the consumers in different countries. Hence it is possible for a firm selling soft drink to use common promotional themes in all the markets. Besides, there are certain other standardised products which are used in the same form, with slight modifications. The promotional themes and programmes may be used in the standardised form or with slight modifications. As against these products, there are certain other products which are not standardised such as ready made garments. Such products are differentiated from market to market. As these products do not satisfy the same need in all markets of the world, the standardised promotional strategy cannot be used, To illustrate, garments in France satisfy the fashion need whereas in developing countries, they meet the basic clothing need. Here the standardised promotional strategy cannot be used in the two markets. A firm dealing in garments should design different promotional strategies and themes for different markets.

3. Media Availability. A media which is easily available in domestic country need not necessarily be available in the foreign market. Though one may generalise that identical media are available in most industrialised countries, one should keep in mind that they may vary in institution quality and communications value. In such circumstances, the promotional message, theme and other properties of the media may be adjusted. But the task of international marketer is compounded where a certain type of media is just not available. For example, in some developing countries, television is not available for commercial communications. India has recently introduced the commercial service on TV network. In such cases, TV cannot be used as a promotion media. Countries having low rate of literact, may not have sufficient number of journals for advertisements. Hence, the marketer cannot make use of journals and may have to be shifted to other available media. The information about media may be available from international advertising agencies, country's diplomatic missions and advertising agencies' associations and the marketer should collect the information before drawing its promotion policy.

4. Financial Considerations. Financial resources of the firm may have serious constraint in deciding the promotion policy. A firm, not having sufficient financial strength, cannot use a strategy involving a heavy expenditure. As against this, a firm having a good financial background, may use any method which may prove useful to the firm. For example, most firms from developing countries like India do not rely more on advertising because it is expensive. They prefer direct mailing to customers in foreign countries or to participate in fairs and exhibitions. These firms, at times resort to consortia advertisements, in foreign markets. Such advertisements are often placed by the Commodity Boards or the Export Promotion Councils. But firms having large financial resources, on the other hand, prefer to use advertising and other sales promotion methods to promote their products in world markets. Thus, financial resources of a firm put a limit on the promotion policy and promotools of the firm.

5. Environmental Constraints. Finally, the firm should evaluate the environmental factors like the level of economic development of a country, the disposable income of the people, consumer's preferences and attitudes towards advertising and sales presentation, competitor's promotion strategies and the legal requirements in a given foreign market. Broadly, a firm should assess the cultural and legal side of the environment and the competitor's strategies followed in that market :

(i) Cultural Environment. The culture of the people in a given market influences their attitudes towards the promotion programme of a company. If people believe that the advertisement is nothing but a bundle of lie, the promotor should avoid this tool. People in some country are against foreign goods because they violate their cultural traditions, the firm would have to adopt a promotion programme which would remove this bias. The marketer should make endeavour to educate the people on the benefits which would accrue to them through the product use over their traditional products. The better way in such cases may be to localise the product. The marketer may sell the product to the agents or distributors in the foreign markets and they may sell it under their brand names in the manner most suitable to the country's culture.

Attitude of the people towards their traditions or the image of a particular product cannot be changed overnight. The people are to be educated to benefits of the product and it is a long-drawn programme. This strategy is beneficial only if the marketer develops a market on long-term basis and has sufficient funds to invest in such long term programmes.

(ii) Legal Constraints. The legal requirements as regards promotion techniques must also be fulfilled by a marketer. Legal system in a target foreign market may be different from that of the domestic country which may seriously affect the promotion decision of the firm. The international marketer must have a clear understanding of such requirements before going for a particular promotion strategy or drawing up a promotion programme. Although these legislations vary from country to country, one may observe that there are certain common restrictions in varying degree in almost all countries. These are:

(a) There are specific prohibitions on advertisements on certain products like wine, cigarettes and tobacco, and certain types of drugs etc. Most countries require that cigarette company must warn their consumers against the injurious effects of smoking hence it is statutorily compulsory to print 'smoking is injurious to health' on all packs and advertisements.

(b) Certain words or expressions that may be mis-interpreted by consumer or may deceive them are prohibited to use.

(x) Some countries, mainly Islamic countries, ban advertisements which are viewed as obscene.

(c) There are legislations which prohibit the promoter to make tall claims about their products. In countries where such legislations do not exists the trade has developed its own code of advertising which acts as a self-disciplinary system of control.

(e) In certain countries, requirements on packaging such as inscribing the name, address, weight and contents of the inside product, should be strictly observed.

The above legal requirements and there may be certain others which may be peculiar to the target market, must be observed by an international marketer before designing a promotion policy for the market. Any carelessness to such provisions may cause harrasment to the marketer.

(iii) Competitors' Promotional Strategy. In designing its promotion policy or strategy for the target market, a firm should not ignore the promotion strategies, policies, programmes and promotools undertaken by the competitors in the market. The firm should study them and then decide on the promotion policy which is better or if not better, it should at least the similar to competitors' policy. This, however, depends very much on the company's resources, culture and attitude of the people, etc.

Thus, the international marketer must consider the above factors into consideration before jumping to any promotion policy. He must not base promotion decision on his hunches or intuition. He should not do what others are doing. He must study and evaluate all the factors relevant to reach a decision for the promotion of his product in the target market.

EXPORT PROMOTION COUNCILS

These are organisations specialised in a particular product or a group of products. Their main objective is to promote and promote export of such commodities or a group of products.

The Export Promotion Councils have been set up under the Indian Companies Act 1956, as non-profit organisations. There are 20 export promotion councils in India, dealing with various commodities. These are being mentioned below:

1. Cotton Textile Export Promotion Council, Mumbai.
2. Engineering Export Promotion Council, Kolkata.
3. Export Promotion Council for Finished leather and leather Manufactures, Kanpur.
4. Gem and Jewellery Export Promotion Council, Mumbai.
5. Handloom Export Promotion Council, Chennai.

6. Apparel Export Promotion Council, New Delhi.
7. Basic Chemicals Pharmaceutical and Cosmetics Export Promotion Council, Mumbai.
8. Cashew Export Promotion Council, Cochin.
9. Chemicals and Allied Products Export Promotion Council, Kolkata.
10. Leather Export Promotion Council, Chennai.
11. Plastics and Linoleums Export Promotion Council, Mumbai.
12. Processed Food Export Promotion Council, New Delhi.
13. Shellac Export Promotion Council, Mumbai.
14. Carpet Export Promotion Council, New Delhi.
15. Wood and Wollens Export Promotion Council, New Delhi.
16. Overseas Construction Council of India, Mumbai.
17. Silk Export Promotion Council, Mumbai.
18. Silk and Rayon Textiles, Export Promotion Council, Mumbai.
19. Spices Export Promotion Council, Cochin.
20. Sports Goods Exports Promotion Council, New Delhi.

Regional and Overseas Offices

Some of these Export Promotion Councils have set up regional as well as overseas offices in the selected countries.

Membership and Working of the Export Promotion Councils

Any exporter of the product coming under the council can become the member if they are desirous of claiming export incentives and assistance of the Council. These councils receive grants from the Government under its various heads.

Each member pays an annual subscription fee. A working Committee elected by the members, elects its chairman and other office bearers. The working committee discusses all the problems relating to the product coming under the council, and necessary action is also taken. Senior officials of the Government, are also appointed on the Working Committee to guide and take part in the deliberations.

Functions of the Export Promotion Councils

(i) Export Promotion. The Export Promotion Councils aid in export promotion works by providing external as well as internal publicity, trade fair participation. It also promotes exclusive exhibitions of specific products.

(ii) Assistance to Exporters. Exporters receive assistance from the Export Promotion Council in understanding and implementing the trade policies and schemes launched by the Government.

(iii) Maintains Liaison. To identify the problems of the exporters, the council maintains an effective liaison with industry and trade. It serves the valuable purpose of a 'link' between the industry, trade and the Government.

(iv) Sends Delegates to Foreign Countries. The council arranges and sends delegation of foreign countries to promote the export of a specific product or a group of products.

(v) Provides Data to the Government. The council collects complete data (concerning a specific product) on export growth, the problems faced by the exporters etc. It presents such data before the Government to evolve policies and programmes for the solution of the problems.

(vi) Assistance through Offices, Branches in Foreign Countries. The council provides assistance to the exporters in consolidating the existing exports and diversifying the new products through new offices opened in the foreign countries. This explores the new potential for exports and lends a very useful service to the small manufacturers who can not go to the foreign countries for the purpose.

ROLE OF EXPORT PROMOTION COUNCILS IN THE FIELD OF EXPORT PROMOTION

An exporter, on being a member of the Export Promotion Council starts getting following utilities from it:

(i) The councils circulate the trade enquiries (received from its commercial representatives abroad) among members much earlier than these are published.

(ii) The publication of the market surveys and research undertaken by the council, in their bulletins provides valuable information to the exporters.

(iii) Plans for display and advertising abroad are prepared by the councils.

(iv) The councils provide valuable advice on finance, banking, insurance, scope of joint ventures, as well as custom formalities.

(v) The councils also provide creditability reports on the status of the suppliers; as well as about their technical competence and capacity.

(vi) The council makes recommendations on the difficulties brought to its notice by the exporters and puts such recommendations before the Government.

(vii) Exporters are assisted in arranging supply of indigeneous and imported raw materials by the councils.

(viii) The councils arrange buyer-seller meetings and get togethers.

(ix) The council also help in establishing tie-ups in the third country exports.

(x) The councils help in resolving trade disputes.

(xi) Arranges programmes of the foreign businessmen visiting the country.

CLASSIFICATION OF EXPORT PROMOTION ORGANISATIONS

Export promotion organisation are concerned with promotion of exports. Many export promotion organisations have been developed in last two decades. We would classify the various export promotion organisation into six different groups. These are Policy and Service support organisation, Commodity Specialisation, Training and Research Institutions, Trading/Service Corporations, Financial Institutions and Institutions to facilitate exports of Small Scale Industries (SSI) and Cottage Industries (CI).

The role of Department of Commerce in ministry of commerce. The department functions through the following six divisions, the economic division, the trade policy division, the foreign trade territorial division, the export products division, the export industries division and the export services division.

Some important organisations set up for export promotion are the Board of Trade, Advisory Council of Trade, Chamber of Commerce, Export Promotion Council, Commodity Boards, Indian Institute of Foreign Trade, Indian Council of Arbitration, etc.

Export promotion councils are non-profit making limited companies registered under the companies Act. There are more than 20 export promotion councils.

Indian Institute of Packaging (IIP) was set up in 1966 with an objective to give guidance and training to Indian exporters in regard to packaging techniques. We would discuss the objective of IIP and its role.

Indian Institute of Foreign Trade (IIFT) was set up by Government of India in 1963. It is an autonomous body registered under the Societies Registration Act. We would discuss the main activities of IIFT.

Another important organisation for export promotion is the Indian Council of Arbitration. It was set up in 1965 as an autonomous non-profit organisation registered under the Societies Registration Act.

Export Inspection Council (EIC) was set up in 1964 to administer quality control and preshipment inspection of export goods. The EIC came into existence mainly to ensure standards of Indian export goods.

The various foreign trade promotion organisations can be broadly classified or grouped as follows:

1. Policy and Service Support Organisations.
2. Commodity Specialisation.
3. Training and Research Institutions.
4. Trading/Service Corporations.
5. Financial Institutions.
6. Institutions to facilitate exports of SSI/CI.

1. Policy and Service Support Organisations

(i) Ministry of Commerce. Ministry of Commerce is the apex ministry at the central level to formulate and execute India's foreign traqe policy, and to initiate various export promotional measures. Under the Ministry of Commerce, the following organisations operate and undertake the role assigned to them:

(a) Board of Trade.

(b) Board of Approval for EOUs.

(c) Inter-Ministerial Committee on Joint Ventures.

(d) States Cell.

(e) DGFT

(f) Director General of Commercial Intelligence and Statistics.

(g) Export Inspection Council.

(h) EPCs/CBs/FIEO.

(i) Indian Trade Promotion Organisation (ITPO).

(ii) Ministry of Textiles. The Ministry of Textiles is primarily responsible for the formulation and execution of foreign trade policy in respect of textile sector including, sericulture, jute and handicrafts, Prior to November 1989, the Ministry of Commerce through its Department of Textiles used to monitor exports of textiles. The following organisations or bodies who work under the Ministry of Textiles in connection with exports - Advisory Boards.

(a) Development Commissioner, Handicrafts.

(b) Development Commissioner, Handlooms.

(c) Textile Commissioner.

(d) Jute Commissioner.

(e) Development Council on Textile Industry.

(f) Jute Manufactures Development Council.

(g) National Institute of Fashion Technology.

2. Commodity Specialisation (Organisations)

The Government has set up a number of commodity organisations which specialise in the export promotion of specified items. Each organisation has certain item(s) under its purview. The commodity organisations are assisted and aided by the Government. These institutions are as follows :

(a) Export Promotion Councils (EPCs).

(b) Commodity Boards (CBs).

(c) Marine Products Export Development Authority (MPEDA).

(d) Agricultural Products Export Development Authority (APEDA).

(e) Federation of Indian Export Organisations (FIEO).

3. Training Institutions

The GOI has also established training institutions, so as to promote India's export trade. Some such prominent institutions are:

(a) Indian Institute of Foreign Trade (IIFT).

(b) Indian Institute of Packaging (IIP).

(c) National Institute of Fashion Technology (NIFT).

4 . Trading/Service Corporations

A number of trading/service corporations have been set up under the Ministry of Commerce, and Ministry of Textiles. They are engaged in import and export of goods (canalised and non-canalised items). The prominent among such institutions are:

(a) State Trading Corporation (STC).

(b) Minerals and Metals Trading Corporation (MMTC).

(c) Mica Trading Corporation (MITCO).

(d) Spices Trading Corporation Ltd. (STCL).

(e) Central Cottage Industries Corporation of India Ltd. (CCIC).

(f) Handicrafts and Handlooms Export Corporation of India Ltd. (HHEC).

(g) Tea Trading Corporation of India (TTCI).

(h) Projects and Equipments Corporation of India (PEC).

(i) National Textiles Corporation (NTC).

(j) Cotton Corporation of India (CCI).

(k) Jute Corporation of India (JCI), etc.

(l) National Handloom Development Corporation (NHDC).

5. Financial Institutions

The financial institutions plays a leading role in the promotion of export trade. Without the active support of financial institutions, the exporters cannot think of exports. The commercial banks and EXIM Bank provides direct finance for export trade. SIDBI provides direct finance to units in small scale sector and tiny sector.

All India financial institutions such as lOBI, ICICI, IFCI, and others provide long term industrial finance for setting up export projects or industries.

The RBI through its departments, *i.e.*,:

(a) Industrial and Export Credit Department ; and

(b) Exchange Control Department, administers various policies relating to export finance/credit and dealings in foreign exchange.

The ECGC of India Ltd., also plays a leading role in promoting exports. It protects exporters against credit risks which may be commercial risks or political risks.

6. Institutions to Support Exports of SSI/CI

The government has established organisations exclusively for small scale industries and cottage industries. The various foreign trade promotional organisations in this respect are:

(a) The Development Commissioner, SSI Organisations (DCSSIO).

(b) Directorate of Industries.

(c) National Small Industries Corporation (NSIC).

(d) State Corporations.

ADVERTISING CAMPAIGN

After the exporting firm takes a decision to use advertising as a tool of promotion, the first step in this direction in is to design a specific advertising campaign. To carry out this task, it must work in close association with the advertising agency appointed to do it.

Three specific Problems

Following three basic questions are to answered *viz.*,

(i) What to communicate? The objectives of the company.

(ii) How to communicate? Identifying the media.

(iii) To whom to communicate? A problem to identify the target buyers.

(i) What to Communicate? It depends on the basic objectives of the firm what to communicate to target buyers. The message and appeal will differ for different objectives. While the ultimate objective of any firm's advertising campaign is to increase sales, the immediate objective may be to popularise the brand name, brand loyalty etc. to achieve sale increase.

(ii) To Whom to Communicate? This is the problem to identify the market segment that involves identifying the target buyers. The advertiser is to find out how, when and where do they purchase, the strength and weakness of the advertiser's products and of the competitors' products etc. The age, sex, income and other relevant market variables for the consumer products decide the segments of the market.

(iii) How to Communicate? This is the problem to decide how to link the above two variables *viz.*, to bring the advertising message to the target consumers in such a way as to get the maximum out of it. It is a question of choice of media to communicate the message (theme) to the target buyers. Out of a number of media available in developed countries, such as television, radio, journals, newspapers, cinemas etc., a particular medium is to be selected on the basis of following criteria:

(a) Coverage. Coverage means the number of potential buyers exposed to the medium. A medium which reaches to the maximum number of buyers, should be given preference taking into consideration the cost of advertising per customer and the sale potential of the market.

(b) Selectivity. Selectivity means popularity among the target consumers. While some journals are favoured only by professionals, some others may have a large number of female readership. Journal for the medium preferred by the customers to whom the product is meant for is the best medium of advertising.

(c) ***Frequency.*** This means: Does it allows to see the advertisement very often to the expected buyers? Does it allow high concentrations of advertising suitability or to support a consumer promotion? A medium with highest frequency is obviously the best.

(d) ***Creative Scope.*** It means: Does it allow the message to be developed as fully as necessary or allow visual inspection? Does it allow colours? Medium with maximum creative scope is the best.

(e) ***Regional Flexibility.*** This means that does it allow the advertising to concentrate on a specific area or flexible enough to have a wider geographic dispersion. The national media should be selected as far as possible taking into consideration the product development in future.

(f) ***Relative Cost of Each Medium.*** The main objective of medium is not only to have the maximum impact but also at least cost. The real cost calculation involves some managerial judgement. The cost of media should be measured per unit. For example, the cost of a medium may be cheap but it may be less effective, therefore the real cost per unit, will be more. So relative cost of medium should be studied.

(g) ***Sociological Factors.*** These should be considered in media selection. In a country where literacy rate is low and printed advertisement may be less effective, T.V. or Radio is the best medium.

Role of Department of Commerce in Promoting Exports

The Department of Commerce in the Ministry of Commerce is the apex body in the six-tier arrangement of the institutional infrastructure created for the promotion of exports in India. This is the primary Government agency and the brain of entire export promotion system in India and is responsible for evolving and directing India's foreign trade policy and programmes including developing trade relations with other countries. It also supervises the state trading in India and is also responsible for devising and implementing various trade promotional, measures and the development and regulation of certain export-oriented industries. It formulates and regulates country's foreign trade policy and is responsible for external trade including commercial relations with other countries, state trading, various trade promotional measures, and development and regulation of certain export-oriented industries and commodities such as tea and tobacco. The department functions through the following six divisions.

Divisions of the Department of Commerce

The Department of Commerce in the brain behind the policy formulation regarding infrastructural facilities. It is also the principal agency to chalk a out the trade policy of the country. It has six functional divisions that assist it in its deliberation and discharge of functions:

(i) The Economic Division. The Economic Division is headed by the economic adviser to the Government of India. The division is responsible for the development of export planning and export strategies and also for the periodic review and appraisal of foreign trade policy. It co-ordinates the functions of and maintains contacts with the other division as well as with other organisations set up under the Department of Commerce to assist the export drive. It also monitors work relating to technical assistance, management services for exports and overseas investments by Indian entrepreneurs.

(ii) The Trade Policy Division. This division is mainly concerned with the development in the international field like UNCTAD, GATT, ESCAP. It has regular contact with the regional groupings like EEC, EFTA, LAFTA etc. and Commonwealth to maintain trade relations. It is also responsible for the tariff and non-tariff barriers imposed by the importing countries on India's exports.

(iii) The Foreign Trade Territorial Division. The division is entrusted with the work relating to the development of trade with different regions and countries of the world. It looks after matters relating to state trading, trade fairs and exhibitions, organisation of trade, commercial publicity abroad etc. Besides, it also maintains a liaison with India, commercial missions and representatives abroad and attends to the connective administrative work as also the protocol functions.

(iv) The Export Products Division. The division is concerned with the problems of production, generation of surplus and market development of different products except with the products under the jurisdiction of the Export Industries division which are exported by India. Though these products administratively continue to be under the ministries concerned, the division is simply responsible for ensuring that exportable surplus is generated on continuous basis and export commitments are met to their full extent besides meeting the home consumption. It also keeps continues watch over the functioning of export promotion councils, commodity boards and other export organisations dealing with the commodities under its jurisdiction.

(v) This Export Industries Division. This division is responsible for the problems connected with the production development and regulation of some select commodities, including tobacco, rubber, and cardamon for export purposes. It also looks after the export promotion activities of certain specified products, including textiles, woollens, readymade garments, coir, silk and handicrafts.

(vi) The Export Services Division. The division deals with problems of export assistance, facilities and grants to Indian industries and exporters to produce more to general export surplus. The functions of this division include replenishment licences, cash assistance, marketing development assistance, export credit, export houses, guidance to Indian entrepreneurs to set up joint ventures abroad, capacity creation in export-oriented units etc.

Apart from the various divisions within the Ministry of Commerce there are a number of executive or advisory agencies functioning under the Ministry of Commerce. These bodies are mainly in the category of attached or subordinate offices, trade promotion institutions, public sector corporations, commodity boards or registered societies. Further, there is an Import Export Trade Control Organisation headed by Chief Controller of Imports and Exports. This office is responsible for the execution of the import and export policies formulated by the ministry. Import and export licensing of iron and steel and ferro alloys is also looked after by this organisation. Its subordinate offices are located at Ahemedabad, Amritsar, Banglore, Mumbai, Kolkata, Ernakulam, Hyderabad, Kanpur, Chennai, New Delhi, New Kandla, Panji (Goa), Pondicherry, Rajkot, Shillong, Srinagar, Vishakhapatnam, Chandigarh, Jaipur, Patna and some other places.

The subjects for which the of Department Commerce of is responsible are enlisted below:

1. General International Trade Policy

(i) International Commercial Policy.

(ii) International Agencies connected with Commercial theory (*e.g.,* UNCTAD, ESCAP, ECA, ECLA, EEC, EFTA, GATT).

(iii) International commodity agreements other than agreements relating to wheat.

(iv) All matters relating to international trade policy agreements relating to what.

2. Foreign Trade

(i) All matters relating to foreign trade including trade negotiations, and agreements (including general Agreement on Tariffs and Trade and Common Wealth Tariff Preferences), trade missions and delegations, trade co-operation and promotion and protection of interests of Indian traders abroad.

(ii) Import and Export Trade Policy and Control Excluding the matters relating to:

(a) Import of feature films.

(b) Export of Indian films, both feature length and shorts.

(c) Import and distribution of cine-films (unexposed) and other goods required by the film industry.

(iii) Chief controller of imports and exports.

3. State Trading

(i) Policies of the State trading and its subsidiaries excluding handicrafts and Handlooms Export Corporation and Central Cottage Industries Cooperation.

(ii) Minerals and Metals Trading Corporation and its subsidiaries.

4. Trading with the Enemy, Enemy Property

(i) Trading with the enemy; enemy firms and enemy property; separations (other than German Industrial Equipment) : Controller of Enemy Trading; Controller of Enemy firms, custodian of Enemy Property for India.

(ii) International customs Tariff Bureau including residuary work relating to Tariff commission.

(iii) Development and Expansion of Export production in relation to all commodities. Products, manufactures and semi-manufactures including the following:

(a) Agricultural produce within the wearing of the Agricultural Produce (Trading and Marketing) Act, 1937.

(b) Marine products.

(c) Fuels, minerals and mineral products.

(d) Industrial products (engineering goods, chemicals plastics, leather products, etc.)

(e) Specific export-oriented products (including plantation crops etc., but excluding jute products and handicrafts) which are directly the charge of this Department.

(iv) All organisations and institutions connected with the provision of services relating to the effort export including:

(a) Export credit and Guarantee corporation.

(b) Export inspection council.

(c) Directorate General of Commercial intelligence and statistics.

(d) Trade Fair Authority of India.

(e) Free Trade zones.

(v) Production, distribution (for domestic consumption and exports) and development of plantation crops, tea, coffee, rubber and cardamon.

(vi) Projects and programmes for stimulating and assisting the export efforts.

(vii) Processing and distribution for domestic consumption and exports of Instant tea and Instant coffee.

(viii) (a) Tea Trading Corporation of India.

(b) Tea Board.

(c) Coffee Board.

(d) Rubber Board.

(e) Cardamon Board.

(f) Tobacco Board.

ORGANISATIONS TO BOOST EXPORT PROMOTION

The Government of India, through the Ministries of Commerce and Industries, has established an integrated structure for servicing and promoting exports. It provides guidance, information and assistance to exporters. The following are the organisations set up for export promotions:

1. The Board of Trade. It is a body consisting of representatives of organised trade and industry. Senior officials of the Economic Ministries of the Government of India are also its members. It meets periodically and discusses the problems regarding country's foreign trade and recommended their solution.

2. Advisory Council of Trade. Public sector trading organisations, RBI, Research and Development Organisation, ECGC, Members of Parliament are its members. It reviews the performance of country's economy in its commercial aspects, mainly concerning exports and imports.

3. Regionl Advisory Committees on Imports and Exports. These are four zonal Committees. North, South, East and West. These committees discuss local problems faced by exporters, importers and manufacturers, relating to import licensing, customs clearance, release of foreign exchange for travel abroad, duty drawback, quality control, pre-shipment export incentives and shipping and transportation etc.

4. Chambers of Commerce and Industries. They play an important role in export promotion. Their activities are mainly the dissemination of information, providing a forum for discussion of problems arising due to policy matter, issue of certificate of origin to exporters, etc.

5. Federation of Indian Export Organisation (FIEO). It was formed by the Government of India to provide an apex co-ordinating agency dealing particularly with problems of general nature, common to all commodities and services.

6. Export Promotion Councils (EPCs). There are 17 such councils in India handling wide range of products. They secure active association of growers, producers and exporters in country's drive for export promotion. They are registered as non-profit organisations under the Companies Act.

7. The Trade Development Authority (TDA). It is the promoter of India's industrial exports. Though it is public sector organisation, it serves the private and the public sector alike. It renders a package of services to an entrepreneur. It is a promoter of new products, markets and export-oriented unit. It also promotes export oriented joint ventures.

8. Commodity Boards. There are in all 9 such boards for different commodities which are tea, coffee, rubber, cardamon, coir, silk, handicrafts and handloom products. They are formed to ganise, develop and promote production and exports along proper lines.

9. Export Houses. In order to develop the capacity, resources, competence and specialisation in the field of export market, the Government of India has started a scheme in 1958 to recognise certain export organisations as export house. In the case of a manufacturfng export house in the small-scale sector, the qualifying export amount is Rs. 25 lakhs (FOB) as exports for products in the select list and Rs. 2 crores for other products. They get the facilities offices, surveys, advertisements and exhibition etc., acquisition by transfer of import replenishment licences.

10. Indian Institute of Foreign Trade (IIFT). It mainly concentrates on areas of market research, training of personnel and dissemination of market information and intelligence in India. It started as an autonomous body registered under the Societies Registeration Act in 1963.

11. Indian Council of Arbitration. Its main object is to promote arbitration as a means of setting commercial disputes and to popularise arbitration among traders.

12. Export Inspection Council (EIC). It tries to maintain quality standards for the products exported from India. Under the Export (Quality Control and Inspection) Act of 1964, the Government of India notified commodities which are subject to compulsory quality control or inspection or both, before shipment. Such commodities should acquire certificates obtained from the EIC.

13. Export Processing Zones. In India, there are two such zones, *viz.*,

(i) Kandla Free Trade Zone (K.F.T.Z.) and

(ii) Santacruz Electronics Export Processing Zone (SEEPZ).

They offer the benefits of duty-free import of capital goods and equipments, exemption from customs, and other counter-veiling duty on raw materials, components, consumable items etc. exemption from central excise duties, advance import licences etc.

14. The Directorate of Exhibitions and Commercial Publicity. It arranges participation in international exhibitions, Indian exhibitions abroad, runs show-rooms in foreign countries and establishes trade centres in important selected markets outside India.

15. The State Trading Corporation of Indian and its subsidiaries. Its main functions are:

(i) Diversification of India's export trade,

(ii) Effecting exports to the existing markets and exploring new markets.

(iii) Maintaining exports of traditional items; and

(iv) Canalising imports of certain commodities.

COMMODITY BOARDS

Commodity Boards have been set up by the Government as a separate organisation to promote the exports of commodities in which they are concerned. The important functions of these Boards (other than the Rubber Board), is to promote export of the commodities with which they are concerned and in this respect they conduct themselves as if they are Export Promotion Councils.

The CBs, are for promoting the exports of specific commodities particularly the traditional commodities including tea, coffee, rubber, spices, tobacco and handloom items. The commodity boards are autonomous bodies and they guide the product development, marketing and export of the respective commodities. The functions and activities of commodity boards are more or less similar to that of EPCs. Following are some important differences between EPCS and Commodity boards:

(a) First the commodity boards look after the export promotion of primary and traditional items of exports while the EPCs look after the export promotion of non-traditional items like engineering goods, computers, chemicals, etc. with promising export potential.

(b) Secondly, the commodity boards are statutory bodies while EPCs are registered bodies under Indian Companies Act.

(c) Thirdly, the commodity boards are concerned not only with export promotion but also with other aspects such as product development etc., whereas EPCs are concerned mainly with the promotion of exports of the respective products.

Commodity boards take active interest in production, development and exports of respective commodities. In addition, other activities like production of new methods of cultivation of commodities, market research, publicity and assistance to manufacturers and exporters are also undertaken by the commodity boards. They act as connecting link between Indian manufacturers and foreign importers. These Boards have opened foreign offices and they participate in international trade fairs and exhibitions. They also undertake market surveys and other research activities. Trade delegations are often sent by these boards for promoting exports. Pre-shipment inspection of export items is also arranged by some commodity boards.

Functions of Commidity Boards

The functions and objectives of the commodity Boards are:

(i) To advise the Government on policy matters such as fixing the quotas for exports, signing of trade agreements with foreign countries etc.

(ii) To undertake promotional activities such as participation in exhibition and trade fairs, opening of foreign offices abroad conducting market surveys, sponsoring trade delegations etc.

(iii) To promote the consumption of the commodities under their jurisdiction by opening their branch offices in foreign countries. For example, Tea Board has opened various promotional unites in foreign countries with a view to organise generic promotion programmes.

(iv) To deal with entire range of problems regarding the commodities under their jurisdiction.

(v) To undertake research activities with a view to develop production, and marketing commodities within the country. Many Commodity Boards have set up their research units. Among them are:

(a) Central Coffee Research Institute.

(b) Rubber Research Institute.

(c) Coir Research Institute at Alleppey.

(d) The Central Sericulture Research Station at Berhampur.

(vi) To impart training to workers engaged in the production of the concerned commodity. The following training centres have been set up by their respective Boards.

(a) The National Coir Training and Design Centre.

(b) Two institutes of Handlooms Technology at Salem and at Varanasi.

They award Diploma to the successful candidates.

Types of Commodity Boards

The Government of India has set up eight commodity boards, the objectives of which are to guide the production and exports of the respective commodities along the right lines.

(i) Coffee Board. The Board was set up under the Coffee Act of 1942 for the development of the industry and the promotion of its exports. The Board has set up a Central Coffee Research Institute and also six coffee demonstration farms. The result of its research activities are made available to coffee growers. The Board inserts special advertisements in foreign trade journals and mass circulation newspaper media. Further, it takes part in trade fairs and exhibitions to further the export of the product.

(ii) Tea Board. This was set up by the Government of India under the Tea Act of 1955, the main objectives of which are the development of the tea industry and the promotion of its exports. The Board has set up offices in India as well as abroad. It is also associated with the Tea Councils set up in the UK, the USA, W. Germany, France, Australia, New Zealand and Canada with the co-operation of other tea-producing countries. The Board also arranges for quality control and pre-shipment inspetion wherever necessary under the Tea Control Order of 1959.

(iii) Cardamom Board. The Board was constituted under the Cardamom Act of 1965 by the Government of India as a statutory body with its headquarter at Ernakulam in Kerala State. It has a foreign office at Brussels, which co-ordinated the exhibitions organised abroad and undertakes promotional campaigns.

(iv) Coir Board. This was set up in 1953 under the Coir Industry Act for the development of the coir industry. It has a Coir Research Institute at Alleppey, as also a National Coir Training and Design Centre. It carries out research surveys, encourages new coir establishments and engages expert weavers to give practical training to the trainees. It undertakes publicity in India and abroad, through mass media and exhibitions.

(v) Rubber Board. This is also a statutory body set up by the Government of India under the Rubber Act of 1947. The Board advises Government on all aspects of the rubber industry, and controls the planning, marketing and acquisition of rubber. One of the important functions of the Board is to promote the development of the rubber industry in India. It deals with the registration of estates, issue of new planting and replanting licences, and other development schemes such as replanting subsidy. It has a Rubber Research Institute with well-equipped laboratories and many publications for the benefit of the industry.

(vi) Central Silk Board. The Central Silk Board was constituted in 1949 under the Central Silk Board Act. The Board undertakes:

(a) The development of the sericulture industry,

(b) The implementation of annual plans and achievement of production and export targets,

(c) The organisation of research, training, seed production, and

(d) The import-export of raw silk fabrics.

Its headquarter is located in Mumbai, and runs the following establishments:

The Central Sericulture Research Stations at Berhampur, Kalimpong, Mysore and Ranchi; and

(vii) The All-India Handicrafts Board. The Board, having its headquarters in Delhi, undertakes:

(a) The running of four design centres at Mumbai, Kolkata, Banglore and New Delhi, and one development centre at Banglore;

(b) To help State Governments in the planning and execution of development schemes;

(c) The development and evaluation of new designs which are commercially viable, and production of proto-type; and

(d) Export promotion measures such as participation in trade fairs and exhibitions, production of films, brochures, catalogues and other promotional aids.

(viii) All India Handloom Board. The Board is doing vigorous work in spreading this cottage industry. There are two institutes of Handloom Technology, one at Salem and the other at Varansi. They conduct diploma courses of 3 years, on successful completion of which students are awarded a Diploma by the Board.

The Board conducts seven weaver centres located in Mumbai, Indore, Varanasi, Kolkata, Mangalari, Bangalore and Madras. These centres carry out research with a view to evolving new and attractive designs for internal and export markets. They also render technical assistance to the handloom industry in the fields of printing, dyeing and weaving. Further, they provide financial assistance and other help to the industry by organising depots abroad and aid in arranging pre-shipment quality-control inspection.

Apart from the above, the Office of the Jute Commissioner, established by the Government of India, renders all possible assistance to the industry and Government in the promotion of export of jute. Similarly, the office of the Textile Commissioner looks after the export promotion of textiles and their derivatives.

INDIAN INSTITUTE OF FOREIGN TRADE

The Indian Institute of Foreign Trade was set up in 1963 as an autonomous body registered under the Societies Registration Act. The main functions envisaged for the Institute are:

(1) Training. The Institute conducts training programmes on various aspects of export trade. Broadly, these fall into three categories, tailored to various needs:

(a) Programmes for senior export marketing executives and Government personnel of India and various developing countries;

(b) Programmes for junior executives and fresh graduates; and

(c) Special training programmes on the basis of requests from various organisations developed to suit their needs.

(2) Research. The research activities of the institute are confined to export trade—mainly in the field of policy formulation and in the field of specific exports, market surveys etc.

Another area in which the Institute has successfully forged ahead is in the field of surveys conducted by it on behalf of the various State Governments to identify commodities from each State which have an export potential. A perusal of these surveys indicates that the Institute:

(a) Identifies the potential products for export from a State,

(b) Investigates the problem faced by such industry in exports,

(c) Studies export marketing problems for such products and finally,

(d) Makes recommendations as to the type of assistance needed for such industry and also indicates various other industries which can be established on the basis of their expert potential arising out of the availability of the raw materials and other expertise in the State. The main activities of IIFT are:

 (a) Training of export management personnel drawn from trade and industry, export institutions, Government departments and trading corporations.

 (b) Undertakes research on various aspects of foreign trade. It also undertakes research on problems referred to it by industry, trade and Government.

 (c) Conduct of market surveys in India and abroad to identify products and countries offering potential for Indian exports.

 (d) Dissemination of information arising from its activities relating to foreign trade.

 (e) Provides consultancy services to business firms in matters relating to foreign trade.

(f) It publishes information through its Journals *i.e.*, Foreign Trade Reviewed (quarterly) and Foreign Trade Bulletin (monthly).

(g) It sponsors candidates selected from industry and trade, export houses trading corporations for higher training abroad in export management.

IIFT has specialised faculty and researchers for undertaking studies in the Indian markets as well as overseas markets and commodity surveys for the benefit of exporting community and export promotion agencies in India.

The institute imparts training to:

(a) Junior executives for one year.

(b) Middle level executives for one to two months.

(c) Senior executives for one to two weeks.

The training covers wide areas in export management such as:

(a) International Marketing.

(b) Trade Policy.

(c) Export Pricing.

(d) Export Promotion Aspects.

(e) Export Finance.

(f) Overseas marketing research.

(g) Overseas Sales Management.

(h) Export Procedures.

(i) Export Regulations etc.

The IIFT has an excellent library where one can refer publications from GATT, UNCTAC, and other publications and periodicals on all aspects of international marketing.

INDIAN COUNCIL OF ARBITRATION (ICA)

In export trade, sometimes a dispute arises between a buyer and seller in which the buyer complains that the seller has not fulfileld the conditions of the contract. These may be due to:

(a) Quality,

(b) Quantity,

(c) Delivery,

(d) Packing,

(e) Specifications, and

(f) Price or due to any other conditions of the contract.

In such cases, arbitration becomes necessary—a procedure which should be acceptable to both the parties.

The Government of India established the Indian Council of Arbitration in 1965, which is registered under the Societies Registration Act as a non-profit organisation.

The main objectives of the Council are:

(a) To publish literature on commercial arbitration cases and allied literature;

(b) To conduct meetings and seminars to acquaint exporters with international law and commercial arbitration;

(c) To render advisory services to the export community with regard to arbitration clauses and allied matters which have to be included in international trade contracts; and

(d) To help in the settlement of trade complaints by providing services for settlement of business disputes by arbitration. For this purpose, the Council maintains a panel of arbitrators.

As is normal in such cases, the help of the Council may be invoked only when there is an arbitration clause in the contract or, in the alternative, when both the parties to the dispute agree to refer the matter to the Council.

The conciliation services of the council are rendered free of charge. However, in cases of arbitration, the fees charged by the Council are nominal. The arbitration proceedings of the Council are governed by the rules of arbitration, which can be obtained from the council.

WORLD TRADE CENTRE

The World Trade Centre was promoted by M. Visvesvaraya Industrial Research and Development centre, a non-profit organisation.

The World Trade Centre was started in Mumbai, the commercial capital of India, in order to promote exports of India, especially that of handicrafts and small and medium scale industries.

The basic idea of starting this World Trade Centre in Mumbai was to bring together all export related agencies at one place. At present, the Centre accommodates offices of EPC's Importers, Exporters, Clearing and Forwarding Agents, Government Agencies, Consultancy firms etc. The Centre also has showrooms where Indian products are exhibited or displayed for Indian and Overseas buyers.

The Centre is presently affiliated to World Trade Centres' Association New York, which presently has 166 members in 56 nations.

Functions of WTC

(1) Research and Development. The WTC assists Indian Exporters and manufacturers in their R & D effort. It publishes a quarterly journal 'World Trade Review' which brings out important aspects of foreign trade.

(2) Seminars and Workshops. The WTC conducts seminars and workshops on foreign trade. This helps the exporters to obtain current information on various markets abroad. By attending such seminars, exporters can device new and better export strategies.

(3) Information. The WTC, also provides valuable information to the exporters through its monthly bulletin Trade Promotion Services' and a quarterly journal 'WTC Intercom'.

(4) Education and Training. The World Trade Centre also conducts short-term courses to educate and train export personnel in various aspects of foreign trade.

(5) Buyer-Seller Meet. The Centre organises and facilitates buyer seller meet, where overseas buyers meet Indian businessmen to negotiate and sign contracts.

(6) Exhibitions. The Centre provides space for display of every kind of merchandise. Exporters can have their exhibitions either permanently or temporarily. A number of items are displayed such as handicrafts, gems and jewellery, leather items, engineering goods, etc.

TRADE FAIR AUTHORITY OF INDIA (TFAI)

The Trade Fair Authority of India (TFAI) has been set up as a Government Company under the Indian Companies Act, 1956. It took over the functions of the erstwhile Directorate of Exhibitions and Commercial Publicity, The Indian International Trade Fair Organisation and the Indian Council of Trade Fairs and Exhibitions. The Trade Fair Authority of India started functioning in March, 1977.

The Indian Council of Trade Fairs and Exhibitions and Trade Fair Organisation.

The objectives of the Trade Fair Authority are:

(i) To promote, organise and participate in industrial trade and other fairs and exhibitions,

(ii) To set up showrooms and shops in India and abroad,

(iii) To undertake trading activities in commodities connected with or relating to such fairs and exhibitions, and

(iv) To develop exports of new items for diversification and expansion of India's exports.

The Trade Fair Authority of India brings out regularly three journals, namely, Udyog Vyapar Patrika (Hindi—Monthly), Indian Export Bulletin (English—Weekly), and Economic and Commercial news (English—Weekly). These periodicals provide authentic information on the country's economy, business possibilities offered by foreign markets, Government trade policies, facilities available for exports and important tenders floated by other countries. They also provide material to Indian Missions for their publicity efforts.

The Authority has been organising wholly Indian exhibitions and India's participation in several international fairs on a countrwide basis.

With effect from July 1981, all fairs and exhibitions, both within the country and outside, are coordinated by the Trade Fair Authority. It is also the sole agency for organising fairs and exhibitions assisted by Marketing Development Assistance.

Recently, TFAI has developed a sprawling exhibition complex in New Delhi called "Pragati Maidan". It is one of the excellent complex for arranging national and international level fairs and exhibitions. Pragati Maidan is one of the best exhibitions complex in Asia. It is now popular as a prestigious trade and cultural centre in the country.

The TFAI plays an important role in promoting exports of non-traditional items. It gives wide publicity to Indian goods in different countries through various media of mass communication and also through fairs and exhibitions. Information about foreign markets and scope for marketing abroad are made available to Indian exporters by the TFAI. The TFAI brings out journals like Journal of Industry and Trade, Indian Exports Service Bulletin and Economic and Commercial News (Weekly). These journals provide authentic information on country's economy, prospects for Indian exports abroad, Government trade policies, export facilities, etc. The TFAI has been organising wholly Indian exhibitions and participates in international fairs and exhibitions. It also brings co-ordination in the fairs and exhibitions organised inside and outside India as it is the only agency for organising fairs and exhibitions assisted by Marketing Development Assistance. The TFAI is playing an important role in projecting the achievements and capabilities as also the image of the country in foreign countries through its publicity techniques and also through participation in international fairs and exhibitions.

FREE TRADE ZONES

The concept of Free Trade Zones has been in existence for a long time. They are very popular and successful in the newly industrialised developing countries of the Far East. India entered this arena with the establishment of Kandla Free Trade Zone in Gujarat and later Santa Cruz Electronic Export Processing Zone (SEEPZ) in Mumbai.

The Government selects a large area if land, preferably close to a port, provides the infrastructure, such as land, water, electricity, and standard construction if necessary for units to be established within the zone. The main facility afforded, to these units are duty free imports of capital goods, raw materials, ancillaries etc. for manufacture and export.

The goods manufactured in the zone can also be supplied to the domestic market upto 25% of the production against valid import licences.

The exports from the Kandla Free Trade Zone amounted to Rs. 107 crores in 1983-84. In the subsequent year 1984-85 the exports amounted to Rs. 150 crores in the first eight months-highest exports since its inception.

The Santa Cruz Electronic Export Processing Zone similarly achieved an export of Rs. 88 crores in 1983-84, and in the period April to December 1984, the exports ammounted Rs. 72 crores, and was well on its way to achieving the maximum exports since inception in the year 1984-85.

In view of the encouraging results, the Government has decided to set up four more Free Trade Zones at Chennai, Cochin, NOIDA (New Delhi) and FALTA (West Bengal).

STATE TRADING CORPORATION AND ITS SUBSIDIARIES (STC)

The STC of India, a public sector agency, was set up by GOI on May 18, 1956. State Trading means the direct participation by the Government in the purchase and sale of goods and commodities both, in internal and external markets.

The main functions of the STC are:

(i) Diversification of, and consequently increases in, India's export trade;

(ii) Exploring of new markets for existing as well as new products; and

(iii) Promotion of long-term export operations and "difficult-to-sell" items.

The STC is also entrusted with products/product groups, the export of which is canalised through it. Similarly, imports of a lot of items are canalised through the STC. Hence, the activities of STC encompasses exports, imports and domestic trade.

It has also set up the Industrial Raw Material Assistance Centre, which imports raw materials in bulk and distributes them to industry "off-the-shelf" at competitive prices. The objective is to extend the benefit of bulk buying to actual users in non-canalised items.

The STC had, moreover, undertaken price support operations at the instance of the Government of India for natural rubber in 1970 and for tobacco in 1972. Growers were assured of remunerative prices, and surplus quantities, mopped up by the STC, were exported.

The export earnings of STC in 1988-89 was Rs. 531 crores as against Rs. 581 crores in 1987-88. The import sales of STC fell from Rs. 3037 crores in 1987-88, to Rs. 2036 crores in 1988-89. Consequently the total turnover of STC of Rs. 2586 crores in 1988-89 was lower than the previous years turnover of Rs. 3646 crores. The decline is primarily attributed to the decline in the import of edible oils.

(i) The Projects and Equipment Corporation of India (PEC). The PEC was formed in April 1971 as a wholly-owned subsidiary of the STC. It took over the Railway Equipment and Engineering Division of the STC. The main objectives of forming the Corporation were:

(a) To boost the export of engineering and railway equipment in established markets;

(b) To penerate new markets;

(c) To promote the export of non-traditional and new products; and

(d) To boost the exports of turnkey projects in the field of railway systems, public utilitise and industrial plants.

Some of the products in which the PEC have negotiated and signed contracts are:

Railway Wagons & coaches, steam an Diesel locals, electrical equipment, garage equipment, pumps and compressors, auto components, hand tools, textile machinery, cycles and cycle parts etc.

(ii) Cashew Corporation of India. This was incorporated in 1970 as a wholly-owned subsidiary of the. STC The main objectives of the corporation are:

(a) To find new markets for the export of cashew kernels;

(b) To establish new sources of the import of raw cashew nuts; and

(c) To ensure an uninterrupted supply of imported raw cashew nuts at fair prices for export-oriented industries.

It may be pointed out that the cashew industry is heavily dependent on imported raw cashew nuts. In order to overcome fierce and unhealthy competition among importers, and also to get the benefit of economic prices on large scale purchases, canalisation of this industry was brought about.

(iii) Handicraft and Handloom Export Corporation of India. The Handicrafts and Handloom Export Corporation of India came into existence in 1962. It is a subsidiary company of the State Trading Corporation. The main objective of the Corporation is to develop new markets and expand traditional ones, thus supplementing and aiding the existing private sector trade in handloom and handicrafts.

Major State Trading Organisations in India

(i) The STC of India Ltd.

(ii) The Projects and Equipment Corporation (PEC) of India Ltd., a wholly owned subsidiary of STC.

(iii) The Cashew Corporation of India Ltd. (CCI), a wholly owned subsidiary of STC.

(iv) The Handicrafts and Handlooms Export Corporation of India Ltd. (HHEC), a wholly owned subsidiary of STC.

(v) The Tea Trading Corporation of India (TICI) a subsidiary of STC.

(vi) Central Cottage Industries Corporation (CCIC), a subsidiary of HHEC.

(vii) The State Chemicals and Pharmaceuticals Corporation of India Ltd., (SCPC), a subsidiary of STC.

(viii) The Minerals and Metals Trading Corporation of India Ltd. (MMTC).

(ix) The Mica Trading Corporation (MITCO), a wholly owned subsidiary of MMTC.

(x) Spices Trading Corporation.

THE MINERALS AND METALS TRADING CORPORATION

This Corporation, known as the MMTC, was established by the Government of India in 1963. It was expected to develop the export of mineral ores and such other products as are assigned to it by the Government from time to time. It was also given the responsibility of importing some essential raw materials for Indian industries.

Of all the main products, it concentrated on the export of iron ore, manages ore, certain grades of coke and coal, ferro-manganese, bauxite, etc. Iron ore occupies a predominant position in this exports. The total exports of the country in iron ore and concentrates are of the order of 28 million tonnes, fetching foreign exchange earnings of Rs. 543 crores in 1988-89. It should be borne in mind that MMTC is responsible only for the export of iron ore other than ore of Goan origin.

On the import side, the Corporation buys non-ferrous metals, fertilisers, certain categories of steel, etc., in bulk quantities at competitive rates for supply to Indian industries.

The various subsidiaries of STC and MMTC were established and expanded with the avowed Government objectives of placing the export and import trade, especially of the products which come under the purview of these organisations, in the public sector with a view to giving a boost to export trade. However, the performance of these Corporations has not come up the levels of export trade expected of them.

❐

12

Export Finance

TERMS OF PAYMENTS IN INTERNATIONAL TRADE

The terms of credit or payments in international trade refer to contractual matters of prior arrangement between the buyer and seller. Their determination depends upon a number of factors including exporter's knowledge of the buyer, buyer's financial standing, the degree of risk involved in receiving payment, speed of remittance, cost involved in receiving payments, exchange restrictions in the importing country, competition in the foreign market the type availability and demand of the merchandise to be exported, the country of importer, new or old account, the availability of freight space to the country of destination and many other considerations.

Terms of Sales v/s Terms of Credit

The terms of sales should be carefully distinguished from the terms of credit. The terms of sales are the conditions of contents, time, place and delivery of merchandise, and only indirectly affect the extension of credit or lengths of time for which the credit is allowed. On the other hand, the terms of credit are the expression of the extent of trust the seller (exporter) is willing to place in the buyer (importer).

An export contract can be deemed to be successfully completed when the exporter gets paid for the goods shipped by him. How he has to receive payment is something which is to be decided during earlier negotiations between the exporter and the importer. There are five methods of payment which involve varying degrees of risk for the exporter. The five methods are:

(i) Payment in advance,

(ii) Open account,

(iii) Documentary bills,

(iv) Documentary credit under Letters of Credit,

(v) Shipment on consignment basis.

The following factors are usually taken into consideration while deciding about the terms of payments:

(a) Exporter's knowledge of the buyer,

(b) Buyer's financial standing,

(c) The degree of security of payment,

(d) Cost involved in receiving payment,

(e) Speed of remittance,

(f) Exchange restrictions in the importing country,

(g) Competition faced by the seller.

Modes or Terms of Payments

There are five modes of payments in international trade.

(1) Advance Payment. When the exporter receives the bank draft or bank advice before the contractual obligation of shipment is fulfilled. The payment may be received either as soon as the order is confirmed or any time before shipment. This method is obviously the most advantageous from exporter point of view. But this form is very rarely adopted and is essential only when the buyer's credit worthiness is open to question. The exporter may be willing to impose the term as a pre-condition only when he knows that:

(a) The goods are in heavy demand, and

(b) The goods are tailor made for the customer, or

(c) Goods are rare.

Even in such cases, compromises are very often made taking into many other considerations. There are certain situations where this type of payment is common, There are some large buying organisations in USA and the continent which have their buying agent all over the world. These agents sometimes pay in advance for the goods procured.

(2) Open Account. Under this method, the exporter sends the invoice and other documents relating to transfer of title and possession of goods direct to the buyer (importer) and on receipt of such documents, the importer remits the amount involved immediately. In case a credit period is allowed the importer will make the payment at the expiry of the credit period.

This method is very simple and avoid many complications and additional charges. The entire risk in this case is of exporter. But this method of payment presupposes that:

(a) There is long established relationship between the importer and the exporter and exporter has faith in him,

(b) The exporter has the necessary financial strength to bear the risk,

(c) There is no exchange regulations in the importing country otherwise payment may not be received in time, and

(d) The foreign exchange regulations of exporting country should permit such an arrangement.

In India, the RBI has permitted this facility for inter-company transactions against 'Round Sum Remittances'.

Thus, under this method of payment, the burden of finance is carried by the exporter and it also carries the real risk for the exporter. Generally, this method is not followed unless parties are well known to each other and there is a keep competition among the sellers.

(3) Documentary Bills. The above mentioned two forms of payment—advance payment, and payments on open account are not very common in foreign trade. The documentary bills, however, is a very common method adopted for payment in international trade. These bills act as a bridge between:

(a) The unwillingness of the exporter to part with the goods until he is paid for, and

(b) The unwillingness of the importer to pay for the support unless he is sure of receiving the goods.

Banks act as a via-media by giving the necessary assurance to both the parties. Under this form of payment, the exporter submits the documents to his bank along with the bill of exchange. The exporter's bank then sends the bill along with the documents to its correspondent bank in the importer's country and presents the bill before the importer either for payment or for acceptance as per terms of the bill. The documents along with bill are full set of bill of lading, invoice and a marine insurance policy. There are two types of documents under this method.

(a) Documents against Payments (D/P), and

(b) Documents against Acceptance (D/A).

(a) Documents Against Payment (D/P). In such cases goods are shipped and the documents of title of goods along with the bill of exchange are surrendered to his bank by the exporter. The bank will send the documents and bill to its correspondent bank in the importer's country. The bank in the importing country will present the documents along with the bill to the buyer and on making the payments of the bill of exchange, will handover the documents to the importer. Until the payments are made, the title to the goods vests with the exporter.

(b) Documents Against Acceptance (D/A). In case of documents are sent to the importer through banker, the banker presents the bill to the importer for acceptance and if he accepts the bill, the bank will deliver the documents of title to the buyer (importer) so that he may take possession of goods. On due date, the bank will again present the bill to the buyer for payment and if payment is received, the collecting banker sends the amount to the exporter through normal banking channels to be credited to his account. Normally under D/A bills the exporter will have to wait for payment till the final payment is received on due date. This may take time and the commercial banks very often discount such acceptances and thus the exporter receives the payment of the bill immediately after shipment of goods.

Both the types of bill—D/A and D/P—are common in export trade, there are various commercial risks which the exporter must take into account before he agrees to accept payment on such basis. Even when the documents are against payment (D/P), the exporter runs the risk of non-payment by the importer. As the documents in this case, will not be handed over to the importer unless he accepts the documents by making the necessary payments. The documents will remain in the hands of the banker and the exporter will not lose possession of and title to the goods. Therefore, he would be able to find the alternative buyers for his goods or in extreme case, ship the goods back to his own country. Though the latter alternative, obviously will be very costly and even in the former, he may have a recourse to distress sales. In the case of D/A bill, the risk is even greater as the importer has already taken the possession of goods which may or may not be in his custody. If he fails to meet his obligation of payment on due date, the exporter will not have any other alternative except to start civil proceedings for the recovery of amount. This course will also prove a costly and time consuming affair. Institutional facilities are available almost in every country which undertake responsibility and provide cover for such commercial risks. In India ECGC (The Export Credit Guarantee Corporation) offers such facilities.

(4) Documentary Credit Under Letter of Credit. This is the most popular form of payment now-a-days. Under this system, the banker of the importer undertakes the responsibility to pay the exporter, under instructions from the importer, if the exporter presents certain shipment and payment documents covering the goods, within a specified period. In effect, the credit of the issuing bank is substituted for that of the buyer. Such written undertaking of the importer's banker to the exporter is known as Letter of Credit (L/C). This will be dealt with in the next question.

(5) Shipment on Consignment Basis. Under this method the exporter makes shipment of goods to overseas consignee/agent without making any claim for payment for the goods shipped but retains the title of the goods with him and also the risk attached thereto even though the possession of goods is with the overseas importer. The payment under such contracts, will be made only when goods are sold. Under such contracts, the risk is of great amount because:

(a) His payment will be due on a date which is quite uncertain as no body knows the date of sale;

(b) If the consignee fails to sell the goods, he may return the goods without any liability and at exporter's expenses;

(c) The price to be realised is also uncertain and will depend upon market condition; and

(d) The consignee may not observe the terms of consignment agreement.

Thus everything is uncertain until the payment is received. But there is an advantage of such agreements that the goods may fetch a handsome price for the goods if the buyer is satisfied with the quality of the product. Two points in this connection may be noted.

(a) Shipment on consignment basis is done only to trusted agents. In India, diamonds, tea, wool and tobacco are usually shipped on consignment basis.

(b) The exporter will have to declare the expected value of consignment in the GR form to meet the requirements of the Foreign Exchange Regulations Act.

Thus, the best form of international payment is the documentary credit against letter of credit and D/P or D/A come to next. All other methods are rarely adopted under terms of contract and under special circumstances.

SOURCES OF FINANCE OF EXPORT CREDIT NEEDS

Both for pre-shipment and post shipment requirements an exporter needs finances. Pre-shipment requirements are short-term requirements where the period of credit does not normally exceed 180 days. The Post-shipment credit needs may be short-term, medium-term and long-term. Medium-term credit is extended beyond 180 days and upto 5 years. Anything beyond 5 years is known as long term credit.

Short-term Sources of Finance

(i) Finance by Importer. In some cases the importer finances the exporter by sending the amount required to meet the pre-shipment credit in advance which can be adjusted against the import price of the goods. The importer may insists upon the letter of credit instead of cash. In both the cases the importer has financed the transaction.

(ii) Finance by Exporter. The exporter has financed the exports when he puts up his own capital or diverts his business funds towards export business, and executes the export order without the help of borrowed funds. The exporter may have an open account with the importer, if they are known and their relations are well maintained. Alternatively he may send the documents against payment or against acceptance after shipping the goods. If documents are against payment with a reasonable time. If the documents are against acceptance, he can discount the acceptance from his banker as soon as he gets it from the buyer after acceptance. Thus the exporter himself finances his short term needs.

Comparatively few manufacturers and professional exporters either have their own capital or wish to employ it in this manner. The rate of interest changed by the bank on export credit or fee for negotiating drafts is quite low and no wiseman will invest his own capital in this manner.

(iii) Finance by Factoring Houses. Factoring houses finance the export trade by discounting the bills of the exporters and they charge discount or commission for their services. They undertake the responsibility of any risk in the discounting of bills and thus particularly offer a good insurance cover for the loses. This method is useful to those exporters whose working capital is limited. The factoring house serves as a mercantile and banking houses which finances manufacturers, exporters, commission house and selling agents through the is discounting of receivables.

(iv) Finance by the Export Middleman. Sometimes the export middlemen, particularly the export merchant, or export commission house, finance export shipment. The manufacturers pay a usually high fee for the services rendered but such middlemen. Credit risks not ordinarily acceptable to banks, are granted by such middlemen. Usually, they turn around and refinance their own drafts through a bank.

(v) Finance by Banks. Banks render valuable services in the international trade providing short term finance to the exporter. Following services are offered by a bank in financing the export credit:

(a) It opens documentary credit account in favour of the exporter at the request of the importer, and issues letter of credit to the exporter. It makes the payment to the exporter on receiving the documents of the goods, imported.

(b) In the exporter's country the bank collects the necessary amount from the importer's bank against letter of credit or against documents of payments on behalf of the exporter.

(c) The bank finances the exporter by discounting the documentary drafts as accepted by the importer.

(d) It provides pre-shipment credits through loans, cash credits and over drafts for exporter's short term needs. In India these are in turn, refinanced by the RBI.

Commercial banks finance the most part of exporter's short term loans in India.

Medium and Long-Term Sources of Finance

By medium-term finance is meant finance for a period exceeding 180 days but not exceeding 5 years. it is provided in the case of durable consumer goods and light capital goods. Long-term finances are provided for a period exceeding 5 years for the sale of heavy capital goods complete plants and turnkey projects.

(i) Buyer's Credit. It is a means of financing an export transaction involving capital goods and equipment of large value or complete turnkey projects on long term credit. In it bank or other financial institution extends the credit facility to the buyer in the supplier's country so that overseas buyer may pay cash for goods imported. The credit facility so extended is guaranteed by the buyer's bank or often extended to buyer's bank itself for the specific purpose in view under two conditions:

(a) If the supplier executes the contract under the terms of contract of sale, he will get the money, and

(b) It involves no transfer of funds from one to another. There is no financial involvement for the seller.

(ii) Supplier's Credit. Under this form of credit the exporter or supplier offers credit to the overseas importer against the reciprocal credits from the commercial banks. In India commercial banks get refinance from the Exim Bank.

The sources of medium and long-terms finances are the following:

(a) Commercial Banks. Commercial banks offer only short-term loans for exports. While extending the short-term and long-terms loan facilities to exporters, they get refinance from the specialised financial institution such as Exim Bank in India.

(b) Export Import Bank. Export import banks finance the medium and long-term export credit needs. Such banks have been set up on USA in 1943 in Japan in 1950 and in India on 1st January 1982. A public sector financial institution in India, it provides medium and long-term loans directly for exports and indirectly to exporters.

(c) Private Export Finance Companies. A number of private finance companies have sprung up in many countries to boost the export trade. They offer medium and long-term loans for export purpose under the terms and conditions agreed upon between the two parties of the finance contract.

(d) International Financial Institutions. Many international banks and financial institutions extend long-term credit facilities especially to under developed countries to expand their industrial base so that they may contribute to world trade. Such institutions are World Bank, International Finance Corporation, Asia Development Bank etc.

EXPORT CREDIT AND FINANCE SYSTEM IN INDIA

(i) Licensed Commercial Banks. In India, the licensed commercial banks generally extend to the exporters short-term credit facilities at pre-shipment and post-shipment stages. Banks enjoy followings benefits for advancing loans to exporters:

(a) An interest subsidy of 1½ percent or refinance from the Reserve Bank of India or the Export-Import Bank.

(b) Guarantees by the ECGC, where a substantial part of risk is covered by the ECGC.

The commercial banks are also authorised to extend medium term and long term credit up to Rs. 1 crore for while they get refinance from the Exim Bank of India. Such loans can be given only to export Indian capital goods or turnkey projects. Long-term and medium-term loans above Rs. 1 crore are directly provided by the Exim Bank after assessing the nature of export, economic status of buyer and the importing country, the period of repayment and the credit risks involved, the project's commercial viability, capabilities of Indian exporter and soundness of importer.

(ii) The Exim Bank of India. It directly extends credit facilities to exporters under its various schemes. Indirectly it provides finances to exporters by refinancing the bills already discounted by the commercial banks. The term finance is generally given to exporters mainly to provide term credit to overseas buyer for the export of capital goods and consultancy services.

(iii) The ECGC. It facilities commercial banks to extend credits to exporters by providing various types of covers for the risks involved in export trade. It also guarantees credits extended by banks to exporters.

(iv) The Reserve Bank of India. It does not contribute directly in financing the export trade. It formulates different policies which help the exporters in getting financial facilities from the commercial banks and financial institutions. It directs the banks and Exim Bank to extend export credits for some particular purpose or at concessions rates or on liberal terms. It has formulated a number of schemes such as Export interest Subsidy Scheme etc.

Various Types of Credit Available to Indian Exporters

(i) Pre-shipment Finance or Packing Credit. It provides the exporters with working capital between the time of the receipt of order and the time of shipment to arrange for production or procurement of goods. Pre-shipment finance is of particular importance to small-scale manufacturers and exporters who do not possess sufficient financial resources to meet the expenditure involved in the production of goods for export.

Pre-shipment finance is normally provided by the commercial banks. As in the case of any other advance, the bank takes into consideration a number of factors before making the necessary advance to the exporter, *viz*,:

(a) Honest, integrity and capital of the borrower,

(b) Exporter's experience in the line,

(c) The bank's experience about the exporter,

(d) The Standing of the foreign buyer,

(e) Security offered,

(f) The margin and the rate of interest,

The security can be provided in the following forms:

(i) Letter of credit,

(ii) Confirmed order as evidence of having received an order,

(iii) Personal bond in the case of party (ies) already known to the banker.

(iv) Relevant policy issued by the Export Credit Guarantee Corporation,

Very often manufacturers might have to supply goods to an export house. In such cases, manufacturers may obtain pre-shipment finance on the basis of a letter from the export house containing:

(a) The obligation of the supplier, and

(b) A certificate that it is not itself claiming the pre-shipment credit.

Pre-shipment finance is provided for a period which would enable the manufacturer to produce the goods for export. The among provided under pre-shipment finance would normally cover the following costs:

(i) Cost of purchase or production,

(ii) Packing including any special packing for export,

(iii) Costs of special inspection or tests required by the importer,

(iv) Internal transport costs,

(v) Port, customs and shipping agents charges,

(vi) Freight and insurance charges if the contract is either C&F contract or a CIF contract, and

(vii) Export duty or tax, if any.

In certain cases the pre-shipment advance is made to finance expected receivables such as compensatory cash assistance, drawback, etc. Where domestic production costs are higher, pre-shipment finance may be higher than the FOB value of the contract to adequately cover the higher domestic costs. Pre-shipment advance may take the form of loan, overdraft or cash credit.

The concessional rate of interest on pre-shipment finance is 9.5 per cent for 180 days from the date of advance. Beyond 180 days but not exceeding 270 days (with prior approval of the Reserve Bank) the rate of interest is 11.5 per cent and beyond 270 days 16.5 per cent.

(ii) Revolving Credit. If an exporter is well known to the banker and his past performance has been satisfactory, the banks are usually prepared to grant revolving pre-shipment credit in connection with successive deliveries. This implies that upon repayment of the first loan, the exporter is automatically granted a corresponding loan on the same terms. This procedure offers the advantage of saving time and cots as the original documents serve as a basis for extended credit.

Packing credit is adjusted out of the post-shipment facility provided by the banks.

Pre-shipment credit may also be provided under a letter of credit with a red clause where advance is granted at the instance, and therefore, on the responsibility of the foreign bank establishing the credit.

In case the goods are to be procured or purchased from a supplier or manufacturer, the banks may open a letter of credit in favour of the suppliers under what is known as 'back to back letter of credit'. This procedure is usually adopted by export houses for getting letters of credit in favour of their suppliers. In such cases credit can be extinguished, by drawing a bill of the export house.

In the case of consignment sales, banks usually establish a special post-shipment credit account which is adjusted when the goods are sold abroad and the sale proceeds received.

(iii) Post-shipment Credit. Post-shipment credits are intended to bridge the financial gap between the time of shipment of goods and the actual payment therefore. Post-shipment credits are also provided by commercial banks against the security of approved shipping documents tendered against letters of credit or otherwise. Post-shipment finance is also provided at a concessional rate.

Post-shipment finance may be provided in one of the following forms:

(i) Export bills negotiated under letters of credit,

(ii) Discounting of bills drawn against shipment of goods-discounting of bills is usually done under limits sanctioned to different customers, and

(iii) An advance against bills under collection.

Banks usually charge a commission according to the rates prescribed by the Foreign Exchange Dealers' Association of India.

The rate of interest is 12 per cent up to 120 days. Beyond this period, the minimum rate prescribed by the Reserve bank is charged.

Repayment of the loan will generally take place when proceeds are received from abroad in conformity with the terms of sale. The position is a little more difficult when documents are to be delivered against acceptance. However, the policies provided by the Export Credit Guarantee Corporation (ECGC) can provide cover for such risks.

Post-shipment loans may be of three types:

(i) Short Term. The period is usually up to 6 months. The loan is provided by banks.

(ii) Medium Term. The period is up to five years and banks provide post-shipment finance in collaboration with the Export Import Bank of India. Medium-term finance is provided for in the case of durable consumer goods and light capital goods.

(iii) Long Term. Long-term loans are provided in the case of sale of capital goods, complete plants and turn-key jobs. The period of credit is usually more than five years.

Banks enjoy certain benefits for advancing loans to exporters. These benefits are:

(i) An interest subsidy of 3 per cent or refinance by the Export Import Bank of India or the Reserve Bank of India.

(ii) Guarantees provided by the Export Credit Guarantee Corporation where a substantial part of the risk is covered by the ECGC.

(iv) Buyer's Credit. It is a means of finance an export transaction involving capital goods and equipment of large value or complete turnkey projects on long-term credit. A loan is extended by a bank or other financial institution in the supplier's country to the overseas buyer who is thus in a position to pay cash for the supplies received. The loan is guaranteed by the buyers bank or often extended to the buyer's bank itself for the specific purpose in view. Two points have to be noted in this connection:

(a) If the supplier fulfils his responsibility, he gets his money.

(b) It involves no transfer of funds from one country to another.

There is no financial involvement for the seller.

Exports on Deferred Payment Terms

Contracts for export of goods against payment to be received partly or fully after the expiry of the period prescribed for realisation of export proceeds (normally 180 days), are treated as deferred payment export contracts. Extension of long-term export credits, especially for large value supply contracts and project exports, is now an accepted marketing strategy. Indian manufacturers also will have to offer such facilities if they have to complete successfully in international markets. Therefore, provision has been made for the extension of medium and long-term credit to finance the sale of Indian capital goods represented by machinery, equipment and related services. The rate of interest charged is 9 per cent.

Any loan up to Rs. 2 crores for financing export of capital goods is decided by a commercial bank which can refinance itself from the Export Import Bank (Exim Bank). In case of export contract above Rs. 2 crores but not more than Rs. 5 crores, the Exim Bank has been given the authority to decide whether export finance could be provided. Contracts above Rs. 5 crores need clearance by the Working Group. The Exim Bank conducts credit appraisal and takes on the major share of financing. The credit appraisal includes assessing the nature of export, economic status of the buyer and the importing country, the period of repayment and the credit risk involved. The various criteria adopted for evaluation of projects are:

(a) Whether the proposed project can be justified on commercial considerations,

(b) Whether the Indian exporter is capable of executing the contract,

(c) Whether the foreign borrower is financially sound to repay the credit according to the proposed repayment schedule,

(d) Whether the projects needing credit are economically viable. There is no maximum limit for the finance to be provided.

Security for deferred credit could be provided by:

(i) Letters of credit,

(ii) Promotes executed by Government buyers/public sector undertakings,

(iii) Acceptable bank guarantees,

(iv) Bills duly accepted by banks, and

(v) Any other security considered adequate.

A Working Group on Export Finance was set up in July, 1975, with IDBI as the focal point (now the Exim Bank) and RBI, ECGC and the bank(s) of the exporters as members. This Working Group is entrusted with the task of evaluation of the proposals of the Indian parties involving more than Rs. 5 crores at the pre-bid stage. The Working Group clearance means package clearance, *viz.*, from the standpoint of export finance, foreign exchange formalities and credit guarantees. In case of large contracts, ministries of Commerce and Finance also are represented on the Working Group.

Under the present regulations, depending on the value of the contract, the credit period can be extended up to 12 years. There are basically two different mechanisms for offering long-term export credit:

(a) Supplier's Credit. Under this system, the Indian exporter will offer credits to the overseas buyer. The exporter can on the other hand, secure reciprocal a credits from the commercial banks which, in turn, can get refinance from the Exim Bank.

(b) Buyer's Credit. In this case, Exim Bank directly extends credits to the importer. The Indian exporters can receive their payments straightway from the Exim Bank. The vital difference between the two schemes lies in the fact that in the former, the exporter is assuming the credit risks, while in the latter, Exim Bank does it.

Payment of Documentary Credit

Export orders or contracts normally stipulate that the buyer should open a letter of credit in favour of the exporter. Once the goods are shipped, the exporter presents the negotiable documents against the letter of credit and receives payment. A letter of credit is an authority for payment for the exporter provided he does not violate any of its clauses.

Payment by a letter of credit (L/C) is not only one of the most secure methods of payment but also the most widely followed in international marketing.

LETTER OF CREDIT

A letter of credit is a letter of payment authority issued by the buyer's bank at the behest of the buyer in favour of the exporter, and stipulates certain conditions, the performance of which, fulfils the contractual obligations of the exporter and entitles him to receive payment. The letter of credit is routed through a bank in the exporter's country referred to as the negotiating bank.

The technical definition of a letter of credit is found in the "Uniform Customs and Practices for Documentary Credits", where it is defined as "any arrangement, however named or described, whereby a bank (the issuing bank), acting on the request and in accordance with the instructions of the customer (the applicant for the credit), is to make payment to or to the order of the their party (beneficiary) or is to pay, accept or negotiate bill of exchange (drafts) drawn by the beneficiary or authorises such payments to be made or such drafts to be paid, accepted by another bank against stipulated documents provided that the terms and conditions of the credit are complied with."

Payment methods through a documentary letter of credit have a number of advantages. These are:

(i) Once the exporter fulfils all the conditions of credit and presents the documents for negotiation to his bankers in his own country, he receives his payment as per the terms of the letter of credit and is entitled to receive full payment for the exports he has made.

(ii) Once the letter of credit is established, the exporter may be reasonably sure that all the import trade regulations of the buyer have been complied with and that the transfer of funds against payment would not normally pose a problem from the exchange control authorities.

(iii) Where the letter of credit is a confirmed and without recourse one, the liability of the exporter ceases, once he has presented the negotiable set of documents and adhered to all the conditions of the L/C.

(iv) A letter of credit in India is an important document, for a commercial bank advances pre-shipment finance, such as packing credit, against the letter of credit.

Parties to Letter of Credit

The various parties connected with the letter of credit are:

(a) Opener. The buyer who makes the application and on whose behalf the credit is opened is called the "opener" of the letter of credit.

(b) Beneficiary. The beneficiary is the person in whose favour the credit is opened; normally, the exporter.

(c) Opening Bank. The bank in the importing country which establishes the letter of credit on behalf of the opener.

(d) Negotiating Bank. Usually beneficiary's bank through which the documents are normally negotiated. It also called the paying bank.

All the above parties have certain rights and responsibilities which are enumerated in detail in the "Uniform Customs and Practices for Documentary Credit."

A few points must be kept in mind while accepting payment through letter of credit. The letter of credit asked for should be:

(i) Capable of confirmation by the negotiating bank;

(ii) Irrevocable; and

(iii) Without recourse.

(i) Conformed Letter of Credit. If the letter of credit by the opening bank is routed through the negotiating bank which adds its own confirmation to the credit, the letter of credit is called a confirmed letter of credit. Confirmation by the negotiating bank entails a definite commitment on its part to carry out the provisions of payment. A confirmed credit thus carried with it the guarantee for payment from two banks—the opening bank and the confirming bank and is therefore a fool proof method of payment.

It should be remembered that the bank in India adds it's confirmation after getting the necessary authorisation from the issuing bank. Another method, which is sometimes resorted to, is for the opening bank to route its L/C through an internationally reputed bank abroad, which adds its confirmation when sending it to the negotiating bank.

(ii) Irrevocable Letter of Credit. This would mean that a letter of credit cannot be modified or cancelled, once it is opened without the consent of the beneficiary. It is thus a firm commitment on the part of the opening bank.

(iii) Without-Recourse Letter of Credit. Under without recourse letter of credit, the opening bank cannot have recourse to the drawer of the bill (exporter) in case payment is defaulted by the opener. An irrevocable letter of credit by itself does not permit the opening bank to have recourse to the drawer. However, as an additional precautionary measure, it is advisable to have without-recourse letter of credit.

(iv) There are two other variations in the letter of credit, which are rarely used by are prevalent in international trade:

(a) ***Transferrable L/C.*** In cases where the export product has to be fabricated partially or completely by a party other than the exporter, a portion or the full value of the letter of credit is made transferrable to the party by means of the transferrable L/C.

(b) ***Red Claused L/C.*** This enables the beneficiary to draw a predetermined value of L/C, as soon as it is established, to enable him to process the product.

Different Types of Letter of Credit

(1) Revocable Letter of Credit. In it the issuing bank clearly states that the credit can be revoked at any time without the consent of or notice to the beneficiary (exporter). Once the credit is revoked, the exporter has no other way out to recover his dues. It is most painful if the exporter comes to know at the last moment or even after shipment, that the letter of credit issued in his favour has been revoked. As the exporter's interest is not protected under this type of credit therefore, it is not very common in export trade. Revocable credits are never confirmed as there are generally addressed to a bank and not to the beneficiary.

(2) The Irrevocable Letter of Credit. It cannot be revoked by the issuing bank. Therefore, the problems attached to the revocable credit do not arise in such credit. The issuing bank is under an obligation to make the payment if the terms of credit are satisfied and the required documents are presented within the fixed period mentioned in the letter of credit. The exporter feels secure that the credit cannot be cancelled or revoked without the consent of or notice to all the parties concerned. According to the uniform customs, all letters of credit should confirm whether they are revocable or irrevocable.

(a) Confirmed Irrevocable Letter of Credit. As the importer and the exporter reside in different countries, the exporter is not familiar with the soundness of the importer's bank, issuing the letter of credit. He wants that a local bank in his country commits itself to make the payment to him as soon as the documents are presented soon after the shipment in order to reduce his payment risk. The commitment for the payment by a local bank on behalf of the issuing bank is called confirmation of letter of credit. The system works as follows:

The importer's bank (issuing bank) asks its correspondent bank in the exporter's country to confirm the original credit as opened by it. The correspondent bank, while advising the exporter about the opening of the letter of credit adds a clause to the effect that.

"The above credit is confirmed by us and we hereby undertake to honour the drafts drawn under this credit on presentation provided that all the terms and conditions of the credit are duly satisfied."

When the correspondent bank adds its confirmation to the irrevocable credit, it becomes confirmed and irrevocable. The exporter is in advantage because the non-payment risk is localised and minimised. But from importer's point of view, it becomes costlier because the issuing bank also charges the commission of correspondent bank from the importer. This is the basic reason why many importers would like to open irrevocable but not confirmed letter of credit.

(b) Unconfirmed Irrevocable Letter of Credit. In it the issuing bank asks the correspondent bank to advise about the letter of credit without confirmation. The exporter need not worry if the issuing bank is well known and of good standing. However, there is a contingency risk involved in unconfirmed credit. When the exporter receives the advice from the local bank that it is willing to negotiate the documents, he collects the payment from the local bank promptly. In such cases bills are usually to be drawn on the issuing bank. The exporter remains contingently liable for this period.

(3) Assignable Letter of Credit. Letters of credit may be assignable or non-assignable. An assignable letter of credit is one which can be assigned by the beneficiary (or in whose favour it is opened) to some other party. It is issued in favour of a representative of the importer/buyer especially when he does not know who will actually be the exporter of the merchandise. Once the representative finds a suitable person or firm (exporter) which is able and willing to ship the goods on the terms specified by the importer, he assigns the letter of credit to the party (exporter) concerned.

(4) Non-assignable Letter of Credit. It is that which cannot be transferred to any other person by the beneficiary *i.e.*, in whose favour, it is issued. Generally, it is opened in the name of the actual exporter after the order is confirmed by the exporter.

(5) Ancillary Letters of Credit (Back to Back Letters of Credit). Based on the original letters of credit these are assisting letters for credit. If the exporter in whose favour the letter of credit is opened, has no funds and no line of credit with a bank and he is unable to by the merchandise ordered, he may request the negotiating bank to open its own letter of credit to third party (the seller of goods) under the identical terms contained in the original letter of credit. If the original letter for credit is irrevocable the bank may issue own letter of credit known an ancillary letter of credit, honour the drafts of the seller on receipts of the shipping documents and cancel the ancillary letter of credit. Thought the exporter presents his draft for the amount of the original letter of credit, he receives only the difference between the amount of the draft and the amount paid by the bank on the draft drawn under the ancillary letter of credit.

Documents Accompanying Letter of Credit

(i) Bill of Landing. It is a document issued by the shipping company acknowledging that the goods mentioned therein have been shipped on board the ship and giving and undertaking that the goods will be delivered in the same condition.

(ii) Commercial Invoice. It is the basic document containing all the relevant information giving description of the goods, price, charges, terms of shipment, mark and number on the package, data, name of buyer and seller etc.

(iii) Insurance Policy. Insurance Policy contains terms of insurance contract.

(iv) Consular Invoice.

(v) Certificate of origin.

(vi) Letter of Hypothecation.

(vii) Certificate of Quality. It is issued by the standard institutions or authorities conforming that the quality of goods exported is according to the terms of contract.

(viii) Certificate of Weight. It is issued by port authorities certifying the weight of goods at the time of shipment.

EXPORT-IMPORT BANK OF INDIA

The Export-Import Bank of India (EXIM Bank) is a public sector financial institution, established on January 1, 1982. It has taken over the various export financing functions of the Industrial Development Bank of India. It was established by an Act of Parliament for the purpose of financing, facilitating and promoting foreign trade of India. It is the principal financial institution for co-ordinating the working of institutions engaged in financing export and import. The EXIM Bank Act also empowers the bank to finance export of consultancy and related services, finance export oriented industries and provide international merchant banking services.

Lending Programmes

The main focus of EXIM Bank operation is on export credits for medium-term and long-term exports. Whenever a buyer of exported goods services from India, is allowed to defer payment, an export credit arises. Deferred export credit is available for the sale of Indian machinery, manufactured equipment and related services. Capital goods eligible for export credit have been identified.

Objectives

(i) To finance exports from and imports into India of goods and services.

(ii) To finance Joint-Ventures in foreign countries particularly in third countries.

(iii) To finance export of consultancy and related services.

(iv) To finance import and export of machinery and equipment on lease basis.

(v) To provide loans to an Indian party so as to enable it to contribute in the share capital of a joint venture in foreign countries.

(vi) To finance export-oriented industries in India.

(vii) To conduct export market studies.

(viii) To undertake limited merchant banking functions such as under writing of stocks, shares, bonds or debentures of companies to parties in connection with export and import.

Resources of EXIM Bank

The authorised capital of the Bank is Rs. 200 crores which can be increased to Rs. 500 crores. Initially its paid up capital was Rs. 50 crores which has been increased to Rs. 147.5 crores, fully described by the Government of India. The Bank can raise its resources from the following:

(i) From the open market by the issue of bonds and debentures,

(ii) From the Government of India.

(iii) From the Reserve Bank of India from its National Industrial Credit (Long Term Operation) Fund.

(iv) From the International markets. It can borrow currency in India or outside India.

To begin with, the whole of the business of Industrial Development Bank of India relating to export financing was handed over to the Exim Bank. As on 31st December 1985 the position of Bank's financial resources were:

(i) Paid up capital of Rs. 100 crores fully subscribed by the Government.

(ii) A long term loan of Rs. 45 crores from the Government of India.

(iii) A loan of Rs. 125 crores from the Reserve Bank of India.

(iv) Outstanding loan of IDBI on transfer of loans to the Bank at the time of its beginning in 1982.

(v) A reserve of Rs. 32.5 crores,

During 1983, the Exim Bank borrowed Rs. 39.4 crores redeemable at par at the end of 13 years, as on 5 the Feb. 1986.

The Government of India has guaranteed the repayment of the principal and the interest on the bonds.

EXIM Bank operates three broad programmes of financing. These are—Loans, Re-discounting the Guarantees.

The Lending and Rediscounting programmes are divided into nine categories as indicated below:

(i) Provide Financial Assistance to Exporters. This enables the Indian exporter to extend term credit to an importer overseas for the purchase of Indian capital goods. The exports include equipment, machinery and related services, projects exports, turnkey projects, construction projects, etc. Export of this nature aries when an Indian company contracts supply agreements for the supply of equipments and services or a project export agreement involving the setting up of a textile mill sugar plant, etc.

(ii) Technology and Consultancy Services. Indian companies borrow funds from EXIM Bank and provide deferred credit to overseas buyers of Indian technology or consultancy services.

(iii) Pre-shipment Credit. This loan of credit is available for companies that have won an export contract for capital goods and are seeking finance to produce the goods which entails a production period exceeding six months.

(iv) Overseas Investment Financing. The bank provides financing where an Indian company establishes a joint Venture overseas, and requires funds towards equity participation.

(v) Overseas Buyer's Credit. This is offered directly to foreign importers for the import of Indian capital goods and relative services with repayment terms spread over a period of years.

(vi) Lines of Credit to Foreign Governments. Lines of credit are offered to foreign governments and foreign financial institutions. Such line provide long-term finance for import of Indian capital goods, and related services.

(vii) Export Bills Re-discounting. This lending programme is available to commercial banks in Indian who are authorised to deal in foreign exchange. Such banks can re-discount their short-term issuance export bills with the EXIM Bank. EXIM Bank provides funds under this programme for a period of 90 days.

(viii) Relending Facility to Banks Overseas. This facility to overseas banks is made available to enable them to provide term finance to importers for import of Indian capital goods. The overseas banks will facilitate the foreign buyer, the EXIM Bank, and supplier to avail of these facilities.

(ix) Refinance of Export Credit. Under this Programme, the commercial banks in India, who are authorised to deal in foreign exchange, can obtain from EXIM Bank 100% refinance of term loans extended for export of Indian capital goods. This credit is limited upto Rs. 1 crore. For contracts above Rs. 1 crore, commercial banks can obtain financing participation under EXIM Bank's other programmes.

New Schemes

Exim Bank has started three new lending schemes to Indian exporters during the year:

(a) Finance for Export Oriented units.

(b) Finance for deemed exports.

(c) Exports Bills (SSI) Rediscounting scheme.

Under the above schemes all financing is in Indian rupees, except otherwise arranged by agreements. Bank charges commitment fees on lending programmes at 1% p.a. on overseas Investment Finance scheme and at 0.5% p.a. in Overseas Buyers Credit scheme and Lines of Credit scheme.

The repayment period under each scheme is flexible according to equipment and project. However, normally it does not exceed 10 years except under pre-shipment credit which depends upon the manufacturing cycle. Under Export Bills Rediscounting Scheme, it is 90 days.

Major Functional Groups

(i) Project Finance Group. It looks after the requirements of Indian exporters engaged in constructions and turnkey project exports.

(ii) Trade Finance Group. It looks after the requirements of exporters of goods without services components.

(iii) Planning Group. It has been assigned the planning work. It provides the economic and financial analysis necessary for the formulation of Exim's corporate strategy. It also analyses these conditions of overseas markets. It identifies foreign markets and the risks involved in exporting goods and services to such markets.

(iv) Overseas Investment Finance Group. It studies the requirements of Indian firms or companies desirous of setting up joint ventures abroad.

(v) Coordination Group. It main function is liaison work. It disseminates information regarding Bank's activities and liaises with institutions related to Exim Bank's activities.

International Contact

Exim Bank has established contacts with international financial institutions and export credit agencies to cofinance the projects which can absorb Indian exports. It has initiated an informations service which provides advance informations to Indian exporters on projects to be financed by IBRD/ ADB and the scope of business job opportunities in such projects.

Exim Bank has set up three foreign offices Abidjan (ivory coast), Washington D.C. and Singapore to identify projects and product export opportunities funded by multilateral agencies. It has also organised a specialist cell at Mumbai to co-ordinate operations with overseas offices to provide advisory and financial services to Indian exporters planning to secure all larger share of projects. It has launched a lending programme to support export from small scale industries. The SSI Exports bills are rediscounted under this scheme.

Terms of Advances

(i) Loans against claims of drawbacks and cash compensatory support. Exporters are require to execute a power of attorney in favour of the Bank so that Bank may collect the amount from the agencies concerned.

(ii) Loans to exporters for more than FOB value of export. The ECGC Export Production Guarantee authorises a commercial bank to advance loans to the extent of 150 per cent of the FOB value of the contract subject to a maximum of 100 per cent of cost of product in the domestic market.

(iii) Loans to 100% EOU. The Bank implemented its lending programmes to support 100 per cent export oriented units, units in free trade zones and deemed profits. It extended financial assistance to export production units with a view to enhancing competitiveness of their products in international markets.

(iv) Credit limit. In general, the basis for fixing the credit limit is the credit needs of the exporter rather than FOB value of the export order.

METHODS OF EFFECTIVE PAYMENT

The most common instruments through which foreign exchange transactions take place are Telegraphic Transfer, Mail Transfers and Bank Drafts and Cheques, Bill of Exchange and Letter of Credit. Foreign exchange dealings of bank involve greater risk than domestic credit extension.

The following are the methods of transferring money from one country to another:

1. Telegraphic Transfer (TT). This is a rare practice of remitting foreign payments through telegram to another person in the foreign countries. Unlike bank draft, the money is deposited with the bankers in India and the Indian banker sends a cable or telegram to the foreign branch to immediately make certain payments to the specific party. Thus, the foreign branch will make necessary payments in foreign exchange to the specific party. In export import trade this practice is not commonly adopted.

Telex are now being used widely for transmitting money between countries. Telegraphic transfer is the quicker method of transmitting funds involving no risk because they are passed between "Gilt-edged" names. As it involves payment of funds at the foreign centres on the same day as the receipt of domestic currency in local centre, no interest or capital risks are involved in TT and its price is considered as the basic rate of exchange between two countries.

2. Mail Transfer (MT). In this method of remittance, an order to pay cash to a third party is made in writing which is sent by mail. This is similar to a telegraphic transfer with the difference that instead of the order being sent by cable it is sent through mail. Mail transfers are issued in duplicate by the issuing bank and they are despatched on the same day as the receipt of payment in domestic currency at the Local Centre. On receipt of the mail transfer order the receiving bank will issue to the beneficiary its own cheque or make payment to the beneficiary.

3. Bank Drafts and Cheques. A bank draft is a pay order issued by a bank on its own branch or correspondent bank abroad. The bank draft or demand draft is handed over to the buyer who sends it to the beneficiary. The beneficiary obtains payment on presentation to the bank on which the draft is drawn. The beneficiary is indicated in the draft or cheque. Banks charge commission for issuing bank draft, and directs the Branch Manager of that country to make payment of specified amount in foreign exchange to the particular party (beneficiary). Bank drafts and cheques are by far the most popular methods of remittances. The only drawback of remittances by draft or cheque is the risk of loss of the draft or cheque in transit and the delay in effecting payment to the beneficiary.

4. Bill of Exchange. A bill of exchange is an order drawn by a person upon a bank or another person asking the latter to make payment to a third party. Bill of Exchange is an important method of payment. It is prepared by the exporter and sent to the importer through a commercial bank along with the documents. On acceptance of bill of exchange or Documents against Acceptance (D/A) the commercial bank delivers, the documents to importer. According to the date specified in the bill of exchange the importer makes payment to the commercial bank in that foreign country and subsequently the payments are received in India.

Foreign Bill of Exchange may be of two types:

(i) Ordinary or Clean Foreign Bill. This is an ordinary bill of exchange and written in case the exporters has sufficient confidence in the credit-worthiness of the importer. This is also called Clean Foreign Bill of Exchange.

(ii) Documentary Bill. When necessary documents to the title of the goods are also sent along with the foreign bill of exchange, it is called Documentary Bill. A Documentary bill may be two types:

(a) *Documents Against Payment.* In this case, the documents are delivered to the importer provided he makes the full payments. The exporter gives clear instruction to the bank that the documents should only be given provided the importer has made the full payment.

(b) *Documents Against Acceptance.* The exporter instructs the bank to delivered the documents to the importer provided the importer accepts the enclosed bill of exchange.

Foreign Bill of Exchange bear the stamps of both the countries. The exporter should affix sufficient stamps while sending the bill and the acceptor of the bill also should affix the stamps according to the rules of his country.

(a) Exchange Rates Regulations. Often the exchange rates fluctuate in the foreign trade, therefore, they can determine the rate of exchange for the maturity date of the bill.

(b) Rules of Interest. The amount of interest is also referred in the bill of exchange. The interest is charged from the date of delivery of the documents till the date of the payment. In the meanwhile, the importer gets the delivery of the goods from the shipping company.

(c) Expenses of Bank. They can clarify in the contract itself that who will bear the bank charges. As a matter of practice all such bank expenses are often borne by the exporter. However, if they wish they can clarify on this point also.

Specimen of Bill of Exchange

Exchange for £ 1,000 13 Bank Lane,
London, May 1, 1994.

Stamp

Sixty days after sight of this First of Exchange (second and third of the same tenor and date unpaid) pay to the Central Bank of India the sum of one thousand pound sterling at the bank's drawing rate for demand drafts on London together with interest at six percent per annum from the date hereof to the approximate due date of arrival of the remittance in London and Bank charges. Value received against 15 bales of cotton piece goods per 15 'Rana Pratap'. Shipping documents attached to be surrendered on acceptance.

For Johney & Co.
Sd. Babar Khan
Director

To,

M/s. Star Traders,
Charni Road,
Mumbai—400004.

A bill of exchange can be a banker's bills or trader's bills; a banker's bill is one issued on a bank while a trader's bill is one issued on a trader. Since a banker's bill is more secure, it commands a better rate as compared to a trader's bill. The purchase price of a bill is the basis of the maturity date of the bill.

5. Letter of Credit. A letter of credit is a letter issued by the buyer's banker in favour of the seller authorising him to draw a bill of exchange upto a particular amount covering specific shipment of goods assuring him or payment against the delivery of the prescribed documents in his own country. Such a letter of credit is known as "banker's letter of credit" or "commercial letter of credit".

The Uniform Customs and Practice for Documentary credits defines a letter of credit as, "any arrangement however named or described, whereby a bank (the issuing bank) acting at the request and in accordance with the instructions of a customer (the applicant or opener of the credit) or is to pay, accept or negotiate bill of exchange (draft) drawn by the beneficiary or authorises such payments to be made or such drafts to be paid, accepted or negotiated by another bank against stipulated documents and compliance with stipulated terms and conditions".

There have been significant developments in the methods of effecting payment of late foreign correspondent banks/exchange houses have started maintaining their accounts (Vestro accounts) with the Foreign Departments of Indian Banks and issued TTs/MTs/ DDs drawn on Indian banks which are payment in Indian rupees. The bank branches of Indian banks, authorised to deal in foreign exchange are spread all over Indian, honour these instruments on different dates by the eh debits on Vestro accounts are raised later, hence these debits have to be "Value dated" to avoid interest loss. The Vestro accounts have to be funded sufficiently and require close monitoring as overdraft cannot be allowed without analysing the balance sheets of the foreign accounts holder. Floats on the accounts of more than 15 days have to be brought to the notice of the management and branches honouring TTs/MTs/DDs issued on Vestro account have to communicate the transactions to the Foreign Departments on the same day, and daily closing balances have periodically to be got confirmed form account holders and reconciled.

ROLE OF COMMERCIAL BANKS TO EXPORTERS

Once goods are a shipped as per term of the contract, the exporter prepares and hands over the full set of shipping documents to the banker together with the duplicate and triplicate copies of the relative GR or PP form. The exporter will receive the payment as per the term of the contract. In cases, where the payment terms are other than through L/C, say documents against payment (D/P) or documents against acceptance (D/A), the exporter is normally paid only after the amenities received from the buyers. Sometimes, the exporter agrees to give credit of 30 days, 60 days or 90 days to the importer. In such a case, the exporter will receive the payment only after the due date of the bills. In such cases, 'Usance Bills' drawn by the exporter and a definite time period has to elapse before the exporter realises full payment for the goods exported.

An exporter can arrange for finance by his bank against export documents, this finance is usually known as 'post-shipment finance' which can be arranged in one of the following five ways:

(1) Discounting of Export Bills. Credit is extended to the exporter against the bill of exchange drawn by human the foreign buyer by discounting the same. The documents and the bill are purchased by the bank and an immediate credit is given to him. The bill can be D/P (Documents against payment) or D/P (Documents against Acceptance) and is usually drawn up to 80 days, this being the maximum period permitted under the exchange control regulations.

Before the bill is discounted by the exporter, the bank usually obtains a credit report on the buyer on whom the bill is drawn through their correspondents in foreign country. A goods credit report is essential for the banks to allow discounting facilities to the exporter. The political and economic situation of the country on which the bill is drawn also plays an important role in the determination of the banker's policy regarding purchase of export bills on that country.

Before accepting bills for discounting, banks, normally ascertain the credit worthiness of the exporter and fix a limit for the credit offered to him. The bills are discounted against the limit fixed. The limit is generally, revolving in nature.

(2) Negotiation of Bills. If the exporter has received a letter of credit in his favour, he has to draw a bill and hands it over to the bank with a request to negotiate the same. Banks do not hesitate to accept bills drawn against letter of credit as they are most secured and there is practically no risk in accepting such bills. The exporter receives payment against his documents and has, therefore, not to block his funds. Before negotiating the bills, the bank will satisfy itself with the exporter's standing, integrity and the past experience of the bank with regard to dealings with the said exporter. The bank if necessary may obtain a guarantee from the exporter that in case the documents are not taken up by the buyer, the exporter will refund the amount on demand.

(3) Consignment Loan. The exporter may, as a special case, export goods on a consignment basis. In this case, there is no sale. Hence, the exporter cannot draw a bill on any body in the country where the goods are sent. The exporter sends the documents to his selling agent through his bank. The exporter receives the payment only after the agent has sold the goods. Hence, exporter receives the payment only after the agent has sold the goods. Hence, exporter's funds are locked up for a considerable period. He can, therefore, approach his bank and request for loan against his documents relating to shipment on consignment basis. Generally, in Indian banks do not give such consignment loans.

(4) Advance Against Bills Sent for Collection. Under this method, banks accept export bills for collection on behalf of the exporters and offer advances against such bills. The banks may give advance varying between 60 to 100 per cent, depending upon credit worthiness of the exporters and integrity. The exporter, while sending bills for collection, must give clear instructions regarding the source of action to be taken in the event of the dishonour of bill, rebate to be allowed in case of early retirement of the bill, whether partial delivery is to be offered etc. so as to avoid delay and further complications.

(5) Advance Against Export Assistance. In addition to the above four methods, Indian banks offer post-shipment advances to the exporter against export incentives offered by the Government. Export incentives, generally take the form of drawback of excise and customs duties. Banks can grant credit against duty drawback for 90 days, free of interest. After the expiry of 90 days, banks charge commercial rate of interest.

❐

Index

J

K

L

M